Communications
in Computer and Information Science   1170

More information about this series at http://www.springer.com/series/7899

Costin Badica · Panos Liatsis ·
Latika Kharb · Deepak Chahal (Eds.)

Information, Communication and Computing Technology

5th International Conference, ICICCT 2020
New Delhi, India, May 9, 2020
Revised Selected Papers

 Springer

Editors
Costin Badica
Computer and Information Technology
University of Craiova
Craiova, Romania

Panos Liatsis
Computer Science
Khalifa University
Abu Dhabi, United Arab Emirates

Latika Kharb
Department of IT
Jagan Institute of Management Studies
Delhi, India

Deepak Chahal
Department of IT
Jagan Institute of Management Studies
Delhi, India

ISSN 1865-0929   ISSN 1865-0937 (electronic)
Communications in Computer and Information Science
ISBN 978-981-15-9670-4   ISBN 978-981-15-9671-1 (eBook)
https://doi.org/10.1007/978-981-15-9671-1

This Springer imprint is published by the registered company Springer Nature Singapore Pte Ltd.
The registered company address is: 152 Beach Road, #21-01/04 Gateway East, Singapore 189721, Singapore

Preface

The International Conference on Information, Communication and Computing Technology (ICICCT 2020) was held on May 9, 2020, in New Delhi, India. The conference was held virtually due to the COVID-19 pandemic. ICICCT 2020 was organized by the Department of Information Technology, Jagan Institute of Management Studies (JIMS) Rohini, New Delhi, India. The conference received 220 submissions and after rigorous reviews, 24 papers were selected for this volume. The acceptance rate was around 10.9%. The contributions came from diverse areas of information technology and were categorized into two tracks, namely (1) data communication and networking and (2) advanced computing using machine learning.

The aim of ICICCT 2020 was to provide a global platform for researchers, scientists, and practitioners from both academia and industry to present their research and development activities in all the aspects of data communication and networking and advanced computing using machine learning.

We thank all the members of the Organizing Committee and the Program Committee for their hard work. We are very grateful to Dr. Anupam Basu, Director of the National Institute of Technology, Durgapur, India, as general chair, Dr. Panos Liatsis, Professor and the Interim Chair of the Department of Computer Science at Khalifa University in Abu Dhabi, UAE, as program chair, Prof. Costin Badica, Professor of the Department of Computer Science, University of Craiova, Romania, as the keynote speaker, Dr. Santosh Biswas, Associate Professor of the Department of Computer Science and Engineering at the Indian Institute of Technology, Guwahati, India, as session chair for Track 1, and Dr. Sunil Kumar Kopparappu, Senior Scientist (R&D) at TCS Innovation Lab, Mumbai, India, as session chair for Track 2.

We thank all the Technical Program Committee members and referees for their constructive and enlightening reviews on the manuscripts. We thank Springer for publishing the proceedings in the *Communications in Computer and Information Science* (CCIS) series. We thank all the authors and participants for their great contributions that made this conference possible.

August 2020

Praveen Arora
Latika Kharb
Deepak Chahal

Preface

Organization

General Chair

Anupam Basu — National Institute of Technology, Durgapur, India

Program Chair

Panos Liatsis — Khalifa University, UAE

Conference Secretariat

Praveen Arora — Jagan Institute of Management Studies, India

Session Chair for Track 1

Santosh Biswas — IIT Guwahati, India

Session Chair for Track 2

Sunil Kumar Kopparappu — TCS Innovation Lab, India

Conveners

Latika Kharb — Jagan Institute of Management Studies, India
Deepak Chahal — Jagan Institute of Management Studies, India

Technical Program Committee

Rastislav Roka — Slovak University of Technology, Slovakia
Siddhivinayak Kulkarni — MIT World Peace University, India
P. Chenna Reddy — Jawaharlal Nehru Technological University Anantapur, India
Razali Yaakob — Universiti Putra Malaysia, Malaysia
Noor Afiza Mohd Ariffin — Universiti Putra Malaysia, Malaysia
Malti Bansal — Delhi Technological University, India
M. Babu Reddy — Krishna University, India
Ahmad Khan — COMSATS University Islamabad, Pakistan
Mohd Abdul Ahad — Jamia Hamdard, India
Rizwan Rehman — Dibrugarh University, India
Shahab Shamshirband — Iran University of Science and Technology, Iran
Atul Gonsai Gosai — Saurashtra University, India
Shamimul Qamar — King Khalid University, Saudi Arabia

P. Subashini	Avinashilingam University for Women, India
Partha Pakray	National Institute of Technology Silchar, India
Azurah	Universiti Teknologi Malaysia, Malaysia
Anazida	Universiti Teknologi Malaysia, Malaysia
Chan Weng Howe	Universiti Teknologi Malaysia, Malaysia
C. Shoba Bindu	JNTUA College of Engineering, India
S. Pallam Setty	Andra University, India
K. Madhavi	JNTUA College of Engineering, India
Janaka Wijekoon	Sri Lanka Institute of Information Technology, Sri Lanka
Hanumanthappa J.	University of Mysore, India
K. Thabotharan	University of Jaffna, Sri Lanka
Kamal Eldahshan	Al-Azhar University, Egypt
Tony Smith	University of Waikato, New Zealand
Abdel-Badeeh Salem	Ain Shams University, Egypt
Khalid Nazim Sattar Abdul	Majmaah University, Saudi Arabia
H. S. Nagendraswamy	University of Mysore, India
S. R. Boselin Prabhu	Anna University, India
S. Rajalakshmi	Sri Chandrasekharendra Saraswathi Viswa Mahavidyalaya, India
Anastasios Politis	Technological Educational Institute of Central Macedonia, Greece
Subhash Chandra Yadav	Central University of Jharkhand, India
Uttam Ghosh	Vanderbilt University, USA
Wafaa Shalash	King Abdulaziz University, Saudi Arabia
Etimad Fadel	King Abdulaziz University, Saudi Arabia
Oleksii Tyshchenko	University of Ostrava, Czech Republic
Hima Bindu Maringanti	North Orissa University, India
Froilan D. Mobo	Philippine Merchant Marine Academy, Philippines
Latafat A. Gardashova	Azerbaijan State Oil and Industry University, Azerbaijan
Wenjian Hu	Dynamic Ads Ranking, Facebook, USA
Muhammad Umair Ramzan	King Abdulaziz University, Saudi Arabia
Areej Abbas Malibary	King Abdulaziz University, Saudi Arabia
Dilip Singh Sisodia	National Institute of Technology Raipur, India
P. R. Patil	D.N. Patel College of Engineering, India
Jose Neuman Souza	Federal University of Ceará, Brazil
Nermin Hamza	King Abdulaziz University, Saudi Arabia
R. Chithra	K.S. Rangasamy College of Technology, India
Homero Toral Cruz	University of Quintana Roo, Mexico
J. Viji Gripsy	PSGR Krishnammal College for Women, India
Boudhir Anouar Abdelhakim	Abdelmalek Essaâdi University, UAE
Muhammed Ali Aydin	Istanbul University Cerrahpasa, Turkey
Suhair Alshehri	King Abdulaziz University, Saudi Arabia
Dalibor Dobrilovic	University of Novi Sad, Serbia

A. V. Petrashenko	National Technical University of Ukraine, Ukraine
Ali Hussain,	Sri Sai Madhavi Institute of Science and Technology, India
A. NagaRaju	Central University of Rajasthan, India
Cheng-Chi Lee	Fu Jen Catholic University, Taiwan
Apostolos Gkamas	University Ecclesiastical Academy of Vella of Ioannina, Greece
M. A. H. Akhand	Khulna University of Engineering & Technology, Bangladesh
Saad Talib Hasson	University of Babylon, Iraq
Valeri Mladenov	Technical University of Sofia, Bulgaria
Kate Revoredo	Departamento de Informática Aplicada, Brazil
Dimitris Kanellopoulos	University of Patras, Greece
Samir Kumar Bandyopadhyay	University of Calcutta, India
Baljit Singh Khehra	BBSBEC, India
Nitish Pathak	BVICAM, India
Md Gapar Md Johar	Management and Science University, Malaysia
Kathemreddy Ramesh Reddy	Vikrama Simhapuri University, India
Shubhnandan Singh Jamwa	University of Jammu, India
Surjeet Dalal	SRM University, Delhi-NCR, Sonepat, India
S. Vasundra	Jawaharlal Nehru Technological University, Anantapur, India
Manoj Patil	North Maharashtra University, India
Rahul Johari	GGSIPU, India
Adeyemi Ikuesan	University of Pretoria, South Africa
Pinaki Chakraborty	Netaji Subhas University of Technology, India
Subrata Nandi	National Institute of Technology Durgapur, India
Vinod Keshaorao Pachghare	College of Engineering Pune, India
A. V. Senthil Kumar	Hindusthan College of Arts and Science, India
Khalid Raza	Jamia Milia Islamia, India
G. Vijaya Lakshmi	Vikrama Simhapuri University, India
Parameshachari B. D.	GSSS Institute of Engineering and Technology for Women, India
E. Grace Mary Kanaga	Karunya Institute of Technology and Sciences, India
Subalalitha C. N.	SRM Institute of Science and Technology, Kanchipuram, India
Niketa Gandhi	Machine Intelligence Research Labs, USA
T. Sobha Rani	University of Hyderabad, India
Zunnun Narmawala	Nirma University, India
Aniruddha Chandra	National Institute of Technology Durgapur, India
Ashwani Kush	Kurukshetra University, India
Manoj Sahni	Pandit Deendayal Petroleum University, India
Promila Bahadur	Maharishi International University, USA
Gajendra Sharma	Kathmandu University, Nepal

Rabindra Bista	Kathmandu University, Nepal
Renuka Mohanraj	Maharishi International University, USA
Eduard Babulak	Institute of Technology and Business, Czech Republic
Zoran Bojkovic	University of Belgrade, Serbia
Pradeep Tomar	Gautam Buddha University, India
Arvind Selwal	Central University of Jammu, India
Atif. Farid. Mohammad	University of North Carolina at Charlotte, USA
Maushumi Barooah	Assam Engineering College, India
Prem Prakash Jayaraman	Swinburne University of Technology, Australia
Kalman Palaggi	University of Szeged, Hungary
J. Vijayakumar	Bharathiar University, India
Jacek Izydorczyk	Silesian University of Technology, Poland
Pamela L. Thompson	University of North Carolina at Charlotte, USA
Arka Prokash Mazumdar	Malaviya National Institute of Technology Jaipur, India
R. Gomathi	Bannari Amman Institute of Technology, India
Zunnun Narmawala	Nirma University, India
Diptendu Sinha Roy	National Institute Technology Meghalaya, India
Nitin Kumar	National Institute of Technology Uttarakhand, India
B. Surendiran	National Institute of Technology Puducherry, India
Parismita Sarma	Gauhati University, India
Manas Ranjan Kabat	VSS University of Technology Burla, India
Anuj Gupta	PEC University of Technology, India
Md. Alimul Haque	Veer Kunwar Singh University, India
Abdullah M. Al BinAli	Taibah University, Saudi Arabia
Subhojit Ghosh	National Institute of Technology Raipur, India
Rohini Sharma	Panjab University, India
Alessio Bottrigh	University of Eastern Piedmont, Italy
Sunita Sarkar	Assam University, India
Sonal Chawla	Panjab University, India
Anurag Jain	Guru Gobind Singh Indraprastha University, India
Matt Kretchmar	Denison University, USA
Sharad Saxena	Thapar Institute of Engineering and Technology, India
Dushyant Kumar Singh	Motilal Nehru National Institute of Technology, Allahabad, India
R. I. Minu	SRM Institute of Science and Technology, Kattankulathur, India
M. Murali	SRM Institute of Science and Technology, Kattankulathur, India
Rajesh Mehta	Thapar Institute of Engineering and Technology, India
Vibhav Prakash Singh	Motilal Nehru National Institute of Technology, Allahabad, India

Contents

Data Communication and Networking

Advanced Computing Using Machine Learning

Data Communication and Networking

Mobility Aware Bandwidth Aggregation Scheme for Heterogeneous Links of Multi-Interface Mobile Node

Vimal Kumar[1,2]([✉]) [iD] and Neeraj Tyagi[2]

[1] IMS Ghaziabad UP, Ghaziabad, India
vimalbaghel@gmail.com
[2] MNNIT Allahabad, Prayagraj, UP, India
{vimal,neeraj}@mnnit.ac.in
http://www.imsghaziabad.ac.in/, http://www.mnnit.ac.in/

Abstract. Now a days, the mobile nodes are multiple interface enabled and each interface has its own maximum bandwidth. The utilization of bandwidth of each interface is upper bounded by its maximum theoretical bandwidth in a given frequency band. Therefore, a need arises to look for alternative solutions to use more bandwidth than the maximum limit of bandwidth of currently in-use interface of mobile node while accessing the Internet. Specifically, more bandwidth is needed in live video streaming applications. When these interfaces are simultaneously active, there is an opportunity to use them for a single packet flow from a server by aggregating the bandwidth of all the interfaces of MN. In this work, we proposed a bunch of mechanisms to realize bandwidth aggregation of simultaneously active interfaces WLAN and LTE of MN using proposed architecture of multi interface controller. These bunch of mechanisms are mobility aware modified scheduling for mobility scenarios, a scheduling sequence technique to decide priority of an interface, and a RTT-based technique to reduce the packet reordering at receiver. The proposed work can be useful to fully exploit the available bandwidth of all the interfaces of MN simultaneously in a mobile and heterogeneous network. The simulation results show the comparison of the proposed work with the state of art work in terms of throughput when individual interfaces of MN are separately used and when all of its interfaces are simultaneously used. Approximately, 42% improvement in average throughput is achieved in comparison to existing techniques of bandwidth aggregation. Packet loss is reduced upto .01%. A significant reduction of upto 98% in packet reordering is observed as compared to the state of art work.

Keywords: Bandwidth · Multiple-interfaces · Aggregation technique · MIC · Heterogeneous networks · Throughput · Delay element · Packet re-ordering · LTE-WLAN Inter-operation

1   Introduction

Bandwidth utilization of an interface has been a research issue specifically in the area of wireless and mobile networks. Number of interfaces per mobile device,

ⓒ Springer Nature Singapore Pte Ltd. 2020
C. Badica et al. (Eds.): ICICCT 2020, CCIS 1170, pp. 3–20, 2020.
https://doi.org/10.1007/978-981-15-9671-1_1

have increased in this era of mobile revolution. The environment for such multi-interface mobile node is becoming more and more heterogeneous as shown in Fig. 1. In this type of heterogeneous environment, each interface of mobile node has certain amount of bandwidth to offer for different services on the mobile device. The bandwidth requirement may not get fulfilled with one interface in some download-intensive applications such as live video streaming. If multiple interfaces can become simultaneously active, a better idea is to use the available bandwidth of all the interfaces simultaneously to fulfill this high demand of download-intensive applications. This idea requires aggregation of bandwidth of all the interfaces and the solution of the issues occurred due to bandwidth aggregation and simultaneous use of multiple interfaces for the same application (TCPUDP flow). The major challenge in realization of this idea, is to schedule packets from one application at sender end and redirect them through WLAN and LTE interfaces corresponding to their IP addresses. Also the packet stream corresponding to WLAN and LTE is to be reassembled at the receiver end. Bandwidth aggregation is the process of bundling the bandwidth of each physical wireless interface and creating a virtual interface. Such virtual interface has a bandwidth greater than or equal to the sum of bandwidths of all individual wireless physical interfaces of the mobile node. In the mobility scenario, bandwidth aggregation can be more beneficial because, even when only one interface is having signal above threshold, the service still continues. Therefore, reliability increases with the bandwidth aggregation, in mobility conditions. The most difficult task of bandwidth aggregation, is to face heterogeneous interfaces, as shown in Fig. 2. Figure 2 shows the MN, an access point (through which wi-fi interface of MN is associated with Internet via WLAN), LTE base station (also known as eNodeB, through which LTE interface of MN is associated with Internet 4G LTE cellular network). The proposed multi-interface controller (MIC) is working at MN to activate the bandwidth aggregation and at server side as aggregator. In such a wireless and mobile environment, the packets are transmitted on unreliable wireless medium, which affects the required QoS for the running application at MN. By using all wireless interfaces simultaneously, higher throughput can be achieved. Security is another advantage of simultaneous usage of all wireless interfaces. One possible consequence is to do the reordering of the packets at MN, due to their arrivals through different interfaces. In this work, the packet reordering problem is solved by proposing a multi-interface controller (MIC). A detailed architecture of MIC is proposed in the coming section.

The rest of the paper is organized as follows: Sect. 2 covers the related work. Section 3 describes the contributions of the paper, and formulation of problem. Section 4 discusses the proposed solution using MIC and the architecture and components of MIC, packet reordering using delay element and minimization of packet reordering using round-trip-time (RTT) based algorithm. Mobility aware modified earliest deadline path first (EDPF) [3] packet scheduling is discussed in Sect. 5. Performance evaluation and discussion of results is given in Sect. 6. In the end, conclusion and future work are given in Sect. 7.

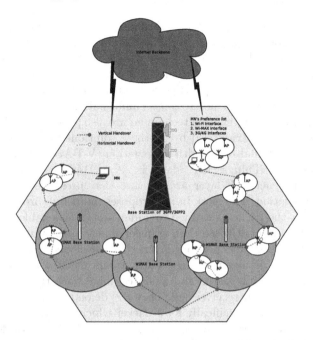

Fig. 1. Environment for multi-interface Enabled MN [10]

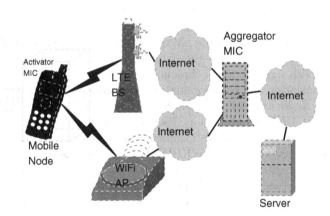

Fig. 2. Bandwidth aggregation scenario: a multi-interface controller at MN and server

2 Related Work

Bandwidth aggregation techniques are proposed across different levels of protocol stack in the literature. However, the majority of the work is done at transport and application layers, such as in [7–9,11,19,20]. The application layer bandwidth aggregation techniques do not include the solution of reordering of packets and cross-layer information, but these techniques provide load balancing among interfaces. Majority of transport layer solutions provide both sender and receiver based IP packet reordering. Some work has also been done at the network layer like [2,4]. The proposed solution in these works, uses the proxy and buffering techniques. In our proposed work, there is no use of proxy and minimal use of buffering. These solutions also provide packet reordering and load balancing at both sender and receiver but no cross-layer information exchange. Some of link layer based bandwidth aggregation techniques are also proposed in the literature, like [21]. Adaptation metrics used by all these solutions are delay, packet loss, and bandwidth. A virtual bandwidth aggregation (V-BAG) scheme is proposed in [5] for Internet of Things (IoT) data. In [2], a BAG scheme was proposed which consists the network layer architecture that uses a network proxy for bandwidth aggregation. The work in [4], proposes multi-link proxy which transparently extracts the packets destined to a multi-interface enabled mobile node. [18] has proposed a a multi-path data transfer solution which uses a multi-path layer between transport and network layers. [18] developed a multi-path transport protocol which divides the single path stream of data at sender end and redirects towards multiple paths and again combine back the multi-path data stream into single path at receiver end. They [18] defended their work by designing a scheduling scheme specifically for a packet which is undelivered or delayed on a particular path by reallocating it another path. In the work done by [17], the authors have proposed a device-centric bandwidth aggregation mechanism which optimizes the process of bandwidth aggregation on their self developed testbed consisting the android devices. The work of [1], describes the physical layer technique of carrier aggregation (CA) for LTE-Advanced CA applications. The [1] worked to implement the physical layer level aggregation of fragmented spectral resources to multiply the channel capacity. [15] proposed a physical layer bandwidth aggregation technique to aggregate the bandwidth of visible light communication and RF communication systems. This technique overcomes some of the disadvantages of visible light communication while works in combination with RF Communication. Packet reordering is the main challenge in the implementation of bandwidth aggregation. In [16], reorder density(RD) and reorder buffer-occupancy density(RBD)are considered as two packet reordering parameters to quantify the performance. RD is defined as the number of out of order packets in a sequence of packets arriving at the receiver. RBD is defined as the frequencies of the buffer-occupancy, normalized to non-duplicate packets in the sequence. Bandwidth aggregation can be adaptive or non-adaptive according to variable or constant link and traffic conditions [16]. The adaptive bandwidth aggregation is considered in our proposed work.

3   Contributions and Problem Formulation

The objective of this work is to schedule the packets on two active interfaces, WLAN and LTE and reduce the receiver-based packet reordering. The aggregated throughput, packet reordering and packet loss has been compared with state of the art work and significant improvement has been recorded. This work is focused on the observation of throughput, and packet loss. The throughput, is compared in following cases:

1. When all the packets are delivered through WLAN interface of MN.
2. When all the packets are delivered through LTE interface of MN.
3. When all the packets are delivered through proposed aggregated virtual link of capacity equal to sum of individual capacities of the two interfaces.
4. Comparison of proposed throughput with the state of the art research.

3.1 Contributions

The motivation for this work comes from the availability of multiple wireless interfaces (like 3G/4G/5G, WLAN and Wi-MAX etc.) in a mobile node (MN). The main contributions of this work are as follows:

1. Mobility aware modified packet scheduling mechanism
2. MIC architecture and its components
3. MIC assisted bandwidth aggregation
4. Use of delay element and RTT-based algorithm for minimization of buffer requirement and packet reordering at receiver end

3.2 Problem Formulation

Since packets are sequenced using sequence numbers and if some packets with greater sequence numbers reaches the receiver earlier than some packets with smaller sequence numbers, the packet reordering is needed at receiver before delivering the packets to the application. The data can not be delivered to application until the missing packets arrives at MN. Now the question should be raised that how the packet scheduling should be done so that these missing packets are zero or minimal? The answer of this question can be given by answering another question which as follows: To understand the scenario, as shown in Fig. 3, let there are 2 links p_0 and p_1 and has bandwidth of 100 Mbps and 10 Mbps respectively. When the packet is sent through link p_0, it reaches MN in 1/10th time as compared to when it is sent through link p_1. If link p_0 is busy and p_1 is free at an instant, whether the packets should be sent through link p_1 or the packets should wait until link p_0 becomes free? The solution of this question is discussed in Sect. 4.3 using Algorithm 1.

Using multiple interfaces of a mobile node simultaneously, gives an opportunity to improve the throughput by aggregating the bandwidth of all the interfaces [6]. Bandwidth aggregation is defined as a process of grouping the individual bandwidths of multiple interfaces to create a logical interface of high bandwidth that can satisfy the demand of applications that require larger bandwidths. A multi-interface equipped mobile node has interfaces which correspond to different bandwidths and operators. In this work, we have used a mixture of network layer and transport layer approach to aggregate the bandwidth. In this approach, the use of multiple IP is hidden from TCP/UDP and upper layers, as shown in

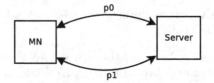

Fig. 3. Illustration of reordering minimization

Fig. 4 by using IP-in-IP encapsulation [14] at sender end (NAT at MIC) and a limited size buffer at receiver end (MN). Although, in some scenarios, the MN becomes overloaded, which is a limitation of this work.

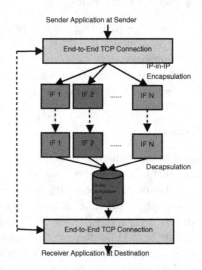

Fig. 4. Hiding the use of multiple IPs from TCP

From literature, as given in [3, 6, 16, 20], to aggregate the bandwidth, there is an assumption that all the WLAN's access points and LTE's eNodeB should be in the control of the same administrative system. In the proposed technique, the BS/AP need not be under the control of single administrative system. The work done in [17], the link qualities are not estimated in a central manner which sometimes creates jittery conditions of links. In our proposed work, a link observer is a component of MIC which periodically, estimates the link qualities and helps timely diversion of the packets.

4   Proposed Solution

In this section, the investigated problem is solved using the middle level MIC architecture which is used to handle the packet scheduling on multiple interfaces. The operational steps of the packet scheduling and the components of MIC architecture are given in Fig. 5.

The scheduler schedules the packet on one of the interface according to modified earliest deadline path first (EDPF) [3] with added mobility awareness discussed in Sect. 5.1 and scheduling sequence algorithm written in Algorithm 2. The packet reordering at receiver is done with the help of delay element of MIC and out of order packets are minimized using RTT-based algorithm written in Algorithm 1. To minimize the need of buffer at receiver, any out of order packet is delayed at NAT at receiver side (which requires minimum amount of buffering at NAT at receiver side). As soon as the missing packet arrives, the delayed packets are delivered to application along with the missing packet. Thus the packet eventually reaches to the application. The work-flow of this operation is given in Fig. 5. The Following steps are performed at MIC for scheduling the packets at multiple interfaces:

1. A TCP connection is established between application at MN and server application using the IP address of LTE interface and server IP address.
2. Once the TCP connection is running, the IP address of WLAN interface is sent in the option field of TCP.
3. The server reads the option field in the received TCP segment and intercepts the IP address of WLAN interface of MN and establishes a connection.
4. The packets are scheduled on both connections according to mobility aware modified EDPF, Algorithm 1 and Algorithm 2.
5. Packets are buffered if received out of order at MN, else delivered to application at MN
6. Sequence Number (N) which uniquely identifies each packet in the sequence, is used to order the packets.

4.1   MIC Architecture and Its Components

MIC is connected with the Internet gateway that is single hop away from eNodeB and the router of WLAN. It is placed at common gateway which is connected to both eNodeB and AP of WLAN. We call it as aggregator MIC. The MIC at MN, activates the multiple interfaces of MN. The aggregator MIC performs the function of bandwidth aggregation by scheduling the packets. The main responsibility of MIC is to handle the packets arriving from server at its server side interface for down link packets. The packets have to be scheduled on multiple interfaces of MN.

The components of MIC architecture enable the packet level interception of flow. The integrated package of MIC is installed on mobile node. These components in the package are used to create a link to each interface of MN. Through this link, the MN sends the IP addresses of all its interfaces to MIC. If an interface is added or existing interface is removed, this update is communicated to MIC. The internal structure of the proposed MIC modules along with their components is shown in Fig. 5.

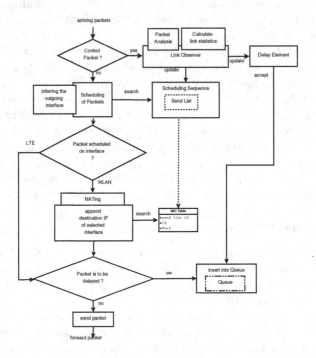

Fig. 5. Operational steps of packet scheduling on two interfaces (WLAN and LTE) and components of MIC

IP Packet Reordering Using Delay Element of MIC. Practically the delay is not same corresponding to two interfaces due to their root characteristics. Therefore, the packets destined to different interfaces may arrive out of order at the NAT installed in MN. To handle the out-of-order arrival of packets, packets must be reordered to deliver them to the TCP. One method of packet reordering is to use buffer at MN as proposed in [2–4]. This method may lead towards packet loss whenever the buffer is full, which results in performance degradation and packet retransmission is to be done. The proposed method here is to insert a additional delay in that path which delivers the packets faster. However, it looks like suppressing the faster interface and promoting the slower interface, but the aggregation of all the paths mitigates this problem and provides reliability, improved performance and robustness. This is achieved with the help of interface observer module. Let us understand the role of this module using delay d_0 and d_1 respectively of two paths p_0, p_1 corresponding to two interfaces. Let $d_0 = 20$ ms and $d_1 = 15$ ms. In such case, packets for p_1 will be delayed by 5 ms. The proposed technique handles packet reordering without modifying the operating system at MN.

Minimization of IP Packet Reordering. With reference to the question raised in Sect. 3.2, the following 4 possibilities occur while solving the scheduling problem on two links p_0 and p_1:

1. If the link with higher bandwidth (p_0) is free and link with lower bandwidth is busy(p_1) then packets are scheduled on p_0.
2. If all the links are free, then packets are scheduled on the link with higher bandwidth(p_0)
3. if all the links are busy, then packets wait until one of link becomes free.
4. if links with higher bandwidths are busy and links with lower bandwidths are free then the packet scheduling is done on the basis of RTT of links to minimize the out of order packets and is the link is chosen using following algorithm:

Algorithm 1. Minimization Of IP Packet Reordering

1: $p0_{RTT} \leftarrow RTToflink0$
2: $p1_{RTT} \leftarrow RTToflink1$
3: **if** $p0_{RTT} \leq p1_{RTT}$ **then**
4:     Schedule Packets on p_0
5: **else**
6:     Schedule Packets on p_1
7: **end if**

Link Observer. This module helps in the scheduling of packets and delay insertion by providing them the required estimates of throughput, delay and other link characteristics. Each interface receives the probe packets from access points/eNodeB to indicate the presence of signal. The time difference between probe packets and their acknowledgement after each 100 ms is considered as time delay to be inserted in a path to handle reordering. Although this method is simple but may be inaccurate in case of congestion. Two main functions are performed in this module of MIC, packet analysis to find the specific packet information and calculation of link characteristics. If it is a control packet, the control information is extracted from the packet. Link characteristics are used to schedule the packet on the link.

4.2 Proposed Role of MIC

In the proposed bandwidth aggregation of heterogeneous interfaces, the major challenge is to unify the packet access through MIC. Unification hides the heterogeneous interfaces from application. Application at MN is connected with MIC through a virtual interface and subsequently with application at server through the Internet and the application is not aware about the presence of MIC at both sides. There are two interfaces of MN, WLAN and LTE. WLAN interface is associated with an access point. The access point is connected with the Internet through a wired LAN and gateway. Since, inside the LAN, the private IP address is allocated to the MN, therefore NATing is needed. The use of NAT keeps the existing infrastructure unchanged which is required to deploy multi interfaces. Although few configurable changes are needed at MN. The NAT is responsible for the packet level striping. Using NAT, the header of the packets is rewritten according to private IPs and ports and redirected to individual interfaces of MN. Again at MN, these packets are combined to reproduce the original packet using NAT. Thus a private network is formed between the NAT server and WLAN interface at MIC of MN, as shown in Fig. 6. NAT tables are maintained at MIC. Using these NAT tables, there is a transparent transfer of a packets between MIC and NAT server. Hence, when packets are scheduled on WLAN interface, NATing is required. If packets are scheduled on LTE interface, the public IP is allocated to the interface and therefore, NATing is not needed.

Initially, when the download-intensive application is initiated, a control packet is sent from MN. This control packet carry the information of interfaces like its type, bandwidth, number of interfaces and IP. The control packet reaches to the server. Using this control packet, MIC at server, extracts the information of the interfaces and use this information in the scheduling of packets on the two interfaces. Thus packets are transmitted on the two interfaces, as per the schedule. When these packets reach at MIC of MN, reordering of the packets may be needed or may not be needed. The reordering is performed at MIC accordingly.

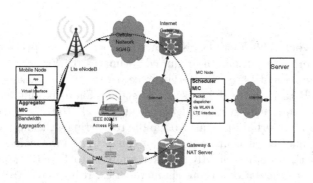

Fig. 6. Proposed topological structure

5   Packet Scheduling Mechanism

The packets are scheduled on path p_0 , and path p_1 corresponding to LTE and WLAN respectively and IP and port of default interface (public IP) are substituted by the IP and port of the destined interface (private IP). In this mechanism, a sequence of packets of same size are used that are sent each second corresponding to each interface to estimate the capacity of each interface. MIC uses the sequence of packets rather than using two back-to-back packets, because it produces more accurate estimates of link capacity. The packet scheduling algorithm considers the estimated link capacity, and interface link selection is done accordingly. The proposed scheduling sequence algorithm is based on weighted round robin (WRR) policy. WRR is used to facilitate controlled sharing of the network bandwidth. WRR assigns a weight to each interface. The weight value is then used to determine the interface for packet scheduling.

Algorithm 2. Scheduling Sequence

$SendList \leftarrow 0$
function GETPARAMETERSVALUE
    $B \leftarrow$ Bandwidth of Interface
    $QL \leftarrow$ Queue Length of Interface
    $PLR \leftarrow$ Packet Loss Rate of Interface
    $SNR \leftarrow$ Signal-to-noise ratio of Interface
    $BER \leftarrow$ Bit Error Rate of Interface
    $RSSI \leftarrow$ Received Signal Strength Indicator of Interface
    $HoF \leftarrow$ Hand-off Frequency of Interface
    for $i = 0 \rightarrow 1$ **do**
        $Wi \leftarrow (B + SNR + RSSI) - (QL + PLR + BER + HoF)$
    end for
    for $i = 0 \rightarrow 1$ **do**
        $WR_i \leftarrow (w_i/w_0 + w_1)$
    end for
    $SendList \leftarrow sort(WR_i)$
end function
Return $SendList$

In the this algorithm, the values of parameters are rated from 1 to 10. In case of B, SNR and RSSI, higher the value, higher the rating. In case of QL, HoF, PLR and BER, higher the value, lower the rating. The weight is calculated for each interface and stored in W_0 and W_1. Using these values, a weight ratio (WR_i) is calculated to normalize the values. These normalized values of WR_i are sorted and stored in a vector (SendList). SendList is returned and is used in mobility aware modified EDPF to schedule the packets.

The Scheduling Sequence algorithm is used to decide the priority of the interface to forward the in-coming packets. In general the algorithm can be extended for more than two interfaces and a pointer may be used to keep track of all the elements of scheduling list which is incremented each time and is reset when reaches the end. Since all the parameters are variable, therefore the weight of each queue is variable and hence the weight ratio is also variable.

5.1   Modified Scheduling Function with Mobility Awareness

EDPF [3] with considerations of wireless propagation delay between BS and MN and handover Information at MIC: Packets between MIC and base stations are scheduled on that available interface that delivers the packet at the earliest to MN. The delay between server and MN is calculated using following Function:

$$d_i^l = MAX((a_i + D_l), A_l) + L_i/B_l + PD_{wl}$$

where

d_i^l = arrival time of ith packet via path l at MN from server,

a_i = arrival time of ith packet at MIC from server

D_l = one way wired delay between MIC and BS.,

A_l = time at wirelesschannel for next packet tx at BS.

B_l = bandwidth of path l at BS.,

L_i = size of the ith arrived packet at MIC from server

PD_{wl} = wireless propagation delay between BS and MN.

Propagation delay is computed using

$$PD_{wl} = \text{length Of WirelessMedium/Propagation Speed}$$

Using modified EDPF, a packet is scheduled on path p according to following criteria:

$$p = l : d_i^l <= d_i^m, 1 <= m <= 2$$

6   Performance Evaluation

The performance of the proposed bandwidth aggregation mechanism is evaluated for streaming of packets. While evaluating the performance of the proposed bandwidth aggregation mechanism, we assume that both the interfaces, corresponding to two wireless technologies are supported by the same provider. We also assume that these two wireless technologies overlap in terms of coverage area. One realistic assumption is that packets are not fragmented between server and mobile node.

6.1 Simulation Setup and Parameters

Table 1. Simulation parameters & considered value

S. No.	Parameters	Value
1	Interfaces	WLAN over path p_1 & LTE over path p_0
2	Bandwidth of p_1	30 (Mbps)
3	Bandwidth of p_0	15 (Mbps)
4	Bandwidth between Server & MIC	greater than or equal to 45 Mbps
5	Delay between Server & MIC	1 ms
6	Delay of WLAN(p_1) Interface from MIC	5 ms
7	Delay of LTE(p_0) Interface from MIC	8 ms
8	TCP Flow for	500 s
9	Packet Size	1500 Bytes

The proposed problem is simulated in NS-2.29 [13] with the mobility package of NIST [12]. The target environment [10] and the considered simulation topology is given in Fig. 2 and 6 respectively. Corresponding to two wireless interfaces, WLAN and LTE, the packet flow is taken for 500 s with initial congestion window (cwnd) at server equal to 50. The maximum burst factor is four times the number of packets that can be sent in response to a single ACK. The start time is uniformly distributed between 0 and 500 s. The other specific parameters and their considered value are shown in Table 1.

6.2 Discussion of Simulation Results

Table 2 shows the average throughput of proposed mechanism and the existing techniques discussed in state of art literature. The average throughput is calculated for the interval of 100 s. Overall, 42% average improvement is recorded in the throughput. The illustration of result of throughput is given in Fig. 7(a) and 7(b). The Proposed aggregated throughput is compared with the referred aggregated throughput using buffering [4, 15, 17] etc. Figure 8 and Table 3 illustrates the results of IP packet reordering using delay element of MIC. Almost, one packet buffering is needed with the proposed technique of bandwidth aggregation. The obtained results of packet loss is illustrated in Fig. 9. The graph shows few stripped packets between server and MN, and corresponding packet loss of the proposed technique and technique using proxy and buffering. Also, the main challenge of bandwidth aggregation is to handle the IP packet reordering and packet loss due to the large buffering needed.

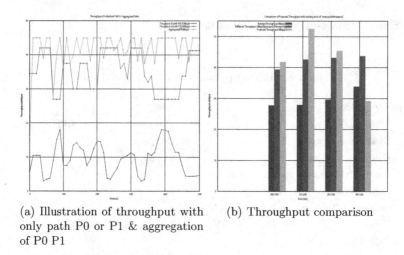

(a) Illustration of throughput with only path P0 or P1 & aggregation of P0 P1

(b) Throughput comparison

Fig. 7. Illustration of throughput: Aggregated paths Vs Individual path & Comparison of proposed aggregated throghput with evensen2009network

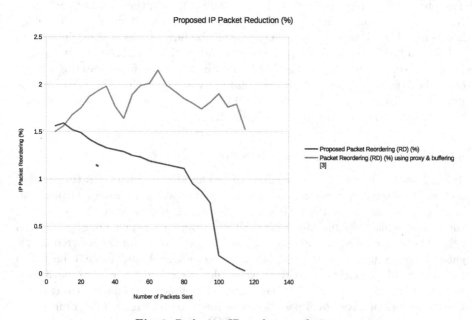

Fig. 8. Reducing IP packet reordering

Effect of Delay Element (DE) on Buffering and Packet Reordering. According to the results obtained, the required packet reordering is significant when the delay element is disabled and packet reordering is nominal (hardly 1 packet is buffered) with the delay element enabled. When the delay element is activated, the buffer requirement is eliminated up to 98% (in terms of number

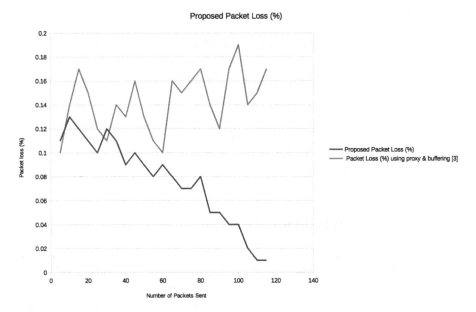

Fig. 9. Reducing packet loss

of packets) which is a significant improvement with respect to the work carried out in [4, 15, 17] etc. In this work, two links corresponding to WLAN and LTE are modeled. The Table 3 shows the number of packets buffered while the delay element is enabled and disabled.

Table 2. Illustration of improvement in Throughput (mbps)

Time(S)	Avg-Throughput		Improvement (%)
	Referred [4]	Proposed	
000–100	27.73	39.30	41.72
101–200	27.90	42.55	52.50
201–300	29.64	43.09	45.38
301–400	30.62	42.33	38.24
401–500	33.82	43.70	29.21

In this work, we assume that all the interfaces are simultaneously active and therefore, ignoring the battery usage, which is the limitation of this work.

Table 3. Reduction in the packet reordering using delay element

# packets sent	Scheduled on		Buffered if DE	
	LTE	WLAN	Disabled	Enabled
5	2	3	2	0
10	4	6	4	1
15	6	9	6	1
20	8	12	8	0
25	10	15	10	1
30	12	18	12	1

7   Conclusion and Future Work

In this work, we proposed mechanism for packet scheduling on simultaneously active multiple wireless interfaces of a mobile node to achieve end-to-end bandwidth aggregation of all interfaces. To solve this problem, we proposed a MIC architecture, a scheduling sequence algorithm to assign weight to each interface, an RTT-based algorithm to minimize out of order packets at receiver, and mobility aware modified scheduling algorithm to make the mechanism suitable for wireless and mobile networks. The result shows that the proposed mechanism improves the average throughput up to 42%, packet reordering is reduced up to 98%. Due to reduced packet reordering, the packet loss is also reduced up to 0.01%. It is evident from the results obtained in the experiments that not only the utilization of bandwidth is significantly improved, the reliability of packet level delivery is also significantly improved by scheduling the packets on the alternative interface in the absence of coverage of currently in-use interface. The proposed mechanism improves the throughput without modifying the servers or the intermediate infrastructure. The use of delay element has reduced the requirement of large buffers. The consideration of wireless propagation delay in scheduling algorithm EDPF, made the packet scheduling more suitable for wireless and mobile scenario. There is a strong need of intelligent routing function to be deployed in the Internet to support the proposed work more efficiently. Also, limitation of this work is that no packet fragmentation is allowed and more battery power usage is needed due to simultaneous use of multiple interfaces. Therefore, intelligent routing, packet fragmentation and optimal use of battery power are subjects of future work.

References

1. Cao, Y., Sunde, E.J., Chen, K.: Multiplying channel capacity: aggregation of fragmented spectral resources. IEEE Microw. Mag. **20**(1), 70–77 (2019). https://doi.org/10.1109/MMM.2018.2875631
2. Chebrolu, K., Raman, B., Rao, R.R.: A network layer approach to enable tcp over multiple interfaces. Wirel. Netw. **11**(5), 637–650 (2005)

3. Chebrolu, K., Rao, R.R.: Bandwidth aggregation for real-time applications in heterogeneous wireless networks. IEEE Trans. Mobile Comput. **5**(4), 388–403 (2006)
4. Evensen, K., Kaspar, D., Engelstad, P., Hansen, A.F., Griwodz, C., Halvorsen, P.: A network-layer proxy for bandwidth aggregation and reduction of ip packet reordering. In: 2009 IEEE 34th Conference on Local Computer Networks. pp. 585–592. IEEE (2009)
5. Gwak, Y., Kim, Y.Y., Kim, R.Y.: V-bag: A virtual bandwidth aggregation scheme for internet of things data. Int. J. Distrib. Sens. Netw. **13**(4), 1550147717700898 (2017). https://doi.org/10.1177/1550147717700898
6. Habak, K., Harras, K.A., Youssef, M.: bandwidth aggregation techniques in heterogeneous multi-homed devices: a survey. Comput. Netw. **92**, 168–188 (2015)
7. Habak, K., Youssef, M., Harras, K.A.: An optimal deployable bandwidth aggregation system. Comput. Netw. **57**(15), 3067–3080 (2013)
8. Hsieh, H.Y., Sivakumar, R.: A transport layer approach for achieving aggregate bandwidths on multi-homed mobile hosts. Wirel. Netw. **11**(1–2), 99–114 (2005). https://doi.org/10.1007/s11276-004-4749-6
9. Kim, D.P., Koh, S.J.: Adaptive congestion control of msctp for vertical handover based on bandwidth estimation in heterogeneous wireless networks. Wirel. Personal Commun. **57**(4), 707–725 (2011)
10. Kumar, V., Tyagi, N.: Optimal ranking-based discovery and selection of wmat using information service of ieee 802.21 in mobile wireless heterogeneous networks. In: Proceedings of the International Conference on Advances in Information Communication Technology & Computing. pp. 1–7. AICTC 2016, ACM, New York, USA (2016). https://doi.org/10.1145/2979779.2979813
11. Magalhaes, L., Kravets, R.: Transport level mechanisms for bandwidth aggregation on mobile hosts. In: Proceedings Ninth International Conference on Network Protocols. ICNP 2001. pp. 165–171. IEEE (2001)
12. NIST Mobility Package used for Network Simulator NS-2.29. https://www.nist.gov/services-resources/software/simulation-models-ns-2
13. The Network Simulator NS-2. http://www.isi.edu/nsnam/ns/
14. Phatak, D.S., Goff, T.: A novel mechanism for data streaming across multiple ip links for improving throughput and reliability in mobile environments. In: INFOCOM 2002. Twenty-First Annual Joint Conference of the IEEE Computer and Communications Societies. Proceedings. vol. 2, pp. 773–781. IEEE (2002)
15. Pratama, Y.S.M., Choi, K.W.: Bandwidth aggregation protocol and throughput-optimal scheduler for hybrid rf and visible light communication systems. IEEE Access **6**, 32173–32187 (2018). https://doi.org/10.1109/ACCESS.2018.2844874
16. Ramaboli, A.L., Falowo, O.E., Chan, A.H.: Bandwidth aggregation in heterogeneous wireless networks: a survey of current approaches and issues. J. Netw. Comput. Appl. **35**(6), 1674–1690 (2012)
17. Sharafeddine, S., Jahed, K., Fawaz, M.: Optimized device centric aggregation mechanisms for mobile devices with multiple wireless interfaces. Comput. Netw. **129**, 1–16 (2017). https://doi.org/10.1016/j.comnet.2017.08.026
18. Syariati, F.M., Choi, K.W.: Optimal concurrent multipath data transfer for bandwidth aggregation in heterogeneous mobile networks. Wirel. Personal Commun. **107**(3), 1383–1400 (2018). https://doi.org/10.1007/s11277-018-5969-x
19. Tsao, C.-L., Sanadhya, S., Sivakumar, R.: A super-aggregation strategy for multi-homed mobile hosts with heterogeneous wireless interfaces. Wireless Netw. **21**(2), 639–658 (2014). https://doi.org/10.1007/s11276-014-0794-y

20. Wu, J., Shang, Y., Cheng, B., Wu, B., Chen, J.: Loss tolerant bandwidth aggregation for multihomed video streaming over heterogeneous wireless networks. Wirel. Personal Commun. **75**(2), 1265–1282 (2014)
21. Yaver, A., Koudouridis, G.P.: Utilization of multi-radio access networks for video streaming services. In: 2009 IEEE Wireless Communications and Networking Conference. pp. 1–6 (2009). https://doi.org/10.1109/WCNC.2009.4918018

Time Series Missing Value Prediction: Algorithms and Applications

Aditya Dubey$^{(\boxtimes)}$ (iD) and Akhtar Rasool (iD)

Maulana Azad National Institute of Technology, Bhopal, India
dubeyaditya65@gmail.com

Abstract. In today's era, in many applications, a huge amount of data is produced. In data mining, these valuable data are processed to provide valuable trends. Unfortunately, in practice, the missing values in the collected data occur frequently and it yields a major challenge to precise the data analysis. The requirement of complete data of the observation becomes important for performing analysis. A series of techniques have been implemented for predicting these lost values. However, many of the existing predicting lost values methods can be either infeasible or could be inefficient. Conventional methods, for example, deletion, mean and mode imputation are not suitable to handle the missing values as those methods can cause biased predicted data. Selected time series predicting methods are outlined in this paper. Implementation of algorithms time series prediction is illustrated and discussed. This paper aims to compare predicting methods and determine which technique is frequently used along with its drawbacks and strengths.

Keywords: Imputation · Multivariate · Time series · Univariate

1 Introduction

In today's world, trillion bytes of data are produced every hour in a day. About 80 percent of the available data have been produced within the last few years. For example, each social networking site normally has over a billion active users. Hence, it is obvious that gigabytes of data are generated each day by the data driven company. With the invention of information technology and communication technology, the capability of data generation has never been so enormous. This large volume data is of complex, heterogeneous and diverse dimensionality. Being autonomous, each data source collects and generates information without relying on any centralized control i.e. distributed and decentralized control.

In many real applications, time series data is the most common kind of data explored. Time series data constitute the observed values at a regular interval of time [1]. This time series data are classified as either continuous or discrete [4]. Examples of continuous time series data include a sinusoidal signal. Example of discrete time series data includes daily crude oil price, atmospheric conditions of an area. The sensors generating time series data could be GPS, RFID sensors, smart phone sensors, infrared sensors, ultrasonic sensors, temperature sensors, humidity sensors, etc. For example, time series data of trajectory provide positioning of the vehicles at a regular interval of time.

© Springer Nature Singapore Pte Ltd. 2020
C. Badica et al. (Eds.): ICICCT 2020, CCIS 1170, pp. 21–36, 2020.
https://doi.org/10.1007/978-981-15-9671-1_2

In the personal medical care system, multiple sensors are deployed to detect multiple temporal attributes like heart rate, blood pressure and sleep quality. In the environmental monitoring system, multiple atmospheric variables ranging from temperature cloud cover dew point humidity and wind speed are measured in real time. Depending on the number of attributes, time series data are classified as univariate and multivariate. Examples of univariate time series data include Indian railway ticket confirmation dataset where the number of waiting lists transformed to confirmation is recorded for each working day. Figure 1 represents the multivariable time series having missing data. X_1, X_2, ..., X_n represents the various sensors and T_1, T_2, ..., T_n represents the time instantly. In the power grid system, multiple sensors are deployed to monitor the status of main power transformers and it generates multivariate time series data by observing the content of various diagnostic gas sensors. A variety of sensors are used to generate time series data.

By mining the time series data, important facts and critical information can be extracted. There have been thousands of research methods proposed on the indexing, classification, clustering, and segmentation of the time series data. While observing the values by the sensors there could be an absence of recorded values. This missingness either could be due to technical fault or human errors [10]. If an observation device breakdowns there could be missing values in the observed data. Similarly, missed values are caused by the respondents who cannot reply to the question posed in an assessment taken manually [2, 3]. However this missingness occurs unexpectedly in the observed time series data, there should be a method to handle these missing values at the preprocessing step of the data mining. Missing data availability in the dataset directly influences the research models' validity, reliability, and generalizability.

A large range of data mining and statistical techniques were suggested to approximate the missing values of the time series dataset. These predictive techniques either focus on predicting the missing data from a single source that is univariate or could not deal with the missingness in a multivariate time series dataset. The proposed methods for predicting the missing values depend on the missing percentage [11, 12, 14]. There is a requirement of a method which predicts even when the missing percentage varies i.e. from 1% to 90%. The predicting methods are evaluated over the dataset. The original data set is divided into two partitions, where one is used for training the model whereas the second one is used for testing the model. Some percentage of data is deleted at random to create test data sets.

In this paper, Sect. 2 describes the background studies exemplifying the types of missingness. Section 3 shows the traditional methods used in the prediction such as deletion and hot deck. Section 4 explains the algorithms based on which many research are being proposed today. In Sect. 5, efficiency measuring methods for prediction are discussed. Section 6 concludes this paper by providing the issues commonly found in the methods.

	T_1	T_2	T_3	T_4 ....
X_1	1.6	1.8	?	1.9
X_2	2.4	?	2.7	2.9 ....
X_3	?	0.4	?	0.6
X_4	8.3	?	8.5	8.6
$\vdots$		$\vdots$		

Fig. 1. Example of a multivariable time series dataset having missing values.

2   Background Studies

A classification scheme for different kinds of missing data has been developed by Statisticians. Rubin (1976) categorized the three kinds of missingness which include missing completely at random (MCAR), missing at random (MAR) and not missing at random (NMAR) [5–7]. A variable is said to be MCAR if the missingness probability is equal for all the units, in other words, there is no dependency of missingness on any other variable [7–9]. Missing data is classified as MAR when the probability of missingness relies upon one or more than one variable from the present data rather than on the data that is missing itself. NMAR is the most challenging type of lost data to handle, which is often described as non-ignoring because statisticians cannot identify the cause of the missingness. MCAR is regarded as the easiest form of data missing. Mellenbergh et al. [24] explained on many causes for missed patterns and also mentioned how specific missed patterns in the data collection stage can be reduced.

In many applications dealing with numerical data over the years, time series prediction has been performed. The forecast can take three distinct periods as Short term period, Midterm period and Long term period. The short term missing data prediction is focused on duration of less than three months while the midterm prediction is focused on a time interval of three months to one year and the long term is considered for the period of the time of more than one year. Many methods have been developed to predict depending on the time duration and data type.

The aim of this paper includes exemplifying different missing data handling methods when assessing datasets contain the missing data, demonstrating the working of different methods in actual practice, providing the demonstration related to differential results that may be preferred when preferring one method over another.

3   Conventional Methods

Early days used traditional prediction methods using mathematical equations and methods to predict the missing data [5]. The use of advances in distinct techniques and automation methods will further strengthen these fundamental techniques.

3.1   Data Deletion

It suggests deleting the missing column or instances of observations if incomplete data is present in the dataset. It is classified into two categories namely listwise deletion and pairwise deletion [5, 6]. Listwise deletion also known as complete case analysis, removes the observation if it contains any missing data on a variable. Only the complete instances of the observations are considered for the analysis which provides researchers a clean dataset. If one or more than one values of the instance are missing then a full instance of observation is removed, this causes a reduction in the quantitative strength of the dataset. The method should only be used in case of MCAR missing data since it removes potential patterns. Aiming to reduce the fall of listwise deletion, pairwise deletion also known as available case analysis examines all the cases where variables of significance are available, thereby maximizing present data through analytical bases. However, the pairwise deletion requires data to be MCAR. The difficulty arises when the missing data is MAR or MNAR.

3.2   Zero Imputation (ZI) and Average Imputation (AI)

In zero imputation, zeros are substituted for all the missing values. Though it is a simple method but not efficient in the situation when missing value percentage available in the dataset is large enough to affect the analysis of the data. AI is the same as ZI, but the missing values in this technique are substituted by the average of the corresponding featured data. Another variation, mean imputation also recognized as concept mean imputation can be used for a small set of missingness. This method replaces the missing values by mean obtained from other respondents measured values. Also known as unconditional mean imputation is not suggested since it arbitrarily reduces the data variability indicating false normal deviations and standard error.

3.3   Imputation Procedures

Imputation procedures may generate a complete set of values for the missing data and it does not take into account the implications of the consequences of the imputation techniques. Imputing is a process in which missing values are replaced with certain values (for different methods the origin values also differ). Single imputation includes constant value imputation, Arithmetic Mean imputation, Zero imputation, Maximum Likelihood (ML) estimated mean and median substitution, Hot and Cold Deck imputation, Last and Next Average imputation, Last Observation Carried Forward (LOCF) imputation and regression imputation. Multiple imputation produces more accurate results as compared to single imputation procedures. Multiple imputations make use of the Bayesian algorithm, which produces the complete set of predicted values for each missing value. McKnight et al. prove that count of imputations lies from 5 to 10. For MCAR and MAR missing data, multiple imputations prove to be a better approach. Multiple imputations comprise three phases namely imputation, analysis, and pooling step.

3.4   Mode Imputation

The value having the highest occurrence in the dataset attribute is replaced by the missing value. The methodology is oblivious and is usually not recommended for datasets. But due to convenience, mode imputation is frequently used where it is impossible to implement complicated methods.

3.5   Bayesian Approach

To impute the missing discrete attributes two methods relying on the Bayesian techniques are implemented. The first technique is used to substitute the missing value with an item that has the highest posterior probability. The second technique substitutes the missing value with the probability equal to the subsequent likelihood. These two approaches use prior and posterior probabilities to calculate the missing values efficiently. However, the attributes that are missing and having dependency must be discrete. NMAR missing data is used for the Bayesian approach.

Table 1 shows various conventional estimation procedures having their benefits and limitations to use it. Computational cost represents the time complexity required to conduct the procedure. Missing variables can be of the type numerical or categorical. Low computation cost represents that the time complexity required for the procedure is less. Medium computational cost represents the time complexity is neither high nor it is low. Similarly high computational cost represents the time complexity to be higher as compared to other methods.

Table 1. .

Estimation technique name	Pros and Cons					
	Primary strength	Secondary strength	Primary limitation	Secondary limitation	Type of missing variables	Computational cost
List-wise deletion	Unbiased to dataset having massive observations	Simplified implementation	Excessively biased with a small dataset	Not utilize all the available information	Numerical & categorical	Very low
Pair-wise deletion	Utilize all the provided information	Permits mining of incomplete data set	Confined information is obtained	Difficult to calculate the degree of freedom	Numerical & categorical	Very low
Last observation carried forward	Valid for variables not substantially changed over time	Simplified implementation	Associations among attributes are not maintained	Can cause infeasible sample instances	Numerical & categorical	Very low
Sequential hot-deck	Variance is not decreased artificially	Imputation is based on the measured data	Do not rely on strong hypothesis search	Can cause infeasible sample instances	Numerical & categorical	Very low

(*continued*)

Table 1. (*continued*)

Estimation technique name	Pros and Cons					
	Primary strength	Secondary strength	Primary limitation	Secondary limitation	Type of missing variables	Computational cost
Random dot-deck	Variance is not decreased artificially	Premises of distribution are not necessary	Do not rely on a strong hypothesis search	May result in infeasible sample instances	Numerical & categorical	Very low
Nearest complete hot-deck	Variance is not decreased artificially	Non-parametric method	Any possible combination has to be calculated	Weak imputation due to increased missing values	Numerical & categorical	Very low
Random assignment	Variance is not decreased artificially	Imputation is derived from the measured data	May induce infeasible sample instance	Does not maintain associations between attributes	Numerical & categorical	Very low
Linear regression	Utilizes limited information required for imputation	The number of infeasible sample instances are decreased	The model generates better imputation	Depends upon the linear relationship	Numerical	Medium
Logistic regression	Utilizes limited information required for imputation	The number of infeasible sample instances are decreased	The model creates too well behaved imputation	Restricted for molding only 2 classifications	Categorical	Medium
Multiple-linear regression	Utilizes all the information required for imputation	The number of infeasible sample instances are decreased	The model creates too well behaved imputation	Small sample size based model, if missingness percentage is high	Numerical	Medium
Multiple imputation	Impartial imputation	Sustainable model quality	Needs missing data to be MAR	Few standardized number of imputed data set	Numerical & categorical	High

4 Prediction Methods

4.1 K Nearest Neighbor Based Prediction Technique

Troyanskaya et al. [20] proposed the K-Nearest Neighbors imputation method. The original data set is partitioned into training and testing set. Let the training data sample be A which contains n instances and Y is the missing data sample.

Algorithm1: K nearest neighbors

Input: Time series dataset D with missing values.
Output: Dataset with predicted values.
1: Initialize the parameter K
2:**for** j= 0 to n do
3:     Calculate eucl_dist(A[j], y)
4:     Sort the lengths calculated in descending sequence depending on range measurements
5:     Obtain top K elements from the sorted array
6:      Find the frequently used class among the top K elements
7:     Return predicted class value
8: **end**

The distance measurement used can be Pearson correlation or variance minimization. However, the Euclidean distance found to be a better norm, but sensitive to outliers. The outlier impact could be overcome by using the log transformation of the data. Optimum K choice relies probably on the average cluster size of the dataset. For the noisy data, if the value of K increases, the accuracy of prediction decreases. The inconveniences in using KNN include choosing the distance function and for the most comparable cases the algorithm searches throughout the complete dataset

4.2   Bayesian Autoregressive Based Prediction Technique

Choong et al. [22] proposed an algorithm that makes use of autoregressive model based missing value estimation. The suggested method works well if many missing values exist at a specific time level or the whole time point is lacking.

Algorithm2: Autoregressive

Input: time series dataset D with missing values.
Output: Dataset with predicted values.
1:**Repeat**
2:     Search K-related data from the observed data
3:     Calculate Autoregressive coefficients
4:     Measure the missing data using the Autoregressive Model
5:**until** convergence

The method considers the vibrant conduct of the time series where the current instance of the data may rely on the previous instance. The mechanism of this method involves finding the K number of similar instances from the time series dataset then calculating the Auto Regressive coefficients of K-similar instances and finally, calculating the missing values using the AR model. The steps are repeated iteratively until the convergence condition is achieved. The strongly correlated instances of the data have the same AR coefficients. There are however a few heavily interdependent cases.

The co-expressed data are determined based on Euclidean distance which has proved to be superior to others. In the first phase, the missing values are put to 0. The forward-backward linear prediction method is employed. The convergence condition is the distinction between the imputed value of the present iteration and the last one. One of the limitations of this method is when the dataset is too small (lower than ten points). Only evenly sampled time series data can be used with the algorithm.

4.3 Genetic Algorithm Based Prediction Technique

GA is used to solve hard issues with an approximation, whose applications range from biology to computer science [6, 12]. Biological derived terminology has been used such as initial population, fitness function, selection, crossover, and mutation to provide an optimal solution to a difficult problem. Among solutions to evolving problems, GA considers learning as a competition. Each solution is examined by a fitness function to find out if the examined alternative contributes to the following problem formation. In the following algorithm, t_i represents the time instance.

Algorithm3: Genetic algorithm
1:**Begin**
2:    $t_i \leftarrow 0$
3:    initialize Population (t_i)
4:    evaluate Population (t_i)
5:    while (termination_condition is false) do
6:    **Begin**
7:        $t_i \leftarrow 0$
8:        select Population (t_i) from Population (t_{i-1})
9:    alter Population (t_i)
10:       evaluate Population (t_i)
11: **end**
12:**end**

After the execution of the algorithm by various genetic operators, optimal operators are chosen to execute the experiment with the greatest outcomes. Lobato et al. [16] proposed a multiobjective genetic algorithm imputation (MOGAImp). This imputation algorithm relies on the concept of NSGA-II. In most applications, the operators of the genetic algorithm are very simple and easy to perform computation. However, the calculation of fitness can have a higher computational time. To solve this issue, parallel approach can be used to decrease the processing time without disrupting the work of any algorithm. By assigning each calculation to thread, the fitness processing time can be reduced.

Algorithm4: Multiple Objectives Genetic Algorithm

Input: Dataset (D) containing missing values, GA parameters
Output: dataset containing predicted values
1:**for**attr = 1 to n do
2:    pool (attr) ←list attribute values (attr);
3:**end**
4: P_0←initialize_population (pop_size, pool)
5: D_0←imputed_dataset (P_0,pool)
6: [O_{acc}, O_{RMSE}] ←evaluate objectives (D)
7: P_0←non dominating sort by NSGA-II (P_0,O_{acc},O_{RMSE})
8:**for** t←1 to maximum_generations do
9:    Q_t←apply_genetic_operators(P_{t-1},O_{acc},O_{RMSE})
10:   D_t←imputed_datasets(Q_t,pool)
11:   [O'_{acc}, O'_{rmse}] ←evaluate objectives(D_t)
12:   R_t←P_{t-1}UQ_t
13:   P_t←survivors_selections_by_NSGA-II(R_t, O_{acc}, O_{rmse})
14:**end**
15:F←Paretofront(P_t)
16:**return**imputed_datasets(F, pool)

The solutions pool consists of all the possible values ordered lexicographically. The decoding process maps the index of the genotype so that the value revealed will be used in the phenotype. The codification strategy was used to provide an abstraction of the data type that will allow the algorithm to manage both types of attributes i.e. continuous and categorical attributes. Secondary, categorical strategy presents a data structure applicable to genetic operators.

4.4 Fuzzy Rough Set Theory Based Prediction Technique

The use of a fuzzy rough set theory combined with the nearest neighbor has been demonstrated for classifying the data by Jensen et al. Fuzzy-rough set theory enables the imputation procedures to be applicable in the situation when there is uncertainty in the data [1]. They do not require the iteration through the algorithmic steps. This is crucial since a stopping criterion is not needed when searching for a good solution is usually difficult. User defined parameter values which can be erroneous are also not required by the fuzzy rough set theory. Simplicity, ease of use and effectiveness allows this method to be used in the presence of noise and to deal with the missingness. The initial presumption for the missing values is not required. Fuzzy similarities among the instances are calculated and decisions are made based on this. The algorithm used not only to predict the continuous but also the distinct decision feature values that consisted of the dataset. The model uses KNN algorithm combined with fuzzy rough lower approximation and fuzzy rough upper approximation.

Algorithm5: Fuzzy Rough Set based algorithm

Input: D, training data;
    f, decision feature;
    p, object for which the algorithm predicts value;
    R, a fuzzy tolerance relation.
Output: Predicted value for p.
1: **Begin**
2:    N←getNearestNeighbors(p,K)
3:    initialize X1←0, X2←0
4:    **For** each z ϵ N do
5:        M←((R↓Rfz)(p)+(R↑Rdz)(y))/2
6:        X1←X1+M*d(z)
7:        X2←X2+M
8:    **end**
9:    **if** (X2>0)
10:       output (X1/X2)
11:   **else**
12:       output (Σd(z)/ |N|)
13:   **end**
14: **end**

In step 5, ↓ and ↑ represents the fuzzy rough lower approximation and fuzzy rough upper approximation respectively. To discover the similarity among the objects, similarity measures are being used by the fuzzy rough set theory. $R(0 \leq R \leq 1)$ is known as fuzzy tolerance relation if following conditions apply to all a and b in X. $R(a, a) = 1$ and $R(a, b) = R(b, a)$.

The missing data handled in this algorithm is MCAR. The algorithm is analyzed for the missing percentage of 5%, 10%, 20% and 30% missing data. The dataset is normalized by min-max normalization at the preprocessing step. For better performance of the algorithm, the parameters must be carefully selected which includes a number of neighbors, implicators, t-norm, fuzzy quantifiers, similarity analyzer.

4.5   Interpolation Based Prediction Technique

Chiewchanwattana et al. [21] carried out a research to handle missingness in the dataset by introducing an interpolation method based on pattern characterization known as varied-window similarity measure (VWSM) method. It is focused on the concept that time series data that are a manifestation of natural phenomenon contains many sets of similar time series subsequences. The imputation is performed by searching for a complete subsequence which is similar to subsequence of missed value sample and thereby imputation is done from this complete subsequence. The approach suits in those application domains where signals are the manifestations of physical systems. A data sequence is randomly divided into size K subsequences. Let v_1 subsequence contains the missing values. For imputing the missing data, many trials of different partition sizes of v_1 are required to find an approximate sequence. v_j subsequence having higher similarity to v_1 subsequence, helps to impute the missing values in subsequence v_1. v_t subsequence represents the target subsequence having some missing data. The other subsequences $v_{q \neq t}$ represents the referential subsequences.

Algorithm6: Similarity based algorithm

Input: Time series dataset (D) containing the missing values Dm
Output: Dataset containing the predicted values.
1: Initialize variable M containing the index numbers of the missing data
2: Values in the dataset are normalized in the range [0, 1]
3: Missing values are set to a random number in the range [0, 1]
4: Initialize counter variable C=0
5: Initialize positive threshold T=0
6: **Repeat**
7:     **For** all missing data Dm where m ∈ M
8:     Set the size of partitioning window K (if time series data is classified as a cyclo-stationary signal then K = period length, else K= 3)
9:     Initialize estimated value
10:    Initialize a counter variable g =0
11:    Initialize temporary variable T= 0
12:    Initialize sum variable S= 0
13:    **Repeat**
14:        Initialize a target subsequence, vt containing values from $D_{m - \left\lfloor \frac{K}{2} \right\rfloor}$ to $D_{m + \left\lfloor \frac{K}{2} \right\rfloor}$

15:        Construct groups of equal size K, by partitioning from $D_{m - \left\lfloor \frac{K}{2} \right\rfloor + 1}$ down to D_1

16:        Construct groups of equal size K by partitioning from $D_{m + \left\lfloor \frac{K}{2} \right\rfloor + 1}$ up to D_N

17:    For a group, P having reference subsequences vq containing the least distance $\left(\beta_j \right)$
18:        For subsequence j in P, calculate the missing value using
$$\hat{D}_m^{v_t} = D_m^{v_q} - \frac{1}{2}\left(D_{m-1}^{v_q} - D_{m-1}^{v_t} \right) - \frac{1}{2}\left(D_{m+1}^{v_q} - D_{m+1}^{v_t} \right)$$
19:        Calculate $T = \sum_j \left(\left(1 - \beta_j \right) \times D_m^j \right) / \sum_j \left(1 - \beta_j \right)$

20:        Calculate S=S+T
21:        Update the number of iterations, g=g+1
22:        Increment K, K=K+1
23:    **Until** number of groups becomes 1
24:    Calculate $\hat{D}_m = S/g$

25:    Set $D_m = \hat{D}_m$

26:    **End**
27:    Increment the cycle count, C=C+1
28:**Until** the maximum of allDm, such that $\hat{D}_m^{(C+1)} - \hat{D}_m^{(C)} \leq T$

In many real application datasets, it is not suitable to fix the window length K to a constant. $D_m^{v_t}$ represents the missing value at the time m of the target subsequence v_t $D_m^{v_q}$ represents the value at the time m of the reference subsequence v_q. It is assumed that v_q is having the same shape as that of v_t. To impute the missing value $D_m^{v_t}$ from $D_m^{v_q}$, four neighbor values $D_{m-1}^{v_t}$, $D_{m+1}^{v_t}$, $D_{m-1}^{v_q}$ and $D_{m+1}^{v_q}$ are involved. In step 19, β defines the distance between two subsequences. The β fluctuates with the change in K; the variance becomes higher when the subsequence length is larger.

Table 2. Comparison between different imputation methods

Researcher	Method	Data set	Performance measure	Compared method	Strength and limitations
Galbraith et al. [23]	Autoregression based estimator for ARFIMA model	–	RMSE	Maximum likelihood	**Strength**- It provides an alternative solution for estimating ARFIMA parameters suitable to stationary as well as non-stationary processes. It performs robust across a range of stationery (including 'antipersistent') and non-stationary values of the long-memory parameter d; that is $-1/2 < d < 1$; and thus no prior information of the non-stationarity or transformation to the stationarity region is required. Relying on the concept of AR approximations representing quite general processes, the technique seems comparatively resistant to misspecification
Troyanskaya et al. [20]	KNN impute and SVD impute	Three microarray data sets	NRMSE	Row average	**Strength**- From a biological point of view, KNN impute provides a precise estimate for missing values in genes belonging to tiny, narrow clusters. The SVD based evaluation of missing data for such genes could be incorrectly predicted if they are not comparable with any of eigengenes used for regression. **Limitations**- With an expanding percent of missing values, the KNN imputation results in fewer deteriorations in performance. KNN imputation technique is more stable as compared to SVD about the type of data used to estimate the data, which is more effective in non-time series or noisy data. The selection of appropriate parameters(for example number of nearest neighbors) is a significant issue. For the non-optimal fraction number of missing values, the SVD based approach presents a sharp decline in the performance

(*continued*)

Table 2. (*continued*)

Researcher	Method	Data set	Performance measure	Compared method	Strength and limitations
M. K. Choong et al. [22]	Autoregressive	DNA microarray time series dataset	NRMSE	KNNimpute, zero imputation, row average method, LL Simpute, BPCA, and FRAA	**Strength**- The majority of the time series dataset is more than 10 instances, so the algorithm is effective in many circumstances. The method will only be used for uniform samples of data. **Limitations**- If the size of the time series is too short (less than ten points), (2) There aren't too many linear equations; so it is not possible to dependably use it
Sridevi et al. [11]	Autoregressive	Stock dataset, sales dataset, and weather dataset	NRMSE	KNN impute method, row average method, and mean imputation	**Strength**- Performs better in the case when there are many missing values in a specific column, even if the complete column is missing
Aydilek et al. [6]	Optimized fuzzy c-means with support vector regression and a genetic algorithm	Glass, haberman, iris, musk1, wine and yeast datasets	RMSE, the Wilcoxon rank-sum statistical significance test	Fuzzy c-means genetic algorithm imputation, support vector regression genetic algorithm imputation and zero imputation.	**Strength**- Fuzzy c means provides a better framework to identify changing class structures. For noisy data or data having outliers, the concept enhances the imputation efficiency by having flexible and creatable nature. **Limitations**- The training of support vector regression is an important task. Before imputing the kernel type and performance criterion have to be specified. For getting better-imputed data, feature selection and dimensionality reduction approaches may also be implemented; for example, includes the implementation of principal component analysis followed by support vector training for reducing the training time
Lobato et al. [16]	Multi-objective genetic algorithm	30 machine learning datasets from UCI repository	RMSE and classification accuracy	Concept most common attribute value for symbolic attributes; global most common attribute value for symbolic attributes, and global average value for numerical attributes; weighted imputation with KNN	**Strength**- The objective is to decrease the bias induced due to missing data. Although most techniques of imputation are limited to one type of attribute i.e. categorical or continuous, moreover, they usually sample with incomplete instances. 1) it can deal with conflicting evaluation measures; 2) the technique is appropriate for datasets having mixed attributes; 3) the proposed technique considers information from instances having missing values and the model building.
Watada et al.	Genetic rough set	Japan stock index	RMSE	Fuzzy time series model	**Strength**- the recurrent fuzzy relationship hidden in the time series dataset is utilized. Rule-based algorithm, the rough set concepts are used so that reasonable and understandable rules can be generated

(*continued*)

Table 2. (*continued*)

Researcher	Method	Data set	Performance measure	Compared method	Strength and limitations
Amiri et al. [1]	Fuzzy rough set	27 datasets obtained from the KEEL dataset repository	RMSE	Bayesian PCA, concept most common, Fuzzy K means, K means, KNN impute, LLS impute, Most common, SVD impute, SVM impute and WKNN impute and expectation maximization	**Strength**- Techniques using the concept of fuzzy rough are capable to handle uncertainty in the dataset. The methods based on this concept have desirable characteristics including robustness and noise tolerance. **Limitations**- The time complexity of the algorithm is an issue. For identifying the most similar instances of the dataset, comparing each instance of the dataset is a time-consuming procedure

5 Efficiency Measuring Methods

When a certain model is applied to a certain time series dataset, the dataset is first split into two sections that are training set and testing set. Training observations are applied to build the required model. Frequently for validation purposes, a small fraction of the training set kept and is called the validation set. Preprocessing is carried out through standardization of the data, logarithmic or other transforms. Box-Coxx transformation is a very popular method. Once a model is built, it will be used for prediction generation. If needed, the expected values are converted to the initial scale by the reverse transformation. In many practical circumstances, due to the basic significance of the prediction of time series dataset, adequate attention must be given to select a specific model. That is why many efficiency procedures are proposed for estimating the predictive performance and comparison of distinct models. In every definition that comes ahead, D_i is the actual value, P_i is the predicted value and error $E_i = D_i - P_i$.

5.1 Root Mean Square Error

It represents a root mean square deviation of the predicted values. Since the negative and positive signed errors that have been recorded do not compensate each other, MSE provides an overview of the error during prediction. It detects severe errors that happened during prediction. RMSE points out that the overall prediction error is greatly influenced by big errors that are considerably more costly than tiny errors. RMSE is also subject to scale shift and data transformations happened at the preprocessing. The less the RMSE, the stronger will be the prognosis. For n number of missing values, RMSE is defined as-

$$RMSE = \sqrt{\frac{1}{n}\sum_{i=1}^{n} E_i^2}$$

(1)

5.2 Normalized Mean Square Error

NMSE is a structured error test as well as efficient to assess the exactness of a model's prediction. The less the NMSE, the stronger will be the prognosis. NMSE gives no insight into the overall error whether they are positive or negative. Vast errors are much costly than low errors. For n number of missing values, NMSE is defined as-

$$NMSE = \frac{1}{\sigma^2 n} \sum_{i=1}^{n} E_i^2 \qquad (2)$$

Here, test variance $\sigma^2 = \frac{1}{n-1} \sum_{i=1}^{n} (D_i - \overline{D})$ and $\overline{D} = \frac{1}{n} \sum_{i=1}^{n} D_i$

Table 2 describes the various prediction proposed during the last few years. The table also describes the strength and limitations of each method. It has been seen that most of the methods use RMSE and NMSE for comparing the accuracy of their method.

6 Conclusion

In this paper, the procedures capable of predicting time series missing data have been discussed. However, in each of the techniques we investigated, we found at least one of the following drawbacks: (1) the predictions are partly failed, particularly if missing values are within the wide gaps; (2) lack of prediction uncertainty quantification; (3) absence of well documented open source software which helps the usage and development of the technique used; (4) non-scalability of the dataset having a larger number of attributes and instances, particularly by choosing methods that avoid efficient parallelism; (5) requires more time for methods having higher complexity that require large scale storage; (6) most of the methods deals with the homogenous dataset; (7) accurate parameters selection for the working of algorithm.

References

1. Amiri, M., Jensen, R.: Missing data imputation using fuzzy rough methods. Neurocomputing **205**, 152–164 (2016)
2. Yozgatligil, C., Aslan, S., Iyigun, C., Batmaz, I.: Comparison of missing value imputation methods in time series: the case of Turkish meteorological data. Theor. Appl. Climatol. **112**(1–2), 143–167 (2013)
3. Wu, S., Chang, C., Lee, S.: Time series forecasting with missing values. In: 2015 1st International Conference on Industrial Networks and Intelligent Systems, pp. 151–156 (2015)
4. Sitaram, D., Dalwani, A., Narang, A., Das, M., Auradkar, P.: A measure of similarity of time series containing missing data using the Mahalanobis distance. In: Proceedings of the 2015 2nd IEEE International Conference on Advances in Computing and Communication Engineering, ICACCE 2015, pp. 622–627 (2015)

5. Little, R.J.A., Rublin, D.B.: Statistical Analysis with Missing Data, pp. 381–386. Wiley, New York (1987)
6. Aydilek, I.B., Arslan, A.: A hybrid method for imputation of missing values using optimized fuzzy c-means with support vector regression, a genetic algorithm. Inf. Sci. (NY) **233**, 25–35 (2013)
7. Afrianti, Y.S.: Imputation algorithm based on copula for missing, pp. 252–257 (2014)
8. Briggs, A., Clark, T., Wolstenholme, J., Clarke, P.: Missing presumed at random: cost-analysis of incomplete data. Health Econ. **12**(5), 377–392 (2003)
9. Malatinszky, Á., Centeri, C., Podani, J., Engloner, A.I.: Book reviews. Commun. Ecol. **8**(1), 129–131 (2007). https://doi.org/10.1556/ComEc.8.2007.1.15
10. Yuan, Y.: Multiple imputation for missing data: Concepts and new development, pp. 1–13. SAS Institute Inc., Rockville, MD (2010)
11. Sridevi, S., Rajaram, S., Parthiban, C., SibiArasan, S., Swadhikar, C.: Imputation for the analysis of missing values and prediction of time series data. In: 2011 International Conference on Recent Trends in Information Technology, pp. 1158–1163 (2011)
12. Tang, J., Zhang, G., Wang, Y., Wang, H., Liu, F.: A hybrid approach to integrate fuzzy c-means based imputation method with genetic algorithm for missing traffic volume data estimation. Transp. Res. Part C Emerg. Technol. **51**, 29–40 (2015)
13. Zhu, X., Zhang, S., Jin, Z., Zhang, Z., Xu, Z.: Missing value estimation for mixed-attribute data sets. IEEE Trans. Knowl. Data Eng. **23**(1), 110–121 (2011)
14. SreeDhevi, A.T.: Imputing missing values using Inverse Distance Weighted Interpolation for time series data. In: 6th International Conference on Advanced Computing, ICoAC 2014, pp. 255–259 (2015)
15. Strike, K., El Emam, K., Madhavji, N.: Software cost estimation with incomplete data. IEEE Trans. Softw. Eng. **27**(10), 890–908 (2001)
16. Lobato, F., et al.: Multi-objective genetic algorithm for missing data imputation. Pattern Recogn. Lett. **68**, 126–131 (2015)
17. Azadeh, A., et al.: Optimum estimation of missing values in randomized complete block design by genetic algorithm. Knowl. Based Syst. **37**, 37–47 (2013)
18. Shao, C.: An interpolation method combining Snurbs with window interpolation adjustment. In: 2014 4th IEEE International Conference on Information Science and Technology, pp. 176–179 (2014)
19. Bańbura, M., Modugno, M.: Maximum likelihood estimation of factor models on datasets with arbitrary pattern of missing data. J. Appl. Econ. **29**(1), 133–160 (2014)
20. Troyanskaya, O., et al.: Missing value estimation methods for DNA microarrays. Bioinformatics **17**(6), 520–525 (2001)
21. Chiewchanwattana, S., Lursinsap, C., Chu, C.H.H.: Imputing incomplete time-series data based on varied-window similarity measure of data sequences. Pattern Recogn. Lett. **28**, 1091–1103 (2007)
22. Choong, M.K., Levy, D., Yan, H.: Study of microarray time series data based on Forward-Backward Linear Prediction and Singular Value Decomposition. Int. J. Data Min. Bioinf. **3**(2), 145–159 (2009)
23. Galbraith, J.W., Zinde-Walsh, V.: Autoregression-Based Estimators for ARFIMA Models. CIRANO, Série Scientifique, Scientific Series (2001)
24. Mellenbergh, G.J.: Missing data. Counteracting Methodological Errors in Behavioral Research, pp. 275–292. Springer, Cham (2019). https://doi.org/10.1007/978-3-030-12272-0_16

FPGA Based Design of Speech Encryption and Decryption for Secure Communication

Rahul Saini$^{(\boxtimes)}$ ⓘ, Mayank Jain ⓘ, Manish ⓘ, and Kriti Suneja ⓘ

Department of Electronics and Communication,
Delhi Technological University, Delhi 110042, India
rahulsaini25899@gmail.com, jmayank612@gmail.com,
manish123me@gmail.com, kritisuneja@dtu.ac.in

Abstract. Data in any form, such as speech, image, video, text etc. need to be transferred against various threats. Such information need to be modified in such a form that even if someone gets an access to it, he will not be able to understand it i.e. it needs to be encrypted before transmission and must be decrypted at receiver side in order to ensure data security. Breaching of sensitive data by fraudsters may impose a potential cost in terms of money, time and efforts. Many approaches have been taken in this direction to attain such security among which chaos based encryption is relatively newer one. Chaotic systems are highly secure and reliable system for encryption. The chaotic systems are highly sensitive to initial conditions and their values dramatically change with the change in initial conditions. This work intends to improve the existing cryptology methods utilizing chaotic circuits. Also, a standalone hardware design which can be used as a part of portable chips for online encryption and decryption is the main objective of this work. In this paper, we have proposed an FPGA based chaotic system with modified logistic encryption algorithm in order to reduce processing time in comparison to that of software. The synthesis results clearly show that the hardware implementation of logistic encryption outperforms the software based implementation and thus can be used in portable devices as a chip.

Keywords: FPGA · Speech · Chaotic · Hardware · Encryption · Decryption · Hamming code · Software · Communication · Logistic mapping · Sampling

1 Introduction

In this era, when data is everywhere, including mobiles, computer, servers etc. and the need to transfer this massive amount of data from one device to another requires information security. This data may include sensitive information which is prone to hacking threats, for e.g. military data, bank data, personal details. While transferring such data, one of the major problems is security. To meet the ever-increasing demand of secure system for communication, data storage, transfer of data, etc. lots of methodologies have been developed one of such method is chaotic system. There are various factors or features which lead to the·advancement in the methods and approach to chaotic system. These systems provide a high degree of randomness based on initial values. Chaotic systems are

© Springer Nature Singapore Pte Ltd. 2020
C. Badica et al. (Eds.): ICICCT 2020, CCIS 1170, pp. 37–49, 2020.
https://doi.org/10.1007/978-981-15-9671-1_3

generally non-linear and dynamic in nature. Their dependence on initial states lead to the formation of eye- catching butterfly diagrams, which confirm their randomness. Its randomness finds application in many fields including communication system [1, 2], cryptography and encryption [3, 4], image processing [5], medical applications [6] etc. Because of its randomness, its applications are expending in other areas also. Chaos method for encryption also solves the problem of high computational requirement of some standard encryption methods like AES [13] resulting into its applications in real time and power constraint environments [12]. For this paper, we have used chaotic system for speech encryption, being difficult to predict, which is one of the most important aspect of encryption, chaotic system seems one of the best candidate for this application. Many algorithms and methods are developed to implement such system depending upon various need and applications some of them includes logistic mapping [4], henon chaotic mapping [7], chua circuits [8] etc.

In this paper, we have implemented Logistic Mapping, which is one of the ways to have a chaotic system (on FPGA). We have encrypted speech data and also added hamming code, which provides the facility of error detection and correction. The whole process has been implemented using binary numbers, since digital form has additional feature of noise immunity as compared to analog world. The primary focus of this paper is to use an independent hardware encryption unit for secure transmission process having a reliable and noise free communication.

The codes were written in Verilog HDL. Basic binary speech data is provided by MATLAB. Xilinx is used to obtain the encrypted data by logistic mapping along with 11 bits hamming code facility in which 15 bit is to be read to rectify a single bit error if any, thus adding an extra secure reliable data communication system having two noise immunity features which are first being inherit nature of digital values with second layer of hamming code. Target device used in XILINX Vivado is xc7x1140tflg1930-1 from Virtex-7 family having 1100 IOBs and 712000 LUTs.

This paper has organized as follows: Sect. 2 gives the description of logistic mapping and hamming code. Section 3 explains the methodology adopted in implementation of the whole encryption and decryption system. The simulation and synthesis results have been justified in Sect. 4. Lastly, Sect. 5 concludes the paper.

2 Logistic Mapping for Chaotic Behavior

2.1 Logistic Mapping

Logistic mapping is one of the most popular ways to implement chaotic systems. In similarity with a general chaotic system, it provides high degree of randomness which is highly sensitive to initial conditions [9] It provides lesser complexity and a large range of parameter values for which we can obtain butterfly diagrams.

Basic equation of one dimensional logistic mapping is given in (1) [4]:

$$x_{n+1} = \mu x_n (1 - x_n) \tag{1}$$

Where μ is the logistic parameter having range (0, 4] signifying the extent of chaotic behavior shown by the system and n is an integer which signifies number of iterations to be performed. When μ is less than 3, The generated sequence is not fully mapped in interval [0, 1] and output has an almost constant value but when its value is increased and μ is closer to 4, the ergodicity distribution in the generated chaotic sequence is better in the interval [0, 1]. As μ is increased from 3, output splits or bifurcates until it shows chaotic behavior at μ = 4, or we can say that when μ is in range of (3.57, 4) it shows highly random nature as shown in bifurcation diagram of Fig. 1. When μ = 4, the generated chaotic sequence is fully mapped over the entire [0, 1] [4]. {X_n} are sequence elements [11] or simply it contain values given by Eq. 1 iteratively. Thus for logistic mapping X_0, initial value of sequence element X_n and μ are seeds to the above equation. Values of these initial parameters affects the ergodicity distribution and as a result the final sequence too. Thus, the effectiveness and reliability of chaotic system also depends on initial values.

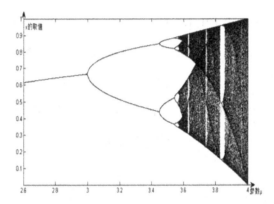

Fig. 1. Bifurcation diagram [4]

In this paper we have used the logistic equations given by Liu Bing and Fu Die [4] to have better logistic mapping which is given as follows in (2):

$$x_{n+1} = \begin{cases} 4\mu(0.25 - x_n)^2, x_n \in (0, 05] \\ 1 - 4\mu(0.75 - x_n)^2, x_n \in (0.5, 1] \end{cases} \quad (2)$$

Where μ and n are defined in same way as above.

2.2 Hamming Code

Hamming code is one of the oldest and most popular and reliable source of error detection and error correction of a single bit error. It is very useful in case of data transmission when there is a probability of bit error. In that case, splitting data into small bunches and applying hamming code will be very helpful in data correction. In this paper we have implemented 15-bit hamming code in which we have taken 11-bit of data along with four parity bits in order to detect and correct error [10]. Format of 15-bit hamming code is given as {P1, P2, D3, P4, D5, D6, D7, P8, D9, D10, D11, D12, D13, D14, D15} where D's are data bits and P's are parity bits.

Procedure for calculating parity bits P's are as follows:

$$P1 = XOR\ (D3,D5,D7,D9,D11,D13,D15); \tag{3}$$

$$P2 = XOR\ (D3,D6,D7,D10,D11,D14,D15); \tag{4}$$

$$P4 = XOR\ (D5,D6,D7,D12,D13,D14,D15); \tag{5}$$

$$P8 = XOR\ (D9,D10,D11,D12,D13,D14,D15); \tag{6}$$

At receiver side, correct data bits are obtained by first checking which bit is in error, given by C ($15 \geq C \geq 0$, where C = 0, signifies no error) and then complementing that bit position.

$$C1 = XOR\ (P1, D3, D5, D7, D9, D11, D13, D15); \tag{7}$$

$$C2 = XOR\ (P2, D3, D6, D7, D10, D11, D14, D15); \tag{8}$$

$$C3 = XOR\ (P4, D5, D6, D7, D12, D13, D14, D15); \tag{9}$$

$$C4 = XOR\ (P8, D9, D10, D11, D12, D13, D14, D15); \tag{10}$$

$$C = \{C1,C2,C3,C4\}; \tag{11}$$

3   Methodology

This section explains about the details of procedure we have followed in this paper. This starts from MATLAB where we have read original audio files. After that using MATLAB this data is first shifted to make it positive this is followed by quantization. Finally quantized data is converted into binary file in which it is divided into various rows and columns (size of each column is n * m * b, where n is number of rows, m is number of column and b is number of bits used for each element in matrix used in Verilog code). This division is done because we have a very large string of binary values 0 and 1 and FPGAs don't have infinite IOBs to incorporate this amount. Thus data is provided in piece by piece format, for e.g., when n = m = 8, then it signifies 64 numbers to be processed, b in column signifies each number in bits where a number can vary from 0 to 255. If we have set b = 8, it turns out to be same range as in decimal format. This data is stored into a text file which can be read by Xilinx for further processing. Rows in binary file are created as per data size.

Once we have the data in binary format, we can start the encryption process which is initiated by reading data into a memory in Xilinx during initialization period, then row by row data is sent into module, i.e. top module, where data encryption gets started. Since most of the FPGAs cannot process floating point type data, we need some other method to implement previous algorithm in Verilog. This can be done by simple scaling by multiples of 10 so that the decimal value obtained remains negligible compared to retained value. We have done this by multiplying it with 106 which gives new equations as shown in (12). Since with iterations this would lead to a very large number X_n, it is modulated by some specific number depending on range parameter which we have set to 256 and the comparison has been with range itself. Ranges also have significant impact on our code and randomness of further processing by positioning and xor data.

$$X_{n+1} = \begin{cases} \left(4(25 - X_n)^2\right) \% (range * 2), & X_n < (range) \\ \left(1 - 4(75 - X_n)^2\right) \% (range * 2), & X_n \geq (range) \end{cases} \quad (12)$$

Then we have used this data to shuffle our main data blocks. First we have obtained suffulePosition (a variable) from logistic mapping by setting μ, n, X_0 and m (where X_0 is the initial value of logistic mapping), then we have block size equal to n * m for every data having b data bits (even each X_n is b bit wide) i.e. we have same number of suffulePosition data and main data having exactly same number of bits, then suffulePosition is used to shuffle indices of every data block.

This completes our first part of encryption. Then next step is to perform logical XOR operation of shuffled data with xor data, which is obtained by logistic mapping with different parameters μ and X_0 in which block size is kept same as data block.

The whole process of encryption followed by error detection and correction part i.e. hamming code can easily be understood with the help of flow charts given in Fig. 2, 3, 4, 5, and 6.

Process begins with (after getting samples from MATLAB and reading those samples in XILINX) generating random position whose flow chart is given in Fig. 2. For complete process, let's assume we have taken n number of rows and m number of columns having each cell b bit wide. Process of generating positions and xor data starts by defining μ and X_0 parameters which marks starting of logistic encryption having equations defined by (12). With the help of loop, array containing above data is created. We have taken different initial parameter for both generating position and generating xor data. Each iteration follows equations defined by (12).

Then getting random position data or posn_data and random XOR binary sequence or xor_data, main encryption process starts. Here posn_data shows where ith index of array is shifted like if first element for n = m = 8 matrix size is 53 then first index of data array will be moved to that position, in this way whole data sequence is shuffled. After shuffling, shuffled data is XORed with xor_data which completes encryption process. This process is shown in Fig. 3.

After getting encrypted data next process is to convert encrypted data into 15 bit hamming code. For each iteration, 11 bits of encrypted data is taken then parity bits P1, P2, P3 and P4 are generated as per equations given in hamming code section. These 11 bits are then merged with 4 bits to form single error correcting hamming code. It may happen that encrypted data is not in multiple of 11, thus data is padded with zeros. Here hamm_itr signifies hamming iterations which is equal to padded data which is multiple of 11 divided by 11 thus it shows number of bunches of 11 bit in encrypted data.

Now data must be processed in order to obtain original data, first hamming code must be removed. This can be done as per Fig. 5. While removing hamming code, checking for any bit error occurred is done. If there is an error, that error bit is complemented/negated (this bit is given by C), this process happens for every 15 bits received.

Then last step and most important step in whole process is to obtain original data from encrypted data. This requires the exact same posn_data and xor_data to decrypt received data. This starts by first logical XOR of encrypted data with xor_data. Then using posn_data, shuffled data is de-shuffled. Thus original data is obtained from encrypted data. Flowchart shown in Fig. 6 explains this step.

3.1 Flow Charts

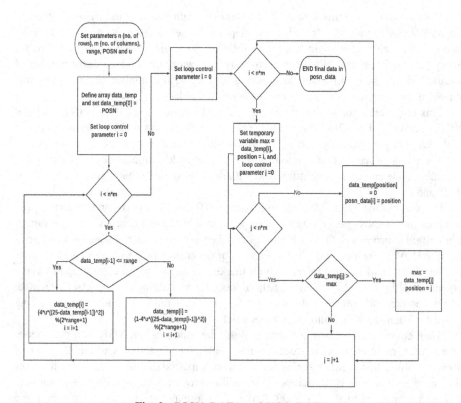

Fig. 2. POSN_DATA and XOR_DATA

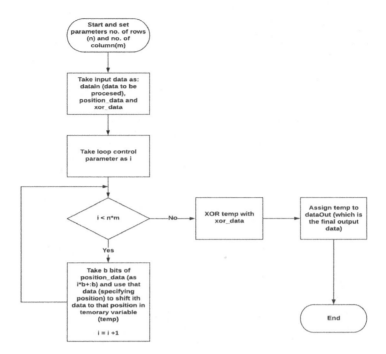

Fig. 3. Logistic encryption

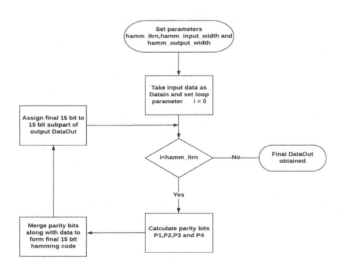

Fig. 4. Hamming code

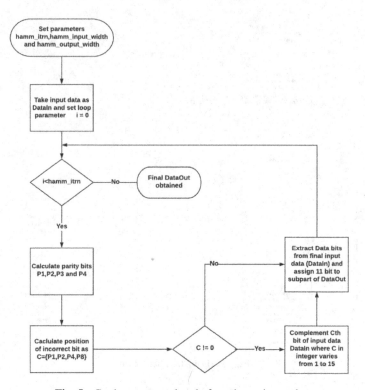

Fig. 5. Getting encrypted code from hamming code

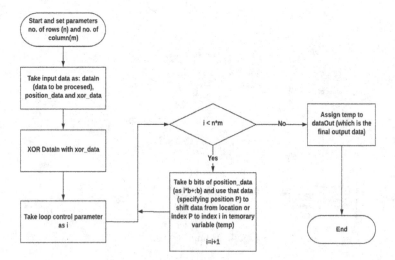

Fig. 6. Decryption algorithm

4 Simulation Results

All the simulations have been performed in MATLAB R2018a. and hardware based simulations have been performed in Xilinx where target device was xc7x1140tflg1930-1 of Virtex-7 family having 1100 number of IOBs and 712000 number of LUTs.

For this paper, we have taken values of X_0 and μ, in Eq. 12, as 30 and 351 respectively for position data and 20 and 379 respectively for xor data.

4.1 MATLAB Simulation Results

In this section all the MATLAB simulation results are given. In these simulation results, y-axis represents Amplitude and x-axis represents samples. In Fig. 7 shows the samples of input audio file taken in MATLAB at 44100 Hz frequency.

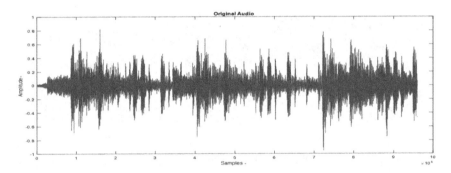

Fig. 7. Original input speech signal

The above signal is then quantized in amplitude and shifted by adding a DC value so as to make all samples positive. This is done to have ease in converting samples into binary files. As seen in Fig. 8 that quantization has a very small impact on overall waveform of input audio file.

Then the quantized signal/waveform is processed with encryption algorithm as explained earlier. The results for encrypted wave are given in Fig. 9, it can be seen that it is very much different from original audio file.

Then the encrypted signal is decrypted using methods discussed earlier as corresponding results are shown in Fig. 10. These results are exactly same as original audio file with no loss of any sort of data.

4.2 Simulation Results of Xilinx Vivado

In Verilog, data is being processed sequentially (in form of samples). Image given in Fig. 12 shows the simulation results of a single sample.

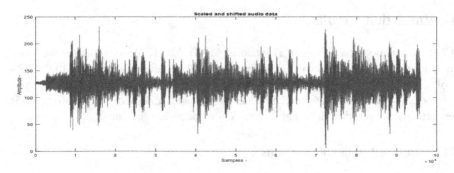

Fig. 8. Shifted and quantized speech signal

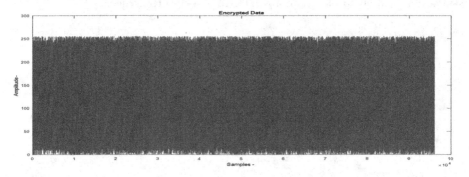

Fig. 9. Encrypted speech signal

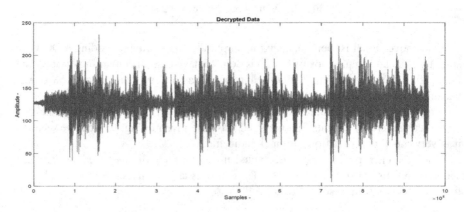

Fig. 10. Decrypted speech signal

Here, 'dataln' is a 1×128 bit vector, which represents input data matrix of 4×4 where each element is 8 bit long. 'enc_out' is encrypted data. 'hamm_out' is the actual data, which will be transmitted. This is hamming coded form of encrypted data.

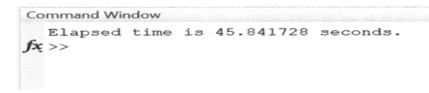

Fig. 11. Execution time taken by MATLAB

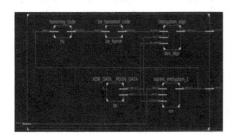

Fig. 12. Xillinx simulation output

At receiver side, 'hamm_out' will be received. Then after error detection and correction (if any) this data will be converted into 'dehamm_out'. 'dehamm_out' is obtained by removing hamming parity bits (de-hamming process) from received data. This is now same as 'enc_out' (encrypted data). Now this data will be decrypted and stored in 'dec_out'.

Figure 11 shows the execution time of the MATLAB. Schematic is given in Fig. 13 and hardware utilization is given in Figs. 14, 15, and 16 and Table 1.

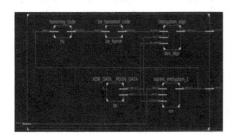

Fig. 13. Block diagram of whole process

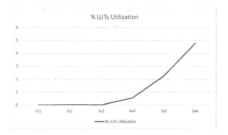

Fig. 14. LUT utilization

Results have shown that delay increases almost linearly with increasing dimensions n and m of block while LUTs and IOBs utilization increases exponentially.

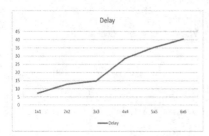

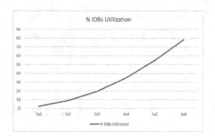

Fig. 15. Graph for delay   **Fig. 16.** Graph for IOBs

Table 1. Hardware utilization and delay for different values of n * m

n × m	IOB's (Available)	LUT's (Available 712000)	Delay (ns)
1 × 1	24(2.18%)	...	7.318
2 × 2	96(8.73%)	64(0.01%)	12.866
3 × 3	216(19.64%)	133(0.02%)	14.92
4 × 4	384(34.91%)	3899(0.55%)	28.52
5 × 5	600(54.55%)	16117(2.26%)	35.43
6 × 6	864(78.55%)	33967(4.77%)	40.464

5   Conclusion

In this paper, we have shown the effectiveness and reliability of the chaotic system for secure communication. We have gone through basic properties of chaotic system and its sensitivity on initial values, which lead to butterfly diagrams and hence provides a strong way to its implementation in field of encryption. Then with various examples, it has been shown how logistic system being a chaotic system alters the content that makes it very difficult to understand unless a person has exact initial parameters. MATLAB and XILINX simulations results are shown which clearly states how fast is hardware implementation in comparison to software ones and justifies the fact to have a separate hardware module for speech encryption. Also synthesis results show hardware utilization for Virtex-7 is very less and hardware utilization increases exponentially with increasing size of data n and m. Chaotic systems are so effective that they are expanding in other fields also. Future work may include having highly chaotic system providing a wide range of input parameters thus improving its efficiency tremendously and seeking its features to other applications.

References

1. Chien, T.I., Wang, N.Z., Liao, T.L., Chang, S.B.: Design of multiple accessing chaotic digital communication system based on Interleaved chaotic differential peaks keying (I-CDPK). In: 2008 6th International Symposium on Communication Systems, Networks and Digital Signal Processing Year (2008)
2. Venkatesh, S., Singh, P.: An improved multiple access chaotic communication system using orthogonal chaotic vectors. In: 2011 International Conference on Communications and Signal Processing Year (2011)
3. Pich, R., Chivapreecha, S., Prabnasak, J.: A single, triple chaotic cryptography using chaos in digital filter and its own comparison to DES and triple DES. In: 2018 International Workshop on Advanced Image Technology (IWAIT) (2018)
4. Bing, L., Die, F.: An image encryption algorithm of scrambling binary sequences by improved logistic mapping. In: 2017 IEEE 17th International Conference on Communication Technology (ICCT) (2017)
5. Lou, Y., Hu, T.: A novel image security system based on cellular automata and improved chaotic system. In: 2012 5th International Congress on image and Signal Processing (2012)
6. Cohen, M.E., Hudson, D.L., Anderson, M.F., Deedwania, P.C.: Using chaotic measures to summarize medical signal analysis. In: Proceedings of the 1st Joint BMES/EMBS Conference. 1999 IEEE Engineering in Medicine and Biology 21st Annual Conference and the 1999 Annual Fall Meeting of the Biomedical Engineering Society (1999)
7. Abdullah, H.N., Abdullah, H.A.: Image encryption using hybrid chaotic map. In: 2017 International Conference on Current Research in Computer Science and Information Technology (ICCIT) (2017)
8. Liu, Z.-S., Wu, S.-L.: Synchronization of two unsmooth chua chaotic circuits through numerical optimization. In: 2013 6th International Conference on Natural Computation (ICNC) (2013)
9. Tripathi, S.K., Soundra Pandian, K.K., Gupta, B.: Hardware implementation of dynamic key value based stream cipher using chaotic logistic map. In: Proceedings of the 2nd International Conference on Trends in Electronics and Informatics, ICOEI 2018 (2018)
10. Singh, A.K.: Error detection and correction by Hamming code. In: 2016 International Conference on Global Trends in Signal Processing, Information Computing and Communication (ICGTSPICC) (2016)
11. Garcia-Bosque, M., Pérez-Resa, A., Sánchez-Azqueta, C., Aldea, C., Celma, S.: Chaos-based bitwise dynamical pseudorandom number generator on FPGA. IEEE Trans. Instrum. Meas. **68**, 291–293 (2019)
12. Sayed, W.S., Tolba, M.F., Radwan, A.G., Abd-El-Hafiz, S.K.: Speech encryption using generalized modified chaotic logistic and tent maps. In: IEEE International Conference on Industrial Technology (ICIT) (2018)
13. Lian, S.: Multimedia Content Encryption: Techniques and Applications. CRC Press, Boca Raton (2008)

A Survey of Network Attacks in Wireless Sensor Networks

Rishita Verma$^{(\boxtimes)}$ (ORCID) and Sourabh Bharti (ORCID)

Department of Information Technology, Indira Gandhi Delhi Technical
University for Women, Kashmere Gate, Delhi 110006, India
rishitaverma@gmail.com

Abstract. In Today's modern world, with the advent of advances in Technology. Wireless Sensor Networks (WSN) is an emerging and the most widely used medium for communication due to its large number of advantages over traditional wired networks. WSN consists of thousands of sensor nodes which are connected to each other in a network. However, WSN are more prone to security threats and attacks because WSN have very low memory, power and computation capabilities. WSN are susceptible to various types of attacks which can occur on any layer in the protocol stack. But network layer is more prone to the attacks. Therefore, we are focusing on network layer attacks in this paper.

Keywords: Attacks · Wireless Sensor Network · Security · Spoofing · Selective forwarding · Black hole · Sink hole · Wormhole · Acknowledgement spoofing

1 Introduction

WSN is an interconnection of hundreds or even thousands of sensor nodes that are geographically dispersed over a wide area. The sensor nodes in WSN have data acquisition and data processing capabilities which enables them to record and monitor the physical and operational conditions of real world environment and this collected data is reported to a central node at a regular and timely interval. The conditions of real world environment which WSN measure includes wind, temperature, air quality index, pressure etc.

WSN have a large domain of applications that includes intrusion detection, power system monitoring, traffic monitoring, Gas monitoring to very critical applications such as Disaster emergency response, forest fire monitoring, Tsunami detection, Military battlefield surveillance, air pollution monitoring, Healthcare application and so on.

However, as we know that every network regardless even if it is a wired network or if it is a wireless network, is susceptible to attacks. WSN is no different. WSN have very low memory, power and computation capabilities. Therefore we cannot apply heavy algorithms requiring large memory and computational power to WSN which makes the attacks on WSN more severe and dangerous than attacks wired networks.

WSN are often deployed in open environments where they interact with the people, which makes them more prone to malicious attacks. The attackers can use this as an advantage to compromise the security of network. For example, the attackers can flood

C. Badica et al. (Eds.): ICICCT 2020, CCIS 1170, pp. 50–63, 2020.
https://doi.org/10.1007/978-981-15-9671-1_4

the network with large amount of traffic consisting useless or old messages which will consume all the memory and battery power of the nodes and halt the communication in the network. Therefore, security of the WSN is a major concern and proper defenses are required to counter the attacks [1].

2 WSN Model

WSN consists of four components: Sensor nodes, Sensor field, Sink, Base station [2] (Fig. 1).

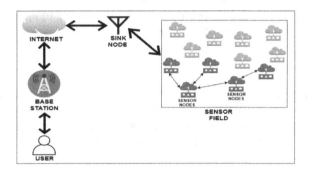

Fig. 1. WSN components.

Sensor nodes collect, process, and transmits the data and information to the sink node and they are placed in a region called Sensor field. The data collected by the sensor node is received by sink node. Base Station excerpt information from the sensor nodes and also transmits information back to the nodes in the network.

3 Security Requirements of WSN

WSN are the networks in which data and information is exchanged among various sensor nodes of the networks. This information is mission critical for some application and needs to be protected from any malicious attack. There are some security requirements of WSN which needs to be followed and satisfied for the secure transmission of information among the nodes and the network. This section describes the security requirements of WSN:

3.1 Data Confidentiality

Confidentiality [3] refers to protecting the access of sensitive data from unauthorized parties and only authorized parties can access this data.

Data confidentiality in WSN implies that the data exchanged and transmitted between the sensor nodes should be kept secret and it should only be understood by the sending and receiving nodes. Violation of confidentiality can lead to eavesdropping, snooping attacks etc. Encryption is used to counter confidentiality threats.

3.2 Data Integrity

Integrity [3] refers to ensuring that the data has not been modified or altered by unauthorised party and the source of the data is trustworthy.

Data Integrity in WSN implies the protection of data from unauthorized or unpermissible modifications. Data should be in the same state as sent by the sender node when it is received by the receiver node. Data integrity assures unauthorized modifications and also modification in an unauthorized way. Data integrity includes source integrity i.e. the reliability and trustworthiness of source of the data and Data integrity i.e. the reliability and trustworthiness of data. Violation of integrity can lead to Modification/Alteration, spoofing threats etc.

3.3 Availability

Availability [3] means that the data/service accessible to all the authorized parties anytime and anywhere. Availability ensures the timely and reliable access to and use of data to authorized nodes in the WSN. Failing to do the same will lead to denial of service attack, In this attack the authorized nodes are not able to access the network because of deliberate manipulation of the resources by an attacker to make the network service unavailable to the authorized nodes.

3.4 Authentication

Authentication [3] refers to verifying the identity of the sender. Authentication in WSN implies that the sender node of the data is the one that it claims itself to be, not some imposter which is sending the messages by spoofing the original sender. Violation of authentication will lead to spoofing threats.

3.5 Authorization

Authorization [3] is defined as the process of specifying the access rights of various resources in a network. Authorization refers to giving access to data and various resources to only the authenticated nodes. Authorization occurs after authentication and this access depends on different rights given to a particular authenticated node.

3.6 Data Freshness

Data freshness [3] in WSN implies that only new messages should be transmitted and no can replay old messages that are already transmitted again in the sensor network. Failing to achieve this will lead to replay attacks. Data freshness can be ensured by adding a nonce or a timestamp by adding time of the message.

4 Taxonomy of Attacks

WSN have very limited resource capabilities and generally, an attacker have more powerful tools and mechanisms to attack a node or even the whole sensor network. Furthermore, an attacker can spoof, alter, intercept or steal the network packets which can lead to security breach in the whole network.

In this section we discuss various categories of attacks on WSN (Fig. 2).

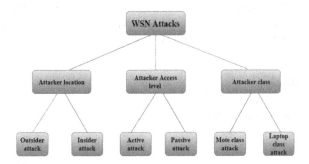

Fig. 2. Taxonomy of attacks

4.1 Outsider vs. Insider Attacks

Outsider Attacks

In this attack [4], the attacker node is an unauthorized node which is not a valid participant of the network. The attacker can intercept the network packets by listening to the frequency range of the target network.

Insider Attacks

In this attack [4], the attacker node is an authorized node of the network. An attacker or compromised node can be a sensor node which is being controlled or reprogrammed by an attacker or it can be device such as a computer or laptop which have more capabilities such as larger memory, larger RAM etc.

4.2 Active vs. Passive Attacks

Active Attacks

In this attack [4], the attacker's goal is to alter, modify or harm the network. Active attack targets the integrity and the availability services in the network. For instance, masquerading as a genuine or legal node in the network to gain access in the network and obtaining the information. Now this obtained information will be altered or modified by the adversary for harmful purposes.

Passive Attacks

In this attack [4], the attacker's goal is to eavesdrop and sniff the information to gather insights about the network. The attacker does not alter, modify or harm the network. The information gathered is then used to launch further attacks and harm the network.

4.3   Mote Class vs. Laptop Class

Mote Class
In this attack [4], the attacker uses the same type of devices as the sensor nodes to launch the attack on the network. The attacker devices have the same memory, power and computation capabilities as the sensor nodes.

Laptop Class
In this attack [4], the attacker uses the devices which have higher capability than the sensor nodes to launch the attack on the network. The attacker devices have high resource capabilities than the sensor nodes.

5   Protocol Stack

There are various attacks at each layer of the protocol stack possible in WSN that are shown in Table 1.

Table 1. Various types of WSN attacks at each layer.

Layer	Attacks [1]
Application layer	1. Attacks on reliability 2. Malicious code attack
Transport layer	1. Injects false messages 2. Flooding 3. Desynchronization 4. Data integrity 5. Energy drain
Network layer	1. Spoofing 2. Selective forwarding 3. Sinkhole 4. Sybil 5. Wormhole 6. Hello flood 7. Acknowledgement spoofing 8. Neglect and greed 9. Homing attack 10. Misdirection 11. Blackhole
Data link layer	1. Collision 2. Internet jamming
Physical layer	1. Eavesdropping 2. Node tampering 3. Hardware hacking

6 WSN Network Layer Attacks

6.1 Spoof, Altered or Replayed Routing Information

In this attack [4–6], the attacker may spoof or impersonate one entity by another and it fools a victim by making it believe that it is communicating with a different entity.

In WSN, an attacker can disrupt the normal functioning of the network. This can lead to generating false error messages, changing routing routes, generating routing loops, attracting or discarding messages from certain sensor nodes & participating the sensor network.

Spoofing attack can be prevented by using Message Authentication Code (MAC) with the message. The receiver can verify the authenticity of the sender by generating MAC using the same hash function and the secret key.

Replaying attack can be prevented by including time stamps or nonce with the messages.

6.2 Selective Forwarding Attack

In this attack [4–6], the compromised or malicious node may forward only selective messages or drop all the messages that it receives. This will lead to disruption in the communication of the sensor network or the network will halt completely.

We can prevent this attack by detecting malicious node in the network and removing them or by finding an alter path in the network. Another way of defense is to use multiple paths in the network to send messages (Fig. 3).

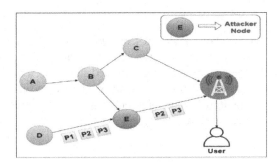

Fig. 3. Selective forwarding attack

6.3   Sinkhole Attack

In this attack [4–6], the attacker entices all the network traffic to a particular compromised node which is reprogrammed and controlled by the attacker. The attacker can achieve this goal by providing a high quality routing path which have more battery power and other capabilities to reach the base station. Further, this will lead to all the neighboring nodes into believing that such a high quality path exist and they will forward all their packets to this compromised or malicious node. Now, this malicious node contains forwarded packets of nearly all the nodes in the network and the attacker can modify, tamper or launch other attacks on the sensor networks. One such attack is selective forwarding attack in which the node will selectively forward the packets or completely drop them (Fig. 4).

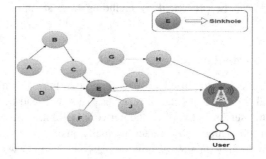

Fig. 4. Sinkhole attacks

6.4   Sybil Attack

In this attack [4–6], a malicious node presents itself to the other nodes by using multiple identities. This attack reduces the efficiency and effectiveness of certain schemes such as fault tolerance, dispersity, distributed storage or replicas. For example in the case of achieving redundancy to safeguard against availability threats, the attacker node can present itself using multiple identities and lures the victim into believing that a certain level of redundancy has been achieved (Fig. 5).

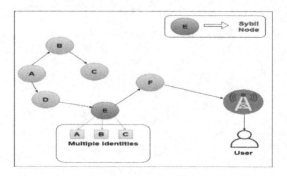

Fig. 5. Sybil attacks

6.5   Wormhole Attack

A wormhole [4–6] can be defined as a link which have low latency and this link exists between two segments of sensor network. The attacker replays message in these two portions of the network. An example of this attack is, a single node transmitting messages between two adjacent nodes. A variant of this instance includes a node forwarding message between two non-adjacent nodes or nodes which exists in different parts of the network.

This attack can also lead to sinkhole attack because the attacker can lure the nodes into believing that it is just one or more node away from the base station or sink node and also by creating a virtual high-quality path to the base station.

Wormhole attacks can be detected and prevented by a mechanism called packet leashes. There are two type of leases namely Geographic and Temporal leashes (Fig. 6).

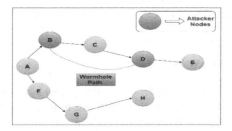

Fig. 6. Wormhole attack

6.6   Hello Flood Attack

The basis for this attack [4–6] is that in WSN, many routing protocols make a false assumption i.e. when a node send hello packets to announce itself, then the nodes assume that they are in the radio frequency range of that particular node and that particular node is a neighbour node. An attacker can also send hello flood packets by using high power transmitter and lures all the nodes into believing that they are neighbours to the sender node and the attacker can also provide a high quality path to the base station. Now, most of the nodes would be selecting this high quality node to forward packets to base station but in reality the forwarded messages are sent to the attack unknown which may or may not forward all the packets. One defense mechanism against this attack is to verify the bi directional link in the network (Fig. 7).

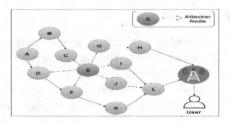

Fig. 7. Hello flood attack

6.7 Acknowledgement Spoofing Attack

The basis for this attack [4–6] is that in WSN, many routing algorithm used acknowledgement to ensure that the messages are received successfully by the receiver. A attacker node in the network can spoof or impersonate the acknowledgement of the packets which are destined for the neighbouring nodes. The motivation for this attack is to provide false information or to convince the victim that a dead note is alive or degrading the energy of the nodes.

6.8 Neglect and Greed Attack

Neglect and Greed attack [5] can be defined as the type of attack in which the attacker or malicious nodes receives the network packets but refuses to forward them or it will forward the packets of higher priority which is determined by this malicious node itself. The effect of this attack depends upon the location of the malicious node and the network region size

6.9 Homing Attack

In this attack [5], the attacker just observes the roles and finds out the location of various nodes in the network such as the nodes near to the base station. The attacker do not modifies or alters the packets. Homing attack is a form of passive attack in which the aim is to gather insights about the network resources which would be useful for launching further attacks on the network.

6.10 Misdirection Attack

In this attack [5], the attacker node misguides or misleads its neighbouring nodes by displaying false or incorrect routing information. Also the packets received by this node will not be transmitted to the intended receiver. This attack causes disturbance in the communication of the network and lead the network in a confused state.

6.11 Blackhole Attack

Blackhole attack [5] is mostly used in combination with the selective forwarding attack. In this attack, a malicious node in the network simply drops all the packets which are received by it; creating a black hole in the network. In this black hole no messages are transmitted in the network which will lead to the disruption of communication in the network.

7 Observations

Attack	Effect on network performance	Defenses	Threats to security services	Location of attacker	Type of Attack	Attack class	Comments/observations
Spoof, altered or replayed routing attack	Generation of false error messages, changing of routing routes, Generating routing loops, alteration or discarding messages from certain sensor nodes [6]	Spoofing attack can be prevented by using Authentication mechanisms (e.g. MAC) [4]. Replaying attack can be prevented by using Timestamps and nonce	Authenticity, integrity, confidentiality	Outsider/insider	Active	Mote class/laptop class	WSN is more vulnerable to spoofing due to the deployment of WSN in open environments. One common defence approach for spoofing is by using authentication mechanisms but implementing these mechanisms is also difficult due to the resource limitations of WSN
Selective forwarding attack	Disruption in communication in the network, or complete network halt [4]	Selective Forwarding attack can be prevented by detecting malicious nodes (probing) and removing them or by selecting an alternate path or by using multiple paths [4]	Confidentiality, availability	Insider	Active	Mote class	Selective forwarding attack is an attack in which the malicious node increases the data loss in the network by selectively forwarding the data packets or by dropping them. This attack is even more difficult to detect because the malicious node selectively forward some packets in the network to make the sender node believe that the packets are sent by not completely disrupting the communication
Sinkhole attack	Disruption in communication in the network, or complete network halt, Energy degradation in the network [4]	Sinkhole attack can be prevented by detecting malicious nodes, or by using multiple paths	Confidentiality, integrity, availability	Outsider/insider	Active	Mote class/laptop class	Sinkhole attacks are very severe for WSN because the attacker gets control of all the data packets and he/she can tamper, modify or alter the data for malicious purposes which is even more harmful for mission critical applications(e.g. Military applications etc.)

(*continued*)

(*continued*)

Attack	Effect on network performance	Defenses	Threats to security services	Location of attacker	Type of Attack	Attack class	Comments/observations
Sybil attack	Reduces the efficiency of routing algorithms, fault tolerance, dispersity, distributed storage in the network [6]	Sybil attack can be prevented by monitoring the network, or by using Authentication mechanisms [4]	Availability, authenticity	Insider	Active	Mote class/laptop class	Sybil attack causes very serious deterioration of security services WSN because in this attack the malicious node uses multiple identities in the network which is direct threat to the authenticity services. In some critical applications this can lead the network in a confused state such as in Disaster response application the attacker can create a false emergency situation by using malicious nodes with multiple identities or by failing to report an emergency situation which required an immediate response
Wormhole attack	Changing of routing routes, creation of routing loops, sending false information to nodes [1]	Wormhole attack can be prevented by a mechanism known as packet leashes, or by using Authentication mechanisms [4], or detecting malicious nodes (probing)	Confidentiality, authenticity	Insider	Active	Mote class/laptop class	Wormhole attack is a very harmful attack in WSN due to its nature of creating a low latency link between two or more nodes in the network. Wormhole attack become even more difficult to detect and prevent when used in combination with the selective forwarding, blackhole or Sybil attacks
HELLO flood attack	Energy degradation in the network, creation of false routing paths, changing of routing routes [1]	Wormhole attack can be prevented by verifying the bidirectional link, or by using Authentication mechanisms [4]	Availability, authenticity	Insider	Active	Mote class/laptop class	In this attack, the attacker uses the advantage of the naïve assumption of the nodes i.e. the nodes send Hello packets to introduce themselves in the network. However, the attacker can use a high computation device to send this message to all nodes and introduce the malicious node as their neighbour. Also the defence mechanisms all requires high computation capabilities which are not supported by the WSN

(*continued*)

(continued)

Attack	Effect on network performance	Defenses	Threats to security services	Location of attacker	Type of Attack	Attack class	Comments/observations
Acknowledgement spoofing attack	Sending false information to nodes, energy degradation in the network	Acknowledgement spoofing attack can be prevented by verifying the bidirectional link, or by using Authentication mechanisms [4]	Availability, authenticity	Insider	Active	Mote class/laptop class	This attack targets the authenticity and availability of the nodes in the network. In this attack, the attacker's goal is to leave the network in a confused state by providing incorrect data and also making the victim believe that a node is alive
Neglect and greed attack	Affects the efficiency of Dynamic source routing (DSR), Depends upon the location of malicious node and network size [5]	Neglect and greed attack can be prevented by using Authentication mechanisms, or detecting malicious nodes (probing) [5]	Authenticity, availability	Insider	Active	Mote class	The motivation for this attack is to target the availability of the nodes and to increase information loss in the network. The attacker forwards the data by maintaining a priority list and by sending it according to this list
Homing attack	Attacker gathers information about critical nodes, gateway for launching other attacks	Homing attack can be prevented by encipherment techniques [5]	Confidentiality	Outsider/insider	Passive	Mote class/Laptop class	In this attack, the attacker only reconnaissance information about the critical nodes such as nodes closer to the base station to launch an attack. This attack opens door for the attacker to launch further harmful attacks
Misdirection attack	Generation of false error messages, changing of routing routes, sending false information to nodes, creation of routing loops, infinite delay [5]	Misdirection attack can be prevented by monitoring the network for intruders	Availability, authenticity	Outsider/insider	Active	Mote class/laptop class	In this attack, the attacker misguides the nodes to send the data to nodes other than the destination nodes. This creates false information and increases data loss. In some applications such as location finding services due to this attack false route will be sent to the user
Blackhole attack	Disruption in communication in the network, increasing the information loss [1]	Blackhole attack can be prevented by monitoring the network for intruders, or using Authentication mechanisms, or detecting malicious nodes	Confidentiality, availability, authenticity	Insider	Active	Mote class/laptop class	In this attack the malicious node simply drops all the packets to be sent and leads to a halt in communication in the network. Availability service is targeted in this attack

8 Conclusion

As we know, that providing security to any system is a cumbersome task. And also referring to the 12 security principles [8], there is no such thing as absolute security. Therefore, we have observed that WSN is also susceptible to various types of attacks at different layers. We have provided various solution for different threats in our paper. However, all the attacks and threats cannot be eliminated. Further research is needed for providing more secure solution for WSN.

References

1. Tomić, I., McCann, J.A.: A survey of potential security issues in existing wireless sensor network protocols. IEEE IoT J. **4**(6), 1910–1923 (2017). Author, F., Author, S.: Title of a proceedings paper. In: Editor, F., Editor, S. (eds.) Conference 2016, LNCS, vol. 9999, pp. 1–13. Springer, Heidelberg (2016)
2. Karakaya, A., Akleylek, S.: A survey on security threats and authentication approaches in wireless sensor networks. In: 2018 6th International Symposium on Digital Forensic and Security (ISDFS), pp. 1–4. IEEE (March 2018). Author, F.: Contribution title. In: 9th International Proceedings on Proceedings, pp. 1–2. Publisher, Location (2010)
3. Singh, U.R., Roy, S., Mutum, H.: A survey on wireless sensor network security and its countermeasures: an overview. Int. J. Eng. Sci. Invent. **3**, 19–37 (2013)
4. Wang, Y., Attebury, G., Ramamurthy, B.: A survey of security issues in wireless sensor networks. IEEE Commun. Surv. Tutor. **8**(2), 2–23 (2006)
5. Ioannou, C., Vassiliou, V.: The impact of network layer attacks in wireless sensor networks. In: 2016 International Workshop on Secure Internet of Things (SIoT), pp. 20–28. IEEE (September 2016)
6. Karlof, C., Wagner, D.: Secure routing in wireless sensor networks: attacks and countermeasures. Ad Hoc Netw. **1**(2–3), 293–315 (2003)
7. Shi, E., Perrig, A.: Designing secure sensor networks. IEEE Wirel. Commun. **11**(6), 38–43 (2004)
8. Breithaupt, J., Merkow, S.: Information Security Principles of Success. Part of the Certification/Training Series, pp. 3–15 (2014)
9. Dubey, R., Jain, V., Thakur, R.S., Choubey, S.: Attacks in wireless sensor networks. Int. J. Sci. Eng. Res. **3**(3), 1–4 (2012)
10. Sen, J.: A survey on wireless sensor network security. arXiv preprint arXiv:1011.1529 (2010)
11. Zou, Y., Zhu, J., Wang, X., Hanzo, L.: A survey on wireless security: technical challenges, recent advances, and future trends. Proc. IEEE **104**(9), 1727–1765 (2016)
12. Panda, M.: Security threats at each layer of wireless sensor networks. Int. J. Adv. Res. Comput. Sci. Softw. Eng. **3**(11), 61–67 (2013)
13. Yang, Q., Zhu, X., Fu, H., Che, X.: Survey of security technologies on wireless sensor networks. J. Sens. **2015**, 1–9 (2015)
14. Akyildiz, I.F., Su, W., Sankarasubramaniam, Y., Cayirci, E.: A survey on sensor networks. IEEE Commun. Mag. **40**(8), 102–114 (2002)
15. Walters, J.P., Liang, Z., Shi, W., Chaudhary, V.: Wireless sensor network security: a survey. In: Security in Distributed, Grid, Mobile, and Pervasive Computing, vol. 1, p. 367 (2007)

16. Perrig, A., Stankovic, J., Wagner, D.: Security in wireless sensor networks. Commun. ACM **47**(6), 53–57 (2004)
17. Chan, H., Perrig, A.: Security and privacy in sensor networks. Computer **36**(10), 103–105 (2003)
18. Chen, X., Makki, K., Yen, K., Pissinou, N.: Sensor network security: a survey. IEEE Commun. Surv. Tutor. **11**(2), 52–73 (2009)
19. Newsome, J., Shi, E., Song, D., Perrig, A.: The Sybil attack in sensor networks: analysis & defenses. In: 2004 3rd International Symposium on Information Processing in Sensor Networks, IPSN 2004, pp. 259–268. IEEE (April 2004)
20. Pathan, A.S.K., Lee, H.W., Hong, C.S.: Security in wireless sensor networks: issues and challenges. In: 2006 8th International Conference Advanced Communication Technology, vol. 2, p. 6. IEEE (February 2006)

LiFi Based Scheme for Handover in VANET: A Proposed Approach

Chinmoy Sailendra Kalita[(✉)] and Maushumi Barooah

Department of Computer Application, Assam Engineering College,
Guwahati, India
chinmoykalita81@gmail.com, maushu@gmail.com

Abstract. A wireless network connecting a group of vehicles irrespective of it
being stationary or mobile constitutes Vehicular ad hoc networks (VANET).
Traditionally VANET has been exploited for safety of drivers and pedestrians
on the road, but now is been also utilized as an infrastructure for intelligent
transport systems (ITS). Communication in VANET has always led to frequent
handoffs as it is dependent on the vehicular speed along with the number of road
side units (RSU) present and the available bandwidth range. These frequent
handoffs may affect the throughput, packet delivery and quality of services
(QoS). This paper presents detailed taxonomy of different handover processes in
VANET and has laid down a comparative study based on their characteristics
and features. Here a proposal has been put forward on Light Fidelity (Li-Fi)
based handover scheme involving decision making based on certain quality
parameters and active network lifetime.

Keywords: Point of access · Mobile station · Quality of service · Road side
unit · Communication · Li-Fi

1 Introduction

VANET in the last few decades have gained immense popularity and find their use in a
wide range of applications in today's world including the area of ITS for applications
like traffic management, navigation, collision warnings and real time media. VANETs
can be compared to MANET as both are ad-hoc networks [5]. However, speeds of
vehicles in VANET is significantly faster as compared to the mobile nodes in MANET
[10] and are not limited by any battery or storage constraints. Some characteristics of
VANET include their rapidly changing topology due to the frequent change in positioning of the vehicles and the network area could range from a small city to the entire
country. Due to the speeding vehicles the communication network in VANETs are
short lived and has resulted in frequent handoffs [12]. So, there is a need to transfer the
network traffic from one channel to the other within a network to prevent packet losses
and delay for the communication channel.

Most of the state of art work for handoff in VANET includes vertical, horizontal,
hard, soft, imperative, alternate, downward, upward, client-network assisted handoffs
[14]. In some of the works the researchers have considered decision algorithms,
mobility of the nodes, clustering and different technologies such as LTE (Long Term

C. Badica et al. (Eds.): ICICCT 2020, CCIS 1170, pp. 64–71, 2020.
https://doi.org/10.1007/978-981-15-9671-1_5

Evaluation), WiMax (Worldwide Interoperability for Microwave Access), two antenna approach [16]. Li-Fi technology as one of the prominent emerging technology based on wireless visible light communication can be very efficiently utilized to help achieve communication in an heterogeneous network and can perform handoff at a comparatively less cost [18]. We will be looking for Li-fi technology for vertical handover in heterogeneous networks in this paper (Fig. 1).

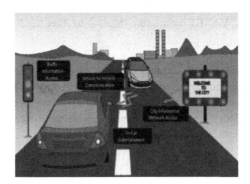

Fig. 1. LiFi in Vanet (Swami Vijaykumar et al., 2017)

In this paper a study on detailed taxonomy on various handoff processes along with a proposed work illustrating the use of Li-Fi technology in a heterogeneous network for achieving better handoff. The paper has been framed as follows: Sect. 2 includes the background study trailed by the literature review on the different handoff schemes. Section 3 shows comparison table of the various handoff processes and Sect. 4 includes the proposed work for handoff and Sect. 5 concludes the paper.

2 Background Study

This section will look into VANET architecture and the state-of-the-art researches. There are three types of VANET architecture which are: Wireless Local Area Network (WLAN), complete ad-hoc network and hybrid-mode network. The WLAN is called Vehicle-to-Infrastructure communication (V2I) using WLAN or access point connected to road side units (RSUs) to gather information. Second type is referred as Vehicle-to-Vehicle (V2V) communications takes place between vehicles through the on board units (OBUs)which is based on Dedicated Short Range Communications (DSRC). The third category it combines both the V2V and V2I modes of communication (Fig. 2).

Handoff is the scheme whereby the network traffic can be transferred from one area of coverage to another area of coverage disconnected due to the shorter range of the outgoing channel [16]. The handover process [14] consist of the following main phases: *Network discovery and analysis*: This phase includes scanning for wireless networks and analyzing their signal quality based on received acknowledgement, *Handoff decision*: Here decision is taken regarding when and with which access point

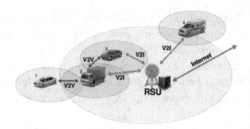

Fig. 2. VANET architecture (Mossobrio R. et al., 2017)

the handoff needs to be performed. *Handoff execution:* This phase performs the actual transfer of routing information to another channel.

Classifications of Handover based on type are: Horizontal handover and Vertical handover, Hard handover and Soft handover, Imperative handover and alternate handover, Downward handover and Upward handover, Network-based handover, Client-based handover, and client assisted handover.

2.1 Literature Review

This section shows some of the state of the art work of different handoff schemes by researchers.

Roberto Baldessar et al. [4] provided a strategy where every vehicle is outfitted with two antennas for transmission and receiving signals. The reception apparatus that is in charge of the handoff checks the signal quality of the BS (Base Station) and if found to be within its signal range vehicle and BS are registered to one another. Handoff method will be performed and after a timeframe the front reception apparatus will be supplanted with new one. In the paper by T. Arnold et al. [6] provided a scheme allowing to trade the IP address from vehicles moving in both directions for the handoff process. V. Devarapalli et al. [8] utilizes Mobile Router (MR) for correspondence with the BS. It has two MRs one at the front called as front MR and another is at end called as back MR. Front MR is in charge of handoff and back MR is in charge of the services to the system. As the load is divided across the MRs the total overhead on the individual vehicles is reduced but there are situations if a high speedy vehicle overtakes the front MR and this may lead to alternate handoff. Here in the work of Pack, S. et al. [2] divided the vehicles on the road into three types with one vehicle performing the handover with another vehicle type broadcasting messages in the network with information on vehicles exiting the network. Supporting this strategy the works of Kuan-Lin Chiu et al. [1] and Toshiya Okabe et al. [3] stated that some APs qualified as Preferred APs perform early handoff very efficiently. The functioning of the RV is particularly important in this approach but is a bit complex as compared to other methods. Zhang et al. [9] showed an approach making clusters of vehicles moving on the road with a group head, which conveys messages straightforwardly to the main station whereas intra cluster vehicles exchange information with the head of the cluster.

In work of Kafle, V.P. et al. [7] provided a scheme whereby during a handover different vehicular nodes can exchange messages and information with successive vehicles in the network along with its sub network and simultaneous exchange of packets takes place. Absence of vehicular nodes could effect this scheme and can also halt this process. For modeling the speed of the vehicle Esposito et al. [11] in their work demonstrated a handover will not really yield a higher throughput when a vehicle experiences another network interface system with higher information rate. Siti S et al. [13] in their work based on vertical handover used a decision algorithm for the handover. Radhwan et al. [15] in their work explicitly talks about the impact speed and LTE on handover.

Wang et al. [17] in their work proposed a dynamic load balancing scheme in an environment where both WiFi and Li-Fi are present. It takes into account the mobility of the nodes and the handover signaling overheads. The Li-Fi access points provide a better packet delivery ratio as compared to WiFi and also provide easy handoff. As it is a hybrid network the overall throughput of the network is dependent on the individual throughput of both Li-Fi and WiFi network which may lead to network partitioning.

3 Comparison

The table below shows the comparison of the various handover schemes (Table 1):

Table 1. Comparison of handover schemes

Sl. no	VANET protocol	Advantages	Disadvantages
1	Two antenna approach	It is fast and reduces the network overhead	It is expensive replacing antennas
2	IP passing	It does not require maintenance	It is dependent on DHCP
3	Network Mobility (NEMO) based	It reduces the overhead on individual vehicles	It fails for any vehicle having a higher speed overtakes front MR
4	Vehicular fast handoff scheme (VFHS)	Reduction in loss of packets	The handover is complex
5	Early handoff mechanism	It is connected to the APs all the time	Unnecessary scanning reduces energy
6	Cluster based handoff	This reduces the overhead on individual	Frequent changes of the cluster head results in instability
7	Cooperative mobile router based handover (CoMoRoHo)	Less overhead on packet delivery	May cause traffic in the vicinity of less routers present
8	Speed based vertical handovers	It increase throughput in vertical handovers	May lead to jitter in network for high speed vehicles
9	Handover decision algorithm based on multiple criteria	Using decision algorithm increase enhanced performance	It works only for heterogeneous networks
10	Optimum handover decision technique VANET-LTE	It provides better QoS in almost all scenarios	It is specific to certain LTE based VANET models
11	Hybrid protocol for dynamic load balancing	It improves the QoS and the network throughput	It may lead to network partitioning

4 Proposed Work

Most of the works presented by researchers are based on radio wave spectrum. However, in this work the authors have tried to exploit the spectrum of light waves using Li- Fi technology whose bandwidth is very high as compared to the latter. Also, the onboard Li-Fi units have built in modem which modulates, receives and transmits the signal. It starts with the Li-Fi sensors fitted to the vehicles periodically broadcasting "Hello messages" to its one hop neighbours, When an AP receives a "Hello messages" it sends back unicast message to the sender with its node information which includes its speed, direction, position, number of vehicles per km and timestamp. Based on the number of replies received by the sender the received signal strength (RSS) and net-work occupancy are calculated. These gives the active network lifetime (A_TL) which is used to assign priority values to different AP's, with the high A_TL value AP assigned the priority value 1 and so on. The AP's with their priority value are entered into the AP_list table and this list is updated every time A_TL value is found for successive AP's. If any vehicle in a network finds that its A-TL value is less than the Active network lifetime threshold (A_Th)then the serving AP (sAP) can perform handover with the target network AP (tAP) as provided from the AP_list table. The list is updated as the sAP is flushed from the AP_list table.

A pseudo code and a flow chart showing the sequence of steps in the algorithm has been presented below:

4.1 LiFi Based Handover Algorithm

Input : Source vehicle or AP scanning for better network to perform handover

Output: Transfer the network from serving AP to another AP.

Parameters:
1. RSS
2. Network Occupancy(NO), which gives the number of vehicles present in the network.
3. Node info (NI) constituting speed,direction, position, no of vehicles/km, timestamp.
4.Active network lifetime threshold (A_Th).
   Parameters (1) and (2) help determine the active network lifetime (A_TL) used to prioritize the target networks for performing handover.

---

1. Begin

2. The source vehicle(sv) or current AP gathers information of available networks.

3. For i=1 upto n-hop neighbours,

4. sv broadcast " Hello messages" to its 1 –hopneighbour vehicles with NI consisting of fields (speed,

   direction, position, number of vehicles/km, timestamp).

5. If (neighbour vehicles receive the Hello message= true)

        it replies by sending an unicast message with its node info.

6. Else

        vehicle discard Hello message.

7. Depending on the number of replies messages received in timestamp order calculate the RSS and NO.

8. If source vehicle does not receive any reply message go to step 3 and increment i++-> next sv.

9. Using the RSS and NO values, calculate the A_TL and prioritizes the different AP's upto N-hop neighbour.

10. AP's are assigned priority(AP_{Max} = Priority(m), AP_{Max-1}=Priority(m+1)...AP_{Max-n}=Priority(m+1))and stored in AP list

11. If (A_TL<A_Th)

        execute handover with AP from AP list

else

        continue with same AP.

12. Update AP list.

13. End.

The algorithm described above for handover in vehicles considers RSS, NO, NI and the A_Th into consideration, which further helps to categories the vehicles with different priority values for better handoff. This work needs to be experimentally examined with the help of a simulation model using NS-2 environment, with Li-Fi as the communication medium and considering vehicular traffic at road cross-section. Authors are of the belief to get favourable results as Li-fi is proven to be better option than other prevalent communication mediums and also many parameters have been taken into consideration to have an efficient handover (Fig. 3).

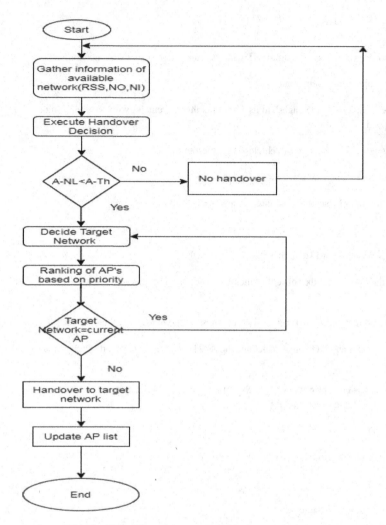

Fig. 3. Flowchart of the proposed handover algorithm

5 Conclusion

This paper has represented a state of art survey on various handover schemes in VANET which stands as one of the most promising technology in the field of ITS. Most of the works are based on cross layer and vertical handover techniques. This proposed work on handover using Li-Fi technology would help researchers to understand the existing handover schemes and work towards development of a newer and a better approach.

The future work would be to simulate the model and compare the result with some standard state of art research work.

References

1. Chiu, K.-L., Hwang, R.-H., Chen, Y.-S.: A cross layer fast handover scheme in VANET. In: IEEE International Conference on Communications, IEEE ICC 2009, Dresden, Germany, 14–18 June 2009 (2009)
2. Pack, S., Choi, Y.: Fast handoff scheme based on mobility prediction in public wireless LAN systems. IEE Proc. Commun. **151**(5), 489–495 (2004)
3. Okabe, T., Shizuno, T., Kitamura, T.: Wireless LAN access network system for moving vehicles. In: 10th IEEE Symposium on Computers and Communications, ISCC 2005, La Manga del Mar Menor, June 2005 (2005)
4. Baldessari, R., et al.: Car-to-Car Communication Consortium, "C2C-CC Manifesto," Version 1.1 (August 2007). http://www.car-to-car.org/fileadmin/dokumente/pdf/C2C-CCmanifesto20070924v1.1.pdf
5. Zeadally, S., Hunt, R., Chen, Y., et al.: Vehicular ad hoc networks (VANETS): status, results, and challenges. Telecommun. Syst. **50**, 217–241 (2012). https://doi.org/10.1007/s11235-010-9400-5
6. Arnold, T., Lloyd, W., Zhao, J.: IP address passing for VANETs. In: IEEE International Conference on Pervasive Computing and Communications (PERCOM), Hong Kong, pp. 70–79, March 2008 (2008)
7. Kafle, V.P., Kamioka, E., Yamada, S.: CoMoRoHo: cooperative mobile router-based handover scheme for long-vehicular multihomed networks. IEICE Trans. Commun. **89**, 2774–2784 (2006)
8. Devarapalli, V., Wakikawa, R., Petrescu, A., Thubert, P.: Network Mobility (NEMO) Basic Support Protocol. Internet Engineering Task Force (IETF), RFC-3963 (2005)
9. Liang, W., Li, Z., Zhang, H., Wang, S., Bie, R.: Vehicular Ad Hoc networks: architecture, research issues, methodologies, challenges and trends. Int. J. Distrib. Sens. Netw. **2015**, 1–11 (2015). Open access article
10. Zhang, Z., Boukerche, A., Pazzi, R.: A novel multi-hop clustering scheme for vehicular ad-hoc networks. In: 9th ACM International Symposium on Mobility Management and Wireless Access (2011)
11. Esposito, F.: On Modeling Speed-based Vertical Handovers in Vehicular Networks, Technical report BUCS-TR-2010-032, Computer Science Department, Boston University, 7 September 2010
12. AL-Hashimi, H.N., Hussein, W.N.: PMIPv6 assistive cross-layer design to reduce handover latency in VANET mobility for next generation wireless networks. Netw. Protoc. Algorithms **7**(3), 1–17 (2015)
13. Salihin, S.S., Noor, R.M., Nissirat, L.A., Ahmedy, I.:VANET handover based on LTE-A using decision technique. In: FCSIT 2017, pp. 9–17 (2017)
14. Saini, M., Mann. S.: Handoff schemes for vehicular ad-hoc networks: a survey. Int. J. Innov. Eng. Technol., 86–91 (2010)
15. Abdullah, R.M., Zukarnain, Z.A.: Enhanced handover decision algorithm in heterogeneous wireless network. Sensors **17**, 1626 (2017). www.mdpi.com/journal/sensors
16. Chang, Y., Ding, J., Ke, C., Chen, I.: A survey of handoff schemes for vehicular ad-hoc networks. In: ACM Proceedings of the 6th International Wireless Communications and Mobile Computing Conference, pp. 1228– 1231, July 2010 (2010)
17. Wang, Y., Videv, S., Haas, H.: Dynamic load balancing with handover in hybrid Li-Fi and Wi-Fi networks. In: 2014 IEEE 25th Annual International Symposium on Personal, Indoor, and Mobile Radio Communication (PIMRC), Washington, DC, pp. 575–579 (2014)
18. Bildass Santhosam, I., Divya, D., Priyanka, R.: VANET based intelligent transportation system using Li-Fi technology. IOSR J. Electron. Commun. Eng. (IOSR-JECE) **12**, 30–32 (2017). e-ISSN: 2278-2834, p- ISSN: 2278-8735

Dual-Level Security with Spiral Mapping [DLSSM] Scheme for Secure Covert Transmission of Speech Signals in Various Indian Languages

P. L. Chithra[1]([⊠]) and R. Aparna[2]([⊠])

[1] Department of Computer Science, University of Madras, Chennai, India
chitrasp2001@yahoo.com
[2] S.S.S. Shasun Jain College, Chennai, India
aparna.r@shasuncollege.edu.in

Abstract. Security is essential to safeguard confidential data. Data in the form of signal, image, text etc. … can be hacked by intruders. Dual-Level Security with Spiral Mapping [DLSSM] Scheme is proposed to secure the secret data in unsafe medium. DLSSM encompass cryptography and steganography along with strong spiral mapping technique. Cryptographic techniques converts the secret data into cipher data, by which hacker doesn't understand any information even if they get the data. Spiral mapping method enhances the level of security provided to the secret signal. Steganography hides the secret data within another covering file with no traces of the hidden secret data. Hence, dual level security scheme strengthens the system in covert transmission. Speech signals of various Indian languages from IL-LDC and standard corpus are taken as samples to analyse the proposed DLSSM scheme effectiveness. Standard voice signals are considered as input to prove the novelty of the method. The proposed method [DLSSM] is compared with existing systems to prove its efficiency.

Keywords: Speech signal encryption · Spiral mapping · Windowing · Covert communication

1 Introduction

Voice signals carry data in a scalar form. Even a very short speech signal holds a very huge scalar set of data. Handling the enormous data is a very critical task. Speech signals are vulnerable in nature. Hence, adding on to the task of handling, enforcing security makes voice processing tougher. Encryption process is usually classified into Symmetric Key and Asymmetric Key method. Algebraic notations and theory of computational complexity are considered as the basics for performing cryptographic techniques. Security and privacy are the most vital part of data. Steganography technique embeds the secret signal in covering signal without leaving any suspicion of hidden signal. There are many situations were confidentiality plays important role. In those cases, cryptography and steganography are considered for achieving data security. Here, we propose a methodology which combines the two strong techniques to promote the efficiency of the system. Hence, it is referred as dual level security scheme. As mentioned above, the speech signals contribute to a huge scalar set of data, windowing and cosine transformations are carried to make the huge dataset manageable. Spiral mapping algorithm is enforced on the huge dataset to produce a strong cipher signal. Encrypting the dataset into cipher dataset such that, the cipher dataset should not have any or having minimal resemblance with original dataset is very essential. It is equally important to decrypt the dataset to original version in order to reveal the secret audio message in the receiver's end. Hence, cryptography (encryption & decryption) process is implemented to produce the performance analysis report.

The spiral mapping technique is very unique and an add-on feature of this proposed system as it is used to shuffle the dataset to produce the crypto-data signal. The cipher dataset should be strong enough to overcome the robustness, brute force attack and should retain the secret data within the embedded voice signal. This spiral mapping technique has the very good quality of producing the strong encrypted cipher signal and at the same time it can be decrypted to revert back the original secret signal. Hence, this process is very important.

Various speech signals from different language corpus are considered to analyze the efficiency of the proposed method. As, Indian languages have sacrosanct discrimination between each other, we executed the system with various Indian languages. The results obtained are compared by performing correlation test, SNR test and spectrogram analysis for depicting the strength of the proposed methodology. Signals in various languages such as Tamil, Hindi, Malayalam, Odiya, Punjabi and Bihari are considered. All these speech signals are taken from IL-LDC, Indian Languages – Language Data Consortium. IL-LDC is a renowned speech signal corpus widely accepted for performing research in the area of voice signal processing. Comparative Analysis is performed to highlight the efficiency of the proposed method. Few input audio signal samples are also taken from the standard TIMIT corpus and OGI-MLTS corpus.

The remaining of this paper is organized as follows. Section 2 is devoted to brief about related existing work carried in the same field so far. Section 3 is to focus on proposed methodology with proposed technique, spiral mapping technique, signal intensity, histogram, Algorithm, PFD (Process Flow Diagram), spectrogram. Detailed description about the steps in PFD is elaborated in Sect. 4, followed by Sect. 5 and Sect. 6 which showcases the performance analysis and comparative analysis with experimental results respectively. Finally, conclusion is presented in Sect. 7.

2 Related Work

The process of scrambling the original signal into cipher signal is known as encryption. The reverse process is decryption. Cryptographic functions are used for encryption process. Cipher signal generated should be strong enough to withstand the attacks but should reproduce the original signal at the receiver's end. Encryption scheme is mainly classified into symmetric encryption and asymmetric encryption. Symmetric encryption is associated with secret key and based on large number of factorization & mathematical functions. Asymmetric encryption is related with combination of private & public keys. Many techniques have been devised for generating the keys for encryption. Chaotic based encryption & decryption [1] depends on non-linear deterministic functions which makes the keys non guessable. Hence, cipher signals produced based on the generated keys ensures the security of the system. Analysis of secret keys for cryptography [2] is carried and six various security properties have been identified such as triple, triple+DHE, asym-ir, asym-ri, sym-ir and sym-ri. Security protocols are analyzed for secret signal communication.

Windowing & CAT transformation have been discussed in [3] where speech signals in 1D converted into 2D for further processing. Speech signals are in analog form. It can be used as such or can be converted into digital for performing the research. Analog speech waveform is considered for secure transformation where the analog signals hold large digital data. The best part of dealing the speech signal in analog form [4] is that, the same voice transmission channel can be used for transmitting encrypted speech without the need of codec. As the signal in analog form holds larger data, segmentation process helps in processing. Random number generation [5] plays a vital role in confusion & diffusion of data, which makes the system very secure. CAT mapping technique [1, 5] devised by Arnold, facilitate in identifying new position for the signals considered in 2D. Transformation of discrete signal is essential in many situations. To name a few, CNT (Cosine Number Transformations) [6], DCT (Discrete Cosine Transformation) [3, 5], FFT (Fast Fourier Transformation) are widely used in the field of signal processing. Encryption carried with 2D chaotic maps are elaborately discussed in, where a detail description about logistic map [1, 7], baker map and henon map [7] is given. Transmission in digital speech processing deals with AES (Advanced Encryption Scheme) and DES (Data Encryption Scheme), whereas in analog, the bandwidth complexity of the channel is considered. Corpus signals are taken from the standard databases, which are used to carry the research work in a very high professional way. Voice signals refer to any audio speech signal with energy function. IL-LDC, TIMIT database, TIMIT-Digit are considered for analysis.

Voice signal processing should also take the pronunciation/ accent of the particular sample. Though the language remains the same, pronunciation might vary, as there are plenty of ways to speak in same language. Different regional people pronounce the same language in different style. Hence, it should also be considered. Phoneme and phonetic classification of signals depends on various parameters. Indo-Aryan speech samples are considered to define the features such as MFCC (Mel Frequency Cepstral Coefficients, PLP (Perceptual Linear Prediction, LPCC (Linear Prediction Cepstral Coefficients) [8]. Salient phonetic features of Indian languages in speech technology has been clearly given in [9]. Plosives, pitch variation, phonetic articulation [9] holds a strong uniqueness for different languages and very important for building a LID (Language Identification) System. Effectiveness of cryptographic algorithms such as

FDS (Frequency Domain Scrambling, blowfish algorithm, Fuzzy commitment, Duffing map, LFSR (Linear Feedback Shift Register), BSS (Blind Source Separation) [10] are compared to identify the better algorithm for voice signal processing. By the principle of Kerckoff, it is understood that the efficiency of encryption scheme is not measured by the obfuscated code, but by the unpredictable secret key [11]. Two-dimensional chaotic maps [7, 12] used for generating symmetric ciphers depends on the structure of permutations induced by baker map where confusion of data is performed by bernoulli shifts does give good results for 2D data. Chaotic map cryptographic is well suitable for symmetric encryption. Likewise, PCA (Parallel-key Cryptographic Algorithm) [13] suits well for asymmetric encryption with CBC (Cipher Block Chaning) and ICBS (Interleaved Cipher Block Chaining). Cryptography, Steganography and Watermarking are the pillars of data security and authenticity. Application of Cryptographic and Steganographic techniques in multimedia files is given in [14] and AES is proved to be the quickest and safest than triple DES. Multiple secret keys strengthen data security. DCT (Discrete Cosine Transform) & DST (Discrete Sine Transform) with masking & permutation generates multiple secret keys [15] to encrypt the signal into ciphers. Permutation and substitution of covet speech samples using secret keys along with various mapping techniques such as logistic map, CAT map belongs to chaotic-based techniques [1, 16] exhibits pseudorandom behavior. Other chaotic systems, Lorenz and Rossler also showed great results by generating unintelligible ciphers [17] with permutation and substitution concepts. Conventional algorithms (AES, DES, TDES) are not appropriate to give high security but inclusion of multi layer scheme with crossover and mutation [18–20] produced good results with logistic and CAT map. SNR (Signal-Noise Ratio), PSNR (Peak Signal-Noise Ratio), Correlation, Cross Correlation, NSCR (Number of Sample Change Rate), UACI (Unified Average Changing Intensity) are the main measures used to check and provide evidence for the competence of the system. Segmentation of speech data into smaller segments makes the speech signal manageable [21, 22] and hence the information in the signal can be secured. Encryption of speech signals using chaotic scrambling techniques are explained in [23, 24], and the audio signals can be safeguarded. Speech signals are obtained in time domain and it has to be considered in frequency domain [25] for further processing, so as to obtain effective results. In this research work, proposed method is compared with existing methods [1, 6] and the analysis is tabulated.

3 Proposed Methodology

Secret audio signal and the covering signal are digitalized for convenient handling of data in it. The proposed method encompasses data shifting, windowing, transformation and embedding techniques. Hence, makes the methodology a very strong approach. As the signal carries secret data and to be transferred in unsecured medium, it has to be encrypted before sending. The reversal process of encryption is decryption, which is to be done in the receiver's end with utmost accuracy to revert back the original secret message from the encrypted cipher signal. Secret signals selected are encrypted to get cipher signal, which is then hidden within a covering signal without leaving any traces of secret signal in it. In this paper, we suggest a method of securely embedding ciphered covert signal on a covering audio signal. The ciphering process is strengthened with spiral mapping and the embedding processing is supported with normalization.

3.1 Proposed Technique

Process at Sender's End:

Step 1: Read the secret speech signal and covering signal.
Step 2: Digitalize both the signals.
Step 3: Take DCT (Discrete Cosine Transformation) & apply suitable windowing technique to obtain short-term energy function of the secret speech signal.
Step 4: Convert the obtained 1D (One Dimensional) data stream into 2D (Two Dimensional) data stream.
Step 5: Perform Spiral Mapping.
Step 6: Revert back the 2D (Two Dimensional) data stream into 1D (One Dimensional) data stream.
Step 7: Apply the approximation factor applicable to the secret speech signal.
Step 8: Hide the resultant signal within the covering signal.
Step 9: Send the signal in any unsecure medium to the receiver.

Process at Receiver's End:

Step 1: Read the received signal.
Step 2: Digitalize the signal.
Step 3: Separate the covering signal.
Step 4: Apply the approximation factor applicable to the secret speech signal.
Step 5: Convert the audio signal data which is in 1D (One Dimensional) data stream into 2D (Two Dimensional) data stream.
Step 6: Perform reverse Spiral Mapping.
Step 7: Revert back the 2D (Two Dimensional) data stream into 1D (One Dimensional) data stream.
Step 8: Take Inverse DCT (Discrete Cosine Transformation) & apply windowing technique to obtain short-the secret speech signal.
Step 9: Play the Secret audio message.

3.2   Spiral Mapping

1⬤	2	3	4	5
6	7	8	9	10
11	12	13	14	15
16	17	18	19	20
21	22	23	24	25

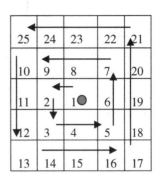

Fig. 1. Original image pixel arrangement   **Fig. 2.** Spiral mapped image pixel arrangement

3.3   Spiral Mapping Pseudo Code

```
START
    SET COUNT=1,FLAG=1
    Find the Mid-Point Coordinates
        SET X,Y    //Transfer data to new POS
    REPEAT Until X=1,Y=1
    LOOP:            //COUNT times
        X=X-FLAG;
        POS(X,Y); //Transfer data to new POS
    EXIT LOOP
    LOOP:            //COUNT times
        Y=Y+FLAG;
        POS(X,Y); //Transfer data to new POS
    EXIT LOOP
        COUNT=COUNT+1;
        FLAG = FLAG*(-1);
END
```

Iteration Results: Sample 5 × 5 Matrix

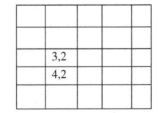

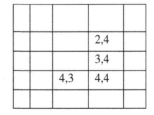

Fig. 3(a). Iteration 1:
MID POINT

Fig. 3(b). Iteration 2:
COUNT = 1, FLAG = 1

Fig. 3(c). Iteration 3:
COUNT = 2, FLAG = − 1

2,1	2,2	2,3		
3,1				
4,1				
5,1				

Fig. 3(d). Iteration 4:
COUNT = 3, FLAG = 1

				1,5
				2,5
				3,5
				4,5
	5,2	5,3	5,4	5,5

Fig. 3(e). Iteration 5:
COUNT = 4, FLAG = − 1

1,1	1,2	1,3	1,4	

Fig. 3(f). Iteration 6:
COUNT = 5, FLAG = 1
Reaches (X = 1: Y = 1)

3.4   Signal Intensity

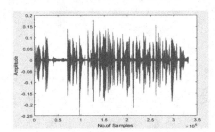

Fig. 4. Base signal

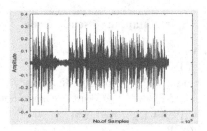

Fig. 5. Secret signal in Hindi

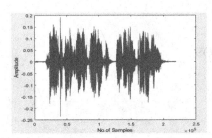

Fig. 6. Secret signal in Malayalam

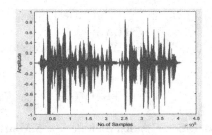

Fig. 7. Secret signal in Odiya

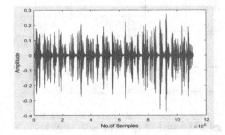

Fig. 8. Secret signal in Punjabi

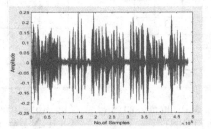

Fig. 9. Secret signal in *Bihari*

3.5   Signal Histogram

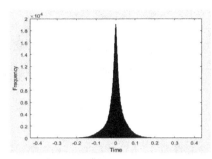

Fig. 10(a). Signal before embedding

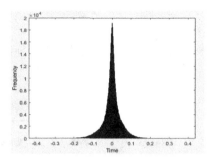

Fig. 10(b). Signal after embedding

3.6   Signal Spectrogram

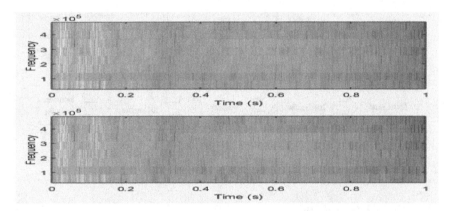

Fig. 11. Covering signal before and after embedding

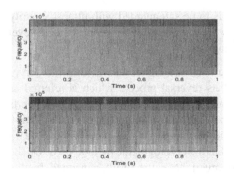

Fig. 12. Secret and encrypted signal

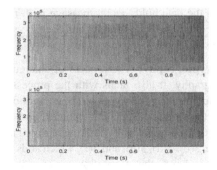

Fig. 13. Secret and decrypted signal

3.7 Process Flow Diagram

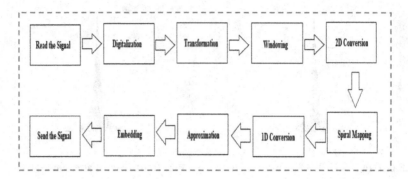

Fig. 14. Encryption process

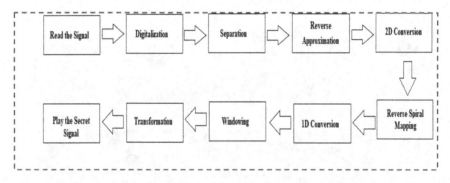

Fig. 15. Decryption process

4 Detailed Description

4.1 Dual-Level Security with Spiral Mapping [DLSSM] Scheme

As the data holds secret message in it, it needs to be safeguarded with utmost security techniques. Cryptography and Steganography are the pillars of the proposed dual-level system, which enhances the security of the signals.

Cryptography: The process of changing the data into cipher data is known as cryptography. It also deals with the process and its reversal process which is referred as encryption and decryption. The encryption should be in such a way it reframes or converts or transforms the data into another form of data which shows minimum or no correlation with the original data. Working of Spiral mapping techniques is shown in Fig. 1, 2, 3(a), 3 (b), 3(c), 3(d), 3(e), and 3(f), which adds credit to the cryptographic method used. On the other hand, the decryption process should revert back the result generated by the encryption process with maximum or full correlation with the original data.

Steganography: Steganography is the practice of hiding secret data within another file without any clue of any concealed data. The efficiency of steganography technique is proportionally related to hiding secret message in another message without any suspicion of hidden data. Using steganographic method is very traditional but here the proposed method is considered to be superior, as it shows exact correlation with original message.

4.2 Step by Step Approach

Digitalization: As the audio signals in the raw form are represented by analog waves, it is very hard to process it. So, the first step is to digitalize the raw analog data into digital dataset to carry the subsequent processing with ease and effectiveness. Digitization or Digitalization comprises of two different process namely, sampling and quantization. Changing the range of continuous data into discrete data with respect to time is known as sampling, and is given by,

$$Ts = 1/fs \tag{1}$$

Where, Ts is to represent time domain and fs is in the frequency domain.

The raw acoustic signal is a range of continuous dataset, which is converted into finite range of discrete data. This process is known as quantization.

Short-Term Energy: The energy of short speech segment is known as the short term energy. Short time energy is a simple, effective holds a vital role in any DSP (Digital Signal Processing) research. The inputs needed for computing the short term energy are the proper speech signal and its sampling frequency beside with the frame shift and frame size. Figure 4, 5, 6, 7, 8, and 9 shows the short-term energy of the input signals. Figure 10(a) and 10(b) shows the histogram analysis of the signal. Using the given sampling frequency value and the number of samples, its frame shift and frame size are computed. For instance, let us consider the sampling frequency is 10 kHz and frame shift and frame size are 10 ms and 20 ms, respectively then the number of samples in a frame will be 200 and number of samples for the considered frame shift will be 100 samples. To work out STE (Short Term Energy) value, the input speech signal is considered in frames of 200 samples with a shift of 100 samples and the energy is computed for each frame. The short term energy values are then plotted as a function of time index. STE of a discrete-time signal is defined mathematically as follows,

$$Energy = \sum_{n=-\infty}^{\infty} |x(n)|^2 \tag{2}$$

Windowing: The process of selecting small set of data from a larger dataset is known as windowing process and it is very essential while dealing with vast dataset such as voice data. Hence, this step is unavoidable in speech signal processing.

Various types of windows are available and we should choose the window which is suitable for further processing. Here, based on the results generated [21, 22], Kaiser window is used for the processing and it is calculated by,

$$\mathcal{M}_0(t) = \begin{cases} \frac{\mu_0\left[\alpha\sqrt{1-\left(\frac{t}{\tau}\right)^2}\right]}{\mu_0[\alpha]}, & |t| \leq \tau \\ 0, & |t| > \tau \end{cases} \tag{3}$$

Where, τ is the window duration,
μ_0 is zeroth order function.

Transformation: In order to proceed with spiral mapping techniques and applying normalization, the considered speech signal has to be transformed into matrix form. Conversion of 1D dataset into 2D dataset is done by setting the r, c values based on the number of values in the windowed dataset.

Sample DataSet

$$\begin{pmatrix}
0.0023 & -0.0033 & -0.0018 & -0.0001 & 0.0000 & \dots \\
-0.0015 & 0.0013 & -0.0001 & -0.0007 & 0.0008 & \dots \\
0.0001 & -0.0009 & 0.0005 & 0.0019 & -0.0007 & \dots \\
0.0016 & 0.0027 & -0.0006 & -0.0011 & -0.0002 & \dots \\
-0.0008 & 0.0002 & 0.0005 & -0.0011 & 0.0007 & \dots \\
-0.0005 & 0.0014 & 0.0009 & -0.0016 & -0.0010 & \dots \\
\dots & \dots & \dots & \dots & \dots & \dots \\
\dots & \dots & \dots & \dots & \dots & \dots
\end{pmatrix}$$

The above given is the representation of a sample dataset. The speech signal will be in scalar form and hence the considered data has to be preprocessed before converting it into 2D form. Identifying the size of square matrix and adjusting the size of the secret signal with covering signal are the preprocessing steps.

Spiral Mapping: This technique adds a new flavor to the methodology and enhances the encryption process, by resulting with a new matrix of data, from which it will not be possible to retrieve the original audio without the knowledge of proper decryption process. At the same time, the obtained signal after decryption process shows higher co-relevance with original signal before encryption. Step by Step working principle of Spiral mapping is shown in Fig. 3(a), 3(b), 3(c), 3(d), 3(e), and 3(f)

Approximation: Normalization factor (η) is an independent factor which can be calculated by the iterative process. The factor is identified based on the secret original signal alone, which makes the encrypted signal perfectly hidden inside the covering signal. The process of hiding the encrypted signal inside the covering signal should be carried in such a way that there should not be any traces of hidden signal, hence the intruder/hacker is without any clue. This makes our proposed methodology superior on other existing methods. SNR (Signal to Noise Ratio) which is calculated by,

$$\text{SNR}(x) = 10\log_{10}\left(\lambda_{\text{signal}}/\lambda_{\text{noise}}\right) \tag{4}$$

Hence the above formula returns the SNR in decibels relative to the carrier in decibels (dBc) of a sinusoidal input audio signal. SNR of secret signal is calculated before & after encryption [3] and the suitable 'η' value is identified.

Embedding: The process of converging two signals is referred as embedding. This embedding of secret signal into an ordinary audio signal secures the secret signal from hackers.

$$z = z_1 + z_2 \tag{5}$$

Where, z_1 is the ordinary base signal within which the secret signal z_2 is embedded in such a way that it is hidden inside but with no traces of it.

Indian Languages: The proposed methodology is experimented with various input signal as secret signals. The secret signal is carefully chosen from different Indian languages, so as to prove that the proposed technique suits well for the high caliber sounds of various Indian languages. Speech signals on Tamil, Hindi, Odiya, Malayalam, Punjabi and Bihari are considered as input signals. Also the Tamil signal used as the base signal exhibits better result.

5 Performance Analysis

The competence of the proposed technique is measured by correlation test. The importance of correlation test is to compare the signals before and after encryption. The encrypted signal should have minimal or no correlation with the original secret signal. At the same time, the correlation between the signal before and after embedding should have maximum. Both the checks are performed and shown in the Table 1. Figure 11, 12, and 13 shows the correlation between the secret-original, ciphered and decrypted signal to prove the performance of the system.

5.1   Signal Correlation

Table 1. Signal correlation

#Covering signal	Secret signal	Signal correlation		
		Before & after embedding	Secret & encrypt signal	Secret & decrypt signal
T1.wav	H1.wav	1	0.0013	1
	O1.wav	1	−9.0603e−05	1
	M1.wav	1	−9.1788e−05	0.9999
	P1.wav	1	1.4379e−05	0.9998
	B1.wav	1	−8.1535e−05	0.9998

Here, we consider signal correlation (Fig. 11, 12, and 13) as the major criteria for proving the efficiency of the system.

Table 2. Normalization value

#Covering signal	Secret signal	Normalization value (η)	SNR value
T1.wav	H1.wav	250	−18.2074
	O1.wav	3550	−18.0874
	M1.wav	120	−15.2806
	P1.wav	150	−18.0305
	B1.wav	235	−20.4683

SNR Value Calculation

Normalization factor plays an imperative role in hiding the encrypted signal without any traces of embedded data. Hence, identifying the η value for each signal is done by reverse iterative method carefully. The parameters required for calculating the η value is independent of the signal which makes the DLSSM system safer. Table 2 shows the calculated normalization value for the considered audio samples in various Indian languages from IL-LDC corpus.

Table 3. Correlation test analysis

#Secret signal	Existing method [1]		Existing method [6]		Proposed [DLSSM] method	
	Encrypted signal	Decrypted signal	Encrypted signal	Decrypted signal	Encrypted signal	Decrypted signal
Audio1.wav	0.0233	0.999	0.0021	–	−0.0020	0.9995
Audio2.wav	0.0384	0.999	0.0036	–	−0.0004	0.9999
Audio3.wav	0.0157	1	−0.0018	–	−0.0002	1
Audio4.wav	0.0119	1	−0.0042	–	−0.0007	1

6 Comparative Analysis

The process of comparing the proposed DLSSM method with existing method and proving that the proposed techniques scores higher values is a way to establish the competence of our system. Table 3 portrays the competence of the proposed method and it is well established that the proposed technique outperforms well than the Existing methods [1] and [6]. Table 1 and 2 contributes the performance analysis while the Table 3 shows the Comparative Analysis of the proposed method. Audio files (Audio1.wav, Audio2.wav, Audio3.wav and Audio4.wav) correspond to the dataset used in existing methods and in our DLSSM method. The overall working mechanism of the proposed DLSSM scheme is depicted in Fig. 14 and 15.

Merits of DLSSM Over Other Methods
The Proposed DLSSM scheme is highly efficient and comfortable than the existing methods [1, 6], which is clearly proved in Table 3. Though the spiral mapping method seems to be less complex and unambiguous, the results prove it to be comparatively stronger than other existing methods [4, 6, 7, 12]. Correlation test results of the encrypted image in [1] and [6] are comparatively less strong than the proposed method. Similarly, the pixels correlations of the decrypted image, also shows closer to 1 in the proposed method. The other advantage of the DLSSM over the existing method is the proposed method deals with inputs of various Indian Languages and all inputs are taken from the standard corpus.

Finally, the proposed DLSSM scores well with the concept of incorporating the most widely used two pillars, Cryptography and Steganography, in a single methodology.

7 Conclusion

Speech signals are the most vulnerable way to communicate secret messages. DLSSM method proves to be the safer way to secure secret information in-spite of using the unsecure communication lines. The spiral mapping techniques used in this DLSSM encrypts the data very well. The preprocessing steps support the core method to enhance efficiency of the cryptosystem used. The embedding process is carried perfectly without leaving any traces of hidden secret signal. Strong cryptography and steganography method proposed give dual level security to the secret signal. Hence, DLSSM (Dual Level Security with Spiral Mapping) can be used to transfer secret speech signal in any unsafe medium with any threat of being hacked. Speech samples from standard corpus such as IL-LDC & TIMIT are considered for experimentation.

Acknowledgment. We owe our sincere thanks to the Department of Computer Science & Applications, University of Madras & Shri Shankarlal Sundarbai Shasun Jain College for consistent support in carrying the research work.

References

1. Sathiyamurthi, P., Ramakrishnan, S.: Speech encryption using chaotic shift keying for secured speech communication. EURASIP J. Audio Speech Music Process. **2017**(1), 1–11 (2017). https://doi.org/10.1186/s13636-017-0118-0
2. Cohn-Gordon, K., Cremers, C., Dowling, B., Garratt, L., Stebila, D.: A formal security analysis of the signal messaging protocol. In: IEEE European Symposium on Security and Privacy, pp. 451–466 (2017)
3. Chithra, P.L., Aparna R.: Voice signal encryption scheme using transformation and embedding techniques for enhanced security. In: IEEE Conference on ICISPC 2018, pp. 149–154 (July 2018)
4. Kohata, M.: Secure speech encryption system using segments for speech synthesis, pp 264–267 (2014)
5. Farsana, F.J., Gopakumar, K.: A novel approach for speech encryption: Zaslavsky map as pseudo random number generator. In: 6th International Conference on Advances in Computing & Communications, ICACC 2016, pp. 6–8 (September 2016)
6. Lima, J.B., da Silva Neto, E.F.: Audio encryption based on the cosine number transform. Multimed. Tools Appl. **75**(14), 8403–8418 (2015). https://doi.org/10.1007/s11042-015-2755-6
7. Mostafa, A., Soliman, N.F., Abdalluh, M., Abd El-samie, F.E.: Speech encryption using two dimensional chaotic maps. In: 11th International Conference on Computer Engineering (ICENCO), February 2016. IEEE Xplore (2016)
8. Aarti, B., Kopparapu, S.: Spoken Indian language identification: a review of features and databases. Sādhanā **43**(4), 53:1–53:14 (2018). https://doi.org/10.1007/s12046-018-0841-y. Indian Academy of Sciences
9. Bhaskararao, P.: Salient phonetic features of Indian languages in speech technology. Sādhanā **36(Part 5)**, 587–599 (2011). https://doi.org/10.1007/s12046-011-0039-z. Indian Academy of Sciences
10. Aparna, R., Chithra, P.I.: A review on cryptographic algorithms for speech signal security. Int. J. Emerg. Trends Technol. Comput. Sci. (IJETTCS) **5**(5), 84–88 (2016)
11. Rajanarayanan, S., Pushparaghavan, A.: Recent developments in signal encryption – a critical survey. Int. J. Sci. Res. Publ. **2**(6), 1–7 (2012)
12. Fridrich, J.: Symmetric ciphers based on two-dimensional chaotic maps. Int. J. Bifurcat. Chaos **8**(6), 1259–1284 (1998)
13. Teerakanok, T., Kamolphiwong, S.: Accelerating asymmetric-key cryptography using Parallel-key Cryptographic Algorithm (PCA). In: 2009 6th International Conference on Electrical Engineering/Electronics, Computer, Telecommunications and Information Technology (2009)
14. Thomas, S.E., et al.: Advanced cryptographic steganography using multimedia files. In: International Conference on Electrical Engineering and Computer Science, ICEECS-2012, pp. 239–242 (2012)
15. Slimani, D., Merazka, F.: Encryption of speech signal with multiple secret keys. In: International Conference on Natural Language and Speech Processing, ICNLSP 2015, pp. 79–88 (2015)
16. Saad, N.A., Eman, H.: Speech encryption based on chaotic maps. Int. J. Comput. Appl. **93**(4), 19–28 (2014)
17. Hato, E., Shihab, D.: Lorenz and Rossler chaotic system for speech signal encryption. Int. J. Comput. Appl. **128**(11), 09758887 (2015)

18. Abdul-Majeed, A.M.: Speech encryption using genetic algorithm and Arnold cat map. Int. J. Comput. Sci. Inf. Secur. (IJCSIS) **14**(12), 911–915 (2016)
19. Dutta, S., Das, T., Jash, S., Patra, D., Paul, P.: A cryptography algorithm using the operations of genetic algorithm & pseudo random sequence generating functions. Int. J. Adv. Comput. Sci. Technol. **3**(5), 325–330 (2014)
20. Jhingran, R., Thada, V., Dhaka, S.: A study on cryptography using genetic algorithm. Int. J. Comput. Appl. **118**(20), 10–14 (2015)
21. Chithra, P.L., Aparna, R.: Performance analysis of windowing techniques in automatic speech signal segmentation. Indian J. Sci. Technol. **8**(29), 1–7 (2015)
22. Aparna R., Chithra, P.L.: Role of windowing techniques in speech signal processing for enhanced signal cryptography, chap. 28. In: The Book Advanced Engineering Research and Applications, pp. 446–458 (2017)
23. Al-Azawi, M.K.M., Gaze, A.M.: Combined speech compression and encryption using chaotic compressive sensing with large key size. IET Sig. Process. **12**(2), 214–218 (2018)
24. Chen, J., Ling, B.W.-K., Feng, P., Lei, R.: Computer cryptography through performing chaotic modulation on intrinsic mode functions with non-dyadic number of encrypted signal. IET Sig. Process. **13**(1), 7–13 (2019)
25. Chen, Y., Hao, J., Chen, J.: End-to-end speech encryption algorithm based on speech scrambling in frequency domain. In: IET Signal Processing, 3rd International Conference on Cyberspace Technology, CCT 2015 (October 2015)

A Novel Energy Aware Resource Allocation Algorithm into a P2P Based Fog Computing Environment

Archita Basu[1]([✉]) [iD], Sujoy Mistry[2] [iD], Satanu Maity[3] [iD],
and Subrata Dutta[4] [iD]

[1] Department of Information Technology, Maulana Abul Kalam Azad
University of Technology, Kolkata, India
architabasu55@gmail.com
[2] Department of Computer Science and Engineering, Maulana Abul Kalam Azad
University of Technology, Kolkata, India
mistry.sujoy@rediffmail.com
[3] Department of BCA, Bengal School of Technology and Management,
Hooghly, India
satanu01@gmail.com
[4] Department of Computer Science and Engineering,
National Institute of Technology, Jamshedpur, India
subrataduttaa@gmail.com

Abstract. Job scheduling, as well as Resource Allocation in the genre of fog computing, are some of the major issues that are required to be efficiently executed. Efficient resource allocation signifies proper scheduling of the user jobs as per resource requirements that lead to fast completion of tasks, which in turn saves energy and time. Resource allocation is a procedure by which the available proficient resources are allocated to the user devices. In this specific paper, we have designed a P2P reliant Fog Computing scenario along with SOA embedded in it and proposed an energy efficient decision-based resource allocation algorithm where resources are allocated in such a way that we get efficient performance from the network. We have also compared our proposed resource allocation algorithm with other standard and recently used algorithms. The outcome of the simulation depicts that our proposed resource algorithm is more efficient in the matter of overall time and energy when collated with the other existing algorithms.

Keywords: Fog computing · Service Oriented Architecture · Peer-to-Peer architecture · Resource allocation · Scheduling algorithms · Energy minimization · Delay minimization · Modeling & simulation

1 Introduction

New emerging technologies such as diverse applications in user devices are developing and flourishing rapidly as a consequence, the user devices are generating a humongous amount of data. These user devices have limited capability of processing, networking,

C. Badica et al. (Eds.): ICICCT 2020, CCIS 1170, pp. 88–97, 2020.
https://doi.org/10.1007/978-981-15-9671-1_7

computing, memory, etc., which makes them incapable of executing complex, memory, or processor-intensive tasks. To resolve these hurdles came a new paradigm known as cloud computing [1]. The enormous data generated by the user devices are dispatched to the clouds, they get processed thereafter and the outcome is dispatched back to the user devices. Humongous time is taken by the data to reach the clouds, get processed there, after that the output is dispatched to user devices. Thus, even in this paradigm, there were issues with latency especially in case of applications like health – monitoring, urgent response, real-time and latency-sensitive applications. There were also issues with bandwidth, network traffic, breakdown of centralized server [2]. To resolve these problems Fog Computing, introduced by CISCO, where network edge devices (switch, router, gateways) namely fog devices collaborate among themselves to bestow a virtual computing environment called fog computing [3]. Fog brings cloud services like computing, storage, applications, etc. nearer to the user devices. Fog computing is helpful for those applications, which are geo-distributed or has low latency requisites such as traffic security, medical, online gaming [4]. Many architectures have introduced and integrated into the fog layer, among them the most demanded and used architecture is the Service Oriented Architecture (SOA) and Peer-to-Peer (P2P) architecture. In SOA service resides in the fog layer until it is not manually removed thus a service can be reused multiple times. SOA facilitates by providing a huge number of services to user devices. P2P provides us with certain advantages, with P2P the centralized concept no more exists, here in P2P each node can act both as a server and as a client [5] (Fig. 1).

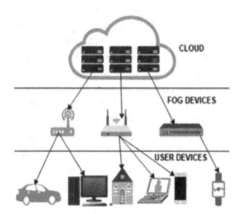

Fig. 1. Layered architecture

This work embraces three approaches. First, is the Service Oriented Architecture (SOA). On the enforcement of this approach, numerous services are got from the fog computing environs. SOA provides a facility i.e. a service resides in the fog layer until it is not manually removed. Thus, it leads to the upsurge in the obtainability of services. Second is resource allocation. Resource allocation is a procedure, which allocates a capable, efficient resource to the user devices from many available resources for proper and energy efficient execution of the tasks, which are incomputable by the user's devices over the internet. This paper proposes a decision based resource allocation algorithm, which comprises two major parameters namely Decision Parameter (DP) and Critical Decision (CD) based on the values of which the resources are allocated for task execution. In scenarios where the value of Decision Parameter of two or more fog devices turns out to be similar, in that case, the fog device with the highest valued critical decision parameter is considered. The advantage of resource allocation is that the user devices need not extend their software and hardware system. In our work, we have introduced an efficient resource allocation algorithm that efficiently allocates resources.

2 Related Work

In recent years, throughout the world, numerous scholars have carried out research on fog computing. The fog layer diminishes the drawbacks of the cloud. Till date many architectures have been proposed, among them, the most popular ones are SOA and P2P architecture. SOA offers innumerable services to distinct components by application module through numerous distinct protocols of communication. Peer to peer collaboration reduces communication latency. In [6] the author has proposed an infrastructure where Fog Computing is merged with intellectual communication protocol which are machine to machine based and the Service Oriented Architecture is also integrated. In [7] the authors have presented SoA-Fog. It is a tri-level structure which proficiently manages data regarding health by the aid of fog devices. In [8], the authors have introduced the idea of cloud/fog facility unification and have proposed a structure for the purpose provisioning of cloud-fog unification. They have also discussed the challenges of unification and have also pointed out some issues for future research. To address the challenges the authors in [9] have used peer-to-peer network for controlling the geo-distributed mobile edge servers, they have also proposed a deadline-conscious, profitable offloading approach. In [10] the authors have proposed a resource allocation architecture and Efficient Resource Allocation (ERA) algorithm. They have compared the existing resource allocation schemes with the algorithm, which they have proposed in terms of cost and overall estimated time and the proposed algorithm has given superior results. In [11] the authors have analyzed the scheduling problem in Fog Computing, focused on how user mobility can influence the performance of an application and how the scheduling techniques like Concurrent strategy, FCFS, Delay–priority can be put in a proper way to upsurge execution depending on the characteristics of the application. In [12] the authors have proposed a task-scheduling algorithm to aid the termination of tasks on time. They have also proposed a resource allocation scheme for the improvement of resource utilization of the fog devices and the reduction of delays in task. In [13] a task-scheduling algorithm based on priority has been designed for application in the fog layer. The proposed algorithm efficiently prioritizes tasks based on the delay tolerance levels. In [14] an algorithm has been presented which is TCaS based on evolutionary algorithm, in Fog as well as Cloud-Fog scenario, compared it with other algorithms namely BLA, MPSO, RR and it was found that TCaS showed the best results. In [15] the authors have proposed a task scheduling scheme on the basis of Hybrid Heuristic Algorithm, which merges the benefits of IPSO and IACO algorithms. The HH Algorithm sorts the difficulties, which the edge devices with restricted computing resources face. Hybrid Heuristic Algorithm was compared with IPSO, IACO, RR and it got superior results. In [16] authors have proposed a bio-inspired optimization approach, which is the Bee Life Algorithm (BLA). BLA showed better results concerning allocated memory and execution time when compared with the Genetic Algorithm and Particle Swarm Algorithm. The authors in [17] have introduced a framework that allows mobile crowdsensing in fog environs. It has a hierarchical scheduling scheme. Simulation outputs have shown that deep reinforcement scheduling is superior in fog computing environs compared to traditional solutions. In [18] a new resource-scheduling algorithm has been proposed on the basis of enhanced fuzzy clustering. After experimentation, outcomes have revealed that the technique increases user satisfaction as well as resource scheduling efficiency. In [19] the authors have reviewed current management and orchestration schemes and their performances in the Fog computing environment. They have also discussed the suitability of the hybrid scheme and how to implement them. Summarizing the related works, we can say certain aspects such as job scheduling, task scheduling, resource allocation, load balancing have not yet been explored much. In this paper, issues like resource allocation and job scheduling have been touched upon.

3   Proposed Algorithm

3.1   System Model

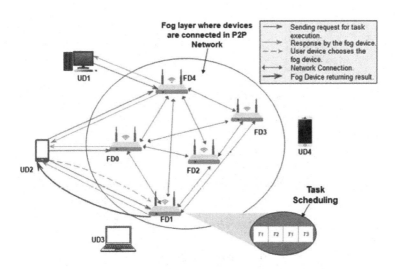

Fig. 2. Diagram of the system model (Color figure online)

In this system model (Fig. 2), we have considered, various User Devices (UD1, UD2...) that want to execute their own incomputable task with the help of local fog devices. Here local fog devices are the ones that are available in the User Device's self-network range. This fog layer, which comprises of heterogeneous fog devices (FD0, FD1…) is having common properties such as processing queue, energy, memory, processing speed, etc. The fog devices are linked among themselves in a Peer-to-Peer (P2P) approach. Therefore, a fog device in the P2P network can play any role at any instance of time like controller, task performer, service provider, etc. Also, the concept of Service Oriented Architecture has been integrated into the proposed system. As a result, a service can reside in this network until it is not manually discarded.

The overall communication and functioning of the proposed system model have been described step by step below and also a supporting sequence diagram is picturized in Fig. 3.

Step 1) Firstly, the user device requests to the local fog devices for self-incomputable task execution.

Step 2) The fog devices that have the requisite service send an acknowledgment, along with certain parameters.

Step 3) Depending on the value of those parameters, the user device chooses the fog device that it perceives to be the most appropriate and well suited based on the values and submits the task there. Thus the resource allocation for that job is done.

Step 4) After, completion of the resource allocation process, that task is again schedule based on a certain algorithm to avoid the process starvation problem. Thereafter, the task gets finally processed.

Step 5) After the tasks execution, the results are sent back to the user device.

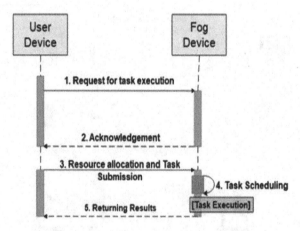

Fig. 3. Steps with sequence diagram of the functionality

In the specified proposed architecture, we have implemented a decision-based re-source allocation algorithm that efficiently allocates resources. The algorithm has been described in details up next.

3.2   Resource Allocation

Let us consider a task T_i with a size of θ_i and D_i deadline, which is incomputable by user device, therefore the device directs the requests to local fog devices in nearby fog network for execution of that self-incomputable task. After getting the request fog devices reply by sending an acknowledgment message to that requesting device. This acknowledgment reply contains five self-information as follows: (1) is that fog device contains that task as a service or not, (2) average waiting time of tasks (AW_{fd}), (3) ratio of remaining energy and total capacity of energy (RoE_{fd}), (4) status of the processing queue and (5) processing speed (δ_{fd}). After getting the acknowledgment user device make a fair decision of choosing a perfect fog device from where it will get the task result after execution. This decision made by a function (DP) as follows:

$$DP(fd) = \left[D_i - AW_{fd} + EXE_{fd}(T_i) \right] * RoE_{fd} = \begin{cases} +ve \\ -ve \end{cases} \tag{1}$$

If the output of the above equation is negative then it signifies that the output is above the deadline, which indicates that the fog device is unable to finish the task within the task deadline, so it will be simply discarded. Otherwise positive, signifies that the output is below the deadline, which indicates, the task finishes within the task deadline. The user device will choose the fog device, which consists of the highest value of the decision parameter. Here EXE_{fd} is the execution time a task of fd fog device which is calculated by

$$EXE_{fd}(T_i) = \theta_i / \delta_{fd} \tag{2}$$

As per the proposed system model figure (Fig. 2), UD2 sends task processing requests to local fog devices (i.e. FD0, FD1, FD4) [designated by red arrow], then fog devices send back the acknowledgment message [designated by green arrow]. Then the user device calculates the decision parameter and finally selects the suitable fog device (FD1) which signifies it allocates a perfect resource for the execution of task T_i[designated by pink dotted arrow]. Now the problem is that if somehow calculated decision parameter (DP) of more than one fog device arises to be the same. Then a decision will be taken upon the status of processing queue of fog devices. The decision-making algorithm for resource allocation has given below (Table 1):

Table 1. Parameters.

ACK_{fd}	Acknowledgement of the fog device (fd)
VQ	Vacant place of processing queue
LOC[]	For storing the id of a fog device (Initially NULL)
CD[]	Used for critical decision (Initially NULL)
COUNT	For counting purpose (Initially all zero)

Algorithm: Decision-Making Algorithm for Resource allocation

1) **Begin**
2) **For**(each ACK_{fd} from all received acknowledgment) **do**
3)   Calculate execution time EXE_{fd} and decision parameter DP(fd).
4)   Calculate critical decision by CD(fd)= VQ * DP(fd).
5) **End for**
6) Find number of highest decision parameter (DP) containing fog device in COUNT and store fog device id in LOC[ ] list and consider it as perfect resource for execution.
7) **If**(the value of COUNT is more than one) **then**
8)   Find the highest critical decision parameter (CD) containing fog device from LOC[ ] list and consider it as perfect resource for execution.
9) **Else**
10)   LOC[0] considered as perfect resource for execution.
11) **End If**
12) **End**

4 Simulation

4.1 Simulation Setup

This sub-section estimates the performance of the proposed P2P based resource allocation algorithm by the execution of simulations. Here the implementation of the proposed architecture, as well as the resource allocation algorithm using Omnet++ has been delineated. The entire simulator setup has also been defined and eventually, the results have been shown after comparing the proposed resource allocation algorithm with other algorithms such as Round Robin (RR), MCT [20] in terms of time and energy. Results have shown that our algorithm is more efficient compared to RR, MCT. The file trio consisted by the simulator is namely: NED file, CC file, INI File. The description of the entire network like topology, specifications of the network devices, and so on is delineated as a module in the NED file. CC file depicts the behaviors of the device in the network through the functioning module and the INI file deals with the initialization of the network at the beginning of the simulation. For our simulation, we have considered a network that consists of Fog Devices and User Devices. First, each device will be initialized with certain values of the following specifications: CPU cycle, Processing speed, total queue size, number of tasks, task size, total energy, task's deadline.

The values of each of these specifications will be dynamically set during the process of network initialization. For each fog devices in the simulation, the processing speed is set within the range 10–15 GHZ, CPU cycle for processing one-bit data at fog is 2000 cycle/bit, the total queue size is considered to be 5, the energy of each fog device will vary within the range 1000–1200 J, task size is between 2–5 MB, deadline of all tasks is considered to be 20 s. The user device has network bandwidth of

20 MHz. At a particular instance during simulation, three fog devices (Fog2, Fog3, and Fog4) are existing within the range of user device (Fig. 5). To compute the self-incomputable tasks, the user device (ud) would perform resource allocation on the fog devices, which are within the network range of the user device (Fig. 4).

```
"" Initializing network
Initializing module Network, stage 0
Network.fog0: Initializing module Network.fog0, stage 0
INFO (fog)Network.fog0: Network.fog0: Fog Nodes Initialization Start.
INFO (fog)Network.fog0: Network.fog0: Pro_Speed   Queue   F_Queue   Energy   R_Energy   Avg_Wait   Energy_Ratio
INFO (fog)Network.fog0: Network.fog0:    14         5        3       1200      779      2.05087      0.649167
INFO (fog)Network.fog0: Network.fog0: Fog Nodes Initialization Finished.
```

Fig. 4. Output log file of the specifications of fog device

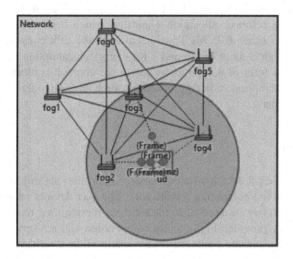

Fig. 5. Fog devices sending back results after task execution

4.2 Simulation Results

We have considered three algorithms for the purpose of resource allocation and compared them. The algorithms are the proposed resource allocation algorithm (PW), RR, MCT. Now after comparison, we have the following results:

Time Consumption	Fog2	Fog3	Fog4		Energy Consumption	Fog2	Fog3	Fog4
PW	9.604604	7.368965	11.90653		PW	399.08	322.08	419.39
MCT		11.54649	13.42487		MCT		372.39	436.16
RR	15.67796	8.761474	4.314838		RR	466.16	338.85	335.54

Fig. 6. Time and Energy consumption of the fog devices using different algorithms

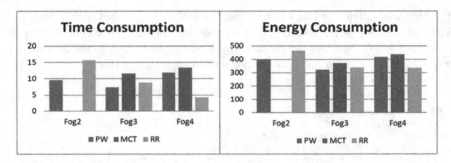

Fig. 7. Comparison of Time Consumption and Energy Consumption using different algorithms

Time consumption constitutes the time taken by the task to get submitted to a specific fog device, get executed there, and the returning of the results after computation back to the User Device. The left part of Fig. 6 and 7 exhibits, the overall time consumption of the resource allocation algorithm which has been proposed, is the lowest compared to other RR, MCT, which proves the efficiency of our proposed algorithm. On the right side of Fig. 6 and 7 the energy consumption simulation results are presented in the form of a table as well as a bar chart. It is clearly displayed the overall energy consumption of our proposed resource allocation algorithm is minimal compared to the others.

5 Conclusion

Here, an energy-efficient decision-based resource allocation algorithm has been introduced in P2P based fog computing architecture. The user devices which are unable to compute certain services because of the scarcity of the required resources to process them, are ultimately provided high-quality computation and are served with the right required results by using the proposed resource allocation algorithm. The parameters which have been taken into concern in the resource allocation algorithm are, if the fog device contains that task as a service or not, the average waiting time of tasks, ratio of remaining energy and the total capacity of energy, the status of the processing queue and processing speed. A comparison of the proposed algorithm has been carried out with algorithms like RR, MCT. It has been found that our algorithm gives the best results with respect to overall time and energy. Security is one of the major issues which have not been explored in our work. A proper theoretical definition of the overall architecture has not been proposed. Our future work will be incorporating proper load balancing in this P2P based fog computing architecture.

References

1. Armbrust, M., et al.: A view of cloud computing. Commun. ACM **53**, 50 (2010)
2. Dillon, T., Wu, C., Chang, E.: Cloud computing: issues and challenges. In: 2010 24th IEEE International Conference on Advanced Information Networking and Applications (2010)
3. Bonomi, F., Milito, R., Zhu, J., Addepalli, S.: Fog computing and its role in the internet of things. In: Proceedings of the 1st Edition of the MCC Workshop on Mobile Cloud Computing, MCC 2012 (2012)
4. Dastjerdi, A., Buyya, R.: Fog computing: helping the Internet of Things realize its potential. Computer **49**, 112–116 (2016)
5. Maity, S., Mistry, S.: Partial offloading for fog computing using P2P based file-sharing protocol. In: Das, H., Pattnaik, P.K., Rautaray, S.S., Li, K.-C. (eds.) Progress in Computing, Analytics and Networking. AISC, vol. 1119, pp. 293–302. Springer, Singapore (2020). https://doi.org/10.1007/978-981-15-2414-1_30
6. Ashrafi, T., Hossain, M., Arefin, S., Das, K., Chakrabarty, A.: Service based FOG computing model for IoT. In: 2017 IEEE 3rd International Conference on Collaboration and Internet Computing (CIC) (2017)
7. Barik, R., Dubey, H., Mankodiya, K.: SOA-FOG: secure service-oriented edge computing architecture for smart health big data analytics. In: 2017 IEEE Global Conference on Signal and Information Processing (GlobalSIP) (2017)
8. Duan, Q., Wang, S.: Network cloudification enabling network - cloud/fog service unification: state of the art and challenges. In: 2019 IEEE World Congress on Services (SERVICES). (2019)
9. Tang, W., Zhao, X., Rafique, W., Qi, L., Dou, W., Ni, Q.: An offloading method using decentralized P2P-enabled mobile edge servers in edge computing. J. Syst. Archit. **94**, 1–13 (2019)
10. Agarwal, S., Yadav, S., Yadav, A.: An efficient architecture and algorithm for resource provisioning in fog computing. Int. J. Inf. Eng. Electron. Bus. **8**, 48–61 (2016)
11. Bittencourt, L., Diaz-Montes, J., Buyya, R., Rana, O., Parashar, M.: Mobility-aware application scheduling in fog computing. IEEE Cloud Comput. **4**, 26–35 (2017)
12. Yin, L., Luo, J., Luo, H.: Tasks scheduling and resource allocation in fog computing based on containers for smart manufacturing. IEEE Trans. Ind. Inform. **14**, 4712–4721 (2018)
13. Choudhari, T., Moh, M., Moh, T.: Prioritized task scheduling in fog computing. In: Proceedings of the Conference on ACMSE 2018, ACMSE 2018 (2018)
14. Nguyen, B., Thi Thanh Binh, H., The Anh, T., Bao Son, D.: Evolutionary algorithms to optimize task scheduling problem for the IoT based bag-of-tasks application in cloud–fog computing environment. Appl. Sci. **9**, 1730 (2019)
15. Wang, J., Li, D.: Task scheduling based on a hybrid heuristic algorithm for smart production line with fog computing. Sensors **19**, 1023 (2019)
16. Bitam, S., Zeadally, S., Mellouk, A.: Fog computing job scheduling optimization based on bees swarm. Enterp. Inf. Syst. **12**, 373–397 (2017)
17. Li, G., Liu, Y., Wu, J., Lin, D., Zhao, S.: Methods of resource scheduling based on optimized fuzzy clustering in fog computing. Sensors **19**, 2122 (2019)
18. Li, H., Ota, K., Dong, M.: Deep reinforcement scheduling for mobile crowdsensing in fog computing. ACM Trans. Internet Technol. **19**, 1–18 (2019)
19. Dlamini, S., Ventura, N.: Resource management in fog computing: review. In: 2019 International Conference on Advances in Big Data, Computing and Data Communication Systems (icABCD) (2019)
20. Khurma, R.A., Harahsheh, H., Sharieh, A.A.A.: Task scheduling algorithm in cloud computing based on modified round robin algorithm. J. Theor. Appl. Inf. Technol. **96**, 5869–5888 (2018)

Network Steganography Using Extension Headers in IPv6

Punam Bedi and Arti Dua[✉]

Department of Computer Science, University of Delhi, Delhi, India
punambedi@ieee.org, arti.batra@gmail.com

Abstract. With the advent of technology, data security over the networks has become a crucial responsibility of organizations these days. One of the techniques to secure data over the networks is through information hiding. The art of hiding data in media files to make it secure from interception is termed as Steganography. Image, Audio, Video, Document, Network packets are different types of medium that are used to hide data within them. On the other hand, where Internet Protocol Version 4 (IPv4) is expected to become obsolete soon due to limited addressing space, Internet Protocol version 6 (IPv6) the next generation protocol, is soon going to take over the internet. In this paper, we propose a network steganography technique which uses Internet Protocol Version 6 packets having zero or more (up to four) extension headers to hide secret data and carry it from one end to other end over a network. Our technique is robust and at present can transfer five bits of covert data per IPv6 packet. This bandwidth can further be increased to few more bits, by increasing the number of extension headers attached to an IPv6 packet up to the permissible limit.

Keywords: Internet Protocol version 6 · Extension headers · Network steganography · Covert channel

1 Introduction

With increased research in the field of Internet of Things and dependency on internet for our day to day life, the usage of the internet has grown all over the world. Subsequently, there is a high need for more number of Internet Protocol addresses. However, due to the limited address space in the Internet Protocol Version 4 (IPv4), which is just 32-bits long there is an eminent need for the world to shift to Internet Protocol version 6 (IPv6), which offers 128-bits long IP addresses. The number of addresses provided by IPv6 is 340,282,366,920,938,463,463,374,607,431,768,211,456 which is enormously large. The IPv6 is expected to solve the limited address problem raised by IPv4 and is sooner expected to replace IPv4.

IPv6 doesn't only solve the problem of limited address space in IPv4, there are many other changes that were done in version 6 of the internet protocol. To list a few, the total number of mandatory fields in IPv4 header is 12 whereas, the number of mandatory fields in version 6 of this protocol is 8. The minimum length of an IPv4 packet is 20 bytes whereas, in case of IPv6 packet the minimum size of base IP header is 40 bytes. Next, IPv4 and IPv6, both can offer addresses which are unicast, multicast.

© Springer Nature Singapore Pte Ltd. 2020
C. Badica et al. (Eds.): ICICCT 2020, CCIS 1170, pp. 98–110, 2020.
https://doi.org/10.1007/978-981-15-9671-1_8

IPv4 supports broadcast addresses which is not supported by version 6 of this protocol. IPv6 supports a special addressing type called anycast address. Further, the fragmentation of IP packets is done at the sender and the forwarding routers in case of version 4 packets. In IPv6, fragmentation is done only at the sender and not at the intermediate routers. The MAC address resolution with IPv4 is done with the help of Address Resolution Protocol, whereas in IPv6, MAC address resolution is done with the help of Network Discovery Protocol (NDP). There are many more differences and we have listed just a few over here. With IPv6 becoming the most vital protocol of future internet, there are vulnerabilities also which pose a threat over internet security.

In this paper, we use Internet Protocol version 6 to implement Network Steganography which basically aims at hiding secret data in this protocol to communicate covertly over a network. As per our knowledge, all the work in Network Steganography that uses IPv6 directly fills covert data in the fields of the IPv6 base header or extension headers. These can easily be detected by analyzing the behavior of various fields of IPv6 base header in usual IPv6 traffic [14]. Whereas, in our technique we use the presence or absence of legitimate and permissible extension headers to communicate covertly which is difficult to identify.

The structure of rest of the paper is as follows: Sect. 2 of this paper describes the background and related work done in the field of Network Steganography and IPv6. Section 3 explains our proposed Network Steganography technique that uses IPv6 packets with its Extension Headers. Section 4 gives detailing of experimental study and results. Section 5 summarizes our work with conclusion and future scope of our work.

2 Background and Related Work

2.1 Network Steganography

Steganography is defined as the art of hiding data in a cover media. The intention behind steganography is to communicate secretly so that no one can intercept the secret message. Many cover medias are used to implement steganography such as Images, Audios, Videos, Documents and Network Protocols. The implementation of steganography that uses network packets that flow over the networks is termed as Network Steganography. Network Steganography has become a recent favorite area of researchers. Network Steganography can be classified on two basis:

1. On the basis of storing covert data in either storage fields or through timing and delays induced between packets.
2. On the basis of number of protocols being used in the techniques.

The first type of classification of Network Steganography classifies the techniques into three categories:

a. Storage Based Techniques: The aim of these techniques is to hide data in the header part or the payload part of a network protocol packet.
b. Timing Based Techniques: The aim of these techniques is to hide data in the interpretations of time gap or delays between two subsequent packets.

c. Hybrid Techniques: These techniques use a combination of above two techniques to hide data in the network packets.

The Second type of classification of Network Steganography classifies the techniques into two categories:

a. Intra Protocol Steganography: These type of techniques uses a single network protocol to implement network steganography techniques.
b. Inter Protocol Steganography: These type of techniques uses more than one network protocol to implement network steganography.

In this paper, we propose a Network Steganography technique that implements inter protocol steganography using storage based technique. The Network Protocol used for implementing Network Steganography in our scheme is Internet Protocol Version 6.

2.2   Internet Protocol Version 6 (IPv6)

The version six of Internet Protocol is the future lifeline of the internet. It is expected to become the most vital protocol over the internet. Figure 1 below shows the basic diagram of an IPv6 packet.

Base Header (40 Bytes)	Payload (Up to 65,535 Bytes)

Fig. 1. IPv6 packet.

RFC 2460 [1] defines the basic structure and fields of Internet Protocol Version 6 Header. The Header format for IPv6 is shown in Fig. 2 below.

Version (4 Bits)	Traffic Class (8 Bits)	Flow label (20 Bits)		
Payload Length (16 Bits)		Next Header (8 Bits)		Hop Limit (8 Bits)
Source Address (128 Bits)				
Destination Address (128 Bits)				

Fig. 2. Base Header of Internet Protocol version 6.

Version: This is a four bits long field that defines the version number of this protocol. The value of this field for IPv6 is 6.

Traffic Class: This is an eight bits long field. Sometimes different data/payloads have different delivery needs. This field defines the delivery requirement of an IPv6 packet. This field was named as TOS (Type of Service) field in IPv4 header.

Flow Label: This is a twenty bits long field. It provides for special handling for a particular flow of data.

Payload Length: This is a sixteen bits long field. This field holds the length of the IPv6 datagram excluding its header.

Next Header: This is an eight bits long field. This field defines the first extension header (if any) present with this IPv6 packet. This basically defines the type of data that is following the base header in the datagram.

Hop Limit: This is an eight bits long field. This field defines the number of hops/nodes that a packet can traverse over a network. It is similar to the Time to Live (TTL) field in IPv4 packet.

Source Address: This is a 128 bits long field. This field specifies the 128 bits Internet Protocol address of the source device.

Destination Address: This is a 128 bits long field. This field specifies the 128 bits Internet Protocol address of the receiver.

Payload: Figure 1 shows the payload part of an IPv6 packet. This payload field in IPv6 consists of zero or more extension headers followed by other protocol headers such as TCP, UDP etc. In IPv4, in place of Extension Headers, options field is used, which is optional in nature.

2.3   Extension Headers

An IPv6 packet consists of a base header as show in Fig. 2, followed by zero or more Extension Headers. The description of each of these headers is defined in RFC 8200 [2]. There are six types of Extension Headers that may be attached to an IPv6 base header. These headers are mentioned as below:

a. Hop by Hop Extension Header
b. Destination Extension Header
c. Routing Extension Header
d. Fragmentation Extension Header
e. Authentication Extension Header
f. Encrypted Security Payload Header

All the extension headers have three mandatory fields: 1) Next Header 2) Length 3) Options Data.

Next Header: This field holds the number value of next header. Table 1 below shows the Extension Header number for some protocols and all six extension headers.

Table 1. Extension Header Types/Protocols with their code values

Extension header Type/Protocol	Code
Hop By Hop Extension Header	0
Destination Extension Header	60
Routing Extension Header	43
Fragmentation Extension Header	44
Authentication Extension Header	51
Encrypted Security Payload Header	50
TCP	6
UDP	17
ICMPv6	58

The IPv6 base header is connected to the Extension header with the help of next header field as shown in Fig. 3. The next header field in the IPv6 base header holds the code value for next Extension Header. The next header field in the next Extension Header holds the code value for the further next Extension Header and so on.

Length: This field contains the length of option data of this option in octets.

Option Data: This field holds the data related to this option.

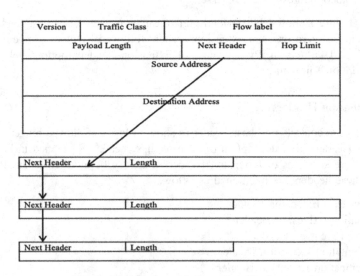

Fig. 3. IPv6 Packet with Extension Headers.

2.4   Related Work

Network Steganography has become an emerging area of research. A lot of work has already been done in this field in the last two decades. Many techniques using different protocols of TCP/IP model such as IPv4, TCP, ICMP, ARP, DNS etc. have been proposed in [3–12] to implement Network Steganography.

In this section, we only discuss the work done related to IPv6. Lucena et al. in [13] proposed 22 covert channels that can be created by directly filling data in IPv6 header. They also discussed the possibility of creation of covert channels by filling data in various Extension Headers that can be added to IPv6 base header. Further, they analyzed the bandwidth of each of the 22 covert channels proposed by them. Researchers in [14] evaluated the feasibility of deploying various covert channels proposed in [13]. Bobade et al. in [15] suggested a covert channel with a bandwidth of 20 bits per packet. They proposed the use of the field called flow label in the IPv6 base header to implement network steganography. They further strengthened this covert channel by encoding data using RSA encryption algorithm. Atlasis in [16] also discussed various security issues as well as the possibility of creating covert channels in IPv6 using the extension headers. In our proposed technique, we used an inter-protocol steganography technique to send data from a covert sender to a covert receiver using the idea of presence or absence of different extension headers for communicating a secret message.

3   Proposed Technique to Implement Network Steganography Using Extension Headers in IPv6

In this paper, we propose a network steganography technique that uses an IPv6 packet as cover media. This IPv6 packet consists of a base header and zero or more (up to four for our technique) Extension Headers followed by a Transport layer header which is either TCP or UDP. To demonstrate our idea of Network Steganography with Extension Headers, we primarily used four extension headers namely Hop-by-Hop, Destination, Routing and Fragmentation Extension Header. The purpose of each of the header is explained as below:

Hop-by-Hop Extension Header: This extension header when used, carries the optional information that needs to be processed at every hop encountered while an IPv6 packet travels from its source to the destination. This is the only extension header that is processed at every node from its source to its destination. The next header field value for this header is zero. If present, this header should be placed right next to the base ipv6 header, which means it should always be the first extension header.

Destination Extension Header: This Extension Header if used, carries the information that needs to be processed by the destination node(s) only. The Destination Header is indicated by a next header value of 60.

Routing Header: This Extension Header when used, specifies the list of intermediate nodes that must be visited while travelling from source to destination. The next header value for indicating Routing Header is 43. The Routing Extension Header further has many types. Type 0 and 1 are deprecated [17]. In our implementation, we used Routing Extension Header with type 2.

Fragmentation Header: This Extension Header is used when a source wishes to send a packet that exceeds the Maximum transmission unit (MTU) value of the path. So the source node fragments the original packet into smaller fragments. This fragmentation is done only at the source node and not at intermediate routers. The next header value for indicating this header is 44.

At the Transport layer, we used two protocols namely Transmission Control Protocol (TCP) and User Datagram Protocol (UDP) to transfer data. The TCP is a reliable and connection oriented transport layer protocol. The UDP is also a transport layer protocol but it is connection-less and unreliable. The next header value of the last Extension Header holds the protocol number of the protocol being used at the transport layer. In case we are using TCP, the protocol number is 6. For UDP, the protocol number is 17.

In our technique, the sender and receiver both agree upon and have a prior knowledge of fixed order of extension header as mentioned below:

1. First Extension Header: Hop-by-Hop Extension Header
2. Second Extension Header: Destination Extension Header
3. Third Extension Header: Routing Extension Header
4. Fourth Extension Header: Fragmentation Extension Header
5. Fifth Extension Header: Transport Layer Header (TCP/UDP)

In our work, we created a covert channel where the presence of an Extension Header with an IPv6 base header in the above said relative order marks a value 1 and the absence of that Extension Header in that same order marks a value 0. For the first four bits, a value of 0 or 1 can be inferred depending upon the absence/presence of the Extension Headers in the above said relative order. For the fifth bit, if the transport layer protocol is TCP, then it is interpreted as a 1, otherwise if it is UDP, it is interpreted as a 0. This channel was capable of sending five bits of covert data. For example, if one wishes to send a bit stream 0000011011 as covert data, it is broken down into two messages of 5 bits each as 00000 and 11011. First the secret message 00000 is sent over this covert channel. For that, the idea is to create an IPv6 base packet at the sender side with no Extension Header and mark the value of next header field in IPv6 as 17 (for UDP). So, a 0 at each of the first four bits is represented by the absence of all the Extension Headers and a value 0 for the fifth bit is represented by the presence of UDP at the transport layer. For the next covert message 11011, IPv6 base header is created followed by a Hop by Hop Extension Header, a Destination Extension Header and a Fragmentation Extension Header with TCP working at the Transport layer. In other words, in the next header field of IPv6 base header put the value 0 corresponding to the Hop-by-Hop Extension Header created in the last step. In the next header field of Hop-by-Hop Extension Header, put the value 60 corresponding to the created Destination Extension Header. In the next header field of Destination Extension Header put the value 44 corresponding to Fragmentation Extension Header and finally in the next header field of Fragmentation Extension Header put the value 6 to associate a TCP header at the Transport layer.

At the receiver's side, both IPv6 packets carrying covert messages are received and scanned carefully for extension headers. Each Extension Header is checked for its presence in the above stated relative order. In the first message, no Extension Header is present which gives an interpretation that the first four bits are 0 and the presence of UDP as Transport layer header is interpreted as 0 at the fifth bit position. So this makes the receiver interpret the first message as 00000. For the second message, all the headers are present in their decided relative order and only routing header is absent so the bit at position three is marked as 0 and the first, second and fourth bit are marked as 1. Further the presence of TCP header at the transport layer confirms the value 1 at the fifth bit. With this, the receiver interprets this message as 11011.

In cases, where one wants to allow sending messages of any bit length which may not be a multiple of five, one can designate the first IPv6 packet to carry the number of padding bits added to the message to make it a multiple of 5. The minimum and maximum number of padding bits required could be 0 and 4 respectively. So in this case the first IPv6 packet can have 5 legitimate values starting from 00000 to 00100. Further IPv6 packets can be used to send the covert data bits. Once the sender has stopped sending IPv6 packets, all the received bits can be combined omitting the number of padded bits from the last received message to decode the actual message.

4   Experimental Study

The environment created to experiment our technique consisted of a covert sender running on Host A, a covert receiver running on Host B of a local area network. Both Host A and Host B have their unique local IPv6 addresses as shown in Fig. 4. The methodology adopted in this paper for experimentation consisted of various steps. In the first step, we inputted five bits of covert message from the user. In the next step, we created a IPv6 base header followed by the needed extension header as per the input message and the fixed order discussed in Sect. 3. Next, we create a TCP or a UDP header at transport layer depending upon the value of fifth bit in the secret message. The legitimate values in mandatory fields of IPv6 base header and the created extension headers is filled and the packet is sent over a local area network to Host B who is the covert message receiver. Host B interprets this IPv6 packet with zero or more (up to

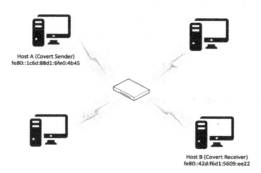

Fig. 4. Network setup for experimentation

four) added extension headers by matching the presence of various extension headers in their specific relative order as specified in Sect. 3.

4.1 Sender Side Methodology

At the Sender side, a python script was written which inputted five bits of secret message from the user. Next, a IPv6 base header is created using scapy [18]. Scapy is a Python library that enables the user to send, sniff, dissect, and forge packets over a network. Depending on the values of these first four bits, the corresponding extension headers are created using scapy as per the order mentioned in Sect. 3. The last bit of the inputted secret message is read to decide weather to create a TCP header or a UDP header at transport layer. A value of 1 indicates TCP and 0 indicates a UDP header. If TCP header is needed port 20 was used as source port and port 80 is used as destination port. These port numbers were selected arbitrarily. The idea is to use the port numbers which are not expected to be in use currently. On the other hand, if UDP header is needed at transport layer, port 53 was used as source as well as destination port in our implementation. The transport header is also created using Scapy library. After creation of these headers appropriate values are filled in mandatory fields like Source Address, Destination Address, port numbers for source and destination, next header value for IPv6 base packet and extension headers etc. After relevant values have been filled in this IPv6 packet, it is sent to the destination over the network.

4.2 Receiver Side Methodology

At Host B, which is a covert message receiver, a python script was created. This script basically sniffed all the incoming IPv6 packets coming from Host A, destined for Host B, having TCP with source port number 20 or UDP with source port number 53. Again, Scapy library was used to sniff and read the received IPv6 packets. The relative order and presence of Extension Headers is interpreted as per the order mentioned in Sect. 3 to decode the covert message sent by Host A.

4.3 Results

The local area network was established with Host A and Host B having unique local IPv6 addresses. The covert messages were inputted from the user as shown in Fig. 5. After applying the proposed technique, the created IPv6 packet was sent to Host B over this network. The technique was tested for all 2^5 combinations for 5 bits of input data. The snapshot for the sender sending two different set of five bits long covert message, one after another is shown in Fig. 5. The first message five-bit code was 11110 and the second message five-bit code was 00011. The sending of these messages was confirmed on Wireshark [19] as shown in Fig. 6. Wireshark is a freely available tool that is used to scan and analyze the packets flowing in and out of a particular device.

On the receiver's side, the covert messages were successfully received and interpreted as per the relative ordering of Extension Headers discussed in Sect. 3. Figure 7 and 8 shows the snapshot of console and Wireshark tool running at the receiver side respectively. Figure 7 shows the receiver process interpreting the message bits. Figure 8 confirms the receipt of the two messages sent from Host A.

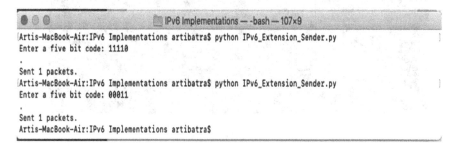

Fig. 5. Sender process

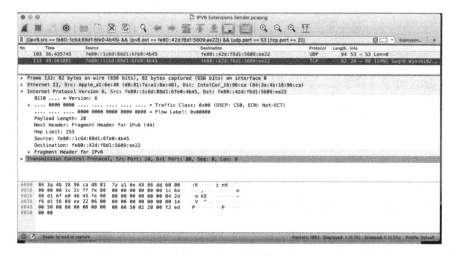

Fig. 6. Wireshark snapshot at the Sender side

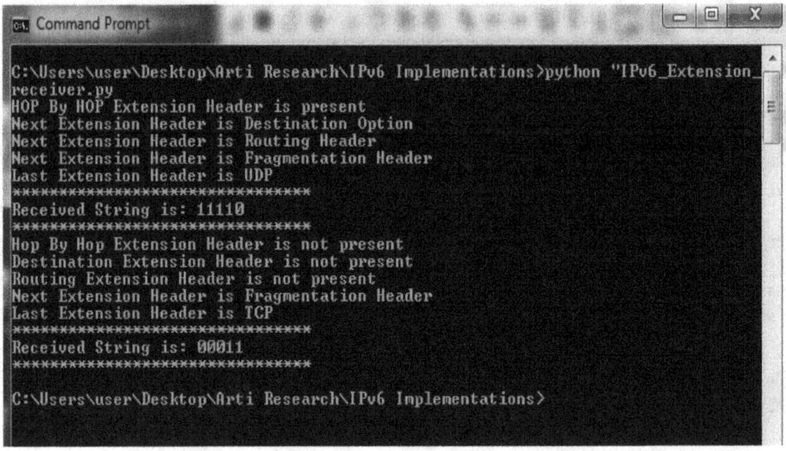

Fig. 7. Receiver process

Fig. 8. Wireshark snapshot at the Receiver side

5 Conclusion and Future Work

In this paper, we successfully implemented a Network Steganography technique using Internet Protocol version 6 and its various Extension Headers. Our technique makes use of the fixed relative order of Extension Headers already known to the sender and receiver. If an Extension Header is present in that relative order, a 1 is marked at its bit position in the covert message otherwise it is marked as a 0. Our technique is robust and undetectable as it makes use of legitimate field values and Extension Headers for covert communications. The current steganography bandwidth of our technique is 5 bits per IPv6 packet with five permissible extension headers. As Scapy, the python library that we used to create IPv6 packets with Extension Headers did not support the creation of Authentication Extension Header and Encapsulating Security Payload Header, thus we had to limit our covert data bandwidth to five bits per IPv6 packet.

This steganography bandwidth can further be extended to two more bits by adding more permissible extension headers like Authentication Extension Header, Encapsulating Security Payload Header over the network. Precisely, we can send one bit of covert data per Extension Header, which depicts a direct relation between number of Extension Headers permissible over a network and steganography bandwidth of this technique.

Further, as IPv6 is still not used widely over the internet, the use of our technique is limited to only those networks which support IPv6 enabled transmissions. Future work can be done to analyze and explore more vulnerabilities in IPv6 to implement new techniques of Network Steganography supporting a wider bandwidth for covert channels over IPv6.

References

1. Deering, S., Hinden, R.: Internet protocol, version 6 (IPv6) specification (1998)
2. Siddiqui, A.: RFC 8200–IPv6 has been standardized. Internet Society, vol. 1 (2018)
3. Mileva, A., Boris, P.: Covert channels in TCP/IP protocol stack-extended version. Open Comput. Sci. **4**(2), 45–66 (2014)
4. Lubacz, J., Mazurczyk, W., Szczypiorski, K.: Principles and overview of network steganography. IEEE Commun. Mag. **52**(5), 225–229 (2014)
5. Rowland, C.: Covert channels in the TCP/IP protocol suite, first Monday. Peer Rev. J. Internet **2**(5) (1997)
6. Szczypiorski, K., Drzymała, M., Urbański, M.Ł.: Network steganography in the DNS protocol. Int. J. Electron. Telecommun. **62**(4), 343–346 (2016)
7. Ahsan, K., Kundur, D.: Practical data hiding in TCP/IP. In: Proceedings of the Workshop on Multimedia Security at ACM Multimedia, pp 1–8 (2002)
8. Kundur, D., Ahsan, K.: Practical internet steganography: data hiding in IP. In: Proceedings of the Texas Workshop on Security of Information Systems, College Station, Texas (2003)
9. Bedi, P., Dua, A.: Network steganography using the overflow field of timestamp option in an IPv4 packet. Presented at 3rd International Conference on Computing and Network Communications, CoCoNet 2019, Trivendrum (2019)
10. Trabelsi, Z., Jawhar, I.: Covert file transfer protocol based on the IP record route option. J. Inf. Assur. Secur. **5**(1), 64–73 (2010)
11. Murdoch, S.J., Lewis, S.: Embedding covert channels into TCP/IP. In: Barni, M., Herrera-Joancomartí, J., Katzenbeisser, S., Pérez-González, F. (eds.) IH 2005. LNCS, vol. 3727, pp. 247–261. Springer, Heidelberg (2005). https://doi.org/10.1007/11558859_19
12. Ji, L., Fan, Y., Ma, C.: Covert channel for local area network. In: Proceedings of the IEEE International Conference on Wireless Communications, Networking and Information Security, WCNIS, Beijing, China, pp. 316–319 (2010)
13. Lucena, N.B., Lewandowski, G., Chapin, S.J.: Covert channels in IPv6. In: Danezis, G., Martin, D. (eds.) PET 2005. LNCS, vol. 3856, pp. 147–166. Springer, Heidelberg (2006). https://doi.org/10.1007/11767831_10
14. Mazurczyk, W., Powójski, K., Caviglione, L.: IPv6 covert channels in the wild. In: Proceedings of the 3rd Central European Cybersecurity Conference, pp. 1–6 (2019)
15. Bobade, S., Goudar, R.: Secure data communication using protocol steganography in IPv6. In: 2015 International Conference on Computing Communication Control and Automation (ICCUBEA), pp. 275–279. IEEE (2015)

16. Atlasis, A.: Security impacts of abusing IPv6 extension headers. In: Black Hat Security Conference, pp. 1–10 (2012)
17. Internet Protocol Version 6 (IPv6) Parameters. https://www.iana.org/assignments/ipv6-parameters/ipv6-parameters.xhtml. Accessed 13 Feb 2020
18. Introduction. About Scapy. https://scapy.readthedocs.io/en/latest/introduction.html. Accessed 12 Feb 2020
19. Wireshark-Go Deep. https://www.wireshark.org. Accessed 12 Feb 2020

Partial Migration for Re-architecting a Cloud Native Monolithic Application into Microservices and FaaS

Deepali Bajaj[1]([⊠]) [iD], Urmil Bharti[1] [iD], Anita Goel[2] [iD],
and S. C. Gupta[3] [iD]

[1] Department of Computer Science, Shaheed Rajguru College of Applied
Sciences for Women, University of Delhi, Delhi, India
deepali.bajaj@rajguru.du.ac.in, ubharti@hotmail.com
[2] Department of Computer Science, Dyal Singh College, University of Delhi,
Delhi, India
goel.anita@gmail.com
[3] Department of Computer Science, Indian Institute of Technology, Delhi, India
scgupta@cse.iitd.ac.in

Abstract. Software development paradigm is transitioning from monolithic architecture to microservices and serverless architecture. Keeping monolithic application as a single large unit of scale is a threat for its agility, testability and maintainability. Complete migration of a monolithic application to microservice or serverless architecture poses additional challenges. Design and development of microservices is complex and cumbersome in comparison to monoliths. As number of microservices increase, their management also becomes challenging. Using serverless platforms can offer considerable savings, however it doesn't work for all types of workload patterns. Many a times, it may be more expensive in comparison to dedicated server deployments, particularly when application workload scales significantly. In this paper, we propose partial migration of monolith application into microservices and serverless services. For the purposes of refactoring, we use web access log data of monolith application. Our proposed architecture model is based on unsupervised learning algorithm and aims to optimize the resource utilization and throughput of an application by identifying the modules having different scalability and resource requirements. This facilitates segregation of services of a monolith application into monolith-microservice-serverless. We have applied our proposed approach on a Teachers Feedback monolith application and presented the results.

Keywords: Microservices · Decomposition · Refactoring · K-means clustering algorithm · Web access log mining · Microservices architecture · FaaS · Serverless

© Springer Nature Singapore Pte Ltd. 2020
C. Badica et al. (Eds.): ICICCT 2020, CCIS 1170, pp. 111–124, 2020.
https://doi.org/10.1007/978-981-15-9671-1_9

1 Introduction

Cloud offers rapid elasticity to commensurate with inward and outward demand and swift setting of virtual servers. Because of these benefits, many business companies from small to medium and large sizes are opting cloud service model for deployment of their web applications. Despite these gains, most of applications deployed on cloud could not reap the complete benefits. As just by dumping the existing legacy applications to a virtualized environment can't be regarded as a true cloud native application. In this scenario, system administrators and developers are responsible for maintenance of software stack on these virtual servers which is a burdensome task for them.

Most of the legacy applications were designed using monolithic architectures. These applications are deployed on cloud web servers as a single codebase consisting of different services/modules. Such applications are convenient to develop, test and deploy till its codebase is small and manageable. As application demand increases or its size grows, maintenance of such monolith applications becomes tricky [1]. In this architectural design, a single defective service can bring down the entire software application.

To resolve these issues of monolithic architecture, a new way of designing software applications emerged which is known as microservices. In microservices architecture, all the business requirements of an application are divided into smaller services. Each service works like an independent component and runs in its own container such as Docker, Amazon EC2 Container Service (ACS), Google Container Engine (GKE), Azure Container Service [2]. Each microservice is designed on single responsibility principle i.e. do just one thing and do it properly [3, 4]. Microservice architectural pattern is free from single point of failure and exercise continuous integration and delivery (CI/CD) practices as each new deployment only affects the microservice being updated and not others [5]. This architecture leverages many advantages like scalability, reliability and agility. Ease of deployment and maintenance, resilience to failure and reduce time to market are also considerable benefits of this architecture. Because of its evolutionary design and inherent advantages, microservice architecture is being embraced by many prime technological companies such as Amazon, Netflix, LinkedIn, SoundCloud, Gilt and eBay [6]. Nevertheless, few drawbacks are also associated with microservices design: (i) since everything is an autonomous service which results in high latency in remote calls between services (ii) testing of microservices based application is very complex (iii) since all services generate their own set of logs so debugging is also painful in comparison to monolithic applications.

Recently serverless computing is also gaining traction. A serverless architecture splits an application into a set of even smaller granular services. In this architectural style, developers don't own the burden of setting and administering servers dynamically based on demand which was an overwhelming task in other two service models discussed previously. Sever and infrastructure management is done by cloud service providers. Because of this ease, an application can be developed at a rapid pace with reduced costs. Developers may write the cloud functions packaged as Function-as-a-Service (FaaS) in a variety of languages (i.e. Python, Java, JavaScript, Go) and selects the triggering events for their function. Resource instance type selection, scalability, deployment options, fault tolerance, logging and monitoring is handled by serverless computing platform. Some of the most common serverless platforms are AWS Lambda [7], Microsoft Azure functions [8], Google Cloud Functions [9] and IBM Cloud Functions [10]. Serverless cloud computing execution model also have certain restrictions [11] (i): FaaS functions have limited execution time and when timeout limit is reached, serverless platform abruptly terminates its execution (ii) Functions connect to cloud backend services across a network interface that consumes significant network bandwidth (iii) Maintaining function state across multiple client calls requires writing the current state to slow storage. Looking at these constraints, services that are stateless, isolated, ephemeral, limited in resource requirements and execution time are perfect use cases for FaaS [12].

Thus all the service models have their own strengths and weaknesses that can be exploited for cloud native applications. To make efficient use of these new architectural styles, several migration techniques have been proposed in literature but they all recommend complete migration of an application into microservices or serverless platforms. These migration techniques can be broadly classified as black box and white box. In white box migration technique, static characteristics of an application like design documents, source code files, revision history etc. are used in migration decisions. In black box migration technique, dynamic characteristics of an application like web access log, user usage log, execution traces etc. are the main attributes which guide the migration process [13].

In this paper, we propose a partial migration approach for re-factoring a monolithic application that allows some services of the application to be deployed as microservices, some as FaaS while the rest of the services may remain in monolithic application. Rationale behind this three-in-one architectural pattern is services that are highly scalable and resource intensive can be implemented as microservices. Stateless, ephemeral, short lived modules can be deployed as FaaS. More precisely, the services that are not very popular and consume limited resources can be easily migrated to a serverless platform instead of using a traditional container based implementation. This approach devoid re-factoring a legacy system to run entirely as either microservices or serverless cloud functions. So it would achieve significant gains in terms of resource utilization and better throughput. Our proposed approach of service model selection in terms of s will yield better optimized performance for a web application. Main contributions of the paper are as follow:

1. Proposed a black-box partial migration approach based on web access log for identifying workload patterns of different modules in a cloud native web application. Dimensions considered for workload identification of a module are its scalability and resource requirements.
2. Devised a selection model that will provide guidance for mapping different application modules to suitable service models (monolithic/microservices/serverless).
3. The proposed approach has been applied on a case study of Teachers Feedback Web Application originally developed as a monolithic application.

2   Related Study

It has become harder to maintain legacy monolithic applications because of tight coupling among their internal software components. Modifying a feature in one component causes ripple effects in several other components as well, leading to increased development time and programmers' effort. To address these issues, decomposition of a monolith has been proposed by researchers. Decomposition is a process of re-factoring existing codebase into small and independently deployable modules to improve maintainability and fault tolerance. However monolith application decomposition is a crucial and complex task [14]. Several research papers have been published describing manual, heuristics based, semi automated and automated techniques for this. But all approaches discussed so far, talk about complete migration of monolith to microservices and serverless architectures. Prime objective of discussing their research work is to understand the strategies available in literature that are used for complete migration of large monolithic applications.

Few researchers have done experiments to compare application performance on different service models. Takanori et al. [15] compared the monolithic and microservices implementation of Acme Air, a fictitious airlines web application. They verified that the response time of client request in microservices is significantly increased than the monolithic for two popular language runtimes Java EE and Node.js. Villamizar et al. [16] compared the running cost of a web application in three different deployment options: (i) monolithic architecture (ii) microservice architecture managed by customer and (iii) microservice architecture offered by cloud service providers. Their experimental results show that microservices adoption helps in reducing infrastructure costs when compared with monolithic architectures. Hasselbring et al. [17] studied and presented different aspects of microservice architecture like scalability, reliability, and agility. Costa et al. [18] discusses the pros and cons of microservice over the monolithic architecture. Balalaie et al. [19] discussed their experience report of the migration process of monolithic system to microservices architecture. They observed that microservices architecture offers more flexibility, scalability and availability but brings in new complexities. Adzic et al. [20] examines cost model of migrating two online application to AWS Lambda architecture and they observed significant cost reductions. Manner [21] discussed two conflicting parameters: cost and performance in terms of FaaS adoption.

Some researchers observed that slicing of monolithic application done on the basis of business domain may not find highly loaded parts of the system [13, 22]. The load predictions done by the software architects may not be enough for more complex use cases and should be supplemented with users' access records for the web pages. Mining web usage logs to dig out useful details regarding user behavior has been investigated in research. Muhammad et al. [13] devised a novel approach to automatically decompose a monolithic application into microservices using web access logs of the application for improved user experience and scalability. They also proposed a dynamic method for the selection of the suitable virtual machine to deploy microservices so as to enhance the performance of microservices. Mustafa et al. [22] suggested black-box based technique that extends utilization of web usage mining techniques and considered non functional requirements like performance and scalability for comparison against monolithic implementation.

All the existing approaches explain about complete migration of monoliths to microservices or serverless architectures using either black box or white box techniques. We did not come across any research work that discusses partial migration of monolithic application to microservices and serverless frameworks. In order to address this research gap, we are proposing a partial migration approach that will refactor an existing monolithic codebase to suitable service model. Our idea is to implement scalable and resource intensive components as microservices and less scalable components with short execution time as FaaS. Components with moderate scalability and resource requirements may remain as monolith. With the best of our knowledge, this is the first and novel approach for re-factoring monolithic systems into microservices and FaaS.

3   Proposed Partial Migration Approach for Re-architecting a Monolithic Application into Microservices and FaaS

Having identified various inadequacies in monolith, microservices and serverless platforms, our partial migration approach identifies services and suggests deploying them on best suited service model. Figure 1 shows the complete view of the partial migration approach for re-factoring a monolithic application to microservices and FaaS.

Our approach is based on mining web server access logs of a monolithic web application to predict the scalability and resource requirements of its various components. This will give an insight about highly loaded services, small independent services that are less scalable (with restricted resources requisite) and services with consistent workload (with predicted resources requisite). Our migration approach involves three main steps:

1)   Preprocessing of Web Access Log
2)   Segregation of URIs
3)   Identification of service models

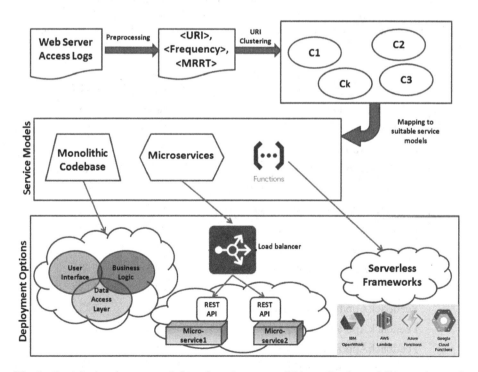

Fig. 1. Partial migration approach for refactoring a monolithic application to Microservices and FaaS

3.1 Preprocessing of Web Access Log

Our approach commences with the collection of web server access log of a monolith web application. The log data must be sufficient enough to reflect the overall application usage statistics. To achieve this, log data should be collected for one complete application execution cycle. This step will ensure inclusion of logs of all services requested by clients so that log mining will obtain unbiased results.

Common format of web server access log file includes Client IP, requested resource URI, time stamp values, HTTP status code, size of document object returned to the client (in bytes) [23]. In addition to default parameters, web servers can be configured to retrieve other log parameters values as well. In our approach, we have used one such configurable parameter i.e. request service time. Value of request response time indicates the time spent to serve a client request (in microseconds) and is also known as request response time (RRT).

Pre-process the collected log data by extracting out only two desired fields i.e. URIs and Request Response Time. The URI frequency from pre-processed logs will reflect scalability requirements and request response time will indicate hardware resource requirements like CPU, disk, network etc. to fulfill a client request.

3.2 Segregation of URIs

From processed log data, segregate all distinct URIs and calculated their frequency of occurrence. Frequency of a URI corresponds to its popularity and thus indicates scalability requirement. Next task is to calculate Mean Request Response Time (MRRT) for each distinct URI. Figure 2 shows sample URIs, their frequency of occurrence and MRRT values.

URIs	Frequency	MRTT
/FeedbackApp/login/	6866	325
/FeedbackApp/	12756	90
/FeedbackApp/feedback/	28716	618
/FeedbackApp/logout/	2016	78
/FeedbackApp/change_password/	4126	92
/FeedbackApp/teacher_analytics/	975	108
/FeedbackApp/teacher_view/	525	515
/FeedbackApp/feedbackStatus/	1020	87
/FeedbackApp/feedbackStatus_view/	510	378
/FeedbackApp/principle_analytics/	413	113
/FeedbackApp/top_five_teachers/	12	973
/FeedbackApp/analytics/	186	606
/FeedbackApp/feedback/VH	6	193
/FeedbackApp/feedback/VH/Chatbot	3	185

Fig. 2. Sample URIs, their frequencies and MRRT values

Our migration approach apply mining technique on processed data to find out similar URI clusters that can be migrated to suitable service models. We propose a URI clustering technique on web access log taking into consideration two clustering parameters (i) mean request response time and (ii) frequency of invocation of each request. We apply URI clustering by partitioning URIs into K discrete clusters {C_1, C_2, ..., C_K} such that the resource and scalability requirements remain uniform within each cluster. Precisely, each partition corresponds to URIs having comparable request response time and frequency of occurrence.

To identify the URIs clusters, we use unsupervised K-means clustering algorithm wherein URIs are partitioned into pre-defined disjoint non-overlapping K clusters. This is a hard clustering technique in which each data point belongs to only one cluster. Our approach also demands that each URI should be a member of only one cluster so we selected K-means clustering algorithm. This algorithm aims to make all the inter-cluster points as close as possible and at the same time, keeping different clusters as distant as possible. Data points corresponding to URIs are assigned to a cluster so that Euclidean distance (sum of squared distance between data points and clusters' centroid) are minimized [24]. Euclidean Distance can be represented in Eq. 1:

$$\text{Euclidean Distance} = \sqrt{(X_F - F_1)^2 + (X_{MRTT} - MRRT_1)^2} \qquad (1)$$

where X_F: Observation value of variable Frequency, X_{MRRT}: Observation value of variable MRRT, F_1: Centroid of cluster 1 for variable Frequency, $MRRT_1$: Centroid of cluster 1 for variable MRRT.

As the scale of measurement of clustering parameters affects Euclidean Distance, so variable standardization becomes essential to avoid biased clustering. Standardization is a method wherein all the parameters are centered around zero and have nearly unit variance. For this we subtracted each dataset value by mean and then divide with standard deviation as shown in Eq. 2.

$$\hat{\chi} = \frac{(X - \mu)}{\sigma} \qquad (2)$$

An elementary step for any unsupervised learning algorithm is to find the appropriate number of clusters into which data must be clustered. The most common method used for K-means algorithm is Elbow Method. We also used Elbow method to calculate the appropriate number of clusters K. We plot WSS value (within-cluster sums of squares) and number of clusters K. The location on the plot that shows a knee bend is considered as an indicator of optimal value of K [25]. WSS is a measure of compactness of a cluster and can be calculated as sum of squared distance between all data points xi of a cluster j and the centroid of cluster j, as shown in Eq. 3.

$$\text{WSS}(K) = \sum_{j=1}^{K} \sum_{x_j \in cluster_j} \left\| Xi - \bar{X}j \right\|^2 \qquad (3)$$

where $\bar{X}j$ is mean in cluster j.

Once we get an optimal value of K, we can implement K-mean clustering to get K number of clusters. URIs that is grouped in one cluster has similarity in terms of scalability and resource requirements.

3.3   Identification of Service Models

In this step, identified clusters are mapped to monolith, microservices and FaaS service models. In general, highly scalable and modifiable components of a monolith are good candidates for microservices. At the same time isolated, ephemeral and independent components are good candidates for FaaS in serverless service model.

Frequency of a URI is proportionate to its scalability need and MRRT value reflects resource usage to serve clients request. We suggest that URIs having high frequencies can be deployed as microservices. Further, URIs with moderate frequency and high resource usage can also be considered for microservices deployment. Similarly URIs having low frequencies and moderate to low resource requirements can be deployed as FaaS. Rest of the URIs can remain in monolithic deployment. Table 1 provides pragmatic guidance about suitable service models.

Table 1. Service model selection on the basis of scalability and resource usage.

Scalability need	Resource usage	Service model
High	High	Microservice
High	Moderate	Microservice
High	Low	Microservice
Moderate	High	Microservice
Moderate	Moderate	Monolith
Moderate	Low	*Monolith/FaaS
Low	High	Monolith
Low	Moderate	FaaS
Low	Low	FaaS

* Dependent on Cloud Service Provider threshold limits for execution time and resource usage.

4   Case Study

In this section, we will present our case study of Teachers Feedback Web Application which is developed to collect teachers' feedback in a university environment. We have applied our proposed methodology on this system to prove our results. This case study can be considered as a proof of concept (PoC) for our partial migration approach.

4.1   Teachers Feedback Web Application

We have validated our approach using a case study "Teachers Feedback Web Application". In order to fine tune the process of teaching-learning and for establishing a positive learning environment, constituent colleges of the University of Delhi employs a feedback mechanism. In this spirit, we developed Teachers Feedback Web Application (TFWA) to automate the feedback process. TFWA is developed on Model View Controller (MVC) architectural pattern which is a popular web application design pattern. It is developed using Django framework 3.0.2 which is a Python-based free and open-source web framework [26]. Django framework officially supports many database backends like PostgreSQL, MariaDB, MySQL, SQLite. In our implementation we have used SQLite as database backend which is a default option supported by Django. For our PoC we deployed TFWA on Apache HTTP Server 2.4.41 (https).

Different actors of this system are Student, Administrator, Teacher In-Charge and Principal. Students use TFWA to record their feedback at the end of every semester for all teachers. Feedback is collected for all subjects taught by either same or different teachers in a course. Feedback is collected on fifteen different questions where a student can mark her response on a scale of 1 to 5. A special use case has also been implemented in which a visually impaired student can also provide her feedback using a chatbot facility that is being developed using conversation technology via audio messages. Teacher In-Charge of every department can track the status of the feedback process to ensure the participation of all the students. TIC can view and analyze the feedback data from different perspectives i.e. teachers-wise feedback summary/details, subject-wise feedback summary/details and course-wise feedback summary/details.

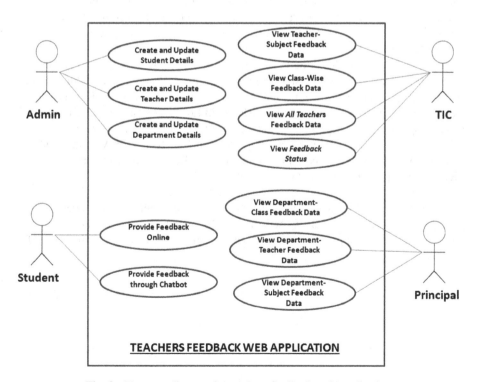

Fig. 3. Use case diagram for teachers feedback web application

Principal of the college can also view and analyze feedback data of the whole college from different perspectives i.e. department-wise feedback summary/details, teachers-wise feedback summary/details, subject-wise feedback summary/details and course-wise feedback summary/details. Principal can also view the top five teachers, as per student feedback, of the college. Administrator of the application can populate students, teachers, departments, courses and principal data into the system by import facility provided in the application. Administrator can also insert or update any of these entities if any correction is required after import operation. Figure 3 shows use case diagram for TFWA.

4.2   Methodology in Practice

Based on the system requirements of TFWA presented above, in this section we have discussed the application of our proposed approach for partial migration as PoC for our case study.

We collected web server access logs of one complete execution cycle of Teacher Feedback Web Application. These logs have feedback from all the students (for all teachers and their respective subjects) and multiple views of feedback data by TIC and principal and hence the entire URI space is collected as per the real usage of application. Next step was to preprocess the web server access logs to retrieve frequency of each URI and its MRRT. Since both parameters differ in their unit and scale which may unduly influence the migration process so we performed variable standardization to transform data to a common scale. This scaling will not distort the differences in original ranges of values. This standardization preprocessing has been discussed in Subsect. 3.2.

To apply K-means clustering technique on our URI space, we need to get an idea about the optimal number of clusters (K) for the K-means algorithm. We addressed this concern by applying the Elbow method in which we iterate the value of K and calculate within-cluster sums of squares (WSS) as shown in Eq. 3. We clearly noticed that WSS value drops sharply when K is smaller than elbow point 3 and decreases slightly afterwards. Therefore, we opted 3 as an optimal value for K in TFWA. Figure 4 shows variation of WSS with an increasing number of K. URI space distribution is shown in Fig. 5 after applying K-mean clustering with K = 3.

Boundaries of the clusters are distinguishable without any overlap. This demonstrates that identified clusters can be implemented in different service models as suggested in Table 1. Figure 5 shows service model selection for TFWA where each data point represents an application URI (a set of sample URIs is given in Fig. 2 for reference).

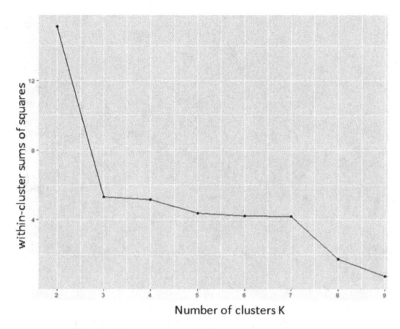

Fig. 4. Elbow method - WSS vs. number of clusters

4.3   Results

In the previous subsections, we have applied our proposed methodology on TFWA. As an outcome, we have identified possible refactoring for microservices, FaaS and monolith deployments. Our findings are as follow:

Microservice Potential Candidates: URIs with high frequency indicate high scalability requirements so can be deployed as microservice architectures. As shown in Fig. 5 cluster C1 contains all the URIs involved in capturing feedback of teachers. Since, *Capture Feedback* functionality of TFWA is a highly scalable component as thousands of students give their feedback in parallel for all teachers taught them in the current semester. So it is a judicious decision to re-factor this component from monolithic code base and implement it as a separate microservice.

FaaS Potential Candidates: URIs with very less frequency and low resource requirements can be mapped to serverless service model. It means services associated with these URIs can be implemented as Function-as-a-Service in a serverless platform. As shown in Fig. 5, cluster C3 contains all the URIs that occurred least number of time in log data. Data points of this cluster represent the URIs of chatbot service. In our application, *ChatBot* functionality to simulate human conversation for providing feedback using voice-based interfaces (speech-to-text and text-to-speech) that is required only for visually impaired students is a good candidate for FaaS.

Other system capabilities of TFWA like *User Authorization*, *Admin Functions* like maintaining department, course, teacher and students details, *Tracking Feedback Status* and various *Feedback Analytics* options available for TIC and Principal can be

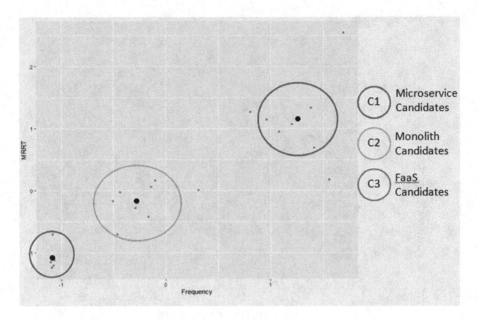

Fig. 5. Identified Clusters and their mapping to service models

considered as monolith candidates as these services have moderate scalability and moderate resource usage requirements. All the URIs of these application capabilities are shown in cluster C2 as shown in Fig. 5.

So our case study establishes our results and validates our proposed approach of partial migration.

Conclusion

In recent years, web applications that require scaling for thousands or millions of concurrent users are becoming common. Traditional enterprise web applications are generally developed as monolith applications, which become hard to develop, test, scale and maintain with time. To alleviate these problems, Microservice and serverless architectures are evolving. Microservices enable creating an application as a collection of autonomous services which interact with each other through lightweight mechanisms like REST API or message bus etc. In a serverless execution model, cloud provider dynamically controls allocation and provisioning of servers. Serverless applications run in stateless compute containers that are event-triggered, ephemeral, and fully managed by the cloud provider itself. Pricing is determined by number of executions at run time and not by pre-provisioned compute capacity as in IaaS solutions.

While re-factoring a monolith application for better scalability and resource utilization, some components of the application can be reorganized as microservices and some as FaaS. Identifying different components of the application that suits to microservice architecture and for FaaS implementation is an unanswered question. To address this issue, we have given an approach that provides pragmatic guidance to system architects to reorganize their monolithic code base into microservices, FaaS and monolith. We applied our proposed technique on a case study "Teachers Feedback Web Application" and proved our approach. Our partial migration procedure uses web server access logs of one complete application execution cycle and then applied unsupervised learning algorithm on these logs to map components that best suits monolith-microservices-FaaS service patterns.

Future Work

In our future work, we will implement above identified services in microservices and serverless architecture to gauge empirically improvement in performance in terms of response time and cost reduction. We are also planning to perform static and dynamic code analysis to identify independent and autonomous services to strengthen the basis of our approach and assess more deeply the benefits of partial migration.

References

1. Iqbal, W., Erradi, A., Mahmood, A.: Dynamic workload patterns prediction for proactive auto-scaling of web applications. J. Netw. Comput. Appl. **124**, 94–107 (2018). https://doi.org/10.1016/j.jnca.2018.09.023
2. Zimmermann, O.: Microservices tenets agile approach to service development and deployment. Comput. Sci. Res. Dev. **32**(3-4), 301–310 (2017). https://doi.org/10.1007/s00450-016-0337-0
3. Fowler, M., Lewis, J.: Microservices a definition of this new architectural term, p. 22 (2014). http//martinfowler.com/articles/microservices.html
4. Mazlami, G., Cito, J., Leitner, P.: Extraction of microservices from monolithic software architectures. In: Proceedings of the 2017 IEEE 24th International Conference on Web Services, ICWS 2017, pp. 524–531 (2017). https://doi.org/10.1109/icws.2017.61
5. Villamizar, M., Garcés, O., Castro, H., Verano, M., Salamanca, L., Gil, S.: Evaluating the monolithic and the microservice architecture pattern to deploy web applications in the cloud (Evaluando el Patrón de Arquitectura Monolítica y de Micro Servicios Para Desplegar Aplicaciones en la Nube). In: 10th Computing Colombian Conference, pp. 583–590 (2015). https://doi.org/10.1109/columbiancc.2015.7333476
6. Garriga, M.: Towards a taxonomy of microservices architectures. In: Cerone, A., Roveri, M. (eds.) SEFM 2017. LNCS, vol. 10729, pp. 203–218. Springer, Cham (2018). https://doi.org/10.1007/978-3-319-74781-1_15
7. https://aws.amazon.com/lambda/
8. https://azure.microsoft.com/en-gb/services/functions/
9. https://cloud.google.com/functions/
10. https://developer.ibm.com/api/view/cloudfunctions-prod:cloud-functions:title-Cloud_Functions#Overview
11. Hellerstein, J.M., et al.: Serverless computing: one step forward, two steps back. In: The 9th Biennial Conference on Innovative Data Systems Research, CIDR 2019, vol. 3 (2019)
12. Spillner, J., Mateos, C., Monge, D.A.: FaaSter, better, cheaper: the prospect of serverless scientific computing and HPC. In: Mocskos, E., Nesmachnow, S. (eds.) CARLA 2017. CCIS, vol. 796, pp. 154–168. Springer, Cham (2018). https://doi.org/10.1007/978-3-319-73353-1_11

13. Abdullah, M., Iqbal, W., Erradi, A.: Unsupervised learning approach for web application auto-decomposition into microservices. J. Syst. Softw. **151**, 243–257 (2019). https://doi.org/10.1016/j.jss.2019.02.031
14. Fritzsch, J., Bogner, J., Zimmermann, A., Wagner, S.: From monolith to microservices: a classification of refactoring approaches. In: Bruel, J.-M., Mazzara, M., Meyer, B. (eds.) DEVOPS 2018. LNCS, vol. 11350, pp. 128–141. Springer, Cham (2019). https://doi.org/10.1007/978-3-030-06019-0_10
15. Ueda, T., Nakaike, T., Ohara, M.: Workload characterization for microservices. In: Proceedings of the 2016 IEEE International Symposium on Workload Characterization, IISWC 2016, pp. 85–94 (2016). https://doi.org/10.1109/iiswc.2016.7581269
16. Villamizar, M., et al.: Infrastructure cost comparison of running web applications in the cloud using AWS lambda and monolithic and microservice architectures. In: Proceedings of the 2016 16th IEEE/ACM International Symposium on Cluster, Cloud and Grid Computing, CCGrid 2016, May 2016, pp. 179–182 (2016). https://doi.org/10.1109/ccgrid.2016.37
17. Hasselbring, W., Steinacker, G.: Microservice architectures for scalability, agility and reliability in e-commerce. In: 2017 IEEE International Conference on Software Architecture Workshops, ICSAW 2017, pp. 243–246 (2017)
18. Costa, B., Pires, P.F., Delicato, F.C., Merson, P.: Evaluating REST architectures—approach, tooling and guidelines. J. Syst. Softw. **112**, 156–180 (2016)
19. Balalaie, A., Heydarnoori, A., Jamshidi, P.: Migrating to cloud-native architectures using microservices: an experience report. In: Celesti, A., Leitner, P. (eds.) ESOCC Workshops 2015. CCIS, vol. 567, pp. 201–215. Springer, Cham (2016). https://doi.org/10.1007/978-3-319-33313-7_15
20. Adzic, G., Chatley, R.: Serverless computing: economic and architectural impact, pp. 884–889 (2017). https://doi.org/10.1145/3106237.3117767
21. Manner, J.: Towards performance and cost simulation in function as a service. In: Proceedings of ZEUS 2019 (2019)
22. Mustafa, O., Marx Gómez, J.: Optimizing economics of microservices by planning for granularity level - Experience Report. In: 2017 Programming Technology for the Future Web, April 2017, p. 6 (2017)
23. Aragon, H., Braganza, S., Boza, E.F., Parrales, J., Abad, C.L.: Workload characterization of a software-as-a-service web application implemented with a microservices architecture. In: Web Conference 2019 - Companion World Wide Web Conference WWW 2019, pp. 746–750 (2019). https://doi.org/10.1145/3308560.3316466
24. Hussain, T., Asghar, S., Masood, N.: Web usage mining: a survey on preprocessing of web log file. In: 2010 International Conference on Information and Emerging Technologies, pp. 1–6 (2010)
25. Bholowalia, P., Kumar, A.: EBK-means: a clustering technique based on elbow method and k-means in WSN. Int. J. Comput. Appl. **105**(9), 17–24 (2014)
26. Forcier, J., Bissex, P., Chun, W.J.: Python Web Development with Django. Addison-Wesley Professional, Boston (2008)

Hand Motion Capturing and Simulation in Medical Rehabilitation Applications

Alexandr Kolsanov[1] , Sergey Chaplygin[1] , Sergey Rovnov[1] ,
and Anton Ivaschenko[2](✉)

[1] Samara State Medical University, Samara, Russia
avkolsanov@mail.ru
[2] Samara State Technical University, Samara, Russia
anton.ivashenko@gmail.com

Abstract. The paper is dedicated to a problem of hand motion capturing as a part of an intelligent solution for medical and social rehabilitation technology based on the implementation of virtual reality with tactile feedback. Based on related works overview it is proposed to use the system of resistive transducers to develop a mechanical construction for tracking the position of fingers. To capture and formalize the hand motor function a number of kinematic and dynamic parameters are introduced. The sensors provide complete description of the hand motor function in the form of independent coordinates of its movement. Based on this approach there is proposed an original tracking system, which gives a new opportunity to provide a complete description of hand mechanics. From the variety of solutions two prototypes were developed and studied: one with conductive cord and arm, next with flexible PCB prototype with the ability to host sensors. In addition to hand motion capturing solution some recommendations are given to improve its simulation in AR/VR environment. The results of research and development prove the possibility to implement the sensor glove for hand functions rehabilitation in medical applications with the required efficiency.

Keywords: Hand motion capturing · Medical rehabilitation · Intelligent systems application

1 Introduction

Medical rehabilitation is one of the perspective areas of trending information, communication and computing technologies application. Considering the perspective of using new technologies to improve the efficiency of medical treatment and social assistance engineers and doctors combine their efforts to introduce new solutions. One of the challenging problems in this area is lowering of permanent movement disability observed in most cases of stroke consequences. In particular, restoration of the upper limb requires long time and many efforts and in most cases does not fully react against the patient's affect.

Hand functioning rehabilitation is a labour intensive process. This is especially actual for full rehabilitation of fine motor skills, whichcommonly remains impossible

C. Badica et al. (Eds.): ICICCT 2020, CCIS 1170, pp. 125–134, 2020.
https://doi.org/10.1007/978-981-15-9671-1_10

and leads to severe restrictions in everyday functioning.To provide adequate and sustainable hand motion capture it is required to implement a modern stack of solutions including the Internet of Things, sensors, augmented and virtual reality (AR/VR) and machine learning. Combination of these technologies allows efficient hand motion fixation and simulation in real time.

This task was deeply studied under the project of development of medical and social rehabilitation technology based on the implementation of virtual reality with tactile feedback, carried by Innovations department at Samara State Medical University. Despite the variety of haptic feedback capturing available in the market currently, there was no good tool for cheap and accurate fixation of finger movements. To overcome this difficulty there was developed an original solution presented below.

2 State of the Art

Despite the fact that virtual reality has recently begun to be used for the rehabilitation of patients with neurological disorders, quite a lot of experience has been accumulated in this area. The most intensively virtual reality is currently used to restore postural stability in patients. As you know, the successful maintenance of body stability during standing, walking and any other movements requires the integration of information from the three main sensory systems: visual, proprioceptive and vestibular [1].

In patients with damage to the sensory and associative areas of the brain, the ability to exclude vision and correct postural stability, relying on internal (proprioceptive and vestibular) sensory signals, is usually impaired [2]. This may be due to both general sensory deficits and impaired brain ability to interpret and integrate the received sensory information. As a result, sensory conflict can cause patients to lose their balance and even trigger a fall.

It has been proven that placing a patient in a virtual space with conflicting sensory inputs is an effective way to improve the sensory adaptation necessary to maintain balance. So, in [3] a patient was trained with vestibular disorders so that he could maintain balance while standing on a moving stable platform. The displacement of the platform forward and backward was accompanied by a change in the position of the virtual space in the mediolateral directions. After several repetitions, the patient's ability to maintain a balance disturbed by incoming conflicting information improved.

It was proved that the use of virtual games developed by the VIVID IREX group helps to restore this type of deficiency in patients with post-stroke hemiparesis and damage to the spinal cord and brain [2]. Patients trained to maintain balance during manipulations with virtual objects, for example, beating virtual balls or catching virtual birds. Moreover, patients with gross motor impairment as a result of a spinal cord injury performed the task while sitting in a wheelchair. All participants in the therapy using virtual games significantly improved stability indicators. In addition, they noted increased motivation, interest and a desire to increase the number of procedures, which is important for the rehabilitation of such patients.

Typical hand functions that are impaired in patients with various brain diseases are the ability to reach an object, manipulate it, and coordinate the movements of two hands. The causes of such disorders can be various, but primarily include muscle weakness, changes in the coordination of movements in the joints and the sequence of inclusion of various muscle groups [4].

To prevent the formation of stable motor compensations that interfere with the final restoration of normal movement, M.K. Holden et al. [2] used virtual reality. During the execution of the movement of the hand, the patient was asked to follow the optimal trajectory, which was shown on the screen. Moreover, the patient had the opportunity to synchronize his movements with a moving final trajectory, and with the movement of a virtual hand on the screen. At the end of the course of therapy, significant improvements in the motor functions of the hand were noted in some patients.

Household functions were also trained using games not specifically designed for neurorehabilitation. For example, the computer game Wishy Washy (Sony's EyeToy), which offers participants to wash virtual windows, has improved not only everyday skills, but also the stability of the vertical posture in older people [4].

Therefore there is currently no suitable solution on the market that supports the up-to-datemethodology of restoration of the hand function. It should be capable of fingers motion capturing and simulation in order to support a set of training exercises regularly performed and repeated to guarantee fast and stable results. The most challenging problem is providing adequate feedback from the sensor glove which contains enough number of sensors to track each phalanx.

3 Technologies Overview

The problem of hand movement simulation requires application of various modern technologies including distributed sensors to capture the fingers, computing system to process the movements and generate virtual scenes and AR/VR devices for interactive user interface. Therefore development of modern position tracking systems is concerned with application of Virtual and Augmented Reality [5, 6] used to visualize the simulated objects and provide necessary feedback.

Location and monitoring services to track the position of hand and fingers in real time are usually implemented using built-in sensors and markers, which are placed on the body, gather the required information about its movements and then transmit it to processing unit with the corresponding chains of signals. The basic requirements for such systems require the sensibility and accuracy of the sensors that allow adequate determination of object position in space and time. In case of use of multiple sensors they should be coordinated and function in real time.

One of the possible ways of human body parts monitoring is based on implementation of mechanical tracking technologies [7, 8], which are based on goniometers. This type of sensors allows measuring the rotation angles of the joints to thus determine the final positions of the monitored objects. Under the context of the problem being solved they can be used to determine position of fingertips in space relative to the hand.

The disadvantages of such systems include the difficulty of alignment (a set of operations to align structures and structural elements along a certain direction) of goniometers with joints, especially those with many degrees of freedom. The centers of rotation of the goniometers do not coincide with the centers of rotation of the joints. Due to this kinematic mismatch, slippage or relative displacement takes place between the goniometer mount and the limb during displacement. Human joints are not ideal: the axis of rotation moves when the angle of rotation of the joints changes. To increase accuracy, appropriate calibrations must be used.

The algorithm of the mechanical tracking systems includes the following:

- the mechanical sensors mounted on the arm provide data on the degree of bending of each joint;
- data is interpreted as a rotation angle;
- data is transferred to the kinematic model of the hand;
- sets of sensors are used that track the movement of the finger mechanically – for example, load cells, servo sensors, etc.;
- a set of sensors is placed on the glove, in some cases in an additional rigid exoskeleton of the hand;
- sensor data are interpreted as rotation angles of the joints and transferred to the kinematic model of the arm.

Mechanical tracing provides comparatively high accuracy and is simpler in construction and production, which can be which can be attributed to the undoubted advantages. The limitations include lower reliability and possible user experience discomfort caused by the necessity to wear on the body sensors and wires. The most illustrative example of such kind of a system is an exoskeleton.

The quality of a mechanical tracking system can be sufficiently improved by using the resistive transducers, which allow improving the basic algorithm the following way:

- sensors on the phalanx give values that are interpreted as stretching;
- stretching according to calibration is translated into the bend angle of a particular phalanx;
- bend angles are mapped onto a kinematic model;
- resistive load cells - resistance changes depending on stretching;
- a set of sensors is placed on the glove.

The advantages of mechanical systems with resistive sensors include higher accuracy, simpler calibration and stability of the data collecting and transmitting processes, relative compactness and lightness of the hardware. The main disadvantage of mechanical systems with resistive sensors is concerned with possible discomfort when using the specifically designed gloves.

4   Hand Tracking and Visualization Features

Hand simulation in medical rehabilitation applications requires tracking of spatial position of fingers and visualization of their movements in 3D scene using VR goggles. Simulation results should look realistic for the user; therefore 3D model of the hand should be built using high-precision three-dimensional mappings in real time. The basic requirement for tracking is the high intuitiveness and naturalness of the interaction, close to that of real-world objects.

To solve medical rehabilitation problems the hand model should consider and reproduce the functional state of the hand. Using one sensor per finger is not enough since it is not able to track typical movements of fingers conducting simple hand actions. Consequently it was proposed to place a separate sensor on each phalanx and coordinate them as the parts of a solid model.

To identify each movement with satisfactory quality there can be introduced a number of indicators. For example, the relative distance of the finger tips comparative to the palm allows understanding possible options of hand positions; and further analysis of its changes makes it possible to improve the level of accuracy and determine the right position and movement.

For rehabilitation purpose it is important to identify the positions of fingers at their maximum flexion, the distance between the tips of the thumb and forefinger when they are closed, and the resulting grip force. The patient usually carries out a number of exercises trying to perform necessary movements to join the fingers in various orders. In clinical practice understanding of fingers relative positioning is used to study various pathological conditions.

Biomechanical parameters for research include:

- angles of abduction of the thumb and little finger;
- range of motion in the wrist and metacarpal joint of the thumb;
- range of motion in the metacarpophalangeal joints;
- bending angles of all fingers;
- the angle of flexion of the wrist joint.

Based on the analysis of these parameters there can be gathered a complete description of hand functioning necessary for diagnostics and rehabilitation procedure organization. Their evaluation requires determination of interdependent coordinates of finger phalanx. The proposed solution requests positioning the sensors located on each phalanx of each finger of the hand as shown in Fig. 1.

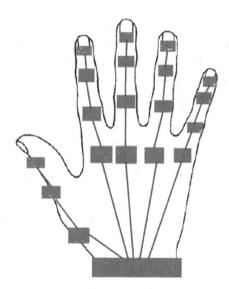

Fig. 1. The location of the sensors on the hand

The sensors should be incorporated into a solid system, capable to associate the measured positions of phalanx and balance the evaluations on order to reduce the error accumulation. The resulting kinematic model is build considering the estimated positions using mathematical laws, which allows providing adequate accuracy and targeting the high immersive effect.

In addition to this, analysis of the tracking history and context of rehabilitation procedure (like e.g. types of required actions that patient performs at certain time) helps improving the quality and accuracy of simulation.

The context of the user's activity can be analyzed at processing stage by and adaptation algorithm and used later to coordinate and correct the results of fingers' movements tracking. This approach allows considering the features of patients' perception as well. Some ideas of the user activity analysis are presented in [9, 10].

Current functional state and movement of the hand is visualized for the patient using virtual reality. Hand visualization itself is a complex task as soon as it requires animation of many fingers positions. Therefore when simulation the process of "grab" some object with the hand in most simulating solutions the hand is not represented itself, but often replaced by the object. Still some visualization of the fingers and their current position provides a greater presence effect and is more preferable for realistic immersion.

This is true in the case of using the Oculus Touch due to ergonomics. However in some projects using Vive with their current version of the controller, the effect sometimes appears that the user does not hold the object with a virtual hand, but the virtual hand itself is holding the object. This probably depends on the specific use cases and the specific angles of rotation of the object and hand.

Moreover, in the option with showing only the object in the hand, there is no sensation of the avatar disappearing or simply losing contact with it (after the disappearance of virtual hands), since at this moment the whole focus is transferred to the object itself.

Possible solutions include developing a "wax" model or representing the hand by a hand of a robot or a special glove. The "empty glove" effect is based on the effect of transparency. The glove takes the shape of the hand and justifies it visually, which solves the problem of the ephemerality of the virtual hand. At the same time it does not require complex visualization and animation with photorealistic effect.

When using VR goggles the real hand position should be synchronized with the simulated virtual hand. However movement of a virtual hand cannot be terminated by other virtual objects in 3D scene. If the hand crosses any geometry in scene it with go through it. Still in case the hand is visually translucent it does not cause any logical dissonance. In addition to this the events of intersection of the virtual hand with other objects in scene can be signalized by means of vibration.

Visualization of the shadow from the hands also helps in determining the position of the hands in space, and also creates a connection between the hands and the virtual environment. Since the user associates virtual hands with him this strengthens his connection with the virtual environment.

The described above implementation features provide the effect of realistic and immersive simulation suitable for hand rehabilitation applications.

5 Implementation Results

Solving the task of computer modeling, hands are represented as a mechanism from a system of bodies connected with each other with certain degrees of freedom of movement. The bones are simulated by separate bodies rotated relatively to each other in a corresponding association considering the spatial orientation of the entire arm. Therefore sensors should capture these positions with lowest possible deviations.

The developed prototypes are presented in Fig. 2.

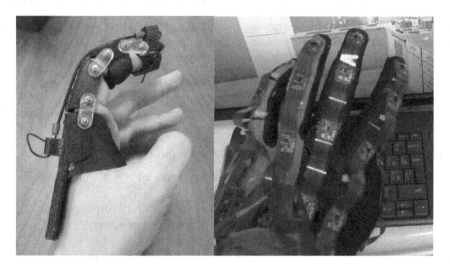

Fig. 2. Prototype with conductive cord and arm (at the left). and flexible PCB prototype with the ability to host IMU sensors (at the right)

To obtain data from the glove, a binary serial data protocol is used. Data is transmitted through a virtual serial port, implemented through the Bluetooth protocol stack.

The main algorithm of data transfer includes the following steps:

1. Activation of the Bluetooth protocol on a personal computer and gloves;
2. Pairing the Bluetooth stack of the personal computer and the Bluetooth glove stack while maintaining the identification of the glove instances (right, left);
3. Coordination of a virtual serial data channel;
4. Initialization of the working status of the serial data channel;
5. Obtaining configuration data for each glove;
6. Obtaining the functional status of electronic equipment gloves;
7. Initialization of the data transfer mode of the glove sensors data stream;
8. Receiving a glove sensors data stream.

Information exchange can be carried out only between the master and slave devices. Each device can be either a master or a slave, and the connection of devices between themselves forms a network called a piconet (personal network) with the following characteristics:

- in one piconet there is only one master device, all the rest are subordinates;
- the maximum number of devices of one piconet simultaneously participating in the transmission of information is not more than 8;
- the total number of devices connected to the master device is not limited;
- at each moment, data can only be exchanged between two devices in one direction.

Set of piconets is formed by overlapping individual piconets, where each device of one piconet can enter another piconet both as a subordinate and as a master.

Basic Bluetooth network states are implemented:

- idle – low power consumption, only the device's clock works;
- connection status – the device is connected to the piconet;
- parking status – the status of a slave device from which it is not required to participate in the piconet, but which should remain part of it.

Intermediate states for connecting new slaves to the piconet include:

- polling – determination by the device of the presence of others within its reach;
- polling search – waiting for a polling device;
- response to the survey – the device that received the survey responds to it;
- request – sent by one device to another to establish a connection;
- request search – the device is waiting for a request;
- response of the slave – the slave responds to the request of the master;
- response of the master – the master device responds to the subordinate after receiving from him a response to the request, neuroplasticity and virtual reality.

The essence of the mathematical model of the hand in the VR environment is to simulate the folding of the phalanges of the fingers by manipulating certain coefficients that characterize the angles between the phalanges (see Fig. 3).

The results of hand motion capturing and simulation are illustrated by Fig. 4.

The proposed solution allows achieving accuracy and adequacy of movements sufficient to satisfy the requirements of medical rehabilitation applications. From some device designed to read the movement of the hand, data is taken, which are converted into corners for the corresponding limbs. These angles are applied to the hand model, after which the simulated arm begins to move in the VR environment identically to the real arm with which the data is taken.

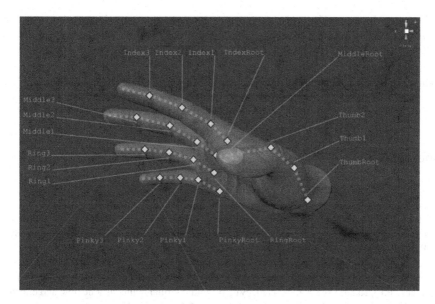

Fig. 3. Handmathematical model in VR

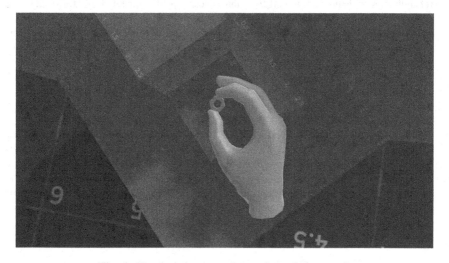

Fig. 4. Hand motion capturing and simulation result

6 Conclusion

Virtual reality solutions with haptic feedback are highly required in medical and social rehabilitation innovations. The sensor gloves that implement mechanical tracking of finger phalanx positions using the resistive transducers provide an increased quality of

hand motion fixation. The most perspective constructions include the one with conductive cord and arm, and the second with flexible PCB prototype with the ability to host
sensors. The proposed solution allows achieving the required accuracy and adequacy.

Acknowledgments. Research is supported by the Federal Target Program "Research and
development in priority directions for the development of the scientific and technological
complex of Russia for 2014-2020", №075-02-2018-1920, Project ID RFMEFI60418X0208.

References

1. Rand, D., Katz, N., Weiss, P.L.: Evaluation of virtual shopping in the VMall: comparison of
   post-stroke participants to healthy control groups. Disabil. Rehabil. **13**, 1–10 (2007)
2. Holden, M.K., Dyar, T.A., Dayan-Cimadoro, L.: Telerehabilitation using a virtual environment improves upper extremity function in patients with stroke. IEEE Trans. Neural Syst.
   Rehabil. Eng. **15**(1), 36–42 (2007)
3. Keshner, E., Kenyon, R., Langston, J.: Postural responses exhibit multisensory dependencies
   with discordant visual and support surface motion. J. Vestib. Res. **14**, 307–319 (2004)
4. Weiss, P.L., Rand, D., Katz, N., et al.: Video capture virtual reality as a flexible and effective
   rehabilitation tool. J. Neuroengineering Rehabil. **1**(1), 12 (2004)
5. Lambercy, O., Dovat, L., Gassert, R., Burdet, E., Teo, C.L., Milner, T.: A haptic knob for
   rehabilitation of hand function. IEEE Trans. Neural Syst. Rehabil. Eng. **15**(3), 356–366
   (2007)
6. Merians, A.S., Tunik, E., Adamovich, S.V.: Virtual reality to maximize function for hand
   and arm rehabilitation: exploration of neural mechanisms. Stud. Health Technol. Inform.
   145, 109–125 (2009)
7. Field, M., Stirling, D., Naghdy, F., Pan, Z.: Motion capture in robotics review. In: IEEE
   International Conference on Control and Automation (ICCA), pp. 1697–1702 (2009)
8. Shi, G., Wang, Y., Li, S.: Development of human motion capture system based on inertial
   sensors 2125. Sens. Transducers **173**, 90–97 (2014)
9. Ivaschenko, A., Kolsanov, A., Nazaryan, A.: Focused visualization in surgery training and
   navigation. In: Arai, K., Kapoor, S., Bhatia, R. (eds.) SAI 2018. AISC, vol. 858, pp. 537–
   547. Springer, Cham (2019). https://doi.org/10.1007/978-3-030-01174-1_40
10. Ivaschenko, A., Kolsanov, A., Chaplygin, S., Nazaryan, A.: Multi-agent approximation of
    user behavior for ar surgery assistant. In: Satapathy, S.C., Joshi, A. (eds.) Information and
    Communication Technology for Intelligent Systems. SIST, vol. 107, pp. 361–368. Springer,
    Singapore (2019). https://doi.org/10.1007/978-981-13-1747-7_34

Efficient Authentication Protocol for Heterogeneous Wireless Networks

Ashish Joshi[1]([✉])[iD] and Amar Kumar Mohapatra[2][iD]

[1] University School of Information Communication and Technology, GGSIPU, Delhi, India
ashishium@gmail.com
[2] Indira Gandhi Delhi Technical University for Women, Kashmere Gate, Delhi, India
mohapatra.amar@gmail.com

Abstract. It is evident from the past literature that in any authentication protocol there is a trade-off between efficiency and security. This paper aims to solve this problem in the domain of heterogeneous wireless networks, by proposing an efficient authentication protocol which operates in two modes namely full authentication and fast re-authentication. This paper proposes a protocol which mitigates the delay in authentication by reducing the number of message excahnges in full authentication procedure and reducing the number of authenticating parties in fast re-authentication procedure. This paper also used hash-chain technique to guarantee safety and freshness of the information. AVISPA (Autmated Validation of Internet Security Protocols and Applications) was used to formally analyse the security of the protocol. Some other existing authentication protocols were also analyzed and compared with our proposed protocol. Our analysis showed that the proposed authentication protocol is efficient while guaranteeing the security and improved performance of the heterogeneous wireless networks.

Keywords: Authentication protocol · Authentication delay · Hash chain · AVISPA

1 Introduction and Literature Review

With the rapid development and advancement of wireless technology, various wireless network types have emerged in order to cater various communication requirements. Some examples of various wireless networks are cellular mobile communication networks, satellite networks, GPRS (general Packet radio service) network, 3 G, VOLTE, wireless local area network (wireless local Area network, WLAN), wireless sensor Network, WSN) and Wireless Ad-hoc networks etc. The current age of computing is known as the information age where heterogeneous wireless networks with different modes, coverage, and bandwidth coexist connected to each other in order to provide backbone to the internet. Each of these heterogeneous wireless networks have their own advantages and

© Springer Nature Singapore Pte Ltd. 2020
C. Badica et al. (Eds.): ICICCT 2020, CCIS 1170, pp. 135–146, 2020.
https://doi.org/10.1007/978-981-15-9671-1_11

complement each other. Seamless integration of these networks have promoted the common development of various technologies. Therefore network applications today needs to keep in mind this integration of different networks [1]. Various researchers have contributed in solving the most crucial issue in heterogeneous integrated wireless networks, i.e the issue of network convergence [2]. With the goal of improving network convergence security, a series of innovations in authentication mechanisms for heterogeneous converged networks have been proposed [3,4]. 4G networks and Lawns are the most widely deployed universal commercial communication networks. The mutual authentication between the users of these two networks has found its place evidently in the research for wireless heterogeneous networks [5]. At present, most of the existing programs are in compliance with 4G and WLAN. 4G [6] related standards, EAP-AKA and EAP-SIM protocols are Presented under the standard. 4G hopes to pass the authentication and key exchange Protocol. They were proposed to protect the security of communication services under converged heterogeneous networks. But in fact, EAP-AKA and EAP-SIM in terms of functionality, efficiency and safety have various gaps which can be filled [7,8] When mobile users roam, neither of the above two protocols can reduce the information exchange between the visited region and the home location [9,10].

The number of information exchanges can cause high delays. Salgarelli et al. [11] Improved the high latency of the above protocol [12] and proposed the W-SKE protocol Negotiation. The main idea of the protocol is to reduce the number of message interactions. Resolving high authentication delays in EAP-AKA and EAP-SIM protocols question. But W-SKE [13] also has the following weaknesses:

1. In this protocol FA (foreign authentication server) cannot be trusted if the node is not trusted. W-SKE cannot prevent FA from making false accounts;
2. The user's anonymity is not considered;
3. The authentication delay is not optimized enough and there is no fast re-authentication process.

The protocol proposed in this paper is based on the protocol proposed by Salgarelli et al., we have proposed an efficient and safer authentication mechanism. The proposed protocol mitigates the weakness of W-SKE and a temporary session key is generated during the authentication process for FA to ensure that the node is available and trustable. At the same time, in order to solve the problem of latency usage of hash chain adds a fast re-authentication process. Afterwards we formally validated the protocol using dole-yao attacker based model over AVISPA tool. The analysis of the protocol proved that it improved the functionality and security of the overall architecture.

2   Proposed Authentication Protocol

The proposed authentication protocol consists of two phases: full authentication phase and fast re-authentication phase. Full certification phase involves MS (mobile Station), AS (access station), FA and HA (Home Authentication server). The secure channel between FA and proxy AA as well as proxy AA and HA is considered foolprof, therefore not covered under this protocol. As the customer roams to a new zone/area or at the current temporary primary session key is changed then full authentication process is performed. Upon completion of full authentication process, the MS and FA share a temporary primary session key. Afterwards they can perform n fast re-authentication during the validity of the temporary primary session key.

The design idea of the agreement is to reduce the authentication delay by reducing the number of message exchange in the full authentication process. The fast re-authentication process is implemented by using the hash chain method. This process only involve the FA, AS and MS thereby reducing the number of participating authentication entities. Even if we assume that the entities in the network are impersonating entities, our protocol can also effectively prevent FA from presenting false bills.

2.1   Full Certification Phase

Abbreviations used:

- YID is the user identity
- SID is the session identity
- TID is the temporary identity used when re-authenticating with FA
- ASID is the identity of the AS
- PRF (pre-defined Key derivation function) is a predefined key generation function
- K_{SMS} is the session key between MS and AS
- $K_{MS,FA}$ is the temporary session master key between the MS and the FA

The certification process in the full authentication phase is shown in Fig. 1. The detailed description of this phase is as follows:

Step 1 MS transmits the session identifier SID (SID is mutually agreed upon by MS and AS) and its unique identification UID to the AS, AS forwards the MS's request (containing UID and SID) to FA. FA issues a challenge $H^n(X_1) : FA$, selects a random number N_1 and calculates $X_1 = Date||N_1$ and a hash value $H^n(X_1)$. Date indicates the current system date, $H^n(X_1)$ Indicates that X_1 is hashed n times. FA also stores X_1 for the purpose of fast-reauthentication process which is performed later on. Date indicates the system date instead of the timestamps, timepstamp is used in the protocol to limit the billing records for the validity period. Only non-expired billing records are kept in the HA database. Therefore the database is not congested and does not require strict clock synchronization.

Step 2 The MS selects a random value N_2 after receiving the message from FA. It calculates $X_2 = Date||N_2$, $H^n(X_2)$ and $AUTH1$. Where $AUTH1 = MAC_{K_{MS,HA}} (H^n(X_1)||H^n(X_2)||UID||SID||ASID||Date)$. MS sends UID, SID, AUTH1 and $H^n(X_2)$ to the AS. AS forwards the response sent by MS to FA.

Step 3 FA uses (UID,SID) pair to find out whether the MS is roaming, and then the response of the MS together with the challenge of FA: The value $H_n(X_1)$ and Date is sent to the corresponding HA through a preset secure channel.

Step 4 HA uses UID to find User's credentials and shared key $K_{MS,HA}$. Then it uses this key and the value received from FA to calculate $AUTH' = MACK_{MS,HA} (H^n(X_1)||H^n(X_2)||UID||SID||ASID||Date)$ and matches value AUTH' to AUTH1 to see if they are equal. If the authentication fails, HA will Send a "reject" message to FA; if the authentication is successful then it calculates AUTH2 and K_{SMS} using session key $K_{MS,FA}$. $AUTH2 = MAC_{K_{MS,HA}}(H^n(X_2)||H^n(X_1) ||UID||SID||ASID||Date)$ and session key $K_{SMS} = PRF_{K_{MS,HA}}(AUTH2)$, $K_{MS,FA} = PRF_{K_{MS,HA}}(AUTH2||TID)$. Finally HA encapsulates AUTH2, TID , $K_{MS,FA}$ and K_{SMS} in AAA protocol format and sends it to FA. HA stores $(H^n(X_2), H^n(X_1), UID, SID, ASID, Date, AUTH1$ as credentials for the billing verification phase.

Step 5 FA processes the response information from HA. FA extracts and stores TID, $H^n(X_2)$ recieved from HA messages, $H^n(X_1)$, AUTH2 and $K_{MS,FA}$ during fast re-authentication and accounting use. At the same time, the FA pass contains TID, AUTH2 and $K_S MS$ The HA message is sent to the AS.

Step 6 The process by which the AS processes HA messages. AS uses K_{SMS} Encrypt TID, and send the encrypted TID and AUTH2 to the MS. The main purpose of TID encryption is to transmit on unreliable WLAN When given to MS, TID will not be intercepted by interested people.

Step 7 MS calculates $AUTH2' = MAC_{K_{MS,HA}}(H^n(X_2)||H^n(X_1)||UID||SID|| ASID|| Date)$. Is it compare with th received AUTH2. If both of them match, MS generates the session key K_{SMS} and $K_{MS,FA}, KSMS = PRF_{K_{MS,HA}}(AUTH2)$, $K_{MS,FA} = PRF_{K_{MS,HA}}(AUTH2||TID)$. K_{SMS} is the current session key between the MS and the AS for decrypt the TID. $K_{MS,FA}$ is the temporary fast re-authentication key between MS and FA.

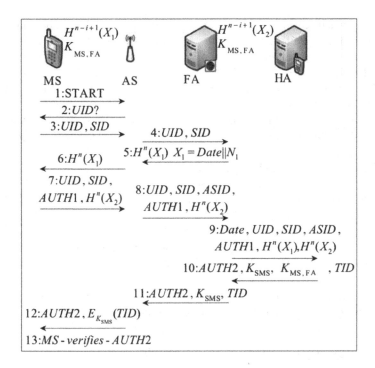

Fig. 1. The proposed full authentication phase

2.2 Fast Re-authentication Phase

When MS and FA perform a complete full authentication process, it outputs a temporary session master key between MS and FA known as $K_{MS,FA}$. During the validity period of $K_{MS,FA}$, as long as the MS is in the coverage area of FA, it can perform n times fast re-authentication with FA. The following mainly introduces the i-th fast re-authentication process of MS.

The fast re-authentication process is shown in Fig. 2, and the specific analysis is as follows:

Step 1 MS and AS pass the MS's session ID and identity authentication ID to AS through a challenge. MS sends its TID, session identity SID and $E_{K_{MS,FA}}(H^{n-i}(X_2))$ to AS, $E_{K_{MS,FA}}(H^{n-i}(X_2))$ table Illustrates the use of the key $E_{K_{MS,FA}}$ to encrypt $(H^{n-i}(X_2))$. AS transmits TID, SID, and $E_{K_{MS,FA}}(H^{n-i}(X_2))$ to FA.

Step 2 The process of FA processing fast re-authentication information: Using TD, FA can verify that MS is a roaming client which require fast Speed authentication. FA retrieves the primary session key from the database $K_{MS,FA}$ and hash value $(H^{n-i}(X_1))$. FA uses the key $K_{MS,FA}$ for decrypting $E_{K_{MS,FA}}(H^{n-i}(X_2))$, then verify whether $(H^{n-i}(X_2))$ is equal to $(H^{n-i+1}(X_2))$. The $(H^{n-i+1}(X_2))$ is the last time (i - 1 Times)

Re-authentication of the hash value stored in FA. If the authentication fails, re-authentication is rejected. If the certification is passed, FA authenticates the customer.

The client (MS) authenticates and updates the hash value $(H^{n-i}(X_2))$ for the use in the subsequent re-authentication. In addition, FA is its client (MS) selects a new new TID, calculate the new session key $K_{SMS} = PRF_{K_{MS,FA}}(H^{n-i}(X_2)||H^{n-i}(X_1))$. After that, FA sends a message. Success message to AS, the message includes newTID, $E_{K_{MS,FA}}(newTID)$, $E_{K_{MS,FA}}(H^{n-i}(X_1))$ and the new session key K_{SMS}.

Step 3 The process by which the AS processes the FA's response: If it is a failed response, then the AS will refuse to connect. If it is a successful response, AS Extract and retain newTID and K_{SMS} and sends $E_{K_{MS,FA}}(TID)$ and $E_{K_{MS,FA}}(H^{n-i}(X_1))$ to MS.

Step 4 The process by which the MS processes the FA's response: MS uses the master session key $K_{MS,FA}$ to decrypt the information and get the newTID and $(H^{n-i}(X_1))$. USING the last $(i - 1^{th})$ re-authentication the FA verify the legality of $H^{n-i+1}(X_1)$ and generate new session key $K_{SMS} = PRF_{K_{MS,FA}}(H^{n-i}(X_2)||H^{n-i}(X_1))$. In addition, The MS updates $(H^{n-i}(X_1))$ to be used for the next re-authentication.

3   Security and Functional Analysis

3.1   Security Analysis

Two-Way Authentication. The protocol proposed in this paper implements Two-way authentication between MS & HA and MS & FA Two-way authentication. HA and MS pass the pre-shared key $K_{MS,HA}$ and mutually authenticate with fresh message authentication code. During the full certification phase, AUTH1 and AUTH2 are considered as authentication tokens to prove the authenticity of MS and HA mutually. This authentication token It is derived from the key $K_{MS,HA}$. The encryption contains new challenge values such as $H^n(X_2)$ and $H^n(X_1)$ for each session . Although $H^n(X_1)$ is generated by FA, but HA can use the Date to verify it freshness. So whenever either MS or HA is forged, neither the authentication process of the message be completed nor the session key be generated.

After a secure channel is established between HA and FA, The authenticity of FA is verified by HA, therefore the connected MS can Verify FA with HA. During the authentication of the MS by FA, because K_{SMS} will not be passed back to the MS, the MS needs to generates the session key K_{SMS}, so that the legitimacy of MS can be confirmed. After completing a full authentication phase, $K_{MS,FA}$ becomes the master key for the temporary session between MS and FAs. In re-authentication phase, MS and FA use this key to decrypt the received information, the authenticity and freshness of information can be achieved through a one-way hash chain. Therefore, FA and MS can mutually authenticate.

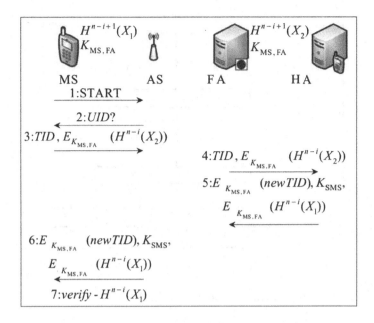

Fig. 2. The proposed fast re-authentication phase

Session Key Update Establishment. In the full authentication process, the session key between the MS and the AS, i.e $K_{SMS} = PRF_{K_{MS,FA}}(H^{n-i}(X_2))$ is generated between MS and FA. The Temporary session key $K_{MS,FA} = PRF_{K_{MS,HA}}(AUTH2\|TID)$ is calculated. The freshness of keys of AUTH2 and $K_{MS,HA}$ is guaranteed by the session key K_{SMS} and temporary session keys $K_{MS,FA}$. Session confidentiality between MS and AS during the fast re-authentication phase is guaranteed through $K_{SMS} = PRF_{K_{MS,FA}}(H^{n-i}(X_2)\|H^{n-i}(X_1))$. The randomness and uni directionality of the hash chain guarantee the security of the session key.

3.2 AVISPA: Automated Protocol Validation

Formal verification is one of the effective techniques for security analysis and protocol design assurance. One of the laws. Most of the formal verification techniques use formal language to model network security protocols. They generally employ analytical methods and assumptions to demonstrate the security of the designed protocol [14]. AVISPA is a type of validation automation tool which is used to verify various types of security-related network protocols [15]. The AVISPA tool set uses High level protocol specification language(HLPSL) to describe the implementation of the entire protocol. HLPSL is a rich, modular, role-based formal language. The process of AVISPA authentication protocol is shown in Fig. 3.

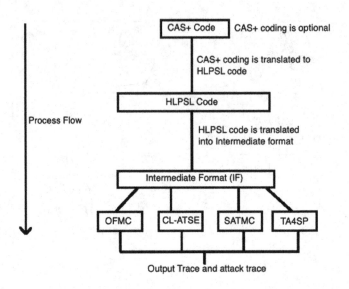

Fig. 3. Analysis process of the AVISPA tool

AVISPA validation follows the following steps:

1. The protocol designer designs the security protocol by using the AVISPA editor entering Variables such as the environment, participant role, verification target, attacker ability, etc. They also specify the expected security attributes of the protocol for role-based attack modeling.
2. The designer either uses CAS+ language to model the protocol or HLPSL. CAS+ language is further translated into HLPSL code. The resulting verification program is saved into a file with the suffix ".hlpsl" and compiled;
3. The AVISPA back ends requires IF(intermediate Format) code as input. These back ends are OFMC(on-the-fly model checker), SATMC(SAT based model checker), CL-ATSE(constrained logic based attack searcher) and TA4SP(Tree automata based analysis). The tool imports the hlpsl file and convert it to the IF file using the HLPSL2IF translator.
4. The imported IF file is fed to the AVISPA back ends model(s) along with the model specification configurations. The model(s) analyzes the IF file and obtains the final ".atk" file, attack trace, intruder simulation and protocol simulation.
5. The resulting output is analyzed to verify whether the security objectives of the protocol are met [16].

We ran the automated validation on our protocol's HLPSL script and got the compilation results as shown in Fig. 4 and Fig. 5. The verification results of OFMC and CL-ATSE indicated that the proposed authentication protocol satisfies the given set of security goals, It can effectively prevent attacks such as replay attack and counterfeiting attack.

Fig. 4. Output of OFMC   **Fig. 5.** Output of ATSE

3.3 Effectiveness Analysis

In order to improve the performance of Heterogeneous networks, reducing the round-trip time(RTT) between the FA and the HA is Very necessary. Table 1 shows the RTT of the full authentication phase of various schemes. It also provides the availability of fast re-authentication mode in the protocol, if present it provides the round-trip time of the fast re-authentication phase.

Table 1. Comparison between RTT of various protocols

Protocol	Round Trip Time	
	Full Authentication	Fast Re-authentication
Our Protocol	1	0
Protocol in [2]	1	Not applicable
Protocol in [1]	3	2
Protocol in [11]	2+	2

As it can be seen from Table 1, our proposed scheme has the lowest RTT during the full authentication phase. The required RTT value is minimal. Due to the fact that during the fast re-certification in the protocol it is not necessary for HA to participate, RTT during fast re-authentication is 0. In EAP-SKE during the full authentication value of RTT is also the smallest, but EAP-SKE does not support fast re-authentication and does not prevent fake bills generation by FA. EAP-AKA protocol requires at least two RTT 's. In fact, in the AKA protocol, when the MS and HA synchronization counter reaches its upper limit, it may take more than 5 round trip times to resynchronize. pre-shared key based EAP-SIM requires 3 RTTs.

In order to evaluate the efficiency of the protocol in more detail and specifically according to the identity authentication delay, $T_{FA,HA}$ represents the authentication delay between HA and FA, $T_{FA,AS}$ indicates between authentication delay between FA and AS, $T_{MS,AS}$ indicates the authentication delay between the MS and the AS. The authentication delay for the W-SKE protocol is $2T_{FA,HA} + 4T_{FA,AS} + 6T_{MS,AS}$, The delay of the full authentication protocol is in this paper is $2T_{FA,HA} + 4T_{FA,AS} + 6T_{MS,AS}$ but the delay of the fast re-authentication scheme is $2T_{FA,AS} + 4T_{MS,AS}$, EAP-AKA authentication delay is $4T_{FA,HA} + 4T_{FA,AS} + 6T_{MS,AS}$. Assuming that $T_{FA,HA} = 100$ ms, $T_{FA,AS} = 30$ ms, $T_{MS,AS} = 5$ ms, the maximum allowable fast re-authentication per full authentication phase is 30, On an average maximum number of fast re-authentications allowed is 20, and Fig. 6 shows the authentication delay in different protocols. It is evident from the results that our scheme significantly improves authentication delay.

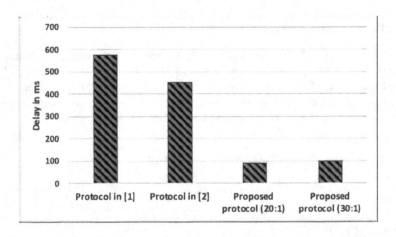

Fig. 6. Average authentication delay for different protocols

If during three repetitions our experiment $T_{FA,HA}$ is set to 100 ms, 150 ms, 250 ms, respectively, We get the output which can be plotted as graph shown in Fig. 7. As it can be seen from Fig. 7, our protocol significantly improves the authentication delay over other compared authentication protocols. When $T_{FA,HA}$ increases, we can see that our proposed exhibits stable authentication delay with little change. Therefore larger the value of $T_{FA,HA}$, the more efficient our protocol becomes.

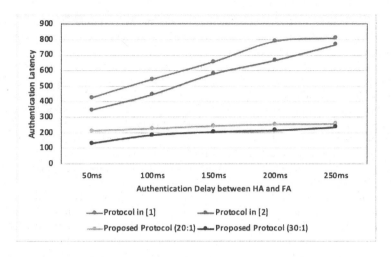

Fig. 7. Effect of Varying HA & FA delay on authentication latency

4   Conclusion and Future Work

With the development of heterogeneous converged network technologies, The need for effective and efficient authentication agreements is increasing. This paper proposed an efficient authentication protocol for converged heterogeneous wireless networks. The proposed authentication protocol reduces authentication delay and increases efficiency by reducing the number of message exchanged by introducing a fast re-authentication process. The number of authenticating entities greatly increases the authentication delay but our protocol proved to work with little delay and ensures the authentication smoothly. Simultaneous use of hash chain method, session key distribution management technology can effectively prevent replay attacks, camouflage attacks, and ensure security of the whole process. We believe that our protocol will get its place in contemporary research due to its unique advantages and wide range of application support.

References

1. Yao, Z., Chuang, L., Hao, Y.: Security authentication of 3g-wlan interworking. In: 20th International Conference on Advanced Information Networking and Applications-Volume 1 (AINA 2006), vol. 2, p. 5, IEEE (2006)
2. Guomin, Y., Qiong, H., Duncan, S.W., Xiaotie, D.: Universal authentication protocols for anonymous wireless communications. IEEE Trans. Wirel. Commun. **9**(1), 168–174 (2010)
3. Lei, L., Wenfang, Z., Yu, W., Xiaomin, W.: A pairing-free identity-based handover ake protocol with anonymity in the heterogeneous wireless networks. Int. J. Commun. Syst **32**(12), e4000 (2019)

4. Santos-González, I., Rivero-García, A., Burmester, M., Munilla, J., Caballero-Gil, P.: Secure lightweight password authenticated key exchange for heterogeneous wireless sensor networks. Inf. Syst. **88**, 101423 (2020)
5. Wei-Chen, W., Liaw, H.-T.: An authentication, authorization, and accounting mechanism for 3g/wlan networks. Secur. Commun. Netw. **9**(6), 468–480 (2016)
6. Ruhul, A., Hafizul Islam, S.K., Neeraj, K., Kim-Kwang, R.C.: An untraceable and anonymous password authentication protocol for heterogeneous wireless sensor networks. J. Netw. Comput. Appl. **104**, 133–144 (2018)
7. Ntantogian, C., Xenakis, C.: One-pass eap-aka authentication in 3g-wlan integrated networks. Wirel. Personal Commun. **48**(4), 569–584 (2009)
8. Na, L., Pubing, S.: Amendment and analysis of eap-aka protocol. Comput. Secur. **10**(6), 30–32 (2010)
9. Mohammad Sabzinejad, F., Muhamed, T., Saru, K., Marko, H.: An efficient user authentication and key agreement scheme for heterogeneous wireless sensor network tailored for the internet of things environment. Ad Hoc Netw. **36**, 152–176 (2016)
10. Li, X., Xiang, L., Ma, J., Zhu, Z., Li, X., Park, Y.H.: Authentications and key management in 3g-wlan interworking. Mob. Netw. Appl. **16**(3), 394–407 (2011)
11. Salgarelli, L., Buddhikot, M., Garay, J., Patel, S., Miller, S.: Efficient authentication and key distribution in wireless ip networks. IEEE Wirel. Commun. **10**(6), 52–61 (2003)
12. Anastasios, N.B., Nicolas, S.: Lte/sae security issues on 4g wireless networks. IEEE Secur. Priv. **11**(2), 55–62 (2012)
13. Chang, C.-C., Hsueh, W.-Y., Cheng, T.-F.: A dynamic user authentication and key agreement scheme for heterogeneous wireless sensor networks. Wirel. Personal Commun. **89**(2), 447–465 (2016)
14. Joshi, A., Mohapatra, A.K.: Authentication protocols for wireless body area network with key management approach. J. Discrete Math. Sci. Crypt. **22**(2), 219–240 (2019)
15. Ashish, J., Mohapatra, A.K.: Security analysis of wireless authentication protocols. Int. J. Sensors Wirel. Commun. Control **9**(2), 247–252 (2018)

A Novel Transformation Based Security Scheme for Multi-instance Fingerprint Biometric System

Deepika Sharma$^{(\boxtimes)}$ and Arvind Selwal

Department of Computer Science and Information Technology Central University of Jammu, Samba 181143, J&K, India
sharmadeepika749@gmail.com

Abstract. The multi-biometric systems (MBS) are being rapidly deployed to address the security issues of uni-biometric systems. However, the security of the MBS still remains an open issue particularly as there are multiple vulnerable points in these systems. In our work, a new region code based hashing scheme (RCHTSS) for template protection in multi-instance biometric system is presented. The RCHTSS uses dual instances of fingerprint biometric modality i.e. the images of index finger from right and left hand. In the case of enrollment step, the fingerprint images acquired from the sensing devices are used to extract minutia local features using a biometric feature extractor (FE) module. The RCHTSS makes use of local region codes to convert real valued feature vector (FV) of the fingerprint image for protection. The RCHTSS utilize weighted matching score level fusion during authentication with higher recognition performance at weight of λ = 0.5. The RCHTSS provides excellent results with comparatively lower false acceptance rate (FAR) as 0.2% whereas false rejection rate (FRR) is 0.05%.

Keywords: Biometric-based systems · Feature fusion · Biometric template security · Multi-instance biometric systems · Bio-hashing

1 Introduction

The digitisation of various business processes in wide range of information technology applications has necessitated the security and integrity of the key information. A reliable and accurate human identity system is required in order to fight the rapid expansion in individuality theft as well as to meet the augmented security needs in a wide range of application areas. The authentication based on PINs, tokens, ID cards, passwords etc. are vulnerable to loss, damage or theft. In order to overcome these problems, the human recognition using biometric based systems is increasingly being deployed in large number of real life applications [Roberts 2007]. With the explosion of biometric based recognition systems, an attacker's benefit in creating a system compromise is also raising. Therefore, the need is to ensure system from attackers and maintaining the integrity of information. A biometric based system suffers from many limitations mainly because of the fact that not all biometric traits satisfy all the characteristics. One of the problems is due to presence of various types of noises during

© Springer Nature Singapore Pte Ltd. 2020
C. Badica et al. (Eds.): ICICCT 2020, CCIS 1170, pp. 147–159, 2020.
https://doi.org/10.1007/978-981-15-9671-1_12

collection biometrical traits from the human body. The performance of the system considerably decreases due poor quality of the raw biometrical information. One more problem is related to presence of small inter-class and large intra-class variation in the biological information of users. For instance, in the case of a face biometrics there are lot of variations present in the trait of a user due to pose change. In the case of biometric, identification accuracy has an upper bound and it creates another challenge. The fingerprint biometrics has an upper limit of up to 10000 users and after that there is possibility that two users may have identical biological traits. Similarly, in the case of hand geometry identification accuracy has an upper bound between 100 to 200 users. The users of biometric based systems are required to be educated, so that their trust may be enhanced. The cost for deployment of these biometric based systems is another factor, which limits its usage in many applications. The vulnerability of biometric systems to variety of attacks is yet another challenge for the researchers. The biometric systems have been spoofed using different ways right from sensor module to attacks on the system database. The biometric systems also create social issues of user's privacy protection. The confidential and personal information of a user is captured during enrollment, which may be further misused. The trust and confidence of the prospective users of a biometric system may be improved, if all the challenges are properly addressed. An attack on template database may result in complete failure of the system and hence its reliability is also another challenge. Furthermore, issue is related to coverage of large user's population for successful deployment of biometric systems [Jain et al. 2008]. For example, AADHAR unique identification in India is multi-modal biometric system, which is capable of covering more than 125 billion population of the country. The organization of remaining of the article is as follows. The Sect. 2 presents a general idea about various biometric template protection schemes. The Sect. 3 presents the proposed novel region code based hashing for template protection scheme. The evaluation result of our proposed RCHTSS scheme in terms of various metrics is provided in the Sect. 4. Finally, Sect. 5 focuses on the main contributions of the proposed technique with conclusions.

2   Background

A feature template is a compact version of the raw biometric modality which contains salient distinctive feature which are crucial for verifying the enrolled user. The disclosure of biometric templates of enrolled users to intruders may breach the security of biometric systems by enabling the representation of the spoofed templates and replay attacks with sensors. Unlike passwords, it is impossible to reject the exposed template and again enrolling the user based on the same trait. Furthermore, there is a possibility of cross-matching the templates stored in different databases and detecting whether the person enrolled across different applications is same or not. In this way the privacy of individuals enrolled in biometric systems is compromised [Jain et al. 2002; Ramu and Arivoli 2012]. The biometrics template security schemes may be categorized into two types such as biometric cryptosystems and transformation based schemes [Jain et al. 2008; Yang and Lei 2014]. The templates generated from transformation based schemes are easily revocable and biometric crypto-systems mainly rely on the error correcting coding theory. The both types of schemes have their own merits and demerits, therefore in case of most of the MBS, a hybrid or mixed schemes are used. The Crypto-system based template security schemes are further classified as fuzzy commitment and fuzzy vault oriented schemes. The transformation based schemes are categorized either as invertible or non-invertible template security schemes (cancellable biometric). A template transformation based schemes transforms the template based on the factors derived from external sources such as keys or passwords. In case of authentication same function is applied to the query template matched with the stored template in transformed domain. The non-invertible transforms were first suggested for face, with succeeding work focusing on fingerprints. The Non-inevitability alone does not provide significant protection. Since fingerprint systems are tolerant of moderate error levels even if, ambiguities can never be resolved, the protection may still not be sufficient. A cancelable biometrics technique involves intentional distortion of biometric traits during enrollment [Roberts 2007; Reddy et al. 2008]. The distortion function is repeatable so that it may be again applied during testing the legitimate user during verification. Further, distortion function is also non-invertible and revocable. Therefore, if template stored in database is compromised, then system administrator may cancel the stored template data and fresh distortion function may be applied on biometric trait to get new template after enrollment [Robert 2007; Prakash et al. 2013; Kindt 2007]. Popular approach of cancellable biometrics involves salting of biometric features with a secret key, non-invertible functions applied to angular tessellation of face or fingerprints biometrics [N. Ratha et al. 2001] and quantized random projections computation from feature vectors [A. Teoh et al. 2006]. A Bio-hashing approach works by converting a given template using large number of random codes, into binary sequences, which are called as bio-hashes [Robert 2007; Prakash et al. 2013]. The random codes are stored in the tokens, which are used during verification. The Bio-hashing involves two important steps namely; randomization and quantization. In [Teoh et al. 2006] used bio hashing for fingerprint biometric system. Here, features were extracted from fingerprint using Fourier Mellin transform framework and integrated wavelet. [Ao and Li 2009] used bio-hashing technique for template protection in infrared facial biometrics. In this case bio-hashes were generated by comparing features with randomly generated thresholds. In [Teoh et al. 2007], proposed a security scheme, where complex numbers were used to generate bio hashes. In this case random vectors and feature vectors are imaginary and real parts respectively. The phase of complex numbers are averaged which are called as bio-phasor and further discretized to generate a bio-hash. One of the limitations, of bio-hashing is that, if key is known to the imposter then matching performance degrades mainly due to quantization of features and reduction of dimensions. Further, drawback of bio-hashing is that it is easy to invert the bio-hashes if key is known to adversary. In this way original template may be recovered from the stored secured template. In a secure sketch approach, a sketch or helper data SS is derived from the given biometric trait B and stored in to the database. A function takes decision after testing whether the query template X is consistent with the sketch SS. The Secure sketches are constructed in such a ways that it draws little information from biometric trait. The fuzzy vault scheme is a key-binding biometric crypto-system that hides a secret K within a huge amount of chaff data. In brief it may be explained as, Ram places a secret 'K' in fuzzy vault and it is locked by using elements from set 'X' of some public universe U. To unlock this vault, and retrieve K, Laxman must represent a set Y, that to a large extent overlaps with X. The fuzzy vaults are invariant to order; meaning X and Y may be arranged in any order. In order to secure K, it may be denoted as polynomial p, specifically encoded with coefficients. A set 'S' of points is generated from p(A) as well as A. Additionally with these points, chaff points Z are created randomly and given to S. [Juels and Wattenberg 1999] introduced a fuzzy commitment technique. Fuzzy commitment techniques involve in the binding secret information, say S, to template T during the user enrolment, which may be recovered during testing of the legitimate user. There are many methods to bind the secrete message and few popular techniques are quantization index modulation (QIM) and ECC. [Nandakumar and Jain 2008] designed a scheme for protecting multi biometric templates in a MBS. It was achieved by generating a single multi-biometric template using feature level fusion and securing the muti-biometric template using the fuzzy vault construct. They applied an existing fingerprint fuzzy vault implementation to secure fingerprint minutiae and proposed a new vault implementation for securing iris codes. A salting transformation based on a transformation key was used to indirectly convert the fixed-length binary vector representation of iris code into an unordered set representation that can be secured using the fuzzy vault. The GAR of 98.2% at a FAR of ≈0.01% is achieved for fingerprint and iris modality in a proposed multi-biometric vault, while the corresponding GAR values for fingerprint and iris individually are78.8% and 88% respectively. [A. Jagadeesan et al. 2010] have generated a secure cryptographic key by using multiple biometrics modalities of an individual providing better security. An efficient technique for creating a secure cryptographic key which is based on MBS (Iris and fingerprint) has been presented. The proposed scheme comprises of three modules namely; Feature extraction, Multi-modal biometric template generation and Cryptographic key generation. At first, the texture properties and minutiae points were extracted from the iris and fingerprint biometrical traits respectively. Afterwards, the extracted features were fused together by using feature level fusion for obtaining the MBS feature template. In the last, a secure cryptographic key with a size 256-bit was generated from the fused MBS biometric template. The experiments were conducted by using the fingerprint images obtained from openly available secondary resources and the iris images were obtained from CASIA Iris Database. The results show that the efficiency of the proposed technique to produce the strong cryptographic keys for achieving the template security. [Ning Wang et al. 2015] have proposed a new MBS template security method which is based on chaotic system and fuzzy commitment. They use an approach of security analysis for a uni-biometric systems leakage. Initially, the thermal images of face were acquired, in order to conquer the counterfeit. Thereafter, the fuzzy commitment code is obtained from the help of an Error Correcting Code (ECC) and by fusing the binarized FVs. Furthermore, the dual iris FVs were encrypted through the chaotic system and then the score level fusion is applied, which is based on Aczél-AlsinaTriangular-norm (AAT-norm) implementation to get the ultimate authentication. In the results, the entropy of both MMBS and UBS information leakage is computed for analysing the security of the proposed scheme. The experiments were conducted on a synthetic MBS database, which combines the challenging CASIA-Iris-Thousand and the NVIE face database. The EER was improved from 0.03 to 0.1163%, whereas the MBS template security is improved from 80.53 to 167.80 bits on the basis of BCH ECC (1,023, 123, 170). [Y.J. Chin et al. 2014] presented a new technique for fusing multiple biometrical traits at feature level to get a combined template and a hybrid template security method was used to secure the fused templates. The proposed method used a FV transformation approach known as "Random Tiling" (RT) and an "equal-probable 2 N discretization" technique. The RT method enabled the revocability of template where as the "equal-probable 2 N discretization" transform the feature elements to binary values as per the area under the genuine interval curve, to provide better security to the template [13]. [Md. Marif Monwar et al. 2009] used a fusion scheme that fuses information presented by the system at rank level. The scheme use PCA, fisher's linear document network matcher (face, ear, signature) and uses a rank level novel fusion for consolidation of matcher results. This method uses highest rank, Borda's count and regression approaches. The proposed method used Eigen face projection for face, as well as fisher face projections. For the ear, it uses Eigen ear projections and for the signature it uses Eigen signature and produces representative codes which are stored in the database. The similar approach is used during the identification phase and matching is done to find the match scores and then rank level fusion applied. The proposed approach was able to get an equal error rate (EER) of 1.12% compared to other similar approaches, which is comparatively lower. [Nagar et al. 2010] have improved the recognition performance as well as the security of a fingerprint based biometric cryptosystem, called fingerprint fuzzy vault. The authors incorporated minutiae descriptors, which capture ridge orientation and frequency information in a minutia's neighbourhood, in the vault construction using the fuzzy commitment approach. The experimental results demonstrates that, with the use of minutiae descriptors, the fingerprint matching performance enhanced from an FAR of 0.7% to 0.01% at a GAR of 95% with some improvement in security as well. [Bin Ma et al. 2014] proposed a framework for enhancing biometric security based on two phase authentication. In this case, the face feature of the user is hidden into the fingerprint image of the same person. Here, wavelet quantisation based watermark is used for embedding the feature of face in fingerprint. The first phase of the system verifies the data credibility. In the second phase, the face watermark was used as additional information for identity by using the subsequent biometric authentication. The proposed scheme starts working at better FAR and provides good performance with additional accurate information of fingerprint. [Chen et al. 2014] proposed an efficient multi-biometric crypto-system integrated with fuzzy extractor. It improves the performance of the MBS in comparison with the uni-biometric cryptosystem. [Karthi and Ezhilarasan 2018] presented a template security scheme for MBS by fusing three biometric modalities such as fingerprint, face and iris. The authors designed a hybrid scheme for securing the templates. The hybrid technique improved the privacy and security of the system. The proposed technique takes the advantages of both biometric cryptosystem and cancelability. The experiments with two databases exhibit that the technique performs better as compared to other existing template security schemes (Table 1).

Table 1. A summary of state-of-the-art template protection techniques

Technique	Biometric trait	FAR/FRR	Authors
Password Hardening	Voice	>2/2	Monrose et al. (2001)
Quantization	Online Signature	1.2/28.0	Feng Wah (2002)
Quantization	Online Signature	0.0/7.05	Vielhauer (2002)
Fuzzy Vault	Fingerprint	0.0/20-30	Clancy et al. (2003)
Bio Hashing	Face	0.0/0.0	Teoh et al. (2004)
Fuzzy Commitment	Iris	0.0/0.42	Hao et al. (2006)
Bio-hashing	Face	0.0002 (EER)	Goh et al. (2003)
Fuzzy Commitment	Iris	0.0/5.62	Bringer et al. (2007)
Bio-Convolving	Signature/Iris	10.81 EER	Maiorana et al. (2010)
Transformation and Quantization	Fingerprint	15% EER	Jin et al. (2012)
Cryptosystem of Fuzzy vault	Fingerprint	0.7-0.01%	C. Moujahd (2014)

3 The Proposed Technique

The outline for proposed technique is depicted by the Fig. 1, here the fingerprint images of a user are captured by a sensing device during enrollment phase. The features are extracted from the acquired images by using feature extraction process. Suppose that the feature vectors of ith user are denoted by X_1^i and X_2^i. Afterward, the Region Code Hashing (RCH) is imposed on FVs and the converted vectors are denoted by X^1_{RHC} and X^2_{RHC}. The fusion at score level is used to combine both the FVs in the matching phase.

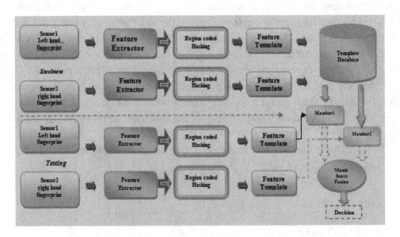

Fig. 1. The framework for proposed RCHTSS template security scheme.

The RCH technique works by dividing the region of interest of the acquired fingerprint images into 8-regions by using an area of 45° for each segment as shown in the Fig. 2.

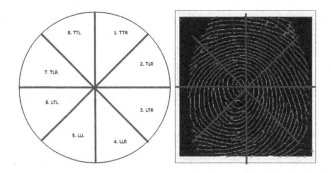

Fig. 2. The segmented regions and the region codes (RC)

In the next phase, a binary code of 3-bits is assigned to each region on the basis of its geometrical shape. The codes assigned to each region are based on the criteria with three positions as shown in the Table 2.

Table 2. The regions with their location in ROI

Region no.	Region location (Top = T, Right = R, Left = L, Low = L')	Binary code of respective location
1.	T, T, R	Right: 1
2.	T, L', R	Left: 0
3.	L', T, R	Low: 0
4.	L', L', R	Top: 1
5.	L', L', L	
6.	L', T, L	
7.	T, L', L	
8.	T, T, 1	

Let us assume that '$b_2b_1b_0$' denotes the segment binary code of three bits. Here the bit 'b_0' denotes left or right portion of the total region w.r.t y-axis. Hence, b_0 denotes the minutia point's located on negative or positive x-axis. The b_1 bit provide information of a segment in a given quadrant. It is assumed that a given segment is present either on lower or upper side. If the given segment lies on upper side then the value '1' is assigned to b_1 or '0' otherwise. The b_2 bit indicate the position of segment across the negative or positive y-axis where a value of '1' or '0' is assigned respectively. The list of regions locations and their respective binary codes are shown in the Fig. 3.

Region No.	Region location/position	Region Code
1	TTR	111
2.	TLR	101
3.	LTR	011
4.	LLR	001
5.	LLL	000
6.	LTL	010
7.	TLL	100
8.	TTL	110

Fig. 3. The Regions with their binary code values

Algorithm1 : RCH Template Security Scheme
Input: The feature vectors X_1^i and X_2^i extracted from feature extractor for user-i, X_c^i.
Output: Encoded template of user-i, X_{RHC}
1.   Start
2.   Let n=| X_c^i |, be the total number of minutia points in a feature vector.
3.   For j=1 to n, perform step 2 to 5
4.   Read jth minutia point from template say $F_i(x,y,\Phi)$, check Φ, perform step 3.
5.   Compute encoded feature $F_i'(x',y',\Phi')$, with case
6.   **Case1 : 0 < Φ ≤ 45**
7.   x'=h(x, TLR)= x+1, x-1, x +1
8.   y'=h(y, TLR)= y+1, y-1, y+1
9. $\Phi'=\tan^{-1}(\frac{x}{y})-\tan^{-1}(\frac{x'}{y'})$
10. **Case2 : 46 < Φ ≤ 90**
11.   x'=h(x, TTR)= x+1, x+1, x+1
12.   y'=h(y, TTR)= y+1, y+1, y+1
13. $\Phi'=\tan^{-1}(\frac{x}{y})-\tan^{-1}(\frac{x'}{y'})$
14. **Case3 : 91 < Φ ≤ 135**
15.   x'=h(x, TTL)= x+1, x+1, x-1
16.   y'=h(y, TTL)= y+1, y-+1, y-1
17. $\Phi'=\tan^{-1}(\frac{x}{y})-\tan^{-1}(\frac{x'}{y'})$
18. **Case4 : 136 < Φ ≤ 180**
19.   x'=h(x, TLL)= x+1, x-1, x-1
20.   y'=h(y, TLL)= y+1, y-1, y-1
21. $\Phi'=\tan^{-1}(\frac{x}{y})-\tan^{-1}(\frac{x'}{y'})$
22. **Case5 : 181 < Φ ≤ 225**
23.   x'=h(x, LTL)= x-1, x+1, x-1
24.   y'=h(y, LTL)= y-1, y+1, y-1
25. $\Phi'=\tan^{-1}(\frac{x}{y})-\tan^{-1}(\frac{x'}{y'})$.
26. **Case6 : 226 < Φ ≤ 270**
27.   x'=h(x, LLL)= x-1, x-1, x-1
28.   y'=h(y, LLL)= y-1, y-1, y-1
29. $\Phi'=\tan^{-1}(\frac{x}{y})-\tan^{-1}(\frac{x'}{y'})$
30. **Case7 : 271 < Φ ≤ 315**
31.   x'=h(x, LLR)= x-1, x-1, x+1
32.   y'=h(y, LLR)= y-1, y-1, y+1
33. $\Phi'=\tan^{-1}(\frac{x}{y})-\tan^{-1}(\frac{x'}{y'})$
34. **Case8 : 316 < Φ ≤ 360**
35.   x'=h(x, LTR)= x+1, x-1, x+1
36.   y'=h(y, LTR)= y-1, y+1, y+1
37. $\Phi'=\tan^{-1}(\frac{x}{y})-\tan^{-1}(\frac{x'}{y'})$
38. $F_i'(x',y',\Phi')$ ← X_{RHC} // Store the transformed minutia
39. Stop

Fig. 4. The matching algorithm

The algorithm 1 describes the working of the proposed Region coded Hashing based template protection scheme (RCHTSS) for converting the given minutia points of a FV to corresponding secured template.

Region Coded Hashing Based Template Security Scheme (RCHTSS)
The RCHTSS algorithm as given in the Fig. 4, works on the basis of distorting the minutia points in the original FP modality to transform the given template to secured feature template. Firstly, RCHTSS works by taking the angular position of each minutia point and then the hashing is applied by using the respective region codes of each region.

4 Results Analysis

The RCHTSS scheme is developed in MATLAB version 7.6.0 (R2008a) and the code for extracting features in fingerprint system is publicly available. The experiments have been carried out on a primary dataset which consists of 288 samples. These samples are collected from hundred subjects of various categories. The right and left hand fingerprint biometric modalities are collected from the heterogeneous population including subjects from various age group, classes and gender. The fingerprint images were acquired from each of the subject for three different interval of time. The fingerprint images of 300 × 300 size were captured with a high quality optical sensing device at a resolution of 500 dpi.

Table 3. The comparative analysis of RCHTSS technique

Sr. no	Technique	FAR (%)	FRR (%)
1.	Fingerprint Cryptosystem of Fuzzy vault	0.7	0.01
2.	Transformation and Quantization scheme	15	15
3.	Face and Palm-print	2.07–3.07 (EER)	2.07–3.07 (EER)
4.	RCHTSS	0.2 (Approx.)	0.05 (Approx.)

For the overall performance of the multi-modal biometric system the weight level fusion is considered as an important parameter. The match score's weight as obtained from both the instances of the modalities plays an important role in the proposed RCH technique. It is clearly shown in the Table 3 that the proposed technique results in low FRR and FAR when both right hand and left hand fingerprints are assigned equal weights ($\lambda = 0.50$). The Table 4 as plotted in the Fig. 5 clearly shows that the FRR/FAR increases when there is an increase in the weights of both the modalities. When the value assigned to 'λ' is 0.65 then the other modality will have the weight equals to 0.35 and FRR/FAR becomes 1.5 and 2 respectively.

Table 4. The Performance measure of the RCHTSS with different λ values

Sr. no	Weight λ	FAR(%)	FRR(%)
1.	λ = 0.30	0.2	0.05
2.	λ = 0.35	0.5	0.08
3.	λ = 0.40	0.6	0.06
4.	λ = 0.45	0.5	0.05
5.	λ = 0.50	0.2	0.05
6.	λ = 0.60	1.25	1
7.	λ = 0.65	2	1.5

The ideal characteristic for a template security scheme, as defined by ISO/IEC24745 biometric system standards, are used for performing the security analysis of this proposed technique. The proposed technique ensures the security of the template at multiple levels such as from generation of template to a time before it gets stored in template database. An intruder tries to compromise the secure templates by updating the templates already stored in the system database. One of the limitation associated with RCHTSS scheme is, it utilizes an invertible transformation function. The proposed technique also ensures greater amount of diversity by developing a broad range of intra-class and inter-class feature templates.

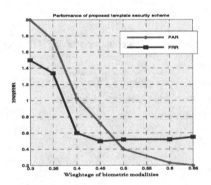

Fig. 5. Trait weight vs. FAR/FRR of RCHTSS

The performance of the proposed technique (RCHTSS) in terms of EER is 4.8% as depicted from the Table 5. But it results in a secured template which requires only 64-bits. The small size of the secured template is good for matching algorithm, but on the other side it becomes easy for an intruder to guess the template. The LOOITS technique is difficult to spoof by an attacker, but it is revocable. The performance of FUOTSS is better in terms of EER which is 3.03% but it results in bigger size template due to which its representation in memory becomes difficult.

Table 5. The Performance comparison of proposed RHTSS scheme

Sr. No.	Scheme	Performance	Template size
1	FUOTSS	3.03%(EER)	Very large
2	LOOITS	4.8%(EER)	Small
3	RCHTSS	~2–5%(FAR)	Medium
4	HYBTSS	~5.06–12.1% (FAR)	Medium

The Fig. 6 clearly shows that, the FAR in case of RCHTSS lies in the range of 2 to 5% but it results in a template size which depends on the size of fingerprint modality. This performance is good and can be further improved if the proposed scheme is applied on hand-geometry and fingerprint modality.

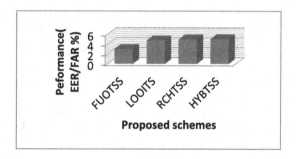

Fig. 6. Comparative analysis of proposed schemes

5   Conclusion

A novel region coded hashing technique was developed for template protection of the user information stored in the central database. The RCHTSS provides an Identification Accuracy of 99.1% with FAR as 0.2% and 0.05% as FRR, which is fairly compared to the other similar existing techniques. In future, the RCHTSS may be tested on the publically available datasets of fingerprint biometrics like FVC2000, FVC 2002 etc. The RCHTSS is revocable in the case when is compromise by an intruder. The proposed RCHTSS may be extended to other similar Multi-instance biometric systems. Moreover, the constraint of the RCHTSS may be addressed by modifying it to as a non-invertible.

Acknowledgement. The author conveys their gratitude to the authorities of Central University of Jammu for providing necessary support for carrying out this work.

References

Roberts, C.: Biometric attack vectors and defences. Comput. Secur. **26**(1), 14–25 (2007)

Jain, A.K., Flynn, P., Ross, A.A.: Handbook of Biometrics. Springer, London (2008)

Jain, A.K., Ross, A., Uludag, U.: Biometric template security : challenges and solutions. Secur. Watermarking Multimed. **4675**(IV), 629–640 (2002)

Ramu, T., Arivoli, T.: Biometric template security: an overview. EURASIP J. Adv. **65**(November), 65–75 (2012)

Prakash, S.: Human recognition using 2D and 3D ear images. Ph.D. thesis IIT Kanpur, February 2013

Kindt, E.: Biometric applications and the data protection legislation. Datenschutz und Datensicherheit - DuD **31**(3), 166–170 (2007)

Ratha, N.K., Connell, J.H., Bolle, R.M.: An analysis of minutiae matching strength, pp. 223–228 (2001)

Teoh, A.B.J., Kuan, Y.W., Lee, S.: Cancellable biometrics and annotations on BioHash. Pattern Recognit. **41**(6), 2034–2044 (2006)

Ao, M., Li, S.Z.: Near infrared face based biometric key binding. In: Tistarelli, M., Nixon, M.S. (eds.) ICB 2009. LNCS, vol. 5558, pp. 376–385. Springer, Heidelberg (2009). https://doi.org/10.1007/978-3-642-01793-3_39

Juels, A., Wattenberg, M.: A fuzzy commitment scheme. In: 6th ACM Conference on Computer and Communications Security, pp. 28–36 (1999)

Nandakumar, K., Jain, A.K.: Multibiometric template security using fuzzy vault. In: BATS (2008)

Jagadeesan1, A., Thillaikkarasi, T., Duraiswamy, K.: Cryptographic key generation from multiple biometric modalities: fusing minutiae with Iris feature. Int. J. Comput. Appl. **2**(6), 0975–8887 (2010)

Chin, Y., Ong, T., Teoh, A., Goh, K.: Integrated biometrics template protection technique based on fingerprint and palmprint feature level fusion. Inf. Fusion **18**, 161–174 (2014)

Nagar, A., Nandakumar, K., Jain, A.K.: A hybrid biometric cryptosystem for securing fingerprint minutiae templates. Pattern Recognit. Lett. **31**(8), 733–741 (2010)

Yang, Y., Lei, C.: Secure multimodal biometric authentication with wavelet quantization based fingerprint watermarking. Multimedia Tools Appl. **72** (2014)

Chen, C., Wang, C., Yang, T., Lin, D., Wang, S., Hu, J.: Optional multi-biometric cryptosystem based on fuzzy extractor. In: Proceedings of International Conference on Fuzzy Systems and Knowledge Discovery, pp. 989–994, August 2014

Karthi, G., Ezhilarasan, M.: Multibiometric template protection using hybrid technique. Int J. Eng. Tech. **7**(4) (2018)

Monrose, F., Reiter, M.K., Li, Q., Wetzel, S.: Using voice to generate cryptographic keys. In: Proceeding Speaker Odyssey 2001, The Speech Recognition Workshop (2001)

Feng, H., Wah, C.: Private key generation from on-line handwritten signatures. Inf. Manage. Comput. Secur. **10**(4), 159–164 (2002)

Vielhauer, C., Steinmetz, R., Mayerhofer, A.: Biometric hash based on statistical features of online signatures. In: Proceeding of the 16th International Conference on Pattern Recognition (ICPR 2002), vol. 1, pp. 123–126 (2002). https://doi.org/10.1109/ICPR.2002.1044628

Clancy, T., et al.: Secure smartcard-based fingerprint authentication. In: Proceedings of ACM SIGMM Multimedia Biometric & App, pp. 45–52 (2003)

Teoh, A.B.J., Ngo, D.C.L., Goh, A.: Personalised cryptographic key generation based on FaceHashing. Comput. Secur. **23**, 606–614 (2004)

Hao, F., Anderson, R., Daugman, J.: Combining crypto with biometrics effectively. IEEE Trans. Comput. **55**(9), 1081–1088 (2006)

Goh, A., Ngo, D.C.L.: Computation of cryptographic keys from face biometrics. In: Lioy, A., Mazzocchi, D. (eds.) CMS 2003. LNCS, vol. 2828, pp. 1–13. Springer, Heidelberg (2003). https://doi.org/10.1007/978-3-540-45184-6_1

Bringer, J., Chabanne, H., Cohen, G., Kindarji, Z'emor, G.: Optimal iris fuzzy sketches. In: IEEE First International Conference on Biometrics: Theory, Applications, and Systems, BTAS 2007, Washington, DC, 27–29 September 2007

Maiorana, E., Campisi, P., Fierrez, J., Ortega, J., Neri, A.: Cancelable templates for sequence-based biometrics with application to on-line signature recognition. IEEE Trans. Syst. Man. Cybern. **40**(3), 525–538 (2010)

Jin, Z., et al.: Fingerprint template protection with minutiae-based bit-string for security and privacy preserving. Expert Syst. Appl. (2012). https://doi.org/10.1016/j.eswa.2011.11.091

Reddy, P., Kumar, A., Rahman, S., Mundra, T.: A new antispoofing approach for biometric devices. IEEE Trans. Biomed. Circuits Syst. **2**, 328–337 (2008)

Teoh, A.B.J., Chong, T.Y.: Cancellable biometrics realization with multispace random projections. IEEE Trans. SMC Part B – Spec. Issue Recent Adv. Biometrics Syst. **37**(5), 1096–1106 (2007)

Monwar, M., Gavrilova, M.: FES: a system for combining face, ear and signature biometrics-susing rank level fusion. In: Fifth International Conference on Information Technology: NewGenerations, (ITNG), pp. 922–927 (2009)

Advanced Computing Using Machine Learning

Smart Parking System to Predict Occupancy Rates Using Machine Learning

Sarthak Garg[1]([⊠])[ID], Pratyush Lohumi[1][ID], and Supriya Agrawal[2][ID]

[1] Department of Electrical Engineering, Shiv Nadar University, Greater Noida, India
{sg485,pl528}@snu.edu.in
[2] Department of Computer Engineering, NMIMS University, Mumbai, India
supriya.agrawal@nmims.edu

Abstract. Car Parking is a significant issue in urban zones in both developed and developing nations. Following the quick incense of vehicle possession, numerous urban communities are experiencing a lack of car parking regions. Keeping in mind that issue, we undergo the study of Frankfurt Car Parking Data. The aim of this research work is to test several prediction strategies to provide the users with information about occupancy rates of parking lots. With the approach of self-sufficient vehicles as the future and automatic car parking features in cars, realizing the occupancy rates of a parking area beforehand can be valuable and can spare a ton of time and fuel. To predict occupancy rates we are using the following prediction models namely Linear Regression, Neural Networks, Support Vector Regression, Decision Trees (Regression) and Ensemble Decision Trees. We have also implemented K-means clustering as we hypothesise that adding one more feature to the dataset for similar instances would help predictive algorithms to fit better on the data. Using this additional feature, we modified the existing dataset D1 (with 3 features) into D2 (with 4 features). We advocate this hypothesis by comparing the results of prediction algorithms on both datasets (D1 and D2). From the results, we found out XGBoost fits the dataset exceptionally well.

Keywords: Frankfurt parking data · Smart cities · Machine learning · Non-parametric algorithm · Regression · Neural network · XGBoost

1 Introduction

Successfully getting an open parking spot in a city is painstaking for private car owners/drivers, and is becoming harder and harder with proliferating numbers of cars on the road [1]. It is much harder in cities with larger populations, majorly in heart of the city or the city centre. A good traffic management is required on this end, a smart city needs to have ways to manage traffic and parking facilities efficiently. A study shows that about 30% of road jamming is contributed by drivers looking for an open parking spot [2].

© Springer Nature Singapore Pte Ltd. 2020
C. Badica et al. (Eds.): ICICCT 2020, CCIS 1170, pp. 163–171, 2020.
https://doi.org/10.1007/978-981-15-9671-1_13

With the advent of autonomous vehicles such as Tesla, these occupancy rates can highly help autonomous vehicles to make informed decisions as to where exactly to park in the auto-park-mode [16,18]. It will also help the drivers to look for the availability of parking spots at their planned destination before hand in turn it will lead to decrease in road jamming and congestion [17]. In this paper we try to address a smart parking solution to this problem using machine learning models, not only we find out the best machine learning model for this data but also get insights about the distribution of the data.

We use Frankfurt Car Parking data [15] obtained from Kaggle which has 4 attributes namely Parking Lot Number(unique number for each parking lot), Day of Week (eg. Monday = 2), Time(time of the day) and occupancy rate (how much percent the parking lot is occupied). We use this data as a Regression Problem and try to find out correlation between X [Parking Lot Number (X0), Time (X1) and Day of Week (X2)] and Y [Occupancy rate] in order to predict Y (occupancy rate) for unseen data X. Less work has been done on this dataset, our aim is to fit a model which is useful for predicting parking occupancy rate efficiently and accurately.

2   Literature Review

The goal of creating a smart parking system which predicts open parking spaces is a popular problem statement and is very well known since decades. Hence, there are many studies related to the problem that we are addressing. Challenges of parking occupancy prediction involve the accuracy of prediction for long terms and how user's behaviour influence the availability of parking spots. Following are some related works.

Xu et al. [3], they designed an app to tackle the problem, called Phone Park, it detects the availability of parking spots through smart phones carried by the car owners/drivers. This does not depend on any sensors and doesn't require any dedicated infrastructure.

Caliskan et al. [4], each parking lot sends out five values through a VANET (Vehicular ad hoc network) which is developed by moving vehicles, which include capacity of the parking lots, time-stamp, parking places occupied, and the rate of arrival of cars, and the rate of parking of cars. Each of these rates are measured and calculated at each parking lot and are transmitted on the VANET.

Zheng et al. [5], authors are using datasets of parking occupany of the cities like San Francisco, USA and Melbourne, Australia. Some machine learning algorithms which they implemented involve Regression Tree, Neural Networks and Support Vector Regression to predict the occupancy rates. Their study reveals that Regression Tree performs best on both datasets and is the least computational algorithm.

Zhao et al. [6], The authors have offered an ingenious method of planning for parking systems. They altered parking planning into a linear problem. They did this by holding the parking queries inside a queue for some time. They developed an estimating algorithm for this linear problem. Simulations show that this problem is efficiently tackled with good results.

Tiedemann et al. [7] developed a system for prediction that provides approximated occupancy rates for parking lots in Berlin, Germany.

3 Dataset and Algorithms

3.1 Dataset Description

This study on done on Frankfurt Car Park dataset obtained from [15]. Dataset contains 1,16,004 instances with 9 attributes. Objective is to predict the occupancy rate which lies between 0 to 1, of parking lots (X0) on particular day (X1) and time (X2). Feature set that we defined is as follows. The input as X = X0, X1, X2 and the output as Y = Oc(t), where Oc(t) is the occupancy rate.

Prediction of occupancy rate is a supervised learning problem and because of having a discrete output, the prediction of occupancy rate is a "regression type of supervised learning".

Table 1. Feature set of the model

S. No.	Feature name	Feature description	Feature notation
1	Parking lot number	Unique Reference Number for different parking lots	x_0
2	Day of week	Sunday = 1, Monday = 2, Tuesday = 3 and so on	x_1
3	Time	H : M is converted to $H + \dfrac{M}{60}$	x_2
4	Occupancy rate Oc(t)	$Oc(t) = \dfrac{Number\,of\,Slots\,Occupied}{Total\,Number\,of\,slots}$	y

Table 1 can be referred to observe different features undergone in this study and their respective descriptions followed by feature notations used in this paper.

3.2 Machine Learning Algorithms

Machine learning algorithms are statistical tools which help us find correlation between variables in a dataset. Dataset consists of a target variable whose value depends upon the corresponding variables called features. In our case features are Time, DOW and Parking Lot number and target variable is Occupancy Rate. The following algorithms/tools are exploited to predict the unknown target variable i.e. Occupancy Rate given a new set of features unseen by the algorithm.

3.2.1 Linear Regression

Linear Regression [8] is a statistical technique which is a regression investigation apparatus that is utilized to anticipate dependent variable or output from a lot of independent factors or traits. Under supervised machine learning algorithms, it is one of the most acclaimed calculations that is utilized for regression problem. For our situation, it isolates the data linearly and gives a continuous output [8].

3.2.2   Support Vector Regression

The essence of SVM [9] lies in graphing the data points in an n-dimensional space (where n denotes the number of features in the dataset) and therefore where each value is plotted, every feature depicts a coordinate in that space. A hyper-plane is then drawn depending upon kernel functions which differentiate the data points to give an output. Therefore, SVM regression is considered a non-parametric technique because it relies on kernel functions. Often used kernel functions is RBF (radial basis function),

$$K(x, \hat{x}) = exp(-\frac{||x - \hat{x}||_2^2}{2\gamma^2}) \tag{1}$$

where x and $\hat{x}$ are the input vectors, and determination of area of influence by support vector is done by γ. To fit SVR, this equation needs to be optimized

$$min_w \frac{1}{2} w^T w + C \sum_i (\varepsilon_i + \varepsilon_i^*) \tag{2}$$

where w is the margin and C is a positive constant. ε and ε^* are the slack variables [9].

3.2.3   Neural Networks

Neural Networks [10] taken inspiration from the human brain are also made out of simpler units called neurons, where each neuron can map basic numerical decisions. Therefore, these simpler units combined in a network can easily map complex mathematical functions and decisions and can provide fair results. A neural network has 3 types of layers: an input layer which is aligned with the type and size of input data, the hidden layer which can be chosen depending upon the complexity of the decisions to be made by the neural network and lastly an output layer which is aligned by the type of output which is expected as per the problem statement. Deep Neural Networks has a denser and more number of hidden layers to map complex data distributions and therefore performing better by learning complex mathematical operations [10].

3.2.4   Regression Tree

Decision Tree [11] works on the principle of splitting the data into branches and creating sub-trees to decrease impurity in classes as the splits happen, therefore it is an iterative procedure as the data is split into smaller groups. A fully-grown tree consists of decision nodes and leaf nodes and each leaf node represents a decision on the numerical output. The first split or the topmost decision node of the tree happens on the most important feature of the dataset and is also called the root node. Every node consists of feature p and split point q, the data can be split/divided in two regions R1 and R2. To find the best splitting point and feature, we need to solve

$$min_{p,q} [\sum_{x_i \in R_{2(p,q)}} (y_i - c1)^2 + \sum_{x_i \in R_{1(p,q)}} (y_i - c2)^2] \tag{3}$$

where the best c1 and c2 are the average values of the corresponding region(R1 or R2) [11].

3.2.5   XGBoost Regression

XGBoost [12] is an efficient and famous implementation of Gradient Boosting Decision Tree (GBDT), a GBDT is based on ensemble learning which exploits decision trees as base classifiers and uses gradient boosting approach for better results. XGBoost model consists of "n" number of decision trees T1, ... ,Tn. For testing, it runs inference on all "n" trees and then adds the inference results obtained.

$$L(\phi) = \sum_i l(\hat{y}_i, y_i) + \sum_k \Omega(f_k)$$

where

$$\Omega(f) = \gamma T + \frac{1}{2}\lambda||w^2|| \tag{4}$$

Here l is defined as a convex loss function which calculated the difference in prediction and actual value. Ω creates a penalty on the complexity of model [12].

3.2.6   Random Forest

Random forest [13] algorithm is a supervised ensemble algorithm. As the name proposes, this technique joins various trees cooperating with arbitrarily picked characteristics from the feature set hence it is called a random forest. This algorithm randomly picks features from the whole dataset while making splits. Therefore, making grown trees uncorrelated to each other which encourages generalization of the dataset and removes overfitting. This process is called feature bagging and makes the model more robust and less susceptible to outliers and missing values. Random forest not only makes the model robust but it also helps to remove the overfitting problem from the picture [13].

3.2.7   K-Means Clustering

K-means [14] is a clustering algorithm which tries to find a local maxima after each iteration. Clustering comes under unsupervised learning approach. By clustering the data points with similar characteristics into one cluster and giving each of them a cluster index/label, these cluster indices/labels can be used as an additional feature in our supervised predictive algorithms. The objective function for the K-means clustering algorithm is the squared error function:

$$J = \sum_{i=1}^{k} \sum_{j=1}^{n} (||x_i - v_j||)^2 = 1 \tag{5}$$

where, Eucledian distance is represented by $||x_i - v_j||$ between a centroid and a point, the iteration is carried on over all k-points in the ith cluster, for all n clusters [14].

4   Experimentation and Results

We have experimented with Linear Regression, Support Vector Regression and other machine learning algorithms mentioned above on Frankfurt car park dataset. We used a non-parametric algorithm i.e. k-means clustering, it enabled us to obtain an additional feature which provided a better fit to the data using the same algorithms and fetched us satisfactory results. "Xclusterindex" is the additional feature which is obtained by clustering. {Xclusterindex $\in [0, 3]$}

We decided to choose k = 4 using the principal that 'k' is chosen at the elbow point (where MSE decreases the most).

Mean Squared Error (MSE) is used to determine the performance of the algorithms, in both training and testing stages. Equation 1 shows the mathematical equation for MSE where yi are the real values measured, fi are the predicted values, and n gives the number of observations.

$$MSE = \frac{1}{n} \sum_{i=1}^{n} (yi - fi)^2 \tag{6}$$

R-Squared (R^2 or the coefficient of determination) is a statistical measure it helps in understanding how well the distribution of data fits with the model(the goodness of fit). 100% indicates that the model explains all the variability of the response data around its mean.

Dataset 1{D1}:- $\{X_{parkinglotnumber}, X_{dow}, X_{time}, Y_{oc(t)}\}$

Dataset 2{D2}:- $\{X_{parkinglotnumber}, X_{dow}, X_{time}, X_{clusterindex}, Y_{oc(t)}\}$

From Table 2: Low Mean Squared error suggests that expected and predicted points are close to each other but another measure is required to figure out how model fits the data which can be explained by R^2. Higher R^2 suggests that regression model aligns better with the distribution of the data and therefore it's a better fit. Linear regression shows the lowest R^2 of 6.5%, which makes it clear that the data is not in a linear distribution, hence low R^2. Random forest fits the data best with the highest R^2 of 91.7%.

Table 2. Results: supervised algorithms implemented on D1

S. No.	Algorithms used	Mean squared error (MSE)	Coefficient of determination R^2
1	Linear regression	0.049	0.085
2	Support vector regression	0.0437	0.634
3	Neural networks	0.0404	0.4685
4	Regression tree	0.0172	0.7622
5	XGBoost regression	0.0060	0.912
6	Random forest	0.0062	0.917

Next we experimented with same algorithms on a new feature set which includes one additional feature i.e. $X_{clusterindex}$, extracted from K-means Clustering, let's observe the results in Table 3.

Table 3. Results: supervised algorithms implemented on D2

S. No.	Algorithms used	Mean Squared Error (MSE)	Coefficient of determination R^2
1	Linear regression	0.069	0.115
2	Support vector regression	0.0216	0.722
3	Neural networks	0.0212	0.612
4	Regression tree	0.0066	0.914
5	XGBoost regression	0.0049	0.951
6	Random forest	0.0058	0.924

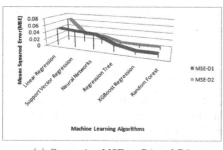
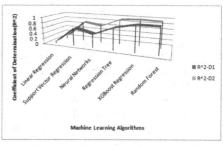

(a) Comparing MSE on D1 and D2   (b) Comparing R^2 on D1 and D2

Fig. 1. Visualizing results of datasets D1 and D2

Implementation has been done on Python 3.6 We progressed from trying to fit our data into linear distribution and then moved on to non-linear distribution and turns out data is well fit using ensemble decision tree methods and XGB Regressor fits best with tree pruning at level 13 and with 30 estimators.

Best performance is shown by XGB Regression with Clustering showing R^2 of 0.951 and MSE of 0.0049 in Table 3.

Figure 1 can be referred to visualize mean squared errors and R^2 of different algorithms respectively.

If we compare Table 2 and Table 3, every cell of Table 3 showcases a better result. Thus, proving our hypothesis that an additional feature extracted using non-parametric algorithm helps the supervised learning algorithm's performance.

5   Conclusion and Future Work

Analysis of parking data collected in large amounts by smart city IOT deployments is essential in order to intelligently manage the infrastructure. In this work, we did an analysis on the parking occupancy data collected from Frankfurt. We employed many different parametric prediction algorithms for the parking occupancy rate and compared relative strengths of these methods. Evaluation revealed that XGboost regressor fits the dataset exceptionally well. Furthermore, we hypothesised that non-parametric algorithm such as k-means clustering would further improve the performance of parametric algorithms and our hypothesis was proven right as we not only obtained reduced MSE but also achieved a higher R^2.

In the future, we would like to add some features/factors into the model that might influence the availability of parking, factors may include social events/gatherings, weather conditions, holidays, traffic flow and vicinity of famous places (malls, tourist spots etc.) near the respective parking area.

References

1. Bélissent, J.: Getting clever about smart cities: new opportunities require new business models. Cambridge Massachusetts USA **193**, 244–77 (2010)
2. Shoup, D.: Free parking or free markets. Access Mag. **1**(38), 28–35 (2011)
3. Xu, B., Wolfson, O., Yang, J., Stenneth, L., Philip, S.Y., Nelson, P.C.: Real-time street parking availability estimation. In: 2013 IEEE 14th International Conference on Mobile Data Management (MDM), vol. 1, pp. 16–25. IEEE (2013)
4. Caliskan, M., Barthels, A., Scheuermann, B., Mauve, M.: Predicting parking lot occupancy in vehicular ad hoc networks. In: IEEE 65th Vehicular Technology Conference: VTC2007-Spring, pp. 277–281. IEEE (2007)
5. Zheng, Y., Rajasegarar, S., Leckie, C.: Parking availability prediction for sensor-enabled car parks in smart cities. In: 2015 IEEE Tenth International Conference on Intelligent Sensors, Sensor Networks and Information Processing (ISSNIP), Singapore, 7–9 April 2015
6. Zhao, X., Zhao, K., Hai, F.: An algorithm of parking planning for smart parking system. In: Proceeding of the 11th World Congress on Intelligent Control and Automation, Shenyang, pp. 4965–4969 (2014)
7. Tiedemann, T., Vögele, T., Krell, M.M., Metzen, J.H., Kirchner, F.: Concept of a data thread based parking space occupancy prediction in a Berlin Pilot region (2015)
8. Schoolfield, R.M., Sharpe, P.J.H., Magnuson, C.E.: Non-linear regression of biological temperature-dependent rate models based on absolute reaction-rate theory. J. Theor. Biol. **88**(4), 719–731 (1981)
9. Smola, A.J., Schölkopf, B.: A tutorial on support vector regression. Stat. Comput. **14**(3), 199–222 (2004)
10. Beale, H.D., Demuth, H.B., Hagan, M.T.: Neural Network Design. Pws, Boston (1996)
11. Breiman, L., Friedman, J., Stone, C.J., Olshen, R.A.: Classification and Regression Trees. CRC Press, Boca Raton (1984)
12. Chen, T., Guestrin, C.: XGboost: a scalable tree boosting system. In: Proceedings of the 22nd ACM SIGKDD International Conference on Knowledge Discovery and Data Mining, pp. 785–794 (2016)
13. Carliles, S., Budavári, T., Heinis, S., Priebe, C., Szalay, A.S.: Random forests for photometric redshifts. Astrophys. J. **712**(1), 511 (2010)
14. Hartigan, J.A., Wong, M.A.: Algorithm AS 136: a k-means clustering algorithm. J. Roy. Stat. Soc. Ser. C (Appl. Stat.) **28**(1), 100–108 (1979)
15. Dataset. https://www.kaggle.com/orgesleka/frankfurt-car-parking-data
16. Jin, J., Gubbi, J., Luo, T., Palaniswami, M.: Network architecture and QoS issues in the internet of things for a smart city. In: 2012 International Symposium on Communications and Information Technologies (ISCIT), pp. 956–961. IEEE (2012)

17. Ramya, M.R., Ravi, S.: International Journal of Engineering Sciences & Research Technology Smart Parking Solutions for Smart Cities Based on Wireless Sensor Networks

18. Zheng, Y., Rajasegarar, S., Leckie, C.: Parking availability prediction for sensor-enabled car parks in smart cities. In: 2015 IEEE Tenth International Conference on Intelligent Sensors, Sensor Networks and Information Processing (ISSNIP), pp. 1–6. IEEE (2015)

Analyzing Fuzzy Phrases for Emotion Detection Using Distance Based Approach

Rahul Gupta⬥, Nikhil Yadav(✉)⬥, Nikhil Sharma⬥, and Raveesh Garg⬥

Delhi Technological University, New Delhi, India
rahulgupta100689@gmail.com, nikhily.725@gmail.com,
nsharma1245@gmail.com, raveeshgarg.garg7@gmail.com

Abstract. With the increasing popularity of social media platforms such as Twitter and Facebook the amount of text data available is humungous. Extracting opinions and polarity from this text data available is a hot topic for research work. Many researchers have developed different methods to tackle the problem of sentiment analysis but the main focus by and large has always been on classifying the general tweets. Meanwhile, a large number of fuzzy phrases that assert significant impact on a sentence's polarity is left untouched. Thus, solving these fuzzy phrases to get membership values for various emotions effectively could widen the scope for sentiment analysis. In this study, we are using one of the most trending topics in India i.e., CAA, NPR and NRC. We are classifying tweets into different emotions to analyze public outlook and then uses the fuzzy sentiment phrases concept to analyze the strength of emotions based on the distance of intensifiers and diminishers from the fundamental words. In our experiment, we got a precision of 0.815 for strong sentiment and 0.713 for weak sentiment, thus showing our method work very well on FSPs.

Keywords: Fuzzy sentiment phrases · Sentiment analysis · CAA · NRC · NPR

1 Introduction

The increasing text data available online and advancement in computational technologies have aided Natural Language Processing (NLP) research to a great extent. The number of social profiles proliferates each day and people express their thoughts, opinions and knowledge on social networking sites. Keeping this in mind, opinion mining becomes an important field of research.

One of the most popular social networking sites which serves as one of the major sources for text data is Twitter. The number of Twitter users have grown exponentially with nearly 500 million tweets posted every day. There are 330 million active users and 145 million daily users and a total of 1.3 billion accounts have been created [1]. Twitter Sentiment Analysis (TSA) is a method used in many research papers in order to mine opinions from text data. Sentiment Analysis is basically the process of calculating and analysing the intentions of twitter users about a topic of interest.

Sentiment generally refers to emotions, attitudes, feelings or opinions of the users. TSA helps various organizations to gather the emotions and opinions of Twitter users

© Springer Nature Singapore Pte Ltd. 2020
C. Badica et al. (Eds.): ICICCT 2020, CCIS 1170, pp. 172–180, 2020.
https://doi.org/10.1007/978-981-15-9671-1_14

and its analysis. A plethora of sentiment analysis tools can be found online that classify the text to a certain category. However, these tools focus on the basic level of sentiment, that is, they generally classify the text into positive or negative (sometimes also as neutral). Our research focuses on going into a finer level of detail and perform Sentiment Analysis at that level. The purpose is to produce more realistic, specific and actionable results with detailed emotion that would help to determine the intensity of the emotion of the user.

In general, most of the research work is done in classifying the general tweets. In some research papers, lexicon-based approach is used i.e. "Domain-Specific Lexicons" has been used in order to improve the accuracy of classification. However, one strategy cannot work in all scenarios and that's why divide-and-conquer approach is more suitable [2, 3], i.e. better results can be attained using an approach focussing on each type of sentence separately. Like in [4] the author suggests how the opinions should be mined from the sentences in which a comparison has been made between different entities and similarly in [5] the author targets the analysis of sentences containing the conditional clauses.

To clearly understand the demerits of the existing methods, we analyse the following example: "The structure of this house is considerably good". In this sentence, there is a phrase that is not clear, namely "considerably good." Many of the former methods would have categorized the sentiment of this sentence as positive as they would have emphasised only on the word "good" without taking into account the impact of the "considerably" into account. Former methods did not consider the impact of fuzzy sentiment phrases on sentiment analysis and handled them as any other phrase. Hence, they do not perform that much good for sentences as shown in example. The thesis [6] discusses the impact of intensifiers and diminishers and how these impacts the emotion of any sentence.

So, this motivated us to classify the tweets accordingly into 4 sentiments namely happy, sad, anger and hate and then determine the fuzzy phrases in each class and determine their fuzzy membership value in order to evaluate the intensity of emotion.

2 Related Works

TSA is a hot topic for researches and a lot of work has already been done in this field. So, in this section we give a basic overview of the work related to our research, which includes pre-processing techniques, ML algorithms and score calculation.

Most of the studies in the field of sentiment analysis is based on general tweets and classifies the tweets in positive, negative and neutral classes [7, 8]. A very limited research has been done on classification of specific type of sentences.

In [9] author proposed Label propagation to generate context-specific lexicons with word embedding algorithm which effectively aids in classification of a particular type of news i.e. financial news into hot/not-hot which further helps in avoiding the problem of dimensionality.

In [10] Jefferson proposed a fuzzy approach in which he used the fuzzy membership values to determine the extent to which a sentence contain a particular sentiment. The algorithm proposed by Jefferson leads to more refined intensities or categories.

In [2] Phan considered a divide and conquer strategy by first categorizing the tweets into FSPs and Non-FSPs and as shown in the result section in [2] this led to a much better categorization. Phan calculated the sentiment score of an FSP by using the sentiment score of words using Sentiword Net library.

In [11] the author has proposed an algorithm for parsing the natural language for evaluating the users' sentiment using the text from social media sites. The paper proposes the steps of parsing and also evaluate the work using data from Twitter social network. Some studies like [3] suggests the embedding of sentiment-specific word and a weighted text feature model which is easy to build, simple and effective and others like [12] focuses on calculating initial word emotion using standard emotion lexicon but does not take into account the fuzzy sentiment phrases. In [13–15] the author presents a survey of sentiment analysis and the various classification algorithms used.

3   The Proposed Method

In this section, we will illustrate the steps for Data acquisition, Pre-Processing, Feature-Extraction, Fuzzy Sentiment Phrases Extraction and Score Calculation.

3.1   Data Acquisition

We aim to study and analyze the trends of the National Population Register (NPR), Citizenship Amendment Act (CAA) and National Register of Citizens (NRC) on twitter and classify them into different emotion categories and the strength of these emotions. In order to retrieve the tweets, we used Tweepy (Python package) to make a dataset of 10,000 English tweets having CAA, NRC and NPR as the hashtag. We have manually labelled the dataset into different emotions and also after detecting FSPs we have manually labelled them as strong and weak emotion.

3.2   Pre-processing

Before proceeding to train the model, the data first needs to be pre-processed in order to assemble the required data in a structured manner so as to achieve a uniform and clean data for sentiment analysis.

Pre-processing of data involves the following steps:

- Removal of duplicate data: This step involves the removal of duplicate data in the dataset in order to eliminate redundancy
- Filtering: This step removes special symbols (e.g. #, @ etc.) and URL links.
- Removal of stop words: Removal of irrelevant words like "a", "an", "is" etc. from the data.
- Tokenization: This involves the separation of text by segmenting it by spaces and punctuation marks thereby forming a bag of words.

Next, to reduce the effect of acronyms and spelling mistakes in our dataset we make use of the Python-based Aspell library7 to carry out spell correction. Then, the FSPs are extracted from the dataset which are then used to analyse to strength of the emotion into two classes namely weak emotion and strong emotion. The workflow of the method used is shown in Fig. 1.

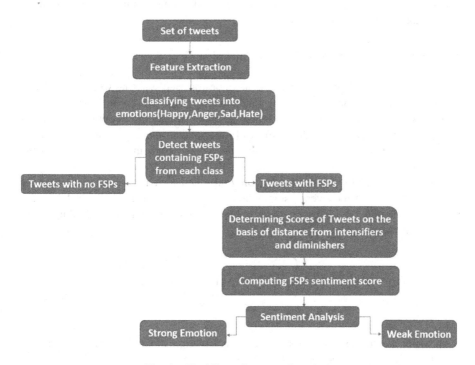

Fig. 1. Workflow of proposed method

3.3 Feature Extraction

In our paper, the information related to the lexicons, semantics and syntactic of words is used as features. The n-grams we used consists of 1-gram, 2-grams, and 3-grams. Every n-grams' corresponding feature value of TF-IDF (term frequency inverse document frequency). is added as a row in the feature vector.

3.4 Fuzzy Sentiment Phrases Extraction

Given below is Table 1 that shows a vocabulary of 71 words containing intensifiers and diminishers.

Table 1. Lexicon content.

Lexicon	#words
Intensifiers	56
Diminishers	15

FSPs are categorized into two main types:

- **Without Negation Word**: If a sentence has a fuzzy word following the fundamental word for example: "significantly good" or "relatively better" or" damn nice".
- **With Negation Word**: Negation Word following the fundamental word for example: "not that good" or "not too bad".

3.5 Fuzzy Score Calculation and Classification

- SentiWordNet 3.0 is used to find a float value for each word between −1 to 1 and this is put in score array for all the fundamental words present in the library.
- In [2] while calculating score of a fundamental word they didn't consider the effect of its distance from the modifier. So, to further extend the approach, our approach focuses on taking into account the distance of the fundamental words from the modifiers.
- Now the scores of fundamental words are multiplied with a value >1 to increase the impact of word in the overall summation and as the distance between the fundamental and modifier increases that constant approaches to 1 hence leading to no impact of the modifier.

$$score[j] = score[j] * \prod_{i=1}^{j-1} \left\{ \begin{array}{ll} 1, & if\ i\ isn't\ a\ modifier \\ \left(1 + \left|\frac{score[i]}{e^{j-i}}\right|\right), & if\ \ i\ is\ a\ modifier \end{array} \right\} \quad (1)$$

- Above is the formula used for the score calculation of fundamental word j. The score array is initialized using SentiWordNet 3.0.

$$SCORE = \frac{\sum_{h=1}^{n} Score[h]}{n} \quad (2)$$

SCORE is the final score of the tweet used.

3.6 Evaluation Metrices

The method proposed uses precision (P), recall (R), and F-score(F1) to measure the accuracy and calculate the results.

These values are calculated as follows:

$$P = \frac{TP}{FP + TP} \quad (3)$$

$$R = \frac{TP}{FN + TP} \quad (4)$$

$$F_1 = \frac{2 * P * R}{P + R} \qquad (5)$$

FP (False Positive): FSPs not belonging to class C but classified as class C.
FN (False Negative): FSPs belonging to class C but not classified as C.
TP (True Positive): FSPs belonging to class C and classified as class C.

4 Observation and Result

First, the tweets are classified into 4 emotion categories (happy, sad, anger, hate).
Figure 2 shows the overall distribution of CAA tweets into aforementioned categories.

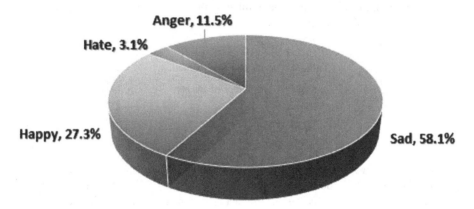

Fig. 2. Pie-chart of tweet analysis

Table 2 shows the number of tweets of each class in test data and train data.

Table 2. Classification result of tweets (on our dataset) for each emotion.

Emotions	Number of tweets (train data)	Number of tweets (test data)
Happy	2454	260
Sad	5231	588
Anger	1036	127
Hate	277	25

As can be seen from Fig. 2, 58.1% of the tweets belong to Sad Category, 27.3% to
Happy, 11.3% to Anger and 3.1% to Hate. The statistics shows majority of classes as
sad and a very few showing hate. The test and train accuracy for the classification of
tweets into various categories is mentioned in Table 3.

Table 3. Accuracy of classifying tweets into emotions using Naïve Bayes Classifier.

Train accuracy	92.7
Test accuracy	91.1

The train accuracy for the classification of tweets into 4 classes using the Naïve Bayes Classifier is 92.7% and test accuracy is 91.1%. This is because of the preprocessing steps performed on the data that results in a better accuracy of our classifier.

Second, we work towards analyzing the intensity of the emotion present in the tweets containing Fuzzy Sentiment Phrases. This is achieved by first dividing the tweets into 2 sets (as represented in the Fig. 1), those containing FSPs and those not containing FSPs. Table 4 represents the number of FSPs and Non-FSPs in the dataset used.

It is clear from the Table 4 that the number of tweets containing FSPs are very less as compared to non FSP tweets.

Table 4. Result of FSPs extraction.

Type	Number of tweets
FSPs	721
Non-FSPs	9279

Third, then the data is analyzed to get the intensity of the emotion by employing Sentiword Net 3.0 to get the scores of individual words and then applying the formula given below to take into account the impact of intensifiers and diminishers in our tweets.

$$score[j] = score[j] * \prod_{i=1}^{j-1}\left(1 + \left|\frac{score[i]}{e^{j-i}}\right|\right) \quad eq.1$$

- Score [j] is the Sentiment Score of fundamental words sentiment.
- Score [i] is the Sentiment Score of Intensifiers and Diminishers.
- The Product is done for intensifiers and diminishers before fundamental word j.

Our approach focuses on taking into account the distance of the fundamental word from the modifiers. The scores of fundamental words are multiplied with a value >1 to increase the impact of word in the overall summation and as the distance between the fundamental and modifier increases that constant approaches to 1 hence resulting in no impact of the modifier.

After calculating the score for each FSPs using Eq. 1 we evaluated the precision, recall and f-score for the classification of FSPs into strong and weak emotion and the results are listed in Table 5.

Table 5. Result of FSPs extraction.

Type	Precision	Recall	F-Score
Strong sentiment	0.815	0.793	0.804
Weak sentiment	0.713	0.742	0.742

As seen from the values shown in Table 5, it is clear that we are able to classify strong sentiment more precisely as compared to weak sentiment since the intensifiers for strong emotion are more prominent.

5 Conclusion

This paper presents a method for analysing the fuzzy phrases. First finding out the type of emotion and making a vocabulary of Intensifiers and Diminishers to be used to detect fuzzy phrases. Second detecting the sentences having fuzzy phrases. Third find the fuzzy membership value and deciding a threshold to classify whether am emotion is strong or not. In our experiment we got a precision of 0.815 for Strong sentiment and 0.713 for weak sentiment, thus showing our proposed method work very well on FSPs.

Also, the work done is unique and novel since any related work could not be found in the literature, specifically on CAA. Therefore, we haven't compared our approach with any other approaches.

References

1. 60 Incredible and interesting twitter stats and statistics. https://www.brandwatch.com/blog/twitter-stats-and-statistics/. Accessed 05 Jan 2020
2. Phan, H.T., Nguyen, N.T., Van Cuong, T., Hwang, D.: A method for detecting and analyzing the sentiment of tweets containing fuzzy sentiment phrases. In: Proceedings of the IEEE International Symposium on INnovations in Intelligent SysTems and Applications, INISTA 2019, pp. 1–6. IEEE (2019). https://doi.org/10.1109/inista.2019.8778360
3. Li, Q., Shah, S., Fang, R., Nourbakhsh, A., Liu, X.: Tweet sentiment analysis by incorporating sentiment-specific word embedding and weighted text features. In: Proceedings of the IEEE/WIC/ACM International Conference on Web Intelligence, WI 2016, pp. 568–571 (2017). https://doi.org/10.1109/wi.2016.0097
4. Ganapathibhotla, M., Liu, B.: Mining opinions in comparative sentences. In: Proceedings of the 22nd International Conference on Computational Linguistics, Coling 2008, vol. 1, pp. 241–248 (2008). https://doi.org/10.3115/1599081.1599112
5. Narayanan, R., Liu, B., Choudhary, A.: Sentiment analysis of conditional sentences. In: Proceedings of the 2009 Conference on Empirical Methods in Natural Language Processing, EMNLP 2009, a Meet SIGDAT, a Special Interest Group of the ACL, Held Conjunction with ACL-IJCNLP 2009, pp. 180–189 (2009). https://doi.org/10.3115/1699510.1699534
6. Strohm, F.: The impact of intensifiers, diminishers and negations on emotion expressions (2017). https://pdfs.semanticscholar.org/d40e/7b7df41a420e1bd456b39cae68726e3a0acb.pdf

7. Go, A., Bhayani, R., Huang, L.: Twitter sentiment classification using distant supervision. Processing **1**, 1–6 (2009)
8. Mohammad, S.M., Kiritchenko, S., Zhu, X.: NRC-Canada: building the state-of-the-art in sentiment analysis of tweets. In: 2nd Joint Conference on Lexical and Computational Semantics (*SEM 2013), Proceedings of the Seventh International Workshop on Semantic Evaluation (SemEval 2013), vol. 2, pp. 321–327 (2013)
9. Yildirim, S., Jothimani, D., Kavaklioğlu, C., Bener, A.: Building domain-specific lexicons: an application to financial news. In: Proceedings of the International Conference on Deep Learning and Machine Learning in Emerging Applications, Deep-ML 2019, pp. 23–26 (2019). https://doi.org/10.1109/deep-ml.2019.00013
10. Jefferson, C., Liu, H., Cocea, M.: Fuzzy approach for sentiment analysis. In: IEEE International Conference on Fuzzy Systems (2017). https://doi.org/10.1109/FUZZ-IEEE. 2017.8015577
11. Luneva, E.E., Banokin, P.I., Zamyatina, V.S., Ivantsov, S.V.: Natural language text parsing for social network user sentiment analysis based on fuzzy sets. In: Proceedings of 2015 International Conference on Mechanical Engineering, Automation and Control Systems, MEACS 2015 (2016). https://doi.org/10.1109/meacs.2015.7414902
12. Jiang, D., Luo, X., Xuan, J., Xu, Z.: Sentiment computing for the news event based on the social media big data. IEEE Access **5**(c), 2373–2382 (2017). https://doi.org/10.1109/access. 2016.2607218
13. Kaur, H., Mangat, V., Krail, N.: A survey of sentiment analysis techniques. In: International Conference on IoT in Social, Mobile, Analytics and Cloud (I-SMAC 2017), pp. 921–925 (2017). https://doi.org/10.1109/i-smac.2017.8058315
14. Rathi, M., Malik, A., Varshney, D., Sharma, R., Mendiratta, S.: Sentiment analysis of tweets using machine learning approach. In: Proceedings of 2018 11th International Conference on Contemporary Computing, IC3 2018, pp. 1–3 (2018). https://doi.org/10.1109/ic3.2018. 8530517
15. Giachanou, A., Crestani, F.: Like it or not: a survey of Twitter sentiment analysis methods. ACM Comput. Surv. **49**(2), 1–41 (2016). https://doi.org/10.1145/2938640

PMM: A Model for Bangla Parts-of-Speech Tagging Using Sentence Map

Prosanta Kumar Chaki[1(✉)] ⓘ, Biman Barua[2(✉)] ⓘ,
Md Mozammel Hossain Sazal[1(✉)] ⓘ, and Shikha Anirban[1(✉)] ⓘ

[1] Daffodil International University, Dhaka, Bangladesh
prosanta35-279@diu.edu.bd, mhsazal80@gmail.com,
anirban@daffodilvarsity.edu.bd
[2] BGMEA University of Fashion and Technology, Dhaka, Bangladesh
biman@buft.edu.bd

Abstract. The Part-of-speech (POS) tagging is mandatory for almost all kinds of Natural Language Processing (NLP) tasks such as Grammar checking, Machine translation, summary writing, sentiment analysis, information retrievals, and speech processing etc. Having very few successful researches on computational linguistics in Bangla language, it still remains the demand for technology. The existing works on Bangla parts-of-speech tagging require large training data set and not applicable for all language styles. In this research, we proposed Prediction Maximization Model (PMM) for Bangla parts-of-speech tagging. We used statistical data for learning and used rule-based analysis. Hidden Markov Model (HMM) is applied with tag mapping and scoring in PMM to maximize the accuracy by using relatively less statistical training data. PMM achieved 95.6% accuracy that is relatively high compared with two other existing POS tagger which claims the nearest accuracy but with the relatively much higher number of training data sets. In our experiment, we used around 14K unique token as training data for PMM and the other two existing systems and PMM performed best.

Keywords: Part-of-speech · Bangla language · Machine learning · Hidden Markov Model · Lexicon · Maps · PMM

1 Introduction

Part-of-speech (POS) indicates the linguistic category of a word that addresses the appropriate syntactic label of each word in a sentence. Besides the demand for communication with other languages through technology, a good POS tagger is required for almost all natural language processing (NLP) applications. That is why it is one of the significant concerns of computational linguistic researchers to have a good POS tagger. Lots of researches have been done in some languages like English, French, and German, which enriched the digital archive of those languages morphologically. As a result, it becomes more accessible to NLP research. Bangla is the fifth most spoken language in the world, but the computational linguistic resources did not develop yet, and the research on this language is not much noticeable. Although the Insufficient

© Springer Nature Singapore Pte Ltd. 2020
C. Badica et al. (Eds.): ICICCT 2020, CCIS 1170, pp. 181–194, 2020.
https://doi.org/10.1007/978-981-15-9671-1_15

amounts of training data, a variety of POS tags, different types of words and many other dependencies made POS tagging complex but some researchers trying to overcome those problems by working hard.

In NLP the Hidden Markov Model is very popular. We have applied the HMM to develop a model for maximizing the accuracy of Bangla POS tagger with error detection and self-correction. As a hybrid approach, we applied both supervised and unsupervised machine learning by using training data sets with some rules. We have analyzed the character level representation to identify the suffixes and the noun. From our training data, the system is taught some words and their tag. Moreover, the representation of the probabilistic relationship between two tags also increases the knowledge of the system for multi-layered analysis. Another essential knowledge that should be learned by the machine is the tag map. This is the representation of a sentence where it's POS tag replaces the words. Tags relation are used for prediction of unknown words and tag maps are used for matching the predicted POS tag with an existing tag map to validate the assigned tag. This system does not require a very large training data set. Having a small data around 14k unique token with around 3k sentences as training data, we achieved 95.6% accuracy in our experiment, and this can be increased up to 98% increasing the training dataset.

2 Related Works

Computational linguistic researchers are working on developing efficient methods and techniques to convert linguistic resource into digital form. Reducing linguistic barrier for human communication is also a result of these types of research. Some of the successful projects are on natural language processing including POS tagging already have done to enrich languages. Some algorithms like Hidden Markov Model (HMM) [1], Support Vector Machine (SVM) [2, 3], Maximum Entropy (ME) [4], Conditional Random Field (CRFs) [5, 6], and hybrid approach [7] are very popular and efficient for POS tagging. Some of Bengali linguistic researcher used those algorithms for POS tagging and they are literally successful. There has a good scope to improve this research to improve the accuracy of Bengali POS tagging.

There are different tag sets based on the purpose of POS tagging. The researchers are flexible to select a tag set based on their necessity. A few tag sets are available for the Bengali language that is proposed by some authors. Paul [8] proposed a tag set having 1070 tags by analyzing Bengali language base on morpho-syntactic view. This tag set is too big and very difficult to use for its dimension of POS tag as an example they showed 39 forms of a proper noun for masculine gender and total 103 tags for the proper noun. Altaf Mahmud et al. [9] reported a POS tag set for the Bengali language where they describe 53 tags based on Penn Treebank design.

Each language has some unique features that can use to identify the unknown tag. Like suffix and prefix is one of those features for many languages as well as the Bengali language. Compound and some are complex word structures are very common in Bengali language and suffixes are the part of those words. For splitting Compound Words the Morphological Analysis [10] is a very useful technique that can identify the suffix. Suffixes play an important role in POS tagging. Seddiqui et al. [11] developed the algorithm for eliminating multiple suffixes using conservative, aggressive, and rule-based approach. On the other hand, most of the proper noun has some unique characteristic. Islam et al. [12] worked on naming word identification for Bengali to UNL translation and they define some rules to find proper noun. These rules have been used in this research.

Researchers tried differently to solve POS tagging problems for the Bengali language to enrich digital information. Dasgupta published an article on the Bootstrapping [13] approach for unsupervised part-of-speech induction by using morphological and distributional information, that is applicable for the Bengali language. Another represents a method for word sense recognition [14] by using a mixture of statistical methods related to POS tagging problems. 86.84% accuracy has been achieved [15] by using SVM and that had increased by one of those authors and his team [16] by using CRF based finally he got 90.3% accuracy. Alam [17] represented a POS tagging system for the Bengali language based on neural network, that does not require any knowledge source for organizing linguistic information. They used LDC data set that is publicly available and get an accuracy of 86%. An experiment on unsupervised Bengali POS tagger for consulting the features works area on this topic has conducted by Ali [18]. In that experiment, they used corpus from CRBLP having 50000 tokens. By using the combination of ME, CRF and SVM classifiers Ekbal [19] created a POS tagger. Using voting techniques they developed that POS tagger base on contextual information with the orthographic word level features. That system was trained by 57,341 token having 27 tags and final gain from this is 92.35% accurate POS tag.

The highest accuracy (95%) have been achieved [20] by using both supervised and unsupervised process using 500 tagged sentence to train the system. That tags known words by using the Hidden Markov Model. Besides this, they applied that extract knowledge from other 50000 words to train their system for better accuracy. Their system deal with 40 tags with considering multiple tags for single words based on application. Another research article [21] shown 93.4% accuracy on Bengali POS tagging. In that article the researchers applied rules for suffix, verb data set and more than 45000 tagged words for learning. That system performed well for 8 different tags.

To maximising the accuracy, we analyze the previous works to point out the main concept and technique they followed. Initially, we have to create or select a tag set that we are going to use. Although there have different tag set developed by some Bangladeshi and Indian Bangla linguistic researchers. The availability of resource was prioritized for selecting the tag sets. Although tag set from CRBLP is more compatible for us but tagged data set are not available for training. Society for Natural Language Technology Research (SNLTR) offered a tagged data set has 32 tags. Additionally, we collected the linguistic features as like as noun identification rules and suffixes rules for our experiment. Finally, we drew a model that we are going to follow by analyzing recent and successful research on POS tagging in a different language. We have considered two other successful research where Dandapat et al. [20] and Hoque et al. [22] claim the maximum accuracy. We implemented those systems to analyze the accuracy of our system by comparing with those.

3 Significant Bangla Linguistic Features

Having a vast range of vocabulary the Bangla language becomes identical by its suffix and prefix that represents the state of words, Part-of-speech and the tense of the sentence. With this, some other features of Bangla language are playing a vital role in POS tagging and morphological analysis. Many of them are considered for our experiment.

3.1 Sentence Structure

Comparing other language like European languages the Bangla is relatively free word order[2] as an example:

I go home Í PRP VB NN
Which is equivalent to some Bangla sentence[2]

আমি (ami) বাড়ি (bari) যাই (zai) (I home go) Í PR NC VM
আমি (ami) যাই (zai) বাড়ি (bari) (I go home) Í PR VM NC
বাড়ি (bari) আমি (ami) যাই (zai) (Home I go) Í NC PR VM
According to Bangla sentence structure all of those three sentence are correct.

3.2 Word Suffix

Some small words can work individually or sometimes tied up with other words are considered as the suffix. Those words often found in compound or complex words. They change the meaning of the root words or represents the state of the words. Those suffixes are mostly placed after the root words. Suffix plays a very crucial role in POS tagging in Bangla language. In this experiment, we will detect the Noun, Adjective, Adverb by analyzing suffix.

3.3 Name Entity Recognition

For each language, there has some common feature for naming words. In Bangla language, a group of words is often used to start a naming group. Some of these types of words place before the main naming words and some place after the main naming words.

3.4 The Length of Words

The length of a word is also applicable to identify POS but not frequently. Some words may have contained multiple words having a different tag but altogether act like a single word. The length of sentence is used for this situation.

4 Machine Learning

For supervise learning we used e a dataset that collected from the 'Society For Natural Language Research'. The tag sets we used also came from this source. Our custom machine learning algorithm runs on these data and updates emission probabilities (word|tag) and transition probabilities (tag|previous tag) for Hidden Markov Model those we named as words lexicon and tag relation sequentially. Besides this, our algorithm creates a tag map used for error detection and correction after POS tagging. We used bi-gram language modeling for tag relation and uni-gram for tag map. For words lexicon, we consider all possible tags for a word which once used.

Figure 1 represents the tag relation or transition probabilities for HMM. By using the following two sentences we create this to illustrate the procedure. And the tag map of those sentences is represented by Fig. 2.

Sentence 1: অফিসে (office)/NC বেরুবার (berubar)/NV সময় (somoy)/NC স্নান (snan)/NC করবেন (korben)/VM কিন্তু (kintu)/CX

Sentence 2: গণমাধ্যমকর্মীদের (gonomadhomkormI)/NC ওই (oi)/DAB বাড়ির (barir)/NC ত্রিসীমানায় (trisimanay)/NC যেতে (zete)/VM দেওয়া (deoa)/NV হচ্ছে (hocCe)/VAUX না (na)/CX

Tag relation from Sentence 1:

a. NC → NV(1), NC(1), VM(1)
b. NV → NC(1)
c. VM → CX(1)

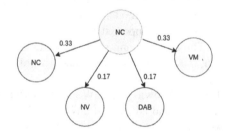

Tag relation from Sentence 2:

a. NC → DAB(1), NC(1), VM(1)
b. DAB → NC(1)
c. VM → NV(1)
d. NV → VAUX(1)

Fig. 1. Transition probabilities

Finalised tag relation from those sentence:

a. NC → NV(1), NC(2), VM(2),
   DAB(1)
b. NV → NC(1), VAUX(1)
c. VM → CX(1), NV(1)
d. DAB → NC(1)

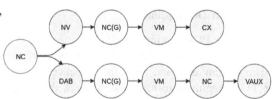

Fig. 2. Tag maps

Tag map for Sentence 1: NC > NV > NC > NC > VM > CX.
Tag map for Sentence 2: NC > DAB > NC > NC > VM > NC > VAUX.

For this supervise learning process we used 2993 different sentences form our dataset. There are 12815 unique words with 32 different tags are in our initial training data. Later, we fed more 1935 unique words to improve the accuracy and to compare with other POS tagging model.

5 Methodology

We have applied different methodologies for POS tagging in our PMM model. Although we used a pre-tagged data set for machine learning that is not enough for perfection. So a set of rules has been implemented for better accuracy. Besides this, we also implement Bangla sentence map to verify the accuracy of our tagger as well as for the correction of the wrong prediction. In this Section, we discusses these complex algorithm step by step to make it easy to understand.

5.1 PMM Model

Prediction Maximisation Model (PMM) represents a set of rules and techniques for Bangla POS tagging. Figure 3 represents the PMM model step by step. In this model, we used the knowledge, which extracted from the training data, with the application of some rules to identify POS tag. The tag map used for error detection and clarification at the end of this model. This works by comparing the tag pattern (tag map base on sentence) that appeared in training data.

The POS tagging starts with the tokenization or splitting sentence into words. At first, this system identifies known words comparing with the lexicon. If matches found then it will use the tag which already known. If not found, it applies Noun rules to detect unknown noun. We have suffix lists for different Parts of Speech (noun, adjective, and adverb). If any suffix form these lists match with the suffix of unknown word's, the word will assign the respective suffix's POS tag. If any words remain unknown then it will apply the Hidden Markov Model (HMM). HMM uses the probabilities and it is not perfect for all the time. We apply the tag map. We introduce this technique to minimize the possible errors of POS tagging.

5.2 System Description

Input text for POS tagging may have some noise or irrelevant data like symbols, extra space, repeating letter, etc. So at first our text analyzer will remove all unwanted elements from text and split the sentence into words which called Tokenisation. The POS tagging algorithm will analyze the words orderly so they will follow the sentence order.

In this hybrid POS tagging system starts with applying the POS tag for known words. In the machine learning step we prepared a lexicon that store all the known words with it's POS tag and frequency. Some words may have different POS tag based on its' application. So initially it considers all the tag is which will analyze at the end of this process.

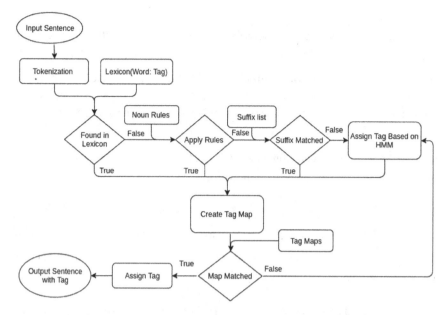

Fig. 3. Prediction Maximisation Model (PMM)

In Bangla culture, some words or group of words indicate religion, caste, or origin. These words appear at the beginning of a name or at the end. It is common to have two or more words in a Bangla paper noun. We have collected those words and the rules, those follow, to identify the naming words. By applying those rules it identifies unknown nouns. Besides this, some suffix also used at the end of some proper, common noun, adjective, and adverb. Our algorithm detects those suffix and assigns the POS tag. Those rules are identical representative Bangla words which are given below.

Rule 1: A group of words are often found at the beginning of a group of naming words like শ্রী(sree), সৈয়দ(soiyod), মোঃ (mO), মোসাম্মৎ (mOsammat), মোছাম্মৎ (mOchammat), আলী (alI), আঃ (a), আব্বদুল (abdul), আব্দুর (abdur), মিঃ (mi), মিস (mis), মিসেস (mises), বেগম (begom), বিবি (bibi), ডক্টর (doctor), ডঃ (d), শেখ (sekh), স্বামী (sbamI), মীর (mIr). These words are the noun and the next one is also a proper noun.

Rule 1A: Some words from the Rule 1 also can place at the end of a naming words group. আলী (alI), বেগম (begom), বর্বি(bibi) etc are among these types of words.

Rule 2: লস্কর (loskor), মর্রিজা (mirja), শাহ (sah), মুন্সী (munsI), দেওয়ান (deuan), গাজী (gaji), কাজী (kaji), খান (khan), চৌধুরী (choudhouI), সরকার (sorkar), গঙ্গোপাধ্যায় (ghongopodZi), মুখোপাধ্যায় (mukhpodZi), পাটোয়ারী (patoyari), পাল (pal), রায় (ray), তালুকদার (talukdar) etc are used as the surname among Bangla people. Bangla surname places at the end of the name. If one of those words found, then previous one is definitely a noun.

Rule 3: Some words are used to describe the objects like road, city, river etc. Some of this type of words are সরণী (sorNI), রোড (roD), স্ট্রিটি (strit) , লেন (len) , থানা (thana), স্কুল (school), বিদ্যালয় (bidZaloy), কলেজ (kolej), নদী (nodi) , লেক (lek) . Those place at the end of the noun as like as a suffix, but it is not a suffix. Sometime hyphen or single space between main words and these word appear and sometime it is not.

Rule 4: Some independent words like(দাদা (dada), বাবু (babu), সাহেব (saheb), কাকু (kaku)) may be added with some naming words.

Rule 5: জনক (jonok), মূলক (mUlok), যোগ্য (zOg), কেন্দ্রিক (kendrik), বাজি(baji), দানি(dani) , ব্যাপী (bZapI), দার (dar), দারি(dari), ইয়ানি(iyani), আনি(ani), বান (ban), মান (man) etc are considered as an adjective suffix. Those usually found at the end of words. So they are useful for identifying adjectives.

Rule 6: We found two adverb suffix (ভাবে (vabe), ভাবেই (vabei)), if those are at the end of any words that word is an adverb.

The suffix is a very common linguistic feature for almost all language. The rules suffix follow to attach with root words are varies from language to language. In Bangla language, this morphological feature is very heard to perfectly identify. The algorithm we used to assign POS tag base on suffix is given below.

Step 0: We have a suffix list and its POS tag.
Step 1: In this morphological analysis system will search if any suffix is in the word.
Step 2: Then it locates the position of the suffix in words if the suffix at the end of the word then executes next steps.
Step 3: Split word into two parts, a first part is stem and second part is a suffix. If the length of the first part is less than two or end with 'ঃ' (hoshonto) (0x09CD) then continue step 1.
Step 4: If the suffix is assigned to any POS tag, apply POS tag otherwise repeat step 1 unless the end of the suffix.

Some words may still remain unknown. The position of those words can be useful to identify the appropriate POS tag. With bi-gram languages modeling, we used Hidden Markov Model to detect those tags. It is not uncommon to assign a wrong tag, so we consider all possible tag for those words based on HMM. Finally, we use error detection and correction it finalises one POS tag comparing with the tag map.

$$\Pr(t_i|\ t_{i-1}) \approx f(t_i|\ t_{i-1}) = \frac{N(t_{i-1},\ t_i)}{t_{i-1}} \tag{1}$$

In equation no 1, ti indicates the unknown tag which next to one known tag ti − 1. This information comes from the second lexicon where tag vs tag probability has been stored. The transition probabilities are based on this equation.

There are four possible states for untagged words base on its' position and the number of untagged words sequentially. We predict POS tag for those in a different way and those have also individual scoring system based on transition probabilities. In the worst case situation, the score will be used.

State 1: When a single untagged word placed between two tagged words.

A word W has no predefined POS tag based on both emission probabilities and rule-based analysis. The previous word of the word W is W1 and the next one is W2 and both of those have known POS tag respectively T1 and T2.

Assume there are n possible tag after the tag T1 and m possible tag before the tag T2 so the possible tag for the word W is

$$T = (n \cap m) \tag{2}$$

For all possible tags has two transition probabilities with the previous one and the next one. Summation of those two transition probabilities will use to predict the probabilities for all possible tag and arrange those on descending order for map matching.

$$S(x) = t1(x) + t2(x) \tag{3}$$

x represents the tag from T, S(x) mentioned the probability score, t1(x) and t2(x) is for describing two transition probabilities.

State 2: There is only one tagged word either before or after the Untagged words.

In this situation, it will single transition probability using the next known word or previous one. t represent both t1 and t2 base on condition. These tags also kept as descending order for map matching, if there are multiple possible tags.

$$S(x) = t(x) \tag{4}$$

State 3: There have multiple unknown words sequentially having tagged words at the stating and ending this block.

In this case, there are two methods we followed basis on the location of the known word. If the known words take place before a group of unknown words, it creates the possible tag list for the first unknown word that can fit after the known words. All possible tags will keep in a list in descending order of transition probabilities. The tag having highest transition probabilities will tack into account initially and rest will be in waiting list. If our verification technique does not allow this POS tag the next tag will consider for that unknown word. The next unknown word will also follow the same way, where the previous tag considered as the known tag although the previous tag is confirmed for that particular word. When all words will have a POS tag, the further analysis will start, which called prediction clarification of map matching. If the sequence of the tags of the sentence (including assumed and confirmed POS tag) is found in our dictionary it confirmed this tag map and the assumed POS tag will confirm for those unknown words in this particular sentence. If matches not found, the POS tag for the unknown words will change form last words to first words and again apply the map matching technique. This process will continue until the match found. While we apply map matching, we count the transition probabilities and store this tag map with this total transition probabilities. If match not found for any combination of assumed POS tag, the tag map which has the maximum transition probabilities will confirm for the sentence.

For a sentence where the known word take place at the end of the unknown words group, same formula will apply. This situation the unknown words tagging starts from last to first.

$$S(x) = \sum_x (t(x)) + t1(x) + t2(x) + \ldots \ldots \tag{5}$$

S indicates the sum of transition probabilities and t indicates the individual transition probabilities.

State 4: There is only tagged word either before or after the Untagged words group.

If there is only tagged word either starting of this word group or the ending then the t(x) will represent either t1(x) or t2(x) and the equation will look like this.

$$S(x) = \sum_x (t(x)) + t(x) \tag{6}$$

When all words will have POS tag the total score S will calculate. And the tag map will create for comparing with the Known tag map to validate.

$$S = \sum_x (Sx) \tag{7}$$

6 System Implementation and Experiment

We implemented a system by using python programming language and natural language processing tools. To test our system, we collected data from some novels and Bangla newspaper. We also maintain a variety of data to get the actual accuracy.

Although our training data size is not such big. We have used only 12815 unique words with tags which are very small comparing the actual amount of Bangla words.

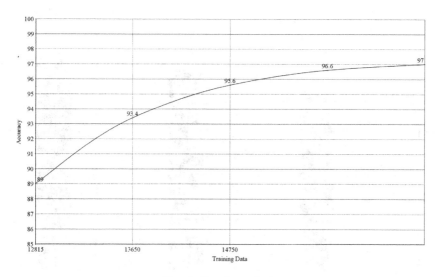

Fig. 4. Results analysis

Besides this, some Bangla words have multiple POS tag base on its position and application which make the words' base POS tagging difficult. Comparing circumstance our model did well in the first attempt we have gotten 2663 accurate POS tag from 2980 words which are around 89%. However, the accuracy has been increased by 6.6%, after feeding more 1935 new words. Although our final accuracy is 95.6% as test result but It can be projected up to 97% by adding new tagged words as training data by analyzing the line graph which shown in Fig. 4. The accuracy.

7 Discussion

Apparently, we have a better accuracy comparing other researches on Bangla POS tagging which have been published. To figure out the actual contribution and achievement we implemented two other systems by using two different models proposed by Dandapat [20] and Hoque [21]. Those two research showed the highest accuracy by using two different methods and both are used in our research with our unique contribution. We used the first author's name to identify their model for discussion purpose.

Sandipan's Model: Dictionary, transition probabilities (tag|previous tag) HMM.
Nesarul's Model: Dictionary, Stemmer, Verb Dataset, and Rules.
PMM: Dictionary, Stemmer, Verb Dataset, Rules, transition probabilities (tag|previous tag) HMM and the Tag map.

PMM Model represents the model we proposed. In our experiment, we used the same learning data for all of the above models and we tested that by using the same data but results are different. We analyze the result by changing the training data amount.

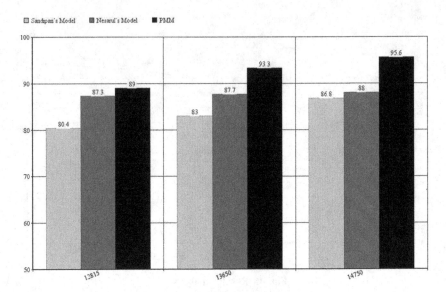

Fig. 5. Result comparison

In each experiment, we used more than 2.5k words. The experiment result shows in Fig. 5. Sandipan's Model and Nesarul's model having lower accuracy comparing their author's claims in this experiment. In our final experiment, PMM model achieves highest 95.6% accuracy whereas Sandipan's and Nesarul's model achieved respectively 86.8% and 88% accuracy on the same training and testing data. The reasons we found that impact on the accuracy of those two models is the amount of training data and the number of tags. However, the training data size less effect on Md. Nesarul Hoque's model comparing two others. Finally, for all three different training data, our PMM works better than others.

8   Conclusions

This paper presents a hybrid model for unknown Bangla word POS tagging, error detection and correction. A powerful tag mapping technology with some rules and some linguistic features as like as suffix have used for ensuring up to 97% accuracy for POS tagging where tested accuracy is 95.6%. This statistical rule base POS tagger can perform well when the sentence is valid and it does not the meter is it complex of a simple sentence. To establish this PMM as better than other models for Bangla POS tagging we compared two other models by using the same data which claim the highest accuracy among published research work and our model performed better.

References

1. Collins, M.: Discriminative training methods for hidden Markov models: theory and experiments with perceptron algorithms. In: Proceedings of the Conference on Empirical Methods in Natural Language Processing, pp. 1–8 (2002)
2. Giménez, J., Màrquez, L.: Fast and accurate part-of-speech tagging: the SVM approach revisited. Ranlp, pp. 153–163 (2003)
3. Tong, S., Koller, D.: Support vector machine active learning with applications to text classification. J. Mach. Learn. Res. **2**, 45–66 (2001)
4. Berger, A., Pietra, S.D., Pietra, V.D.: A maximum entropy approach to natural language processing. Comput. Linguist. **22**(1), 39–71 (1996)
5. Lafferty, J., McCallum, A., Pereira, F.C.N.: Conditional random fields: probabilistic models for segmenting and labeling sequence data. In: ICML 2001 Proceedings of the Eighteenth International Conference on Machine Learning, 8 June, pp. 282–289 (2001)
6. Tseng, H., Chang, P., Andrew, G., Jurafsky, D., Manning, C.: A conditional random field word segmenter for Sighan Bakeoff 2005. Word J. Int. Linguist. Assoc. (X), 168–171 (2005)
7. Altun, Y., Tsochantaridis, I., Hofmann, T.: Hidden Markov support vector machines. In: Proceedings of the Twentieth International Conference on Machine Learning – ICML 2003, pp. 3–10 (2003)
8. Paul, A.K.: A fine-grained tagset for Bangla language. SUST J. Sci. Technol. **21**(1), 1–8 (2014)
9. Junejo, S.A.: Research report on (37), pp. 0–33 (n.d.)
10. Dasgupta, S., Khan, N., Sarkar, A.I., Shahriar, D., Pavel, H., Khan, M.: Morphological analysis of inflecting compound words in Bangla (n.d.)
11. Seddiqui, H., Al, A., Maruf, M., Chy, A.N.: Recursive suffix stripping to augment Bangla stemmer (n.d.)
12. Islam, S., Das, J.K.: A new approach: automatically identify naming word from Bangla sentence for machine translation. Int. J. Adv. Sci. Technol. **74**, 49–62 (2015)
13. Dasgupta, S., Ng, V.: Unsupervised part-of-speech acquisition for resource-scarce languages, pp. 218–227 (2007)
14. Rapp, R.: A practical solution to the problem of automatic part-of-speech induction from text. In: 43rd Annual Meeting of the Association for Computational Linguistics, pp. 77–80 (2005)
15. Ekbal, A., Bandyopadhyay, S.: Part of speech tagging in Bangla using support vector machine. In: Proceedings - 11th International Conference on Information Technology, ICIT 2008, pp. 106–111 (2008)
16. Ekbal, A.: Bangla part of speech tagging using conditional random field. In: Proceedings of Seventh International Symposium on Natural Language Processing (SNLP2007), June 2017, pp. 131–136 (2007). Accessed
17. Alam, F., Chowdhury, S.A., Noori, S.R.H.: Bidirectional LSTMs - CRFs networks for bangla POS tagging. In: 19th International Conference on Computer and Information Technology, ICCIT 2016, pp. 377–382 (2017)
18. Ali, H.: An unsupervised parts-of-speech tagger for the Bangla language (n.d.)
19. Ekbal, A., Hasanuzzaman, M., Bandyopadhyay, S.: Voted approach for part of speech tagging in Bangla. In: PACLIC 23 - Proceedings of the 23rd Pacific Asia Conference on Language, Information and Computation, vol. 1, pp. 120–129 (2009)
20. Dandapat, S., Sarkar, S., Basu, A.: A hybrid model for part-of-speech tagging and its application to Bangla. In: International Conference on Computational Intelligence, December, pp. 169–172 (2004)

21. Hoque, Md.N., Seddiqui, M.H.: Bangla parts-of-speech tagging using Bangla stemmer and rule based analyzer. In: 2015 18th International Conference on Computer and Information Technology, ICCIT 2015, pp. 440–444 (2016)
22. Eddy, S.R.: Hidden Markov models. Curr. Opin. Struct. Biol. **6**(3), 361–365 (1996)

Advanced Machine Learning for Leukaemia Detection Based on White Blood Cell Segmentation

Ishfaq Majeed Sheikh$^{(\boxtimes)}$ ⓘ and Manzoor Ahmad Chachoo ⓘ

University of Kashmir, Srinagar 190006, India
ishfaqmajeed.scholar@kashmiruniversity.net,
c_manzoor@yahoo.com

Abstract. Cancer is a worldwide issue right now. It is generated from blood cells. In fact, the diseases is spread by a change in WBC cells that can cause an unspecified growth in the number of abnormal cells. These immature cells start disrupting the function of normal cells. Processing medical blood images in ML follows a stepwise procedure from pre-processing of blood components to subtype classification. Blood components discrimination, WBC cell identification, noise reduction and cell counting is done by choosing the methodology for segmentation. Its accurate implementation is difficult because of the varying parameters (Size, Eccentricity, Major Arc, Minor Arc and Parameter) of the different WBC types. Usually segmentation is done by extracting nucleus of the WBC cells. Our research is the first that have found some new problems (Division of WBC Nucleus into multiple parts, Distortion in the shape of WBC cell Nucleus, Size Variation and Noise in the form of pixel scratches) associated with the ML methods that remove cell cytoplasm with other blood components (RBC, Platelets and Background) during the nucleus extraction process of WBC cell. Parallelly we have found causes for the mentioned problems, to suggest generic methodology that will produce robust results. Experimental results have shown that methods extracting Nucleus of the WBC cell works only with a certain type of blood images. When we try to generalize the methodology for different types of blood cell images, we are getting the above-mentioned problems. The results had been calculated by the experiments done in MATLAB.

Keywords: ALL-IDB (Acute lymphoblastic Leukaemia – International Database) · ML (Machine-Learning) · DL (Deep-Learning) · WBC (White-Blood-Cell) · RBC (Red-Blood-Cell)

1   Introduction

White blood cells (WBC) are the main component of our immune system. They originate from bone marrow and protects our body from different types of diseases [1]. In human body we have different types of WBC (Lymphocyte, Monocyte, Neutrophil, Basophil and Eosinophil) cells and each subtype have different size and curvature as shown in Fig. 1 to perform normally human body needs specified number or range of

© Springer Nature Singapore Pte Ltd. 2020
C. Badica et al. (Eds.): ICICCT 2020, CCIS 1170, pp. 195–207, 2020.
https://doi.org/10.1007/978-981-15-9671-1_17

values from each subtype of WBC. It can damage huge to a human health if there is a slight deviation from over or under the normal limits in the value of cells. Research in medical field have shown different types of diseases in the form of bacterial infections, Allergy, AIDS, CLL, and ALL grow when the varying range of WBC types present in the hemoglobin met a particular threshold. Among the mentioned diseases associated with different sub-classes of WBC'S cancer has uncontrolled growth in the number of blast cells generated from bone marrow. Every year the deadly disease cast millions of lives through out globe and its number is increasing, by the year 2030 research is predicting that there will be an average rise of around 28.5 million cancer diagnosing cases. India had an estimated 1.6 million cancer cases in the year 2019. World Health Organization (WHO) had given report that 1 in 10 Indians will develop cancer during the lifetime.

ALL is a type of cancer generated from immature or blast lymphocytic WBC. It is one of the most common cancers found in India. Usually patients affected with Leukaemia show multiple symptoms and the specialist suggest a number of treatment methods. All the modes of treatment are effective based on the accurate identification of the disease by the expert specialist. However, these modes of treatment may lead to worse results, if the data collected from patient is not utilized in an efficient manner. Many harmful effects have been observed in some patients because of the lack of exact knowledge (over representation or under representation of molecular data) by expert specialist while identifying the specified disease. Thus, accurate treatment is possible only once we have perfect disease identification, based on the patient's genetic makeup. Many research areas in computer science (Machine Learning, Computer Vision and Image Processing) were explored in the medical field, not only to find automatic disease prediction but also for discovering treatment methods. Recent research has already made efforts in a number of machine learning models to automatize the disease diagnosing process. For detection of cardiovascular disease, the authors have utilized two phase model. At the first phase the authors have assessed the level of risk and the final stage generates advice to the clinicians based on the outcome of the initial phase [1]. For type 1 diabetes mellitus, the authors have used patient's genetic information to develop automatic personalized system [2]. For treatment of colon cancer many approaches were utilized on the DNA microarray and image datasets to suggest treatment methods for the health worker.

Blood test [3] related disease diagnosed by pathologists follows a manual nature which is subjected to multiple failures in terms of complexity of method, time consumption and possibility of error. Thus, disease identification and subtype classification has shifted towards the utilization automatic methods. Nowadays in the advent of technology research efforts are being currently implemented for the medical blood image analysis process, to find automatic computerized solutions, that will not only do the WBC cell identification and counting, but also will calculate accurate results within short time. For this, multiple fields in computer science like pattern based training of models, image characterization and structural based sub-class clustering have been put into effect to do medical blood image examination and diagnose their related diseases.

So many improvements have been found to identify a subtypes, count, class and basic features of WBC cells. Segmentation phase [1] at this step acts as a primary identifier of WBC cells. Because basic features of WBC cells like (Area, Perimeter,

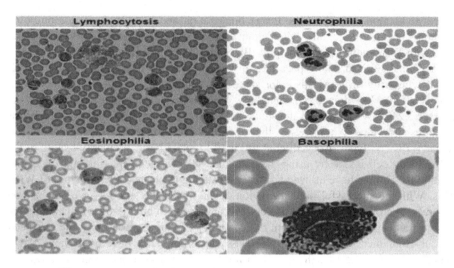

Fig. 1. Structure of different WBC cells present in the Blood sample.

Major Arc, Minor Arc, Eccentricity etc.) can be calculated accurately only once these features will be retained correctly during the nucleus extraction process by the segmentation method. By decoding existing methods and techniques our research has found that considering only WBC cell nucleus (which constitute subpart of the cell) reduces its size and curvature. So, this work is about investigating the methods and techniques (through various experiments) followed at segmentation phase for medical blood images analysis.

2 Literature Review

The existing literature demonstrates various methods which involve different image processing techniques of ML and DL, being currently implemented for the segmentation process of medical blood sample images. The approaches utilized by recent research for medical blood image analysis are elaborated as follows. As the nucleus of WBC blood cell image consists mainly of blue color. FilipNnovoselnik et al. [4] removes the rest of the blood image content as the image noise and deals only with blue part of the blood cell image in the segmentation phase. Figure 2 Shows blood image in which nucleus (blue part) of single WBC cell consists of many segments without connection between them other than the cytoplasm curvature. Processing such blood image at the segmentation phase produces increased count in the number of cells for divided nucleus. D. Umamaheswari et al. [5] deals with region of interest by conserving brightness according to the weight of blood components (RBC and WBC) present in the blood sample image. Basic operations like linear contrast stretching, image subtraction and erosion for filling holes of nucleus had been used to identify the actual scale and curvature of WBC cells present in the blood sample image and perform intra class segmentation. Vonn Vincent Quiñones et al. [6] conducted research in which the authors applied following operations like (conversion from RGB to HSV color space, Extraction of gray scale, Image binarization and blob analysis) the proposed method works normally, only with certain types of blood images and does not perform well with WBC cells like Eosinophil, Basophil and Monocytes. Bilkis Jamal Firdosi et al. [7] has utilized color space L*a*b which represents true human vision and K-Means clustering on it, as this color space may highlight also non-WBC blood components of the blood image. To retain only WBC components the authors have used the average size of WBC cells as threshold and remove all non-WBC components below the threshold value. Nevertheless, the algorithm does not perform efficiently on different WBC cell types. Rosyadi et al. [8] tried to retain basic circularity feature of the WBC blood cell image by using methods like Otsu for segmentation and for classification the authors have utilized K-Means clustering to cluster different types of WBC cells. With the successful implementation of the model the authors have obtained an accuracy of around 67% (which is very less and needs to be improved). Gautam et al. [9] has trained their algorithm from basic features like area, eccentricity and perimeter for sub-component discrimination sub-class clustering. They have used Naïve Bayes classifier for classification (here we can improve the performance of classification by using DL models for classification). Mostafa Mohamed et al. [10] proposed a method that works in two stages one dealing with blood image conversion techniques like (grayscale, threshold to remove non-WBC content, edge detection) and the other represents image texture at the segmentation phase. Putzu et al. [11] color model like CMYK were used by authors from which Y component were extracted to differentiate leukocyte from the other components present in the blood cell image. To identify different types of leukocytes area and size features of the WBC cells were used. Watershed method was adopted by the authors at the segmentation phase. Ongun et al. [12] deform contour around the WBC cells to identify subtypes of WBCs more accurately. To classify WBC cells basic features like shape and texture were used by the authors. Adollah et al. [13] have presented survey of various segmentation methods used for identification and counting WBC cells. Main motive was to do automatic blood cell classification. Nizar Ahmed et al. [3] has utilized Convolutional Neural Network to discriminating different types of WBC'S for sub structural classification. Even though the authors have generated an accuracy of around 81.74%, but the main problem associated with deep learning model is no evidence based proof and Black

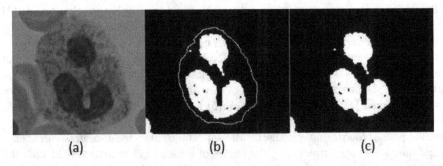

(a)   (b)   (c)

Fig. 2. Segmentation of blood sample image were nucleus of WBC comprises of multiple segments (a) Input blood image (b) Expected segmentation with one object (c) Segmentation by the Method with three objects. (Color figure online)

Box. Rudi Agius et al. [14] has discovered uncertainty estimates from the patient data by adapting Chronic Lymphocytic Leukaemia Treatment model. The modal was capable of generating a precision of 72% and a recall of 75%, here we need to improve the performance metric of a modal.

3 Methodology

Generally, blood sample image content is filled with heterogeneous clusters of WBC'S, RBC'S, Platelets and Background. To detect ALL from the inter cluster blood image data we need to discriminate multiple image components by either applying texture based characterizing of the blood data or the gray level segmentation approach which is based on the visual intensities of the image characteristics (Threshold, canny-edge-detection, sobel-edge-detection and filtering). Techniques that follow gray level intensity methodology require less complexity. Our framework has also utilized gray level intensity-based approach from true color blood image acquisition, blob detection, nucleus extraction and counting of WBC cells. Our main intuition was to analyze various impacts (In the form of Dividing single WBC Nucleus, Distortion in the shape of WBC, Size variation, Noise and Multiple counts for single WBC Nucleus) of ML, on the properties of cells while doing segmentation of blood sample image.

Related methods kept the goal of extraction of nucleus of WBC from the other blood components (RBC, Platelets Background and Cytoplasm). Our approach has utilized the same methodology, but while extracting nucleus we have found some new problems related to the retention of WBC subspace structure. No doubt we are generating an accuracy of around 90%, future research should look towards the retention of basic structure of leucocytes for accurate identification of disease. For that we are extending our work to a vision-based technique for retention of subspace structures. The proposed frame work is depicted as follows.

- Blood related image data is difficult to handle because of the complexity of different cell components, structural variation, their irregular patterns and place of occurrence. Dealing with such congested inter place patterns requires the conversion of vision data from RGB color format to the HSL and gray scale for robust discrimination. For discrimination of nucleus brighter part of the WBC with other blood components (RBC, Background and Cytoplasm) we have retained the luminance information while removing Hue and saturation information. Further blood image is processed to gray level color format. The RGB to HSL conversion is depicted in the Eq. (1 – 3). Its results are depicted in Fig. 3(b).

$$H \begin{Bmatrix} \emptyset, & B \leq G; \\ 2\pi - \emptyset, & B > G \end{Bmatrix}$$

$$\emptyset = arc \, \cos \left\{ \frac{[(R-G)+(R-B)]}{\left[(R-G)^2+(R-G)(G-B)\right]^{1/2}} \right\} \qquad (1)$$

$$L = \frac{1}{\sqrt{3}}(R + G + B) \tag{2}$$

$$S = 1 - \frac{3}{L}[\min(R, G, B)] \tag{3}$$

- To get clear discrimination we adjust the contrast of the converted blood image to the enhanced one by mapping the values of the input intensity image to a new intensity value. Since we got luminance values of L between 100 to 150. We have changed the values of L between 0 to 255 by Eq. (4) Results are depicted in Fig. 3(c).

$$g(x) = \left(\left(\frac{f - 100}{50}\right) * 255\right), \forall 100 \leq f \leq 150 \tag{4}$$

- To make optimal use of the colors available on the gray scale image we did Contrast Enhancement by transforming the values, so that the intensity of the pixels in the resulted blood image approximately matches a specified histogram. Transformation equations. (5), (6) were used and the results are depicted in Fig. 3(d)

$$\text{PDF} p_F(f), 0 \leq f \leq 1. \text{ Range of values for f.} \tag{5}$$

$$g(f) \int_0^f p_f(t)dt. \text{ Transformation function.} \tag{6}$$

$$g \text{ has uniform distribution in the range of } (0, 1)$$

- Except the WBC cell nucleus every blood component present in the blood image is brightened Fig. 3(e). Then we have highlighted WBC Nucleus by subtracting contrast enhanced values from the brightened blood components. Results are shown in Fig. 3(f). Then we have retained WBC cell nucleus with minimum distortion shown in Fig. 3(g).
- For extraction of cell nucleus, we have utilized shape-based threshold algorithm namely Otsu. It is a global optimal threshold algorithm used to find optimal values so that the within class (WBC cell Nucleus) variance is minimal and the between class (RBC, WBC, Cytoplasm and Background) variance is maximum. To get the optimal solution, we have minimized the within class variance. Results are calculated from the Eq. 7, 8 and 9.

$$\sigma^2 = \sum_0^n \frac{(xi - \mu)^2}{N} \tag{7}$$

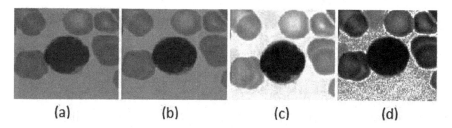

(a)   (b)   (c)   (d)

Fig. 3A. Model results on a test data were labels indicate (a) Input blood sample image. (b) Discriminated Blood components (c) Contrast adjusted blood image. (d) contrast enhancement by matching c to a specified histogram.

$$V_W = \sum_{i=0}^{n} \left(W_i * \sigma_i^2 \right)^1 \tag{8}$$

$$V_B = V_T - V_W \tag{9}$$

$$W_i = \frac{Number\ of\ pixels\ in\ class\ i}{Total\ number\ of\ pixels\ in\ an\ image}$$

x_i is the pixel value, μ is the mean and N is the number of pixels in the image

V_W = within class variance, V_B = Between class variance and V_T = total class variance

- To get approximate number of the WBC from different components of the image data (RBC, Platelets and Background) we have cleaned the processed blood image by removing the noise (small pixel scratches). Noise occurs mainly because of Nucleus extraction process. All the pixels having intensity value less than a particular threshold were removed from the processed blood image. Experimental results are calculated from Eq. (10) and the results are depicted in Fig. 3(h).

$$g(f) = \left\{ \begin{matrix} g_0 f \leq T \\ g_1 f > T \end{matrix} \right\}. \tag{10}$$

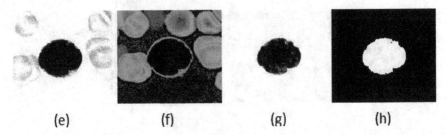

(e)   (f)   (g)   (h)

Fig. 3B. Model results on a test data during nucleus extraction process, were labels indicate (e) Brightened blood components (RBC, Platelets and Background). (f) Highlighted WBC nucleus with some noise. (g) Extracting WBC cell with minimum distortion to nucleus. (h) Output of shape-based thresholding algorithm were between class variance is high and within class variance is low.

4   Results and Discussions

We have found the ML methods that remove cytoplasm of WBC cell with other blood components (RBC, Cytoplasm, Platelets and the Background) did not retain the structure of WBC cell properly. There are different maturity levels of WBC. In the pre mature stage the nucleus of WBC cells consists of a single segment while at the mature stage it gets divided into a number of segments inside the curvature cytoplasm. Removing container cytoplasm at the maturity stage causes nucleus to get divided into a number of parts. The impacts are elaborated as follows.

Problem in Identifying WBC Types: According to [3] each type of WBC cell has different size, curvature and there is little difference in eccentricity between different WBC subtypes. By removing cytoplasm, the algorithm does not differentiate between Eosinophil, Lymphocyte, Monocyte, Neutrophil and Basophil cell types properly Fig. 4 depicts the results.

Problem in Counting the Number of WBC: While counting the no. of WBC present in the blood image we are getting wrong count because of the separated cell Nucleus segments in the blood image. We have tested number of WBC subtypes and the results showed that there was difference between manual counting and automatic counting. An example is shown in Fig. 6. Were the blood image containing only one WBC cell but the model showed three in number. Thus, we should look towards approaches that must retain the subspace geometric structure while extracting Nucleus of WBC.

Noise Reduction Problem: After processing above steps we are getting noise in the form of pixel scratches and there arises a need to remove the noise from the processed blood image. Noise reduction sets some threshold value below which we are removing the content of blood image. Experimental results are depicted in Fig. 5.

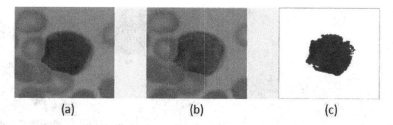

Fig. 4. (a) Input blood sample image of lymphocytic class. (b) Blood image with highlighted nucleus. (c) Output WBC cell with size variation in different class (Neutrophil class).

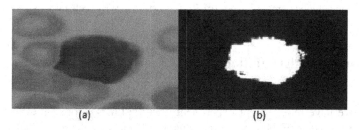

Fig. 5. (a) Input blood sample image of WBC cell without noise. (b) WBC cell with noise at the boundary of nucleus when operations are performed on it.

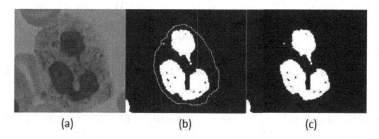

Fig. 6. (a) Blood image with one object single WBC cell (b) Expected count should be single object (c) Model counted three objects for single nucleus.

Distortion in the Shape and Size Variation of WBC Nucleus: The boundary edges of WBC cell nucleus also get affected if the intensity of the pixel scratches present in the blood image is too high, for that we have to set the large value of threshold to get rid of the noise. As shown in Fig. 7 we have increased the threshold value to get rid of noise but in turn we got distortion to the shape of WBC Nucleus.

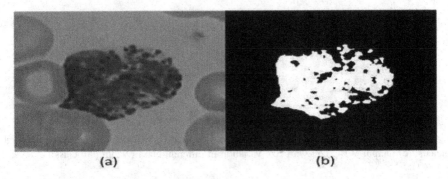

(a)   (b)

Fig. 7. (a) Input blood sample image. (b) Result distorted WBC cell nucleus after removing noise from the blood sample image.

5 Performance Evaluation

We have tested our model on a number of WBC sub classes, to check its consistency and reliability we have repeated our experiment multiple times. From the evaluation perspective performance of the model is presented in Table 1 on the individual WBC subclasses, in terms of performance measures depicted in Table 3 and Table 2 represent the aggregate performance of a model on all sub-classes, in terms of performance evaluation metrics. The proposed methodology was evaluated on 230 different blood sample images, of four different WBC types (Lymphocyte from ALL-IDB Dataset, Eosinophil, Monocyte and Neutrophil from Kaggle dataset). In comparison with existing methods the proposed model has adopted multiple appearance of single WBC cell to get robust discrimination of different components (sub-space structures) present in the blood image. The model has successfully extracted the nucleus of WBC types to analyze various characteristics (Perimeter, Eccentricity, Major Arc, Minor Arc, Circularity and Intensity) for detection of leukaemia. From the evaluation of blood image data on our model we have also calculated the approximate number of WBC'S. Since we have used advanced approaches and mathematical equations to retain the curvature of WBC, but we were unable to extract complete structure. For that we are extending our research to a vision based sub-space segmentation technique that decomposes an input blood sample image to a number of representation vectors, were each representation vector represents a particular sub structures (WBC, RBC, Background and Platelets) of blood sample image. We have used the following metrics for evaluation. TP Models correct approximation or the number of sub-components identified are same as the number is present in the considering class of blood image data, FP wrong approximation of the sub-component data by the model which can indicate a number of cells detected but the same number is not present in the considering class.TN sub-components that are not present in the considering sub-class are also not detected and FN (False Negative) Number of WBC not detected but are actually present in the blood image.

Table 1. Performance on individual WBC types.

WBC type	Accuracy	Sensitivity	Precision	Prevalence	Error rate
Lymphocyte	91.08	94.84	95.83	95.04	8.9
Monocyte	91.66	94.82	96.49	95	8.3
Eosinophil	91.22	98.11	92.85	98.24	8.77
Neutrophil	87.27	90.56	96	90.9	12.72

We have used blood images from multiple Data sources Kaggle (Eosinophil, Monocyte and Neutrophil) and Lymphocytes from ALL-Image Database Base (It has two sub-datasets, dataset (1) Non segmented dataset class of blood images from ALL-IDB it comprises of nearly 130 different images. To identify leukaemia fist we need to discriminate multiple sub-components and then subclass clustering and dataset (2) in which cells are already segmented hence require only classification). We have used random image samples from all of the mentioned datasets. Table 1 describes the performance of model on individual leucocytes.

Table 2. Performance evaluation metrics.

WBC	Total no. images	Automatic count	Manual count	TP	TN	FP	FN
Lymphocyte	80	96	97	92	Nil	4	5
Monocyte	50	55	58	55	Nil	2	3
Eosinophil	50	57	53	52	Nil	4	1
Neutrophil	50	50	54	48	Nil	2	5
Total	230	258	252	247	Nil	10	14

Table 3. Performance measures.

No.	Metrics used for evaluation		
	Parameter	Formula	Value
1	Accuracy: Degree of closeness of a calculated value to its actual value	$\frac{TP+TN}{Total\ data}$	91%
2	Sensitivity: Positive results identified by proposed methodology	$\frac{TP}{TP+FN}$	94.6%
3	Precision: Proportion of subjects that give positive results	$\frac{TP}{TP+FP}$	96%
4	Prevalence: Proportion of data that possesses specific characteristic	$\frac{TP+FP}{Total\ data}$	96.3%
5	Error Rate: Percentage of incorrect prediction in a proposed method	$\frac{FP+FN}{Total\ data}$	0.089%

6 Conclusion and Suggestions

Experimental results showed that, for the task of medical blood image analysis there is a need of generic robust methods that should identify all types of WBC present in the blood sample image. To get accurate results methods for WBC cell identification and counting must focus to retain the sub space structure (cell boundary) of all the WBC types, while removing other blood components (Cytoplasm, RBC, Platelets, and Background). Nucleus extraction process must encompass all the segments of divided WBC (If the WBC Nucleus comprises of more than one part) as one complete cell inside the curvature through erosion, to prevent multiple count for single WBC. When dealing with medical blood image analysis we have to remain careful about every components of the blood image under consideration. Because any mistake in the form of wrong WBC cell count, identifying class of WBC subtypes as different and identifying abnormal WBC cell as normal can lead a damage to the life of a patient directly.

References

1. What are blood tests? National Heart, Lung, and Blood Institute (NHLBI). Blood Dis. Br. Med. J. **2**(3907), 998–999 (1935). http://www.nhlbi.nih.gov/health/health-topics/topics/bdt/. Accessed 2 May 2012
2. Kouris, I., Tsirmpas, C., Mougiakakou, S.G., Iliopoulou, D., Koutsouris, D.: E-health towards ecumenical framework for personalized medicine via Decision Support System. In: Proceedings of the 2010 32 and Annual International Conference of the IEEE Engineering in Medicine and Biology Society, EMBC 2010, pp. 2881–2885 (2010)
3. Ahmed, N., Yigit, A., Isik, Z., Alpkocak, A.: Identification of Leukaemia subtypes from microscopic images using convolutional neural network. Diagnostics **9**, 104 (2019)
4. Novoselnik, F., Grbić, R., Galić, I., Dorić, F.: Automatic white blood cell detection and identification using convolutional neural network. In: 2018 International Conference on Smart Systems and Technologies (SST) (2018)
5. Umamaheswari D., Geetha, S.: Segmentation and classification of Acute Lymphoblastic Leukemia cells tooled with digital image processing and ML techniques. In: Proceedings of the Second International Conference on Intelligent Computing and Control Systems (ICICCS 2018) (2018)
6. Quiñones, V.V., Macawile, M.J., Ballado, Jr., A., Cruz, J.D., Caya, M.V.: White blood cell classification and counting using Convolutional Neural Network. In: 2018 3rd International Conference on Control and Robotics Engineering (2018)
7. Ferdosi, B.J., Nowshin, S., Sabera, F.A., Habiba.: White blood cell Detection and Segmentation from fluorescent images with an improved algorithm using k-means clustering and morphological operators. In: 2018 4th international conference on Electrical Engineering and Information & Communication Technology (2018)
8. Rosyadi, T., Arif, A., Nopriadi, B., Achmad, B., Faridah, F.: Classification of Leukocyte images using k-means clustering based on geometry features. In: 6th International Annual Engineering Seminar (InAES), Yogyakarta, Indonesia (2016)
9. Gautam, A., Bhadauria, H.: White blood nucleus extraction using k-mean clustering and mathematical morphing. In: 5th International Conference- Confluence the Next Generation Information Technology Summit (Confluence) (2014)

10. Mohamed, M., Far, B., Guaily, A.: An efficient technique for white blood cell nuclei automatic segmentation. In: 2012 IEEE International Conference on Systems, Man, and Cybernetics, 14–17 October 2012, COEX, Seoul, Korea (2012)
11. Caocci, G., Putzu, L., Ruberto, C.: Leucocyte classification for leukemia detection using image processing techniques. Artif. Intell. Med. **62**, 179–191 (2014)
12. Ongun, G., Halici, U., Leblebicioglu, K., Atala, V.: An automated differential blood count system. In: International Conference of the IEEE Engineering in Medicine and Biology Society, Istanbul (2001)
13. Adollah, R., Mashor, M.Y., Mohd Nasir, N.F., Rosli, H.: Blood cell image segmentation: a review. In: Abu Osman, N.A., Ibrahim, F., Wan Abas, W.A.B., Abdul Rahman, H.S., Ting, H.N. (eds.) IFMBE, vol. 21, pp. 141–144. Springer, Berlin (2008). https://doi.org/10.1007/978-3-540-69139-6_39
14. Agius, R., et al.: Machine learning can identify newly diagnosed patients with CLL at high risk of infection. Nat. Commun. **11**, 1–17 (2020). https://doi.org/10.1038/s41467-019-14225-8

Design and Development of a Smart Eye Wearable for the Visually Impaired

Tamoghna Sarkar$^{(\boxtimes)}$ (ID), Anith Patel (ID), and Sridhar P. Arjunan (ID)

Department of Electronics and Instrumentation Engineering,
SRM Institute of Science and Technology, Chennai 603203, TN, India
ts3044@srmist.edu.in

Abstract. Accessibility and mobility are two of the major domains with which the Visually Impaired are still struggling. In the 21st century, where everything is termed "SMART", we are yet to reach the acme where we can solve the above problems for the Visually Impaired. People today live in smart homes where everything in the house is connected to a common network. Voice assistants are becoming common in every house and besides, Wearable Technology has taken off in diverse directions which were once considered impossible. This has led to an overall paradigm shift in how humans interact with technology. In this paper, we propose a prototype of an assistive attachable that would help the Visually Impaired, for navigation and orientation. The device has the state-of-the-art implementation of Artificial Intelligence on the edge, Computer Vision and Neural Networks. It performs Real-time Image Cognition frame by frame using the camera on the device, undergoes pre-processing of the images on the edge device and performs classification on our trained region convolutional neural network (R-**CNN**). After Image Recognition is successfully performed, the key features of the surroundings are read out into the ears of the Visually Impaired person through audio feedback. It is expected to provide guided navigation, object information about places, products, and services that are present in the vicinity of the user. The results from the data collected and accuracy has been significantly improved with a recognition accuracy of 96%. The proposed smart wearable device has tested in real-time to prove its usefulness for the Visually Impaired.

Keywords: Visually Impaired · Object Detection · Edge Computing · Mask R-CNN · Artificial Intelligence · Localisation · 3D modelling · Audio feedback · Inter-IC-Sound Interface

1 Introduction

Vision is an important aspect of every human throughout a lifetime. According to the World Health Organization, an estimated 2 billion people globally are visually impaired or are totally blind. Out of the 2 billion people, the classifications are: -

On a global scale, the leading causes for vision impairment and blindness include stroke or transient ischemic attack, glaucoma, detachment of the retina, and so on. By the end of 2020, these numbers are predicted to increase exponentially and get doubled [1].

Therefore, visual impairment can be classified into two parts. Partial Vision Impairment: - wherein a person is blind up to a certain percentage and able to perceive

© Springer Nature Singapore Pte Ltd. 2020
C. Badica et al. (Eds.): ICICCT 2020, CCIS 1170, pp. 208–221, 2020.
https://doi.org/10.1007/978-981-15-9671-1_18

the surroundings in a complete hazy manner and Complete Vision Impairment or a state of complete Blindness.

People distressed with either of them are left in a state of torment and it's an arduous job for them in everyday life as they have to be dependent on others. Accessibility and mobility have always been the utmost conundrums for the visually impaired. Devices existing in the market today are maybe smart assistive devices but evidently not enough to help reduce the pain points of a commensurate, considerable amount of visually impaired people.

Three categories of devices are being developed in order to help Vision Substitution. Vision Substitution: An assistive electronic device with sensors and cutting-edge technology that functions by providing route guides and tries to embellish the mobility of visually impaired people. The three categories for classic electronic devices for the visually impaired are Electronic Travel Aid (ETA), Electronic Orientation Aid (EOA), Position Locator Devices (PLD). These are devices that use SONAR, LASER, sensors for accumulating information about the surroundings, help in pothole detection, gives their location coordinates. In easy words, they are assistive devices [2].

Haptic feedback is used in many of these devices as an alert system. However, these devices have several disadvantages out of which the major ones are stated. Either the devices are too costly which most people can never afford to buy or these devices have a robust size and are too bulky to be carried around. Hence, we cannot totally say that we have been successful in bringing a notable change in the life of the Visually Impaired people. Auditory and Tactile sensors can be deployed for totally blind people. The tactile sensors do not form any obstructions for the auditory sensors, which is the most important unit of perception in every human. Despite that, this approach is avoided due to varied drawbacks and instead of robust sensors we may approach using the synthetic voice or sound as a feedback signal into the ears. This paper is a result of such an approach and an initiative to implement state-of-the art research for the development of a non-intrusive smart attachable in the glasses for visually impaired people [3].

The rest of this paper is organized as follows. In Sect. 2, the Literature Survey is described. Section 3 introduces Materials and methods which includes 3D Modelling of the envisioned attachable, Hardware Platform, the Embedded Detection System on the edge device and the use of Mask R-CNN, followed by experimental results in Sect. 4 and finally conclusions are drawn.

2 Literature Review

Standing in the 21st century, the smart world is one of the most important motivations for most developing countries. We are imminent about amalgamating artificial and penetrative intelligence, Internet-of-Things into ubiquitous things including human behaviour, physical objects around us, social people. Exponentially, we are reaching that state where everything around is ubiquitously intelligent. Without ubiquitous computing, it is very difficult to maintain service support and ambient intelligence. We talk about smart agriculture, smart waste management systems, smart traffic management systems, smart homes, smart devices or wearables. An attempt to convert every ordinary device into a smart with ubiquitous computing is the paramount issue. The leading industries in the world, whether it is an Information Technology company to a core Industry based power plant, everybody tends towards intelligent devices and automation with a motivation to make human lives more comfortable, convenient and informed [4].

Amidst smart devices for daily usage of the normal people, there has also been intense, significant research and development going on for the specially challenged people. Specially challenged people are a part of our society and it's our utmost responsibility that when we think about smart devices all around us, why not implement state-of-the art technology and deploy devices that would make their living smart, comfortable, independent and allow them to have a more immersive experience of their surroundings. There is no usefulness of cutting-edge technology if there is no giving back to society. Some example of some significantly important projects are: -

"Development of a Smart Cane" - Wahab et al. [2] was the chief person behind this research wherein the cane was used mainly for object detection and providing accurate instructions for navigation. Similar, original work was presented by students from Central Michigan University. The system consists of ultrasonic sensors, a microcontroller, a buzzer, and a water detector. It utilizes ultrasonic sensors, fuzzy controllers to detect obstacles around the person and then transfer it to the individual's ears using haptic feedback in the form of vibrations or audio feedback. The cane is basically a sensor-equipped portable device for navigation purposes of the blind people. This device though being able to detect obstacles is not totally non-intrusive as it is robust. It's like the generic canes that the blind people, the only difference being that it has sensor circuitry which makes or smart. The power consumption versus time relationship of the device while the person is on the move is something that has to be looked into [5].

Another prototype, "Fusion of Artificial Vision" demonstrated how Bumblebee stereo cameras were installed on a helmet for video input [6]. The video stream on being captured was processed using the SpikNet recognition Algorithm to locate visual features. These visual features were mapped with GPS coordinates for allowing location services [7].

The Global Position System (GPS), modified Geographical Information Systems (GIS) and vision-based positioning have been implemented for fast localization.

This device comes into the category of Head Mounted Devices for blind but again has a major drawback as its robust structure because the entire setting is done on a helmet that is worn by the blind person. Also, the system has not been tested in actual navigation systems, therefore whether it will ameliorate the navigation system is still unknown.

LASER and SONAR systems have been used with micro-controllers to calculate distances between the object and the obstacle. In addition to that "Obstacle Avoidance using auto-adaptive and Thresholding techniques" using the Kinect depth camera has been tried. But Kinect displayed low accuracy in a short-range and this could directly affect the performance of the system. From the results, it was found out that the auto-adaptive threshold was not able to find distinctions between different objects. Computer Vision methodologies have also been implemented in many research projects for Object Detection, Pothole Detection and so on.

In this paper, we have tried to dive deep into the research aspects, and come up with a Smart Eye Wearable which is expected to solve the drawbacks in most of the mentioned research projects above.

3   Material and Methods

3.1   Three-Dimensional Modelling

Three-dimensional models are 3d-printed using PLA (Polylactic Acid) material for prototyping purposes. We modelled this wearable device for a more effective presentation of the final idea, whether the components we are using fits properly inside the model estimate how much a part or assembly will weigh and obtain its Centre of Gravity. It saves a lot of back and forth wastage in the process of designing final products. Lastly, an idea is always better conveyed when we can present the model to a reviewer physically, instead of trying to make him visualize a vague imaginary picture of the prototype.

The model shown in Fig. 1. is designed in Autodesk Fusion 360. The final project outcome is envisioned to look alike. Due to the already existing availability of assistive devices for the visually impaired that are bulky and are not easy to be carried around while commuting, we decided not to converge towards designing an entirely new device for them, for example, a smart cane, smart helmet with cameras. Instead, design a smart attachable or a wearable that could easily be attached to the spectacles without any extra-hassle. The sleek device attached to the left temple arm and hinges of the rendered design below is the attachable we designed. It is light and could be placed into a purse or pockets eradicating the purpose of carrying something along (Fig. 2).

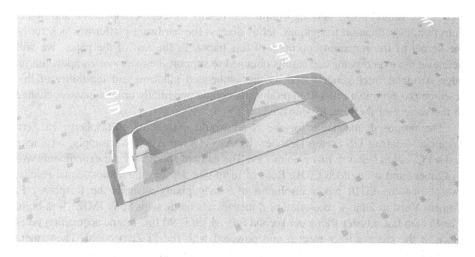

Fig. 1.   3D design of the proposed attachable

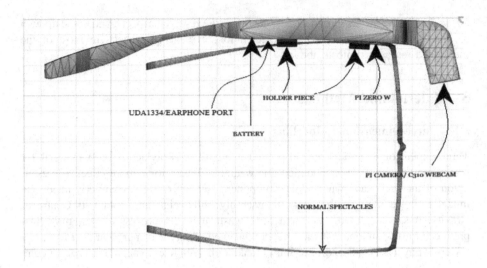

HOLDER PIECE

PI ZERO W

UDA1334/EARPHONE PORT

BATTERY

PI CAMERA/ C310 WEBCAM

NORMAL SPECTACLES

Fig. 2. Labelled representation of components in their envisioned sections

The attachable would consist of the edge device which is Raspberry Pi (R-pi) Zero W in our case. This R-pi would be present vertically along the walls of the device with which a camera would be interfaced. The camera is denoted by small concentric circles in front of the lens of the spectacles. The entire work in this paper is based on Artificial Intelligence on the edge.

3.2   Prototype Hardware Platform

Before we funnel down into algorithms and results for edge computation and object detection, classification techniques, let us discuss the hardware platform which forms the kernel of the remaining portions of this paper. In the rest of the paper, we will delineate the experiments and results obtained to support the theory of computation on edge Artificial Intelligence based on this embedded platform and feasibility of this research project into a full-scaled product that could potentially bring a massive change in the society of the visually impaired.

The proposed attachable for the blind would consist of a Raspberry Pi Zero Wireless, Adafruit I2S Stereo Decoder- UDA1334A, an AC Power supply, a camera, and a PC which behaves like a controller. The camera chosen for the experiments was Pi Camera and a Logitech C310. Both of them can demonstrate almost equal results, except that the C310 has a resolution of 5 megapixels whereas the Raspberry Pi Camera Version 2 has a resolution of 8 megapixels along with Sony IMX219 in-built. The Pi cam has a faster frame per second rate which is 90 fps. Frame acquisition takes place as the camera is connected and powered with the Pi Zero board. The camera captures frame by frame, everything in its vicinity and pre-processes those images on the development board itself. Computer Vision was implemented in the Pi for this purpose. Earlier projects with Computer Vision and object detection have been executed using the Pi 3 and all the higher models, but we chose the Pi Zero W version since we actually designed a 3D model of the attachable and wanted to keep the device lightweight and test the hardware and software in real-time situations. The Pi Zero W has features like 802.11n Wireless LAN and Bluetooth, along with its small size which makes it the best fit for a wearable or attachable development platform.

The board has a 1 gigahertz, single-core Central Processing Unit and therefore it is definite that training the model at the edge or the node is not possible. A GPU is being used for training the model about which we will be discussing in a later section. After Image Captioning is exhibited, the main motive is to provide audio feedback through earphones into the ears of the visually impaired person. To perform this task, the board should be having an I2S interface used for transferring digital audio data between chips. It is also known as the "Inter IC Sound Interface". The RAW/PCM data can be stored on the memory of the micro-controller if the sound file is small and then processed out to the I2S port. The I2S requires accurate clock pulses for working with data back and forth. Though Pi Zero W does not have a direct audio output port like the higher versions, it does support I2S audio output standards on the board. Reconsidering the use case and its size aspects we opted for Adafruit I2S Stereo Decoder-UDA1334A. It is a DAC that processes the data immediately and produces a clear, Analog, stereo line-level output. The pins required for the audio interface of the UDA1334 with the Pi are power pins, ground, DIN, BCLK, LRCLK. The circuit diagram demonstrates the connections clearly between the Pi, UDA1334, the rest of the circuit consists of a camera interfaced with the Pi Zero W and power supply that is connected to the Pi Zero. Finally, the audio output is derived from the audio port of the UDA1334 breakout DAC (Fig. 3 and Fig. 4).

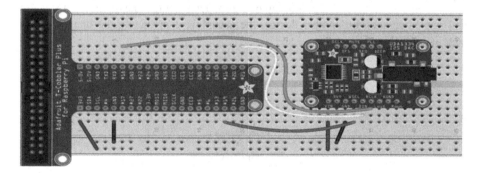

Fig. 3. Circuit connections between Pi Zero W and UDA1334A [https://learn.adafruit.com/adafruit-i2s-stereo-decoder-uda1334a/raspberry-pi-wiring]

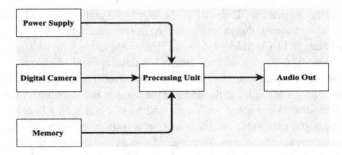

Fig. 4. Block diagram of the system

3.3 Embedded Computation

We are harnessing the power of the edge to perform the computation on a real-time basis. We run the above-mentioned model solely on the embedded computer, in this case, we are using Raspberry Pi, implementing the following flow for the implementation of the first we load the trained model i.e. is trained on the GPU(Graphics Processing Unit), in our case we have used Nvidia TITAN X GPU, usage of the system for training varies from one user to another user. After training, we transfer the weights on the edge device the minimum requirements for this model are 1 GHz of processing and above. Using the system having processing power lower than mentioned can result in the haphazard results. After loading the weights, extraction of the features from the image and conversion of those features into lists and then into string texts for feature to audio takes place, thus the entire process of converting an image to text and text to audio is enchanted here. Since, training of the model is being done on different systems and implementation on another device, the accuracy of predicting the images on the edge is high (Fig. 5).

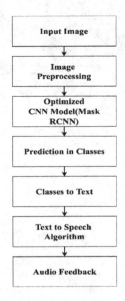

Fig. 5. Flow model of software computation

Object Detection Method. Computer Vision has gained traction in recent years, showing a variety of applications in self-driving cars, security analysis and many more. One of the major applications of this technology is object detection. Object detection aids in pose estimation, surveillance, vehicle detection and so on. Year after year the accuracy of the object detection methods has been increasing exponentially. Various methods and algorithms are tried and tested, like convolutional neural network (**CNN**), region convolutional neural network (R-**CNN**), You Only Look Once (**YOLO**), and so on. For this study, we are implementing the Mask-RCNN framework since it is giving a better overall accuracy in object detection and prediction. Mask RCNN is the extension to the Faster R-CNN method, it adds up the mask as a label to the image giving more accuracy for the output. For our application, we are deploying this model on edge for the real-time detection of the object.

Mask R-CNN. Mask R-CNN uses the two-stage procedure, where the first stage is the same as RCNN i.e. Region Proportion Network (RPN). The second stage is in parallel to predict the class and box, also gives an output in binary for Region of Interest (ROI). This is complementary to the most recent systems where the classification is based on mask predictions.

Formally the loss during the sampling is defined as:

$$L = L_{cls} + L_{box} + L_{mask}$$

The class loss (Lcls) and the bounding box loss (Lbox) are identical as they are defined in Faster-RCNN as well [8]. The mask has Km2 dimensional output for each RoI, which encodes K binary masks of resolution m × m, one for each of the K classes. Here per-pixel sigmoid has been applied and Lmask defined as the average binary cross-entropy loss. For an RoI associated with ground-truth class k, Lmask is only defined on the k-th mask (other mask outputs do not contribute to the loss). L function is optimised in Mask RCNN over other methods so that we can get better and fast outputs (Fig. 6 and Fig. 7).

The masks with a per-pixel sigmoid and a binary loss do not compete with the class and model loss. This is proved in this literature (Fig. 8).

The backbone architecture uses network-depth-features. We evaluate ResNet (Link the citation) and ResNeXt [link the citation] networks having a depth of either 50 or 101 layers. The original implementation of Faster R-CNN with ResNets extracted features from the final convolutional layer of the 4-th stage, which is called C4. Thus, a backbone with ResNet-101, for example, is denoted by ResNet-101-C4.

Implementation. Hyperparameters are set for the existing Faster R-CNN model [9]. We are building on the ImageNet data by adding our customised data set for increasing accuracy according to the environment around us.

Training. RoI is considered to be positive if the ground truth factor is minimum 0.5, thus the mask loss L_{mask} is defined only for positive RoIs. The image pixels are set as 600 × 800 for the training. This method is an image-centric method where the data is predicted based on the image data as the core. The mini-batch has 2 images/GPU and all the images have N sampled RoIs, a ratio of 3:1 of negatives to positives is

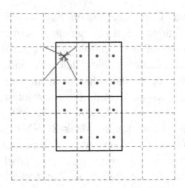

Fig. 6. RoIAlign: the dashed grid represents a feature map, the solid lines an RoI, and the dots the 4 sampling points in each bin. RoIAlign computes the value of each sampling point by bilinear interpolation from the nearby grid points on the feature map [https://arxiv.org/abs/1703.06870]

	backbone	AP	AP_{50}	AP_{75}	AP_S	AP_M	AP_L
MNC [10]	ResNet-101-C4	24.6	44.3	24.8	4.7	25.9	43.6
FCIS [26] +OHEM	ResNet-101-C5-dilated	29.2	49.5	-	7.1	31.3	50.0
FCIS+++ [26] +OHEM	ResNet-101-C5-dilated	33.6	54.5	-	-	-	-
Mask R-CNN	ResNet-101-C4	33.1	54.9	34.8	12.1	35.6	51.1
Mask R-CNN	ResNet-101-FPN	35.7	58.0	37.8	15.5	38.1	52.4
Mask R-CNN	ResNeXt-101-FPN	**37.1**	**60.0**	**39.4**	**16.9**	**39.9**	**53.5**

Fig. 7. Mask R-CNN outperforms the more complex FCIS +++, which includes multi-scale train/test, horizontal flip test, and OHEM. All entries are single-model results. This is the data from the COCO dataset where Mask-RCNN outperformed every other model

Fig. 8. Model running in action in real-time and returning the object with 1.00 probability

mentioned. The C4 backbone value of N is defined as 64 [10] and for FPN it is 512 [9]. Training takes place on a minibatch size of 16 for 160 k iterations, with a learning rate of 0.02, which is decreased by 10 at the 100 k iteration. Weight decay of 0.0001 and a momentum of 0.9 is used. With ResNeXt [11], 1 image per GPU computation is trained and the same number of iterations, with a starting learning rate of 0.01.

Inference. During testing the backbone number for C4 was 250 and for the FPN it was 1100, thus the box prediction branch is running in parallel that is followed by non-maximum suppression. These Mask branches can predict N masks per RoI which is enhancing the label data. The binarized threshold for this model is 0.5.

Application. We will be utilizing this technology to implement in the proposed model where we will be converting the image data into audio output. Further, in this literature, we discuss the overall implementation of the model in the proposed system.

Text to Speech. In our case, we are using GOOGLE Text-to-Speech. Text-to-speech is one of the most important portions of this research project. This is because it is the final stage of the output phase through which the visually impaired person gets to understand the surrounding.

Furthermore, when the live video is being captured and the frames are being processed, the key features of the frames are being extracted using a classification algorithm that is implemented on our deep neural network. The Mask RCNN is also used in numerous cases to solve segmentation problems in Machine Learning and Computer Vision. After the segmentation and classification of key objects in the frames are done, the classes return values as outputs after execution. Those values are converted into string representations.

These strings are demonstrated in a format, "'There is' + person + 'in the frame'". The rearmost step is the conversion of the string data types into speech files. Speech files can be stored as .mp3 or as .wav format and these sound files are then stored. Hence, the conversion from text to speech is completed after the object detection process. The entire process is automated by our python script. The stored audio file is then transmitted as audio feedback in the ears of the visually impaired person through earphones using I^2S (Inter-IC Sound) transmission.

4 Results and Discussions

This project has the implementation of multiple concepts channelling the flow as Image Recording, Object detection from the image, converting objects into the text which is called Image captioning, converting text to audio using Google Text-to-Speech. To make the above flow functional, we used Raspberry Pi Zero W to run the model and software aspects on the board. For image recognition, we get the output in a span of 1–10 s depending on the number of objects in the image. To achieve this performance,

Fig. 9. 3D Printed model along with spectacles

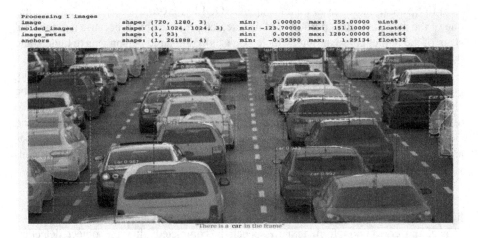

Fig. 10. Output 1 demonstrating image captioning and classification performed in Mask R-CNN

Fig. 11. Output 2 demonstrating image captioning and classification performed in Mask R-CNN

we threaded the neural network to a 1-D array. After the model detects the object from the shutter of images, it converts objects in the image to audio which is achieved in 0.5 s. Thus, making overall system performance ranging from 1.5–10.5 s for performing flow. Along with Raspberry Pi, we use cameras for input and earphones for output (Fig. 9, Fig. 10 and Fig. 11).

4.1 Localization

The above figures prove the feasibility of the Mask R-CNN model. Besides, Image Captioning is also being performed successfully where the details present in the image being fed are being converted into text through suitable localization and segmentation. Figure 12 displays the .Wav sound file being produced after objects in the images are detected, classification is performed and details of the image are converted to strings. Next, the string file is converted into an audio file that may be either be in .Mp3 or . Wav format. This audio file is then sent as an output audio feedback through Text-to-speech services. The output has to be collected from the audio port of the UDA1334A board through an earphone. Therefore, despite the presence of some existing similar research in this area, we claim that the Mask R-CNN model we are using here sees an overall increase in accuracy up to 96%. Reduced latency, computation of the whole process is observed, and power consumed to perform the experiments were very low due to the low power requirement of the Pi Zero board.

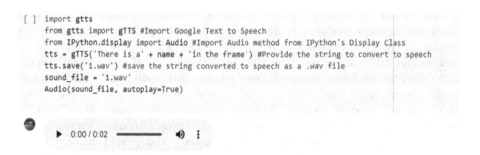

Fig. 12. Text-to-speech execution and generation of .Wav file

Figure 13 demonstrates the quantitative data for the experiment being performed on a real time basis, the model is trained on 5000 images. And we got the output as follows

Objects Labeled	Output accuracy	Time(Average)
Person	96-99%	1.2 sec
Traffic Signals	94-98%	1.443 sec
Car	93-98%	5 sec
Airplane	92-99%	3.5 sec
Motorcycle	95-99.3%	4.3 sec
Fruits	98-99%	1.2 sec
Rocks	84-96%	1.4 sec
Accessories	95-97%	1.7 sec
Bench	91-93%	2.4 sec
Others	75-92%	7 sec

Fig. 13. Quantitative analysis of testing data

From the above results we get the glance of the model working on the system. Where the accuracy produced is reasonable and if more data points for the given samples are used, it could result in increasing the accuracy. In the others section there were various other labels used like 'suitcase', 'frisbee', 'skis', 'snowboard', 'sports ball', 'kite', 'baseball bat', 'baseball glove', 'skateboard', 'surfboard', 'tennis racket', 'bottle', 'wine glass', 'cup', 'fork', 'knife', 'spoon', 'bowl', 'banana', 'apple', 'sandwich', 'orange', 'broccoli', 'carrot', 'hot dog', 'pizza', 'donut', 'cake', 'chair', 'couch', 'potted plant', 'bed', 'dining table', 'toilet', 'tv', 'laptop', 'mouse', 'remote', 'keyboard', 'cell phone', 'microwave', 'oven', 'toaster', 'sink', 'refrigerator', 'book', 'clock', 'vase', 'scissors', 'teddy bear', 'hair drier', 'toothbrush'. etc. more details of the labels can be found in the code.

5 Conclusion

As mentioned earlier in the result, we are able to run the model on a real-time basis on the edge, where we are getting output in the range of 1.2 to 10.5 s, depending on the number of objects in the frame. The model that is implemented, is highly accurate and results to an output accuracy on testing images at around 96%. Apart from Mask-RCNN other techniques were implemented as well where the accuracy and computation time differed. We selected Mask-RCNN over others for the ease of accuracy and time. This device is in the testing phase where the proof of concept works with good efficiency. In this project, we prototyped a device for visually impaired that could have the potential to help them in mobility and orientation related problems. We implemented embedded Artificial Intelligence and Edge Computing to make this device. This device as of now performs conversion of image to text and gives audio output, for further development we plan to integrate OCR (Optical Character Recognition), making an RTOS that is customised for performing activities especially for the blind, add navigation using haptics for ease in mobility. Thus, the overall technology stack of Embedded AI, CNN, and real time systems can help cater visually impaired to enhance their mobility experience.

All the code to this technology is open-sourced and can be found at (www.github.com/anithp/smartglass).

References

1. Tian, L., Tian, Y., Yi, C.: Detecting good quality frames in videos captured by a wearable camera for blind navigation. In: 2013 IEEE International Conference on Bioinformatics and Biomedicine, Shanghai, pp. 334–337 (2013)
2. Elmannai, W., Elleithy, K.: Sensor-based assistive devices for visually-impaired people: current status, challenges, and future directions. https://www.ncbi.nlm.nih.gov/pubmed/?term=Elleithy%20K%5BAuthor%5D&cauthor=true&cauthor_uid=28287451
3. Bai, J., Lian, S., Liu, Z., Wang, K., Liu, D.: Smart guiding glasses for visually impaired people in indoor environment. https://arxiv.org/ftp/arxiv/papers/1709/1709.09359.pdf
4. Ma, J., Yang, L.T., Apduhan, B.O., Huang, R., Barolli, L., Takizawa, M.: Towards a smart world and ubiquitous intelligence: a walkthrough from smart things to smart hyperspaces and UbicKids. Int. J. Pervasive Comput. Commun. 1(1), 53–68 (2005)
5. Wahab A., et al.: Smart cane: assistive cane for visually-impaired people. Int. J. Comput. Sci. 8, 4 (2011)
6. Brilhault, A., Kammoun, S., Gutierrez, O., Truillet, P., Jouffrais, C.: Fusion of artificial vision and GPS to improve blind pedestrian positioning. In: Proceedings of the 4th IFIP International Conference on New Technologies, Mobility and Security (NTMS); Paris, France, 7–10 February 2011, pp. 1–5 (2011)
7. Loomis, J.M., Golledge, R.G., Klatzky, R.L., Speigle, J.M., Tietz, J.: Personal guidance system for the visually impaired. In: Proceedings of the First Annual ACM Conference on Assistive Technologies; Marina Del Rey, CA, USA. 31 October–1 November 1994 (1994)
8. He, K., Zhang, X., Ren, S., Sun, J.: Spatial pyramid pooling in deep convolutional networks for visual recognition. In: Fleet, D., Pajdla, T., Schiele, B., Tuytelaars, T. (eds.) ECCV 2014. LNCS, vol. 8691, pp. 346–361. Springer, Cham (2014). https://doi.org/10.1007/978-3-319-10578-9_23
9. Lin, T.-Y., Dollar, P., Girshick, R., He, K., Hariharan, B., Belongie, S.: Feature pyramid networks for object detection. In: CVPR 2017 (2017)
10. Ren, S., He, K., Girshick, R., Sun, J.: Faster R-CNN: towards real-time object detection with region proposal networks. In: NIPS (2015)
11. He, K., Zhang, X., Ren, S., Sun, J.: Deep residual learning for image recognition. In: CVPR (2016)

GANTOON: Creative Cartoons Using Generative Adversarial Network

Amit Gawade[1]([✉]) [iD], Rohit Pandharkar[1], and Subodh Deolekar[1,2] [iD]

[1] REDX WeSchool, Welingkar Institute of Management Development and
Research, Mumbai, India
{amit.gawade, subodh.deolekar}@welingkarmail.org,
rohitp@media.mit.edu
[2] Research and Business Analytics, Welingkar Institute of Management
Development and Research, Mumbai, India

Abstract. We propose a methodology for generating creative cartoon art. The system generates cartoon by looking at various existing images of cartoon characters and learning about their posture/animation style. The proposed system is creative in nature as it generates unique cartoon art by deviating from the existing styles learned by the algorithm. We build over Generative Adversarial Networks (GAN) with unsupervised learning, which have shown the ability to learn to generate novel cartoons by simulating a given distribution. The proposed model exhibits an ability to generate cartoons which are creative and novel in design. We have conducted experiments by considering around 12K Tom's cartoon images for training purposes. The results show that the increase in number of epochs resulted in better classification accuracy. The proposed system generates the character Tom's cartoons which are novel and we have validated the same by applying Colton's creativity benchmark.

Keywords: Creative art · Artificial creativity · GAN · DCGAN · Artificial Intelligence · Cartoon

1 Introduction

Artificial creativity is the study of developing algorithms which depict behavior of human level creativity. These creative algorithms can be used for creative stuffs, such as inventing mathematical models, generating rhyming, formation of music and paintings. Paintings play an important role to represent emotions. The aesthetic response to the art work is viewed as basic stimulus response by humans. Cartoons are one of such interesting form which we encounter in our day-to-day life [1].

In addition to art attentiveness, their use cases range from publication in printing technology, creating stories for kid's education or from simulation of any fact to movie creation. Likewise, cartoons can be used in various verticals such as marketing, retail, healthcare etc. Similar to other forms of creativity, various famous cartoon images were inspired based on real world situations to depict authentic scenarios in visual form so as to impact spatial learners.

© Springer Nature Singapore Pte Ltd. 2020
C. Badica et al. (Eds.): ICICCT 2020, CCIS 1170, pp. 222–230, 2020.
https://doi.org/10.1007/978-981-15-9671-1_19

Artificial Intelligence (AI) is being used to create different types of art. Various companies are trying to create album-arts. Magenta by Google used to generate new music using AI [2]. GAN's are having wide range of applications such as in-painting [3], image style transfer [4], text to image creation [5].

AI does not experience art, emotions or creativity rather, it learns from patterns of previously known human generated art. Assuming that AI can generate non-existing images from given data, we can say that it has the potential to be an equally important agent of change in the creative world. In this paper we proposed unsupervised learning based method by using convolutional Neural Network (CNN) with GAN to generate cartoon art. The goal is to generate cartoon art that is creative in nature and with unique posture which haven't existed before.

2 Related Work

The proposed approach is motivated from the experiment conducted by Liu [6]. He argued that using GAN he tried to create chair design using image synthesis module and super resolution GAN and came up with a model that creates different designs of chairs from which humans need to select the best-fit.

GAN has showcased good results in image generation and style transfer [3, 4]. Goodfellow [7] explained the architecture of GAN, in this, there is the Generator and the Discriminator, the Generator generates fake samples of data and tries to fools Discriminator. The Discriminator, on another side, tries to differentiate among the actual and fake samples [8]. For the Generator and the Discriminator, the model uses multi-layer perceptron for training. The entire system is trained using back propagation. While conducting their experiment they used MNINST dataset. The Generator uses a combination of Rectifier Linear Activations [9, 10] and sigmoid activations, while the Discriminator network uses maxout activations [11]. To enhance the classification accuracy dropout [12] was applied while training the Discriminator network. With adversarial loss [7] that guides the training process, the Generator can learn the distribution of the training set and then will try to create same distribution from random noise.

Radford explained about Deep Convolutional GANs (DCGAN) [13], like core GANs, Discriminator of DCGAN attempt to categorize images as real or fake, and a generator that tries to generate samples that will be fed to the discriminator trying to mislead it. In this paper he proposed a stable set of architecture with good representation of images. They proposed and evaluated a set of conditions on the architecture and uses convolutional neural network in GAN that makes the architecture stable to train in the most suitable conditions. They named this class of architecture as DCGAN. Use of the deep convolutional network in Discriminators for image classification shows competitive performance with other unsupervised algorithms. The author visualized the filters learnt by GANs and realized that specific filters can be used to draw images.

Ha David in his paper [14] constructed Vector drawing dataset QuickDraw. In this 70 thousand training sample, 2500 validation and 2500 test samples were used. Sketch-RNN has been used to generate sketches which can memorize previous states of drawing. They used Variational Autoencoder [15] to train their model. In their system, the loss function is the sum of two terms, the Reconstruction Loss, and the Kullback-Leibler Divergence Loss [16]. After defining these losses system can generate rough sketches of objects specified in dataset.

Yang Chen in his paper [17] explained the transformation of real world photos to cartoons. For this he proposed CartoonGAN, a GAN framework for cartoon stylization. Two novel losses have been proposed to generate cartoons, the first one is a semantic content loss for high level feature map and the second is an edge-promoting adversarial loss for preserving clear edges.

The existing work has made it possible to use GAN with deep convolutional neural networks to achieve good quality results by generating art forms like cartoons.

3   Methodology

3.1   Architecture of GAN

A GAN structure comprises of two parts, as shown in Fig. 1, the first is the Generator which is trained to generate random images from noise as an output which fools the Discriminator. The Second is the Discriminator D, which identifies whether the image is from the real dataset or from generated one. At last it will predict and display generated images which look like already existing art from the dataset but are the generated ones.

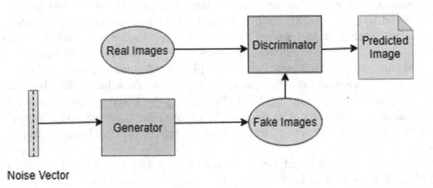

Fig. 1.   General architecture of GAN

Based on the above architecture we proposed a methodology, Fig. 2, which is based on an unsupervised learning approach which generates creative cartoon art which are different from existing art and are novel in nature. The cartoon character Tom from the Warner Bro's cartoon show 'Tom and Jerry' has been used as a prototype for this purpose.

We designed the Generator and the Discriminator networks to outfit the cartoon art generation. In GAN structure, a discriminator function D is trained for reaching generator G.

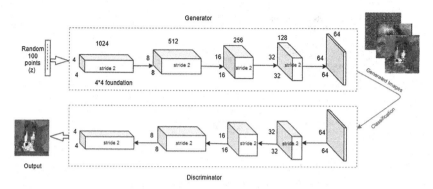

Fig. 2. Proposed methodology

Discriminator. Discriminator has been trained with an actual image dataset and fake data is generated from the Generator. It takes an image as input, passes it through convolutional neural network and produces an output of a possibility telling whether the picture is actual or fake. The Discriminator in a GAN is simply a classifier. Here we have used CNN architecture for the classification purpose.

Generator. The Generator is responsible for creating new images, but these are fake one, likely small photographs of objects. It takes random noise from latent space and tries to generate an image that will try to mislead the Discriminator. By using the Generator network, the Discriminator is used to evaluate whether the input picture is a real cartoon picture or not. The latent space is randomly defined as vector space. Latent space is just random numbers which does not have meaning. From this space we can select 100 random numbers to create fake image.

Training. Training has been divided into two parts: In the first part, by keeping the Generator idle the Discriminator is trained. The Discriminator is trained on real images for 100 epochs, and observed if it predicts it as the correct image. The Discriminator is also trained on the fake generated data from the Generator and observed if it can appropriately predict them as false image which is not like real one.

In the Second part, by making the Discriminator idle the Generator is trained. The Discriminator is trained by the fake data generated by the Generator, we can get its predictions and utilize it for training the Generator and get better from the previous situation to try and mislead the Discriminator. The above process is continual for a small number of epochs and then by hand checked if the fake data appears candid or not. If it appears satisfactory, then the training is stopped up, otherwise, it's allowed to continue for a few more epochs. Following Fig. 3 shows the Generative modeling process where generative model plays an important role in image transformation.

Loss Functions. GANs regenerate a likelihood distribution of a given image. So there should be a loss functions which gives the similarity and dissimilarity between the distribution of the images created by the GAN and the distribution of the actual images. For the Generator and the Discriminator training, loss function is been used. These two

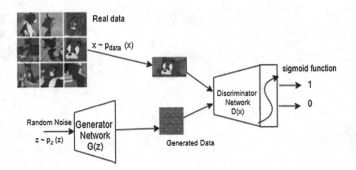

Fig. 3. The generative modeling process

loss functions work mutually to shows a distance measure between the probability distributions. We have used minimax loss function [18] explained below.

Minimax Loss. The paper that introduces GANs explained, the generator and the discriminator will lead to minimize and maximize the following function respectively [7, 18]:

$$min_g max_d \left[E_x \sim p_{data} log D_d(x) + E_z \sim p(z) \log\left(1 - D_d\big(G_g(z)\big)\right) \right] \qquad (1)$$

Here from Eq. 1, $log D_d(x)$ is the Discriminator output for real images and $\log\left(1 - D_d\big(G_g(z)\big)\right)$ is the Discriminator output for the Generator's fake data.

The Discriminator d wants to maximize function such that D(x) is near to 1 and The Generator g wants to minimize function so that D(G(z)) is near to 1. It means the Discriminator is fooled into thinking generated G(z) is real. D(x) is the Discriminator's approximation that shows the probability that actual data x is real. E_x is the expected value over entire real data. G(z) is the Generator's output after given noise z. D(G(z)) is the discriminator's approximation of the probability that a false images is real. E_z is the estimated value for all random inputs. Cross-entropy between the actual and generated distributions derives this formula. This method can be used to implement loss function for both the Generator and the Discriminator [19].

4   Experimental Setup and Results

Python has been used for the implementation of the proposed methodology with Keras framework while TensorFlow is used in background. Around 12K cartoon images of Tom were scraped from online videos to train discriminator model. They are normalized and down scaled to 64 * 64 resolutions. We have used the image Generator of Keras to load images from the computer. We have implemented deep convolutional layers in the Generator and the Discriminator, since most of the GAN based on the neural network architecture give better results.

Instead of using pooling layers we have used stride convolutions in the Discriminator and in the Generator. Batch normalization has been used in both networks. There is no need of normalizing the last and first layer of the Generator and the Discriminator respectively, because of this the model can learn the accurate data distribution and mean.

While designing generator we have used RELU as activation function for all layers except output layer and for output layer tanh activation has been used. LeakyReLU activation has been used in the Discriminator for all layers. We have used Adam optimizer with momentum 0.5.

In every iteration, a batch made up of 64 images are obtained from the original dataset and normalized between −1 and 1. We create one noise vector for each image with size(1, 1, 100) which leads to generate the new image.

The Generator uses noise vectors to generate the fake images. Figure 4 shows the summary of the model with all the learning parameters in every layer.

Layer (type)	Output Shape	Param #
conv2d_5 (Conv2D)	(None, 32, 32, 64)	4864
leaky_re_lu_5 (LeakyReLU)	(None, 32, 32, 64)	0
conv2d_6 (Conv2D)	(None, 16, 16, 128)	204928
batch_normalization_8 (Batch	(None, 16, 16, 128)	512
leaky_re_lu_6 (LeakyReLU)	(None, 16, 16, 128)	0
conv2d_7 (Conv2D)	(None, 8, 8, 256)	819456
batch_normalization_9 (Batch	(None, 8, 8, 256)	1024
leaky_re_lu_7 (LeakyReLU)	(None, 8, 8, 256)	0
conv2d_8 (Conv2D)	(None, 4, 4, 512)	3277312
batch_normalization_10 (Batc	(None, 4, 4, 512)	2048
leaky_re_lu_8 (LeakyReLU)	(None, 4, 4, 512)	0
flatten_2 (Flatten)	(None, 8192)	0
dense_3 (Dense)	(None, 1)	8193
activation_7 (Activation)	(None, 1)	0

Total params: 4,318,337
Trainable params: 4,316,545
Non-trainable params: 1,792

Layer (type)	Output Shape	Param #
dense_4 (Dense)	(None, 1, 1, 8192)	827392
reshape_2 (Reshape)	(None, 4, 4, 512)	0
batch_normalization_11 (Batc	(None, 4, 4, 512)	2048
activation_8 (Activation)	(None, 4, 4, 512)	0
conv2d_transpose_5 (Conv2DTr	(None, 8, 8, 256)	3277056
batch_normalization_12 (Batc	(None, 8, 8, 256)	1024
activation_9 (Activation)	(None, 8, 8, 256)	0
conv2d_transpose_6 (Conv2DTr	(None, 16, 16, 128)	819328
batch_normalization_13 (Batc	(None, 16, 16, 128)	512
activation_10 (Activation)	(None, 16, 16, 128)	0
conv2d_transpose_7 (Conv2DTr	(None, 32, 32, 64)	204864
batch_normalization_14 (Batc	(None, 32, 32, 64)	256
activation_11 (Activation)	(None, 32, 32, 64)	0
conv2d_transpose_8 (Conv2DTr	(None, 64, 64, 3)	4803
activation_12 (Activation)	(None, 64, 64, 3)	0

Total params: 5,137,283
Trainable params: 5,135,363
Non-trainable params: 1,920

(a)   (b)

Fig. 4. Summary of models (a) Discriminator and (b) Generator

We trained the Discriminator with the real images and fake images separately. We then generated noise vectors which were double the size of the batch, that were further used to train the Generator.

Reverse labels has been assigned to the generated images with noise. The discriminator is being misled here and then is trained with the generated images. In every epoch, 3 batches of generated images are saved as .png files and after every 5 epochs, the models are saved in .hdf5 file format. The loss plot is saved at the end of each epoch.

4.1 Generator vs Discriminator Loss During the Training

Figure 5 shows the loss evolution of the Generator and the Discriminator during training, red lines indicate generator loss and black indicates discriminator loss. As batch iterations increase, loss in the Generator and the Discriminator decrease. At last, the distribution of generated images and the images coming from the real dataset are the same. As shown in Fig. 5(a), when iteration is on 120, we can see that the loss in both the Generator and the Discriminator is high as the Generator is creating images from random noise. Figure 5(d) showcases that the loss is decreased as the Generator has learned the Distribution of real images and has successfully fooled the Discriminator. The Generator is able to create a new image which looks like the real image which was taken from the real image dataset.

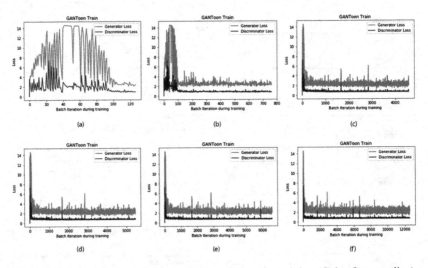

Fig. 5. Generator loss vs discriminator loss during the training (Color figure online)

4.2 Training the Model

Here for training we have used 12k Tom images and for testing we are giving 100 random points from latent space which will generate new image which will look like Tom but it is generated one. The trained generator model was used to generate images from random noise, at epoch 1 by trying different combinations. The proposed model generated impressive images of Tom at epoch 100, few of them have been shown in Fig. 6. Our model generated the following images of Tom using the real images from the show 'Tom and Jerry' as exhibited in Fig. 3.

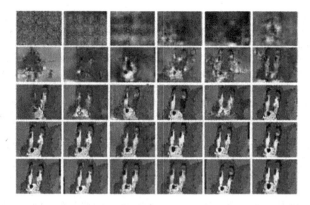

Fig. 6. Sample images generated from a trained generator model.

4.3 Colton's Creative Tripod

The three legs of the Colton's creative tripod [19] represents the behavior's namely skill, appreciation and imagination, and only if all of these are present in the proposed system then it supports the perception of creativity.

We demonstrate above three behaviors in our proposed system as follows:

- *Skill:* The proposed system can generate images which are different from each other but belong to same cartoon distribution.
- *Appreciation:* The system can recognize the good quality cartoon images using GAN which makes the system autonomous in the creative behavior.
- *Imagination:* The proposed system takes a generative approach to create different cartoon images and can generate cartoon postures style which are not seen before.

5 Conclusion

We proposed a system for generating creative cartoons with novel postures. We presented a realization of this system based on a generative adversarial network. The system is trained using a large collection of Tom cartoon images were scraped from online videos to train discriminator model. The proposed system gives evidence that adversarial networks learn good representations of images for unsupervised learning. By improving hyper-parameters and loss function, adding few convolutional layers we can create more accurate postures of Tom cartoons. The system was evaluated based on Colton's creativity benchmark.

References

1. Li, X., Zhang, W., Shen, T., Mei, T.: Everyone is a cartoonist: selfie cartoonization with attentive adversarial networks (2019)
2. Magenta. magenta.tensorflow.org/

3. Gatys, L., Ecker, A., Bethge, M.: Image style transfer using convolutional neural networks. In: Proceedings of the IEEE Conference on Computer Vision and Pattern Recognition, pp. 2414–2423 (2016)
4. Johnson, J., Alahi, A., Fei-Fei, L.: Perceptual losses for real-time style transfer and super-resolution. In: Leibe, B., Matas, J., Sebe, N., Welling, M. (eds.) ECCV 2016. LNCS, vol. 9906, pp. 694–711. Springer, Cham (2016). https://doi.org/10.1007/978-3-319-46475-6_43
5. Xu, T., Zhang, P., Huang, H., Gan, Z., Huang, X., He, X.: AttnGAN: fine-grained text to image generation with attentional generative adversarial networks. arxiv.org/abs/1711.10485 (2017)
6. Liu, Z., Gao, F., Wang, Y.: A generative adversarial network for AI-aided chair design. In: 2019 IEEE Conference on Multimedia Information Processing and Retrieval (MIPR) (2019)
7. Goodfellow, I., et al.: Generative adversarial nets. Adv. Neural Inf. Process. Syst. **27**, 2672–2680 (2014)
8. Dong, G., Liu, H.: Global receptive-based neural network for target recognition in SAR images. IEEE Trans. Cybern., 1–14 (2019)
9. Glorot, X., Bordes, A., Bengio, Y.: Deep sparse rectifier neural networks. In: AISTATS 2011 (2011)
10. Jarrett, K., Kavukcuoglu, K., Ranzato, M., LeCun, Y.: What is the best multi-stage architecture for object recognition. In: IEEE Proceedings of the International Conference on Computer Vision (ICCV 2009), pp. 2146–2153 (2009)
11. Goodfellow, I., Warde-Farley, D., Mirza, M., Courville, A., Bengio, Y.: Maxout networks. In: ICML 2013 (2013)
12. Hinton, G., Srivastava, E., Krizhevsky, N., Sutskever, A., Salakhutdinov, R.: Improving neural networks by preventing co-adaptation of feature detectors. Technical report. arXiv: 1207.0580 (2012)
13. Radford, A., Metz, L., Chintala, S.: Unsupervised representation learning with deep convolutional generative adversarial networks. arXiv preprint arXiv:1511.06434 (2015)
14. Ha, D., Eck, D.: Neural representation of sketch drawings. arxiv.org/abs/1704.03477 (2017)
15. Kingma, D.P., Welling, M.: An introduction to variational autoencoders. arXiv:1906.02691v3. Accessed 11 Dec 2019
16. Kingma, D., Welling, M.: Auto-encoding variational Bayes. ArXiv e-prints, December 2013 (2013)
17. Chen, Y., Lai, Y., Liu, Y.: CartoonGAN: generative adversarial networks for photo cartoonization. In: IEEE/CVF Conference on Computer Vision and Pattern Recognition (2018)
18. Introduction Generative Adversarial Networks Google Developers. Google. developers.google.com/machine-learning/gan/
19. Colton, S.: Creativity versus the perception of creativity in computational systems. In: Proceedings of the AAAI Spring Symposium on Creative Systems (2008)

Handling SQL Injection Attack Using Progressive Neural Network

Rohit Kumar Pathak$^{(\boxtimes)}$ ⑩, Mohit, and Vrinda Yadav

Department of Computer Science and Engineering, Centre for Advanced Studies,
Dr. A.P.J. Abdul Kalam Technical University,
New Campus, Lucknow 226031, Uttar Pradesh, India
`rohit18197@gmail.com, mohitsinghrajput73@gmail.com, vrinda@cas.res.in`

Abstract. Training in machine learning can solve complex problems like catastrophic forgetting. Catastrophic forgetting in machine learning is forgetting the previously known data while training a new model. In this paper, our main focus is to handle the SQL injection attack using Progressive Neural Network. This protects the data that is lost while training a new security model and defends against a new security attack. The proposed technique is a better approach for solving the problem of network security while transferring knowledge from one module to another module. It is found that Progressive neural Network with Naïve based classifier gives an accuracy of 97.897% which is comparatively higher than existing techniques.

Keywords: Catastrophic forgetting · Progressive neural network · Transfer learning.

1 Introduction

Machine learning is one of the most widely used implementation of artificial learning in which a machine is trained to take an appropriate action according to situations and surroundings [3]. Machine learning also enables self learning and knowledge advancement from its surrounding data and after training the machine is independent to take action on the basis of acquired knowledge.

The main focus of this paper is to use Progressive Neural Network model to detect any network security attack,specifically SQL injection attack to check its performance in the field of security, which has not been applied so far.

Naïve based classification method with machine learning for detection of SQL injection attack gives the accuracy of 92.8%, whereas Gradient Boosting Classifier with machine learning gives the accuracy of 97.4% [21].The accuracy can be enhanced with the help of Progressive Neural Network. SQL injection attack is trending in the top 10 vulnerabilities which the society is currently facing [21]. Since SQL query directly interacts with the database, therefore if any SQL attack occurs then the saved data gets compromised.

Firstly we will briefly overview the following: Machine learning, Transfer learning, Catastrophic forgetting, PNN and SQLi attack.

© Springer Nature Singapore Pte Ltd. 2020
C. Badica et al. (Eds.): ICICCT 2020, CCIS 1170, pp. 231–241, 2020.
https://doi.org/10.1007/978-981-15-9671-1_20

1.1   Machine Learning

Machine learning is a technique that turns information into knowledge. In the last few years there is an explosion of data which can remain useless, until and unless it is not analyzed or the hidden pattern remains unidentified. Machine learning is an automatic technique which can easily analyze and find the underlying pattern in any complex data [2]. We analyze and identify pattern of any problem to predict the future event and can perform all complex decision making tasks. The application of machine learning in day-to-day life are listening music, searching on Google or taking any Photo and many more [1].

Fig. 1. Machine learning   **Fig. 2.** Transfer learning

Figure 1 and Fig. 2 shows Illustration of Machine Learning and Transfer Learning.

Example of Machine Learning: Figure 1 shows how models are learned from the information stored in knowledge base. Assuming that model 1 represents knowledge required to detect bugs in a security based application and model 2 represents knowledge required in an automatic driving car. For the purpose of gaining knowledge the model will take information from knowledge base and further process it to train the model. After training model 1, it can detect bugs in security application and model 2 can take action required to drive the automatic driving car.

1.2   Transfer Learning

Transfer learning in machine learning is a concept in which machine uses the existing knowledge of any particular task or similar task with little or no modification just like humans do [20]. If any person knows how to drive a motorbike, then with little addition to knowledge he/she can easily learn how to drive a car in comparison to a person who directly starts learning how to drive a car without any prior knowledge of driving a motorbike. Similar philosophy when applied in machine learning, is any system knows how to defend SQL injection attacks then that system's knowledge can also be used to defend against man-in-the-middle attack [16] with little modification in the existing knowledge.

Transfer learning is a technique in which two or more existing models interact with each other to gain more knowledge and ensure faster learning [5].

Example of Transfer Learning: Figure 2 shows how models are learned from the information stored in the knowledge base and with the exchange of knowledge between them. Assuming that both the model have similar characteristics where model 1 represents knowledge required to drive a motorbike and model 2 represents knowledge required to drive a car. Here, both models require knowledge about how to drive so they will transfer their knowledge to each other so that they need not require learning from scratch [19].

1.3 Catastrophic Forgetting

Catastrophic forgetting is a term that deals with the catastrophic loss of previously learned responses [4]. This is due to transferring of knowledge form existing model to a new model. Catastrophic forgetting works on the concept of transfer learning in which new models are trained with the help of the existing model's knowledge. It is the only reason why artificial neural network does not learn continuously from their surroundings [6]. After catastrophic forgetting, in future when any new model tries to learn the same knowledge then it is not possible due to the catastrophic loss of the same knowledge [18].

1.4 Progressive Neural Network (PNN)

PNN technique to secure the previously existing knowledge, where a dummy model has been taken with some random data, after that we replicate knowledge in dummy model and freeze the base model [22]. This helps to avoid catastrophic loss and can be used in future when required.

The progressive neural network is used to solve a complex sequence of tasks with the advantage of transfer learning. It solves the problem of catastrophic forgetting by providing the lateral connection between the prior knowledge of existing tasks. A PNN contains a list of the interconnected sequence of pre-trained models. Each model of progressive neural network contains several layer having knowledge in it. This model is immune to catastrophic loss.

Example of PNN. Assume that their is a neural network having three interconnected models with three layers each. Knowledge is stored in every layer of the model which can be transferred to the next layer of other models. Figure 3 shows how progressive neural network works in which knowledge is transferred from the first layer of the first task to the next layer of all the other tasks present in that network as input. All layers are interconnected with each other. The last layer of each task is used for classification so its knowledge is not transferred to other tasks.

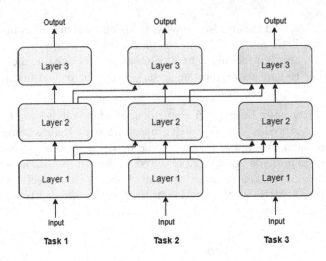

Fig. 3. PNN

1.5   SQL Injection Attacks

Queries manipulation allows attackers to view data which they might not be able to access generally. This data can be sensitive information of users or the data that the application needs to access.

Attackers use this technique to access the data and then modify it permanently or temporarily or in some cases, the full control can be in their hands by changing the original state of the data, contents and behavior [7]. Also, there have been incidents where attackers have escalated an SQL injection attack to compromise the server and the back-end architecture; which has to lead to a denial-of-service attack [17].

SQL Injection Attack. A SQL injection attack can result in unauthorized access to personal data, passwords, credit card or bank related information and many more informative details which couldn't be accessed otherwise and not legal too [21]. There have been pieces of evidence of many high profile breaches which were results of SQL injection attacks like the popular "Bell Canada Breach" of 2014 which exposed openly the data of 40 K customers of "Bell Canada" a telecommunication company in Canada [15].

The benefit to attackers in performing this attack is the modification of query which takes less labour and results are astonishing which can be a billion-dollar data.

As can be seen in the Fig. 4, the attacker watching the network, is waiting for users to make their requests for values from the database. The database is being continuously monitored by him/her in this case where he/she needs some authorized access to request for confidential data from the database via SQL queries. As soon as the user makes a request the attacker knows what values are being requested and the attacker alters the queries to fulfill unethical motives

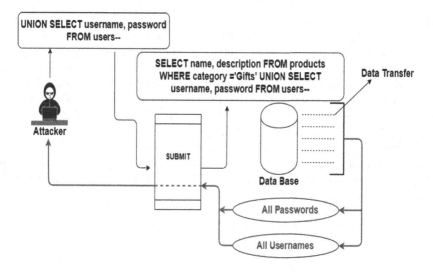

Fig. 4. Example of SQL injection attack

using the union operator, the attacker can combine the result-set of two or more select statements and can request the database in the form of queries and hence can successfully access the important information like usernames, passwords, as was the case with Bell Canada Breach in 2014.

Table 1 enlists various categories of SQL injection attack

2 Experiments

We use Progressive Neural Network which is an existing solution for handling catastrophic forgetting to solve the problem of SQL injection attacks. The progressive neural network was designed to solve catastrophic forgetting problem in transfer learning [8]. In this paper Progressive neural network is used to train machine learning model to detect SQL injection attack Through this model other

Table 1. Categories in SQL injection attack [Chen et al. 2019]

S.No	Research Paper	Contribution
1	Union attack	Attackers can extract data from different database tables
2	Subverting application logic attack	Attackers that can change a query to interfere with application logic
3	The Blind SQL injection attack	The one where the result of the query attacker controls didn't return to the application response

models can be trained to defend against future potential attacks. Since Progressive Neural Network is immune to catastrophic loss so there is very less or no chance of loss of knowledge to train any new model in future [10,11].

A progressive neural network starts with some hidden layers having their weight matrix. In this we take a single column having some random data in its weight matrix, now the actual task's column is frozen before links are established between them and knowledge is transferred. Since the actual column is frozen, there is no chance of loss of knowledge.

Equation 1, below represents Progressive Neural Network where h_i represents hidden layers, W_i is the weight matrix size, U_i represents lateral connections, K represents the total number of columns, I is the number of rows and j is the current column [13].

$$h_i^{(k)} = f(W_i^{(k)} h_{i-1}^{(k)} + \sum_{j<k} U_i^{(k:j)} h_{i-1}^{(j)}) \tag{1}$$

Dataset Used: For the purpose of training Progressive Neural Network model, two datasets from GitHub are considered in this paper: SQL injection detection and SQL injection exploitation. SQL injection detection dataset contain 12 text file having SQL query of size 62.2 KB and SQL injection exploitation contains dataset contain 6 text file having SQL query of size 4.86 KB.

2.1 SQL Injection Detection

To train the progressive neural network against SQL injection attack different parameters are used such as Error based, SQL query, Time based, Union based SQL injection attack [9].

Error based SQL injection is an attack in which the attacker takes advantage of error thrown by the database to know the structure of the database. Sometimes error-based SQL injection attack is itself can enumerate the entire database.

The SQL query is an SQL attack in which the attacker uses the advantage of the loophole that any database has, and by concatenating with malicious code attacker injects desired code.

Time-based SQL is an attack in which the attacker delays the response for a specific period (in seconds) from the server using SQL query.

Union-based SQL injection is those attack in which without having prior knowledge of multiple fields of table in a database can be accessed by the attackers using joints.

2.2 SQL Injection Exploitation

In this dataset, 198 different symbols and characters are used so that progressive neural network modules can be trained on the different possibilities through which any unwanted SQL query can be injected. These symbols are the part of SQL query for gaining the information stored in the user database.

Preparing of the progressive neural network depends on the current characterization method, for example, Naïve Bayes strategy [15]. Credulous Bayes model is an order model utilized in administered discovering that depends on Bayes Theorem [14].

$$P(A|B) = \frac{P(A|B).P(A)}{P(B)} \tag{2}$$

$P(A \parallel B)$= Probability of A being genuine given that B is valid.
$P(B \parallel A)$ = Probability of B being genuine given that An is valid.
P (A) = Probability of A paying little mind to different information.
P (B) = Probability of B paying little mind to other information.

2.3   Training of Progressive Neural Network Model

Trained in sequence, detection and exploitation dataset. Figure 5 shows how the values are stored in the weight matrix after training the progressive neural network by both the datasets (detection and exploitation). The weight matrix stores two values, the index value of the sequence of the trained dataset and future value obtained after training the model based on which the future prediction is enabled.

```
See the caveats in the documentation: http://pandas.pydata.org/
pandas-docs/stable/user_guide/indexing.html#returning-a-view-
versus-a-copy
  self._setitem_with_indexer(indexer, value)
0.4340168988889722
[688.31489307 668.94551805 670.86203388 663.31024959 666.67295203
 697.14951581 701.04458902 704.15908323 707.61393751 702.29483483
 708.64353608 709.74694024 710.75586574 712.4941408  717.21431759
 711.38816495 715.8208448  716.10449828 711.96619491 699.88067843
 707.1399172  706.52013041 715.06877965 717.15279051 718.77639798
 722.76540753 716.5779189  722.75410393 726.21410314 714.90479363
 724.87973081 717.90181132 714.41538621 720.59790374 720.50342326
 722.60938932 711.27484975 715.56659185 707.58604311 711.96994222
 708.92580479 717.894335   718.02896556 702.47908215 715.43946408
 718.50324108 720.92675474 724.24485868 726.94266484 729.99436483
 731.01871304 723.2215697  708.57807798 712.68542721 710.18944108
 696.43592828 694.32167195 699.45971407 705.52302358 683.46884245
 694.37616946 678.09621349 691.73989476 681.46812853 691.95049827
 705.59188409 695.56759408 703.13398644 689.46851969 702.95383334
 705.58650805 702.33294584 695.30484427 677.70897893 682.30733827
 666.07179373 675.72611378 668.2747127  679.51414622 680.75938747
 685.65342099 692.64125213 698.97853498 688.06981902 697.2345625
 699.20673653 690.43703531 696.33452404 700.95096837 694.77982198
 689.09533379 700.26553299 705.68889757 699.13897314 698.15428007
 683.71788894 686.96467559 697.75932967 699.14175609 708.9889412
 710.56905162 712.0908486  715.38059116 711.30238289 707.9924953
```

Fig. 5. Weight matrix

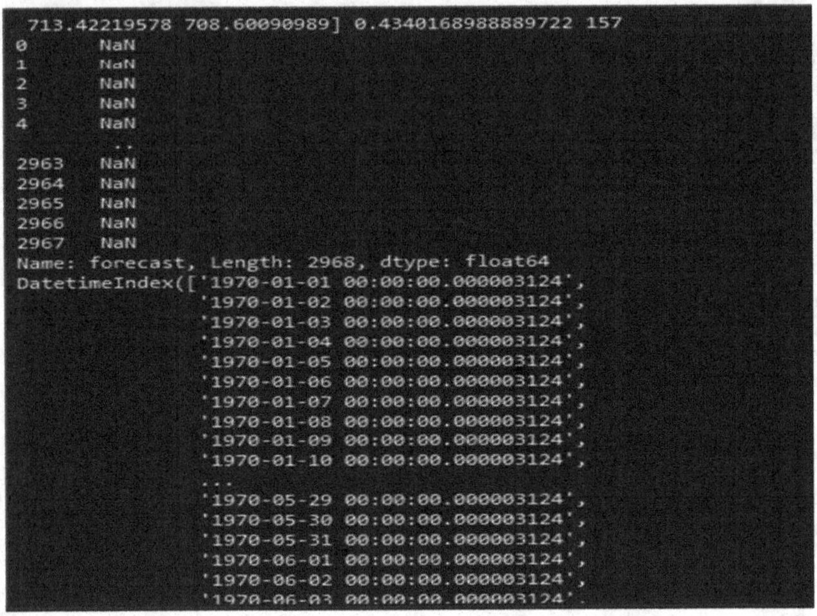

Fig. 6. Deletion of null value from weight matrix

Figure 6 shows how the null value from the obtained result is eliminated from the result. Since null values create problems while predicting the future action of the module so it is very necessary to eliminate all of them. Another reason to eliminate the null value is that it creates a loophole from where the attacker can exploit the attacking intention. After the evacuation of the null values, the weight matrix shows just those sections which contain important information.

3   Results

To assess the efficiency of the proposed work 198 different ways through which SQL injection can be made possible. After doing this we found that approximately 193 were identified correctly. Naïve Bayes method [12] with Progressive neural network gives an accuracy of 97.897% which is greater than the accuracy of Naïve based classification method and Gradient Boosting Classifier with machine learning [21] (Table 2).

Table 2. Comparison between SQL injection detection methods

Parameter	Naïve Bayes method	Gradient boosting classifier	Progressive neural network
Accuracy	92.8%	97.4%	97.897%

Actual Values

		0 **False Positive**	193 **True Positive**
Positive			
	Perdicted Values		
Negative		5 **True Negative**	0 **False Negative**

Fig. 7. Type of errors

The above Fig. 7 shows that out of 198 total sql injection attacks, how many were successfully detected by our machine and how many are not. The "True positive" means successful detection of sql injection attacks performed and "True negative" means inability of the machine to detect the attacks carried.

Here are some output results which shows how proposed experiment works-

3.1 Database Attack

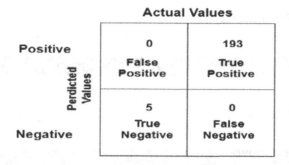

t looks like the back-end DBMS is 'MySQL'. Do you want to skip test payloads specific for other DBMSes? [Y/n] Y
for the remaining tests, do you want to include all tests for 'MySQL' extending provided level (1) and risk (1) values? [Y/n] Y

Fig. 8. Check for database attack

GET parameter 'cat' is vulnerable. Do you want to keep testing the others (if any)? [y/N] y

Fig. 9. Database attack detection

Figure 8 shows that we are checking for database attack whereas Fig. 9 shows the machine has identified the vulnerable point and warn the system. From the above example, we found that due to existing knowledge the machine is able to identify attack.

3.2 Null Value Exploitation

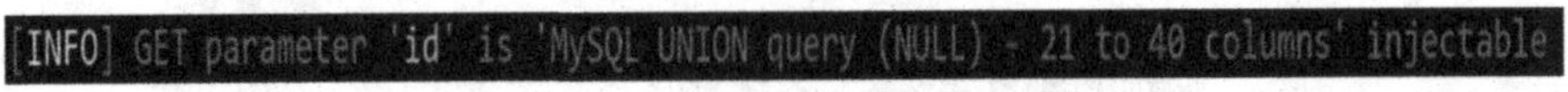

Fig. 10. Null value exploitation

Fig. 11. Detection of Null value exploitation

Figure 10 shows that the attacker try to exploit the null value whereas Fig. 11 shows that the attack has been identified. This is possible because of the knowledge that the machine has, the machine identifies that this query is indeed an attack.

4 Conclusions and Future Work

SQL attack remains one of the most top concern at in the field of cybersecurity [9]. The signature-based technique is no longer reliable for the detection of SQL injection attack. In the field of SQL injection , there is a need to develop a new model which can detect as well as check for the possibilities through which SQL injection is possible.

In this work, we have trained progressive neural network model to successfully avoid SQL injection attack.

Future work will decreasing the complexity and computation cost to reduce the size of weight matrix in the progressive neural network because adding of new column every time increases the weight matrix size.

References

1. Kirkpatrick, J., et al.: Overcoming catastrophic forgetting in neural networks. Proc. Natl. Acad. Sci. **114**(13), 3521–3526 (2017)
2. Parisi, G.I., Kemker, R., Part, J.L., Kanan, C., Wermter, S.: Continual lifelong learning with neural networks: a review. Neural Netw. (2018). https://doi.org/10.1016/j.neunet.2019.01.012
3. Nguyen, C.V., Li, Y., Bui, T.D., Turner, R.E.: Variational continual learning. arXiv preprint arXiv:1710.10628, 29 October 2017
4. Serra, J., Surs, D., Miron, M., Karatzoglou, A.: Overcoming catastrophic forgetting with hard attention to the task. arXiv e-prints (2018)
5. Schwarz, J., et al.: Progress & compress: a scalable framework for continual learning. arXiv preprint arXiv:1805.06370 (2018)

6. Wen, S., Itti, L.: Overcoming catastrophic forgetting problem by weight consolidation and long-term memory. arXiv preprint arXiv:1805.07441 (2018)
7. Sonewar, P.A., Mhetre, N.A.: A novel approach for detection of SQL injection and cross site scripting attacks. In: 2015 International Conference on Pervasive Computing (ICPC), pp. 1–4. IEEE (2015)
8. Ierusalem, A.: Catastrophic importance of catastrophic forgetting. arXiv preprint arXiv:1808.07049 (2018)
9. Chen, Z., Li, M., Cui, X., Sun, Y.: Research on SQL injection and defense technology. In: Sun, X., Pan, Z., Bertino, E. (eds.) ICAIS 2019. LNCS, vol. 11635, pp. 191–201. Springer, Cham (2019). https://doi.org/10.1007/978-3-030-24268-8_18
10. Lee, S.-W., Kim, J.-H., Jun, J., Ha, J.-W., Zhang, B.-T.: Overcoming catastrophic forgetting by incremental moment matching. In: Advances in Neural Information Processing Systems, pp. 4652–4662 (2017)
11. Sarkar, A.M.J., Lee, Y.-K., Lee, S.: A smoothed naive bayes-based classifier for activity recognition. IETE Tech. Rev. **27**(2), 107–119 (2010)
12. Rusu, A.A., et al.: Progressive neural networks. arXiv preprint arXiv:1606.04671 (2016)
13. Schwarz, J., et al.: Progress & compress: a scalable framework for continual learning. arXiv preprint arXiv:1805.06370 (2018)
14. Elovici, Y., Shabtai, A., Moskovitch, R., Tahan, G., Glezer, C.: Applying machine learning techniques for detection of malicious code in network traffic. In: Hertzberg, J., Beetz, M., Englert, R. (eds.) KI 2007. LNCS (LNAI), vol. 4667, pp. 44–50. Springer, Heidelberg (2007). https://doi.org/10.1007/978-3-540-74565-5_5
15. NullCrew attack on Bell Canada was SQL injection and Bell knew weeks ago - NullCrew (update 2) January 20th 2020 (2014). https://www.databreaches.net/nullcrew-attack-on-bell-canada-was-sql-injection-and-bell-knew-weeks-ago-nullcrew/
16. Li, X., Li, S., Hao, J., Feng, Z., An, B.: Optimal personalized defense strategy against man-in-the-middle attack. In: Thirty-First AAAI Conference on Artificial Intelligence (2017)
17. Masse, N.Y., Grant, G.D., Freedman, D.J.:. Alleviating catastrophic forgetting using context-dependent gating and synaptic stabilization. Proc. Natl. Acad. Sci. **115** (2018). https://doi.org/10.1073/pnas.1803839115
18. Paik, I., Oh, S., Kwak, T.-Y., Kim, I.: Overcoming catastrophic forgetting by neuron-level plasticity control. arXiv preprint arXiv:1907.13322 (2019)
19. Weiss, K., Khoshgoftaar, T.M., Wang, D.D.: A survey of transfer learning. J. Big Data **3**(1), 1–40 (2016). https://doi.org/10.1186/s40537-016-0043-6
20. LKindy, D.A., Pathan, A.-S.K.: A detailed survey on various aspects of sql injection in web applications: vulnerabilities, innovative attacks, and remedies. arXiv preprint arXiv:1203.3324 (2012)
21. Mishra, S.: SQL injection detection using machine learning (2019)
22. Rusu, A.A., et al.: Progressive neural networks. arXiv preprint arXiv:1606.04671 (2016)

A Novel Automated Method for Detection of Eye Diseases Using Image Processing on Retinal Images

Amit Kumar Mourya[1]($\boxtimes$) (iD) and Lalita Verma[2]

[1] Electronics and Communication Department,
Mangalmay Institute of Engineering and Technology, Greater Noida, India
mourya.amitkumar@gmail.com
[2] Computer Science and Engineering,
Mangalmay Institute of Engineering and Technology, Greater Noida, India
maanvi6878@gmail.com

Abstract. More than 2.2 billion of people are losing their vision of eye worldwide. These people have vision infirmity due to Cataract, Diabetic retinopathy, Glaucoma, refractive error, macular degeneration etc. In India also there are more than 80 million of people are suffering from moderate visual infirmity. Major problems in the eye diseases are no early symptoms and high cost of treatment, so the diseases get severe. In this paper, I have proposed an automated method of detection of eye diseases in early stages. So the people can cure them before they become severe and incurable. I have considered three main factors which are responsible for vision loss. These factors are Glaucoma, Macular Degeneration and Diabetic Retinopathy. For detection of these diseases Glaucoma, Macular Degeneration and Diabetic Retinopathy several features are extracted which are cup to disk ratio, extraction of blood vessels, optic cup segmentation, optic disk segmentation, brighter part extraction etc. This proposed method has achieved very good results which are verified by the experts. Results mark that the proposed method has very fine accuracy and effectiveness in detection of these diseases over the pre-existing method.

Keywords: Segmentation · Blood vessels extraction · Cup to disk ratio · Glaucoma · Diabetic retinopathy · Macular degeneration

1 Introduction

1.1 Glaucoma

Glaucoma is occurring due to slow progression of damaging of optic nerve. When the flow of aqueous humor in eye is disturbed then the intra ocular pressure is generated which damaged the optic nerve fiber. This results in enlargement [2] of optic cup. People do not have the early symptoms like pain; loss of vision etc. if the optic nerve fiber is damaged once then no treatment can make it healthy. So the early detection is very crucial in the case of Glaucoma eye disease. With the help of early detection, we can halt further damaging of optic nerve. The pixel intensity of Optic disk

© Springer Nature Singapore Pte Ltd. 2020
C. Badica et al. (Eds.): ICICCT 2020, CCIS 1170, pp. 242–251, 2020.
https://doi.org/10.1007/978-981-15-9671-1_21

and cup are greater [1] than the background. The region of optic disk and cup is important [3] for Glaucoma detection (Fig. 1).

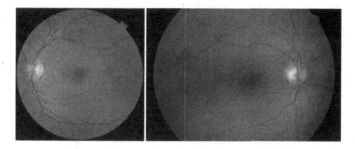

Fig. 1. Retinal image of healthy and Glaucomatous eye.

1.2 Diabetic Retinopathy

It is an eye disease which occurs due to damage of blood vessels by high blood sugar. The blood vessels swell, leak or they can stop passing the blood through it. This leads to change [7] in vision or blindness. If the people do not get treatment on time then it can scar and damage the retina. Adoptive threshold [4] can be used for Diabetic Retinopathy (Fig. 2).

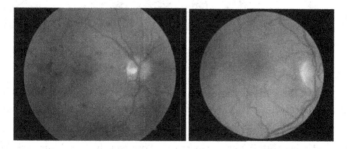

Fig. 2. Retinal image affected by Diabetic Retinopathy and Macular Degeneration.

1.3 Macular Degeneration

In our eye macula is responsible for clear and sharp vision. When the central part of the retina called macula is damaged [10] then this problem occurs. This problem becomes worse with age. Retina has light sensing nerve tissue. It does not cause the blindness but can create severe vision issue.

To analyze the fundus retinal image using image processing techniques is a hot and emerging area for the researchers. There are some image processing methods already exist to detect these diseases. But the existing methods do not give the accurate result to diagnose these diseases. Through this paper we proposed a novel automated method to screen mass population for Glaucoma, Diabetic Retinopathy, and Macular Degeneration.

Paper planning and design is as following. Section 2 will describes the important parameter and terms of the retinal image. Section 3 describes the flow chart of the proposed method which involves the pre-processing, segmentation, post processing and implementation of the Hough Transform. Section 4 will describes the classification of diseases. The paper will end with description of conclusion and future work that can be next area of interest.

2 Description of Retinal Image

2.1 Camera for Retinal Images

This camera is a special featured camera which captures the photograph of eye with high resolution, including the detail of retina, vessels of blood, optic disk and cup, Macular region etc. It has the combination of microscope and camera. It records colored detailed image of interior eye surface.

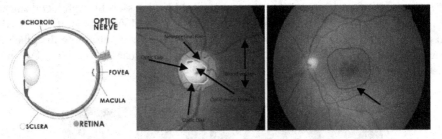

Fig. 3. Various terms in retinal image and region of interest.

Figure 3 shows the various region of intrest in the retinal image. It shows the optic disk and cup, Neuroretinal Rim, vessels, Macula region in the retinal image. The definition of these parts are as following.

- **Neuroretinal Rim (NRR):** It is the region between the cup boundary to the disk. This region mainly consists nerve fiber. Rim thickness to disk diameter is known as Rim disk ratio.
- **Optic disk:** It is brighter part in the retinal image which is elliptical in shape.
- **Optic Cup:** It is the orange pink rim in the center of the optic disk.
- **Macular Region:** It is the pigmented area at the center of retina. It is oval shaped.

For the detection of the Glaucoma, Diabetic Retinopathy, and Macular Degeneration, there are the following changes occur in the eye.

- Area of the optic cup increases
- Damaging of the blood vessels
- Damaging of retinal surface
- Optic nerve head damaged

There are the following difficulties associated with the segmentation.

- Background of the retinal image is not homogenous.
- Width of the blood vessels is varying continually.
- Brightness of the retinal surface is not equal.

Due to all these difficulties, pre-processing of the retinal image is very much important before the segmentation.

3 Detection Process for Proposed Method

(See Fig. 4.)

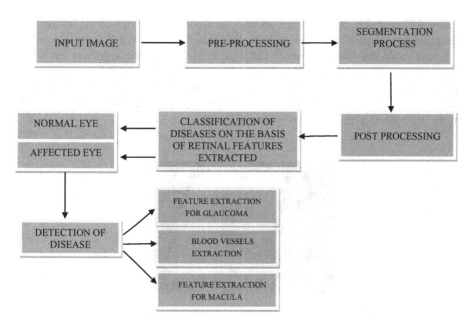

Fig. 4. Flow chart showing detection process.

3.1 Input Image and Pre-processing

A special featured camera is used to take the high resolution images which are taken as the input for the proposed method. All these images are not fit for directly segmentation. So before segmentation I have done the pre-processing of these images. I have taken the histogram of the input image. From the histogram, I come know to know that some pixels belong to optic disk and optic cup have higher intensity value. And some pixels have the less intensity value which belongs to background surface (Fig. 5).

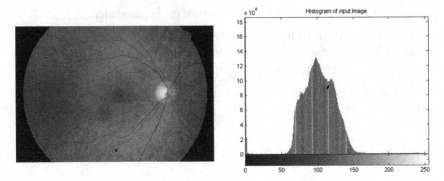

Fig. 5. Input image and its histogram.

Optimal Threshold: By taking the optimal threshold, I have removed the background affect and blood vessels. For the optimal threshold, I follow the following algorithm.

I have taken the initial threshold value T. Then perform the segmentation which produces two group of pixels G1 > T and g2 < T. Then I calculated the average pixel values for G1 and G2 which are T_1 and T_2 respectively. New threshold will be ½(T1 + T_2). These steps repeated till the value of T become stable. The following image is obtained after threshing holding (Fig. 6).

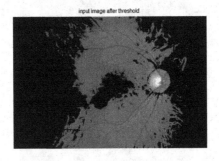

Fig. 6. Input Image after threshold to remove background.

In next step of the pre-processing, I obtained the red channel, blue channel and green channel of the image for the segmentation. Segmentation of optic disk and cup are done from red and green channel image (Fig. 7).

Some time, eye images do not better visible region for segmentation, in such type of cases we formulate an image by applying arithmetic concept over images obtained after threshold (blue and green channel images).

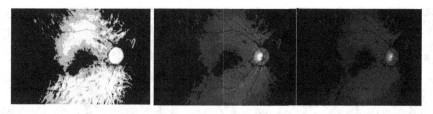

Fig. 7. Images of different channel (Red, Green, Blue) obtained after threshold. (Color figure online)

3.2   Segmentation Process

The segmentation of the Glaucoma and macula, optic cup and optic disk is done for detection. I have focused on higher intensity pixels to segment the region of interest. For the segmentation, the following algorithm is used.

First I have determined the dimensions of input image. All the pixels are counted for levels which are in the histogram of input image. Then a bar graph is drawn for all count. Bar graph is divided into parts. And pixels count for both the part is calculated. I have taken the difference of these counts and the resultant will be the region of interest. For the blood vessels extraction, in first step I normalize the images equal contrast and uniform illumination. In second step blood vessels are extracted using pixel intensity and geometric feature using matched filter. Vessels are differentiated from non vascular region using a neural network classifier. Macula is located at the center of the retina which is marked at a distance of 2.5D where D is optic disk diameter. The center part of the Macula is known as Fovea which is responsible for higher visual acuity. So for the detection of Macula, the diameter of the optic disk is calculated (Figs. 8 and 9).

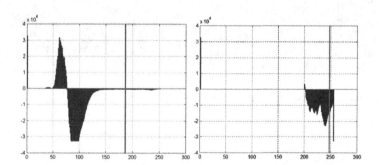

Fig. 8. Difference of histogram for segmentation of optic cup and disk

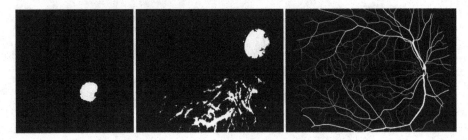

Fig. 9. Segmented cup and disk and extracted blood vessels.

3.3   Post Processing and Feature Extraction

In the post–processing step, the images obtained from segmentation are improved for the feature extraction by removing the other information from the images. I have applied Hough transform to detect the boundary of optic cup and disk. Hough Transform uses a voting procedure for imperfect instances of objects. It can identify line, circle and other figures. To calculate the Hough Transform, a local maximum is determined by an accumulator array. It construct several circles whose center is edge point of boundary with radius r. Accumulator counts number of circles that passes from each edge points. Higher counting point will be the center of the circle. It provides the efficient method for the detection of circle in the input image (Figs. 10 and 11).

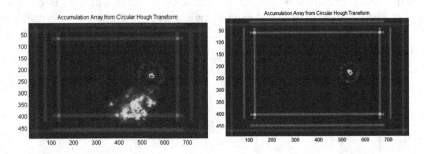

Fig. 10. Output of Hough transforms to detect the center of disk and cup

Different features are extracted after the Hough Transform. They are following.

- Radius: r = (sqrt(Area/π))
- Diameter: D = 2 * r
- Area: A = π * r * r
- Optic cup to Disk Ratio = cup diameter/disk diameter

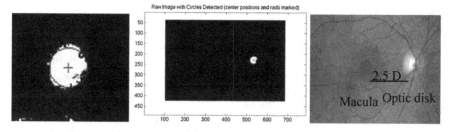

Fig. 11. Detected Optic Disk, Optic Cup and Macula.

4 Classification of Disease

For Glaucoma, cup to disk ratio is determined from the result that come from feature extraction. If the ratio is greater than 0.75 for an eye than the eye is suffer by Glaucoma disease. If the ratio is lesser than 0.75 then the eye will be healthy. To locate the center of macula, optic disk is segmented according to the proposed algorithm. To find center and radius of disk, Hough transform is used. Diameter of the optic disk is calculated for detection of Fovea which is the center of the macula. Generally macula is situated at a distance of 2.5D where the D is diameter of the optic disk. For the diabetic retinopathy, segmentation of the blood vessels is performed in the proposed algorithm. This eye disorder is occurring due to the damaging of the blood vessels in the retinal surface.

The results obtained from the proposed algorithm are verified by the medical expert to check the accuracy and effectiveness of the proposed algorithm. A large Image data base is used for the testing of the proposed method. Some of the tested results is given below (Table 1).

Table 1. Comparison of results of proposed method and expert.

Analysis of output result	Comparison of proposed method result and Medical expert result		
	Proposed method result	Expert result	Compared result
Test Image 1 (Glaucoma)	Normal healthy eye	Normal healthy eye	Positive
Test Image 2 (Glaucoma)	Affected with Glaucoma	Affected with Glaucoma	Positive
Test Image 3 (Glaucoma)	Affected with Glaucoma	Affected with Glaucoma	Positive
Test Image 4 (Glaucoma)	Affected with Glaucoma	Affected with Glaucoma	Positive
Test Image 5 (Glaucoma)	Normal healthy eye	Affected with Glaucoma	Negative
Test Image 6 (Macula)	Affected with Macula	Affected with Macula	Positive
Test Image 7 (Macula)	Normal healthy eye	Affected with Macula	Negative
Test Image 8 (Macula)	Affected with Macula	Affected with Macula	Positive
Test Image 9 (Macula)	Affected with Macula	Affected with Macula	Positive
Test Image 10 (Macula)	Affected with Macula	Affected with Macula	Positive
Test Image 11 (Macula)	Normal healthy eye	Normal healthy eye	Positive

(*continued*)

Table 1. (*continued*)

Analysis of output result	Comparison of proposed method result and Medical expert result		
	Proposed method result	Expert result	Compared result
Test Image 12 (Macula)	Affected with Diabetic Retinopathy	Normal healthy eye	Negative
Test Image 13 (Macula)	Affected with Diabetic Retinopathy	Affected with Diabetic Retinopathy	Positive
Test Image 14 (Macula)	Affected with Diabetic Retinopathy	Affected with Diabetic Retinopathy	Positive
Test Image 15 (Macula)	Affected with Diabetic Retinopathy	Affected with Diabetic Retinopathy	Positive

These results are achieved on the basis of performance of the algorithm over one set of data base. This algorithm is performed over data base that have enough images which are taken High Resolution Fundus Image data base and ACRIMA database. Outcomes of the proposed algorithm are very much promising. On the basis of outcomes which I get after the comparison of expert, the proposed method is significantly having accuracy near to 80%. So the proposed method may be taken as the important development toward automated Retinal image analysis for diagnosing the eye disease.

5   Conclusion

Eye is a precious sense organ. In the world more than 2.2 billion of people are losing their vision due to Glaucoma, Macular Degeneration, and Diabetic Retinopathy. The proposed method have good accuracy to detect these diseases. In the proposed method, different region of interest is segmented and blood vessels extraction is performed. Using Hough Transform, the center and radius of optic disk and cup is calculated. Many other features are extracted for the improvement of the proposed method. Proposed method is verified over a data base that has enough Varity of images. The results are compared with the expert results which show the potential of the method. The proposed method will provide a novel and low cost method for mass screening of people. Future work may contains the extraction of some more features and the classification of the stages of diseases.

References

1. Dutta, M., et al.: Glaucoma detection by segmenting the super pixels from fundus color retinal images (2014). https://doi.org/10.1109/medcom.2014.700598
2. Yin, F., et al.: Automated segmentation of optic disc and optic cup in fundus images for glaucoma diagnosis. IEEE (2012)
3. Bhartiya, S., Gadia, R., Sethi, H.S., Panda, A.: Clinical evaluation of optic nerve head in glaucoma. J. Curr. Glaucoma Pract. https://doi.org/10.5005/jp-journals-10008-1080

4. Ganguly, S., et al.: An adaptive threshold based algorithm for detection of red lesions of diabetic retinopathy in a fundus image (2014). https://doi.org/10.1109/medcom.2014.7005982
5. Nitasha, S., Reecha, S.: Comparison between circular hough transform and modified canny edge detection algorithm for circle detection. Int. J. Eng. Res. Technol. (IJERT) (2012). ISSN-22780181
6. Budai, A., Bock, R., Maier, A., Homegger, J., Michelson, G.: Robust vessel segmentation in fundus images. Int. J. Biomed. Imaging **2013**(Article ID 154860), 11 (2013)
7. https://www.mayoclinic.org
8. https://www.allaboutvision.com
9. https://www.who.int/blindness
10. Marinal, S., Sinha, R.: An unsupervised method for detection and validation of the optic disk and the Fovea. arXiv:1601.06608

Plant Disease Detection: An Augmented Approach Using CNN and Generative Adversarial Network (GAN)

Huzaifa M. Maniyar and Suneeta V. Budihal[(✉)] [iD]

KLE Technological University, Vidyanagar, Hubballi 580031, India
huzzu.maniyar@gmail.com, suneeta_vb@kletech.ac.in

Abstract. The paper provides a framework to classify the plant as diseased or healthy based on the health of the leaf using Generative Adversarial Networks (GANs). Presently the researchers focus on developing a non-invasive method for plant health monitoring and control. Many of the present approaches are towards developing Machine Learning frameworks to address plant disease detection. Although the machine learning algorithms provide improved accuracy, but they lack sample data sets for training the designed model. GAN a Deep Learning architecture is proposed comprising of Generator, Discriminator combinations. The generator is trained to generate new data samples, very close to the original data sample trying to cheat the discriminator. The discriminator is trained to identify the difference between the original and generated sample data as real or fake. The proposed model is trained to provide an accuracy of 98.29% in detection of health of the plant.

Keywords: Generative Adversarial Network (GAN) · Plant disease · Convolutional Neural Network (CNN) · Deep learning (DL)

1 Introduction

Presently the ML along with DL algorithms are attaining better performance in domains of computer vision, image processing, etc. Deep Neural Networks are advantageous as they are capable of exploiting directly the raw data without the use of hand-crafted features. The increased dependency of ML algorithms on the amount of data available for training the designed framework in given architecture limits its application, along with high computational facilities needed, such as Graphics Processing Units (GPU). These features make it possible to train the DNNs and enforce the parallelism. Many algorithms are proposed by ML techniques such as K-means, SVM, Principal Component Analysis, but DL frameworks provide better representative power where the data is passed through several non-linear functions for robust features.

The proposed framework focuses on agricultural application in order to grow crops on a large scale. Plant health is very important for the increased yield. The diseases identified at various stages of plant growth affect health of the plant. Leaves are the better indicators of plant health. The proposed framework is to develop a model for plant disease detection using DNNs. In several recent approaches of plant disease

© Springer Nature Singapore Pte Ltd. 2020
C. Badica et al. (Eds.): ICICCT 2020, CCIS 1170, pp. 252–261, 2020.
https://doi.org/10.1007/978-981-15-9671-1_22

detection, many of the diseases can be identified depending on the dataset of leaf images of the affected plant. Hence, the proposed framework is developed to classify the plant as diseased or healthy based on the modifications in size, shape, colour and other infections in leaf. The challenge lies in training a DNN [1] associated with classification of plant as diseased or healthy using the images of plant leaf.

The proposed framework is developed with GANs and CNNs, popular DL techniques used with increased accuracy for image classification. GANs introduced in [2] are very successful in generating synthetic images that are close to the original images. The major goal in training the CNN model is to generate ample amount of data set may be real or synthetic samples [3, 4] with the same characteristics and training distribution. Supervised learning, a ML algorithm, requires labelled data and large amount of training data set. Hence, the main challenge in applying these algorithms to the agricultural issues is lack of datasets and scarce annotated samples. Collecting the required plant disease data set is not only complex, but requires all the relevant domain people to collaborate and work. The datasets are not available publicly and are the available datasets are applicable to specific problems. This leads to a challenge of class imbalance. In various literature, data augmentation to increase training set and balancing classes are discussed. The diversity and variation achieved from modifications of the images by translation, rotation and scaling is less. It motivates the use of synthetic data to improve recognition and training process along with accuracy, where generated samples enrich the dataset and introduce more variability.

Many strategies have been developed using image processing, but it is needed to apply ML techniques for image processing. It is important that they should be identified by the machines automatically. Plant disease reduces the quality, quantity and in turn the yield. Plant diseases start from very small symptoms and cause damage to the entire yield, causing major financial crises and imbalancing the agricultural economy. The invasive methods are established in the molecular biology and chemistry to identify causal agent of the plant disease precisely. It requires skilled and smart experts to serve the purpose. However, these processes are not accessible to many people and require a thorough domain information and a large amount of investment of time and resources. Currently, the non-invasive solutions available with DL techniques for disease detection have improved the results successfully.

1.1 Literature Survey

Various methods for classification of plant leaf as diseased or healthy have been proposed and high accuracy rates have been achieved. On the other hand, many researchers addressed the plant disease detection. A number of DL architectures have been proposed by many researchers, but CNN [5] is most deployed. Biological nervous and vision systems are the inspiration for development of CNN. It is an unsupervised DL classification model having improved accuracy in classification and recognition. Citrus plant diseases were investigated by [6] and presented a number of articles on plant diseases identification and classification. In the review work, plant disease detection is addressed and discussed various methodologies associated with detecting the disease, that include techniques, challenges, advantages, disadvantages, etc.

The various neural network approaches for plant disease detection using the leaf as the input was discussed in detail in [7]. This work introduces various models, mechanisms, and classifiers used for hyperspectral images processing [8]. Before the advancement of CNNs, traditional ML classification methods, such as SVM [9] and K-Means [10], were used to classify plants as diseased or healthy. In [11] the authors applied image processing for detection of disease in sugar cane plants with threshold segmentation and triangle threshold with average accuracy of 98.60%.

Due to GPUs, AI is growing significantly with the robust set of traditional resources applied by CV techniques [12]. ML techniques have demonstrated improved accuracy in classification and identification of plant diseases. GANs are the promising and better option for training a model that can synthesize fake images. GAN models have generated better synthetic images than previous generative models, and since have become one of the most prevalent research areas. GANs have achieved great acceptance and different variations of GANs have produced high quality realistic images.

Some studies have been encouraged by GANs in image processing [13]. In a research, built on GANs for image-to-image translation, a method for data augmentation to generate new samples via adversarial training is suggested, to increase the data manifold for the estimate of the true distribution. It may lead to better margins between distinct categories of data. In all the above approaches including the other approaches for various tasks in DL in computer vision so far, the availability of large amount of data plays a crucial role for improved classification accuracy. The proposed framework provides an improved performance by starting with small number of original images and gradually generating more plant disease images synthetically using Generative Adversarial Networks (GANs) and feeding those samples to the training set. The proposed framework contributes,

- To design a conditional GAN to generate the synthetic images for data augmentation and CNN for classification.
- To develop methods that can classify the plant as diseased and healthy where other methods have reached less accuracy due to data adequacy.

Section 2 discusses about the various concepts available for the design of the model. Section 3 discusses the implementation details of the synthetic data generated by the GAN network. Section 4 discusses about the obtained results.

2   Proposed Methodology

It includes a brief description of the block diagram of GAN. To be more specific it provides the outline for the design. The methodology includes design alternatives for building a GAN network and finally choosing the best concept among all the variations (Fig. 1).

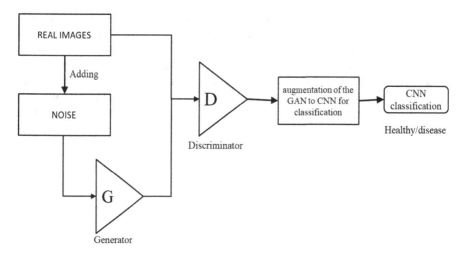

Fig. 1. Functional block diagram of GANs and CNN: Augmenting the synthetic data generated of the plant village dataset for training the model and CNN for classification of plant as diseased or healthy.

2.1 Functional Block Diagram of Generative Adversarial Network

The block diagram gives a brief description about generation of synthetic data using GANs. Initially, a real input block, which consists of the real input images that are taken from plant village database is used. At the later phase noise is added in order to enhance the training capacity of a CNN to generate the new synthetic data and both (real and generated) images are sent to the discriminator, which discriminate the data as real or fake. The whole data (real + fake) is augmented and is given to the Convolutional Neural Network (CNN) for training. Further, the data is split into training and testing and is given to the CNN classifier to classify the plant images as diseased or healthy. A backpropagation algorithm is applied to tune the parameters and adjust them in accordance with the accuracy of the obtained output. Regularization is done in order to minimize the cost function and obtain the highest accuracy.

2.2 Flow Chart for the Proposed Framework to Detect Plant Disease

GAN consists of several layers of implementation. The layers depend upon the designer, generally as the layers of training increases the output will closer to the original input. The total parameters were 58, 102, 67 among those the parameters considered for generation of new data using GANs is 58, 099, 791. The total dataset was split into training and testing. The training samples are given to the various layers of CNN and the result is obtained. The training sample is the synthetic data that is generated by the generator from plant village dataset, which is been deliberately perturbed and given as a corrupted input to the hidden layers. Generator of the GAN generates the new synthetic data, which automatically follows the generation and discrimination process based on the parameters chosen in GAN Network.

Using back propagation algorithm, the generator generates synthetic data in order to reduce the losses. A deep GAN is required, which consists of generator and the discriminator. In order to generate the new synthetic data generator is used and the generator will try to fool the discriminator whereas the discriminator will discriminate the data between real and fake. The aim is to detect the plant as healthy or diseased. GAN is used for the generation of new synthetic data, which is used to train the CNN network, CNN is used for the binary classification in order to classify plant as diseased or the healthy (Fig. 2).

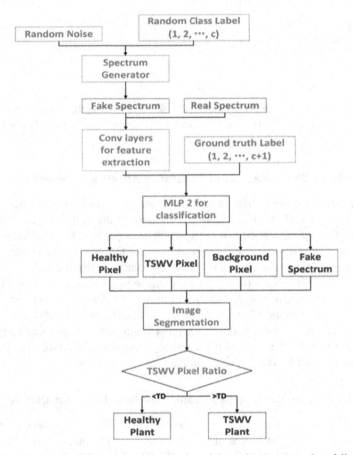

Fig. 2. Flow chart of plant disease detection: It gives the step by step procedure followed in the proposed model.

2.3   Training Strategies

It is desired to use the output from the GAN network to generate the new data for data augmentation for training the CNN network. A network should yield positive output to properly detect a diseased plant. Hence, ReLU activation at the last output layer of CNN is used, which can also accelerate the training speed. An Adam optimizer is used that can adjust the learning rate on each weight parameter, which guarantees effective training. In order to ensure the data detection of plant as healthy or diseased has less loss, a cost function J(w, b) as shown by Eq. (1) is used to calculate the differences between healthy and diseased plant.

$$J(w, b) = \frac{1}{m} \sum\nolimits_{i=1}^{m} (x' - x)^2 \tag{1}$$

2.4   Performance Parameters

Deep neural networks are used as the binary classisfication function. Cross entropy function i.e., CNN is being chosen for the distance function between the input and the output. ReLU activation and SoftMax are used in differnt layers of CNN. Activation functions ReLU function (Rectified Linear Units) ReLU is the most common activation function used in neural networks as in Eq. (2). It returns zero for negative values and one for any positive values. It allows the model to account for non-linearities very well. For input x it returns the value back so we can write,

$$f(x) = max(0, x) \tag{2}$$

The sigmoid function considers any range of real numbers and returns output value in the range from 0 to 1. The sigmoid function produces curve, which will be in the Shape of S. The sigmoid function returns a real-valued output. The first derivative of the sigmoid function will be either non-negative or nonpositive. For SoftMax, the range of output will be from 0 to 1, and the sum of all the probabilities is unity. It returns the probabilities of each class and the target class will have the highest probability. It computes the exponential of the given input and the sum of exponential values of all values of the inputs. Then the ratio of exponential of the input value and sum of exponential values is considered to be the output.

3   Proposed Framework Using GAN

GAN is an unsupervised ML algorithm that consists of Generator(G) and the Discriminator(D). The generator generates new data in accordance with the original data and the generator consists of neural network, which tries to study a guesstimate to identity the function using back propagation algorithm. The generator will try to fool the discriminator by minimizing the noise whereas, the Discriminator will try to identify the generated data is real or fake and the noise will be more in the discriminator. GAN can be built in various ways such as cycle GAN, deep convolutional GAN, stacked GAN, conditional GAN and many more. In this paper building a network-based model that is using conditional GAN is emphasized. Thus, resulting in better accuracy of the model.

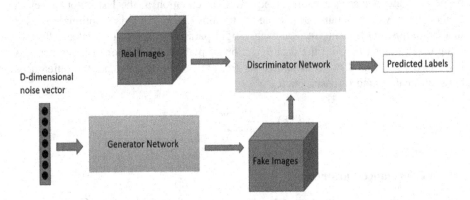

Fig. 3. General representation of a generative adversarial network, which consists of generator and discriminator.

In order to build the model as shown in Fig. 3, many aspects are to be considered. Selection of the parameters depends on optimization and the accuracy of the model. Changes have been made during the training period. The GAN network is the type of data generative model, which includes data argumentation where the functions such as compression and decompression are involved. These functions are automatically learnt, specific in terms of data and are lossy. This means rather than manually being engineered by developers, in almost every context where the GAN is being used the functions are automatically implemented by the neural network. GAN is built concerned with specific data, which means that the data generation algorithm will be able to generate the synthetic data that is only the data similar to trained data. For example, if after training the GAN with the images of pant leaf, the generator of GAN is given with an image of a building, then the generator fails to achieve its goal. GAN learns the functions automatically and the training is made easier. In order to build a GAN three functions are required, such as generator function, the min. max. function and the discriminator function.

To develop a model Google co-laboratory is used as a platform for coding. All the necessary packages are installed on the initial grounds, the data set is directly downloaded from cloud. After reshaping the images, the testing and training samples are shuffled, split and two separate sets of testing and training are created. A noise factor is then added to the training data. Getting started with a CNN, multiple layers of binary classifiers are developed. Three layers are used in GAN where output of the previous is given as input to the above layer and thus accuracy of the model is improved. The equation of the generator of the GAN used to generate the new synthetic data can be expressed as in Eq. (3), Eq. (4) and Eq. (5): At Generator(G):

$$Gloss = \log(1 - D(G(Z))) - \log(D(G(Z))) \tag{3}$$

$$\frac{1}{m}\sum\nolimits_{i=1}^{m} \log\left(1 - D\left(G\left(Z^{i}\right)\right)\right) \tag{4}$$

$$\frac{1}{m}\sum\nolimits_{i=1}^{m} -\log D\left(G\left(Z^{i}\right)\right) \tag{5}$$

The equation of discriminator of GAN to detect the data, which is real and fake can be expressed as in Eq. (6) and Eq. (7): At Discriminator(D):

$$Dloss_{real} = \log(D(X)) \tag{6}$$

$$Dloss_{fake} = \log(1 - D(G(Z))) \tag{7}$$

ReLu is used as an activation function in all the encoder layers. The ReLu function very well accounts for non-linearities, basically it only accounts for positive input values and the negative values will be will be customized to zero, which helps to reduce the dimension and obtain a synthetic image. The CNN classifier layer consists of sigmoid as activation function, which will scale all the negative values to zero and only emphasize the higher values. Adam delta is used as an optimizer, binary cross entropy is used to reduce the classifier losses. The epoch is the duration up till which the training on a particular batch is done.

4   Results and Discussion

Plant village dataset is used to train plant disease detection using GAN with 73 batch size of input noisy images for 25 epochs. The noisy images are obtained by manually adding some Gaussian noise to the input images. It is used as the data augmentation for training the CNN network and increasing the accuracy up to 98.29% as shown in Fig. 5.

4.1   Result Analysis

The following plot shows the result analysis carried out for the architecture, which is trained using GANs and without GANs. Initially, the analysis is done by the architecture without GAN that provided an accuracy of 86.24%. The architecture, which was trained by using GANs generated synthetic data and was able to provide an accuracy of 98.29% and a validation accuracy of 96.12%. Similarly, the losses were also analyzed and was 0.0452 for the model with GAN and the validation losses were about 0.1520 that the system can detect the diseased plant as diseased. In Table 1, the comparative study is listed for the models, which uses the different type of architectures for plant disease detection and the accuracy is mentioned with the corresponding architecture. The proposed model has the highest accuracy of 98.29% as compared to the other architectures (Fig. 4).

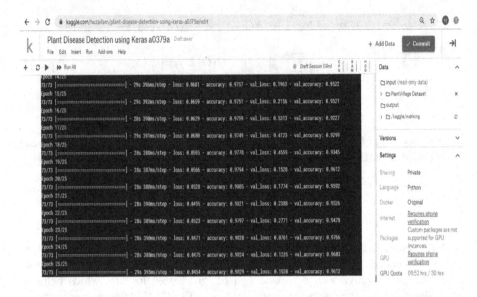

Fig. 4. Screen shot for GAN with losses and accuracy with 25 epochs and 73 batch size.

Table 1. Number of leaf images in the dataset used for training and testing

Sl. No.	Architecture used	Number of trainable parameters	Accuracy in %
1	Conditional GANs	58,099,791/58,102,671	98.29
2	GANs	42,099,791/58,102,671	96.41
3	Others	Comparatively less	86.07

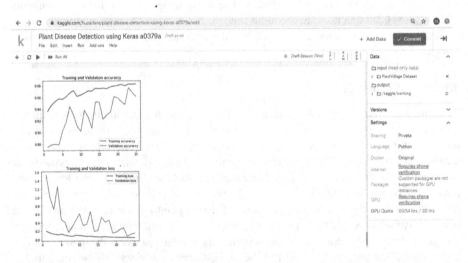

Fig. 5. Screen shot for the accuracy achieved during training and validation and similarly the losses during training and validation.

5 Conclusion

An efficient way to detect the plant as diseased or healthy using the GAN and CNN is discussed with desired level of accuracy. GAN a is proposed trained to generate new data samples, very close to the original data sample trying to cheat the discriminator. The discriminator is trained to identify the difference between the original and generated sample data as real or fake. The proposed model is trained to provide an accuracy of 98.29% in detection of health of the plant as healthy or diseased.

References

1. Salimans, T., et al.: Improved Techniques for Training GANs. ArXiv e-prints (2016)
2. Goodfellow, I., et al.: Generative Adversarial Nets. Adv. Neural. Inf. Process. Syst. **27**, 2672–2680 (2014)
3. Nazki, H., et al.: Image-to-image translation with GAN for synthetic data augmentation in plant disease datasets. Smart Media J. **8**(22019), 46–57 (2019)
4. Zhu, L., et al.: Generative adversarial networks for hyperspectral image classification. IEEE Trans. Geo sci. Remote Sens. (2018)
5. Zhu, H., et al.: Hyperspectral imaging for pre symptomatic detection of tobacco disease with successive projections algorithm and machine-learning classifiers. Sci. Rep. **7**, 4125 (2017)
6. Iqbal, S., et al.: Assessment and molecular characterization of citrus canker causing pathotypes (2016)
7. Golhani, K., et al.: A review of neural networks in plant disease detection using hyper spectral data. Inf. Process. Agric. **5**(3), 354–371 (2018)
8. Moghadam, P., et al.: Plant disease detection using hyperspectral imaging. In: International Conference on Digital Image Computing: Techniques and Applications, pp. 1–8 (2017)
9. Rumpf, T., et al.: Early detection and classification of plant diseases with support vector machines based on hyperspectral reflectance. Comput. Electr. Agric. **74**(1), 91–99 (2010)
10. Al-Hiary, H., et al.: Fast and accurate detection and classification of plant diseases. Int. J. Comput. Appl. **17**(1), 31–88 (2011)
11. Patil, S.B., et al.: Leaf disease severity measurement using image processing. Int. J. Eng. Technol. **3**(5), 297–301 (2011)
12. Ferentinos, K.P.: Deep learning models for plant disease detection and diagnosis. Comput. Electron. Agric. **145**, 311–318 (2018)
13. Fuentes, A., et al.: A robust deep-learning based detector for real-time tomato plant diseases and pest recognition. Sensors **17**(9), 2022–2043 (2017)
14. Pavaskar, S., Budihal, S.: Real-time vehicle-type categorization and character extraction from the license plates. In: Mallick, P., Balas, V., Bhoi, A., Zobaa, A. (eds.) Cognitive Informatics and Soft Computing. Advances in Intelligent Systems and Computing, vol. 768, pp. 557–565. Springer, Singapore (2019). https://doi.org/10.1007/978-981-13-0617-4_54
15. Suneeta, V.B., et al.: Facial expression recognition using supervised learning. In: Smys, S., Tavares, J., Balas, V., Iliyasu, A. (eds.) Computational Vision and Bio-Inspired Computing, (ICCVBIC). Advances in Intelligent Systems and Computing, vol. 1108, pp. 275–285. Springer, Cham (2019). https://doi.org/10.1007/978-3-030-37218-7_32

Compilation of a Social Network Lexicon for Determining the Profile of Authors

Amelec Viloria[1]([✉]), Kevin Parra[1], Marcial Conde[1],
and Omar Bonerge Pineda Lezama[2]

[1] Universidad de la Costa, Barranquilla, Colombia
{aviloria7, kparra7, mcondel}@cuc.edu.co
[2] Universidad Tecnológica Centroamericana (UNITEC),
San Pedro Sula, Honduras
omarpineda@unitec.edu

Abstract. The use of social networks is steadily increasing worldwide. Hundreds of users daily register in the different existing platforms, therefore, the content extracted from the social networks is fundamental for tasks such as sentiment analysis, detection of author profiles, identification of authors, opinions mining, plagiarism detection, calculation of similarity between texts and to develop robust systems that help to make decisions in related areas such as politics, education, economy, among others. This paper provides a lexical aid for the pre-processing of texts posted in social networks evolved for the subsequent languages: English, Spanish, Dutch and Italian.

Keywords: Author profiles · Information and communication · Social network lexicon · Machine learning

1 Introduction

The processing of messages posted on social networks is not an easy task [1]. Messages published on these platforms are generally short (hundreds of words) and do not follow the conventional rules of the language, for example, slang words, abbreviations and emoticons are often used to compose the texts [2]. The phrases taken into consideration as slang and the abbreviations are unique for every language, and therefore, the structures that carry out approaches on social community messages want unique dictionaries [3].

The aim of this study is to compile dictionaries of slang words, abbreviations, contractions and emoticons to help the pre-processing of texts published on social networks. The use of these dictionaries is intended to improve the results of the tasks related to data obtained from these platforms. Therefore, the hypothesis about the task of author profiling is evaluated. The aim of this task is to obtain information about the author of a text, specifically, his age and gender, by analyzing messages published by the author on Twitter [4].

The study is divided as follows: Sect. 2 presents the details of the research carried out in the area of Natural Language Processing and text pre-processing. Section 3 describes the procedure for compiling the dictionaries and their structure. Section 4 presents the

© Springer Nature Singapore Pte Ltd. 2020
C. Badica et al. (Eds.): ICICCT 2020, CCIS 1170, pp. 262–268, 2020.
https://doi.org/10.1007/978-981-15-9671-1_23

evaluation of the task of author profile identification using the developed dictionaries. Conclusions and future research are presented in Sect. 5.

2   Related Studies

This section shows some of the main works that demonstrate the importance of the data pre-processing phase in different automatic text processing tasks. Proper pre-processing leads to proper analysis and helps to increase the accuracy and efficiency of text analysis processes. Some of the challenges encountered when preprocessing social network texts are presented in detail in the study of [5].

In the study developed by [6], the problems related to the processing of messages obtained from social networks are discussed. The authors improved the performance of an open source spell checker on Twitter data by developing an automatic pre-processing system for the normalization of such data. The results reported indicate that the system is capable of decreasing the average error per message from 15% to 5%.

The work carried out by [7] presents some of the pre-processing steps that must be considered to improve the quality of the messages obtained through Twitter. Among the techniques mentioned are: removing URLs, special characters, repeated letters of a word and question words (what, when, how, etc.). This study showed that by performing the steps mentioned above, the result of the sentiment analysis task improves considerably.

The research conducted by [8] used a combination of different pre-processing techniques such as HTML tag cleaning, abbreviation expansion, handling of negation words, stop word removal and use of methods to reduce a word to its root. The objective of this paper is to analyze the feelings about opinions related to films. The authors reported that appropriate text pre-processing can improve the performance of the sorter and considerably increase the results of the sentiment analysis task.

In [9], it is proposed to spell-check the messages found in social networks, including repeated letters, omitted vowels, substitution of letters with numbers (commonly syllables), use of phonetic orthography, use of abbreviations and acronyms. In a data-driven approach [10], a URL filter is applied in combination with standard text pre-processing techniques.

As can be seen, there are various investigations related to the pre-processing of texts published on social networks. In this study, a lexical resource is presented and its importance for the task of identifying author profiles is demonstrated. In the following section, the procedure used for the compilation of the dictionaries is described and examples of their contents are shown.

3   Creation of the Social Network Lexicon

This research includes the analysis and compilation of shortened vocabulary (used in social networks) for the creation of dictionaries in various languages such as English, Spanish, Dutch and Italian. The dictionaries were compiled for these four languages as they are necessary for the pre-processing of tweets for the task of author profile identification.

The type of shortened vocabulary generally used in Social networks may be divided into 3 categories: slang words, abbreviations and contractions [11, 12]. Each category is briefly described below:

- Slang words are structured vocabulary in a given language, which is generally used among people in the same social group. It is a metalanguage used to enrich expressions, and the words have an intact phonological representation. Some examples of slang words found in the Spanish language are bb (baby), xq (why), dnd (where), tb (too), tqm (I love you so much) and xfa (please) [13].
- Abbreviations are orthographic representations of a word or phrase. Also included in this category are acronyms, which are formed from the initial letters of a name or parts of words or phrases. Within this category are the following examples: Architect, Sr. (Señor), NY (New York), kg. (kilogram), Av. (Avenue), among others [14].
- Contractions occur when two words are reduced to one and an apostrophe takes the place of the missing letter. There are many rules among languages to create contractions. However, this research will not take into account any of them. Examples of contractions are: al (a el) and del (de el) [15].

Another type of element that frequently appears in social network messages is the emoticons. Emoticons are typographic visualizations that allow to represent the facial expressions of emotions, that is to say, it is a way to give an emotive load to a text. Two styles of emoticons were included, known as Western and Eastern. The western style is commonly used in the United States and Europe. The emoticons of this style are written from left to right, as if a face is turned 90° to the right. The emoticons shown below belong to this style: :-) (smiling face), :-/ (doubtful face) and :-o (surprised face). On the other hand, the eastern type emoticons are popular in East Asia and unlike the western style, the eastern emoticons are not rotated. In this style, the eyes are often seen as an important characteristic expression. Some examples of this style are (ˆvˆ) (smiley face), ((+ +)) (doubtful face) and (o.o.) surprised face [16].

The study includes a collection of shortened vocabulary and emoticons that are generally used in social networks. The process of compiling the dictionaries is described below [17]:

1. Search and identification of web sites that are used as sources for the extraction of slang word lists, abbreviations and contractions in the four languages (English, Spanish, Italian and Dutch).
2. Manual or semi-automatic extraction of all slang words, abbreviations and contractions along with their respective meanings from each website in the different languages.
3. Identification and merging of all the files of the same category. Cleaning, formatting and standardization of each file, eliminating duplicates. Manual verification of the meaning of each dictionary entry.

Through the process described above, twelve dictionaries were created, divided into four languages, one for each category (slang words, abbreviations and contractions). The dictionaries are available for free on the website, where there is also a brief description of the dictionaries, a list of websites used for the collection of the three categories of vocabulary for the four languages, and the list of websites used to obtain the emoticons. In the case of the slang word dictionary in Spanish, entries were also included from the work of [18], in which a manual extraction of slang words from a collection of Twitter messages was performed.

Each dictionary has been saved in a specific file, with the factors ordered alphabetically and the facts is coded the use of columns separated via way of means of a tab. The first column corresponds to an access of phrase slang, abbreviation or contraction, relying on the character of the dictionary, and the second one column corresponds to the which means of the corresponding access.

Table 1 affords the facts of every dictionary, in which it is able to be visible that there's a massive wide variety of slang phrases to be had for English and Spanish, even as for Dutch and Italian, the wide variety of entries is lower. On the opposite hand, it is able to be visible that there's a big wide variety of abbreviations withinside the Dutch language. The overall wide variety of entries withinside the social networking lexicon is 7,422.

Table 1. Number of entries in each dictionary.

Dictionary type	Dutch	Italian	English	English
Abbreviations	1,325	110	1,401	603
Slangs	300	401	1,314	1,003
Contractions	16	62	151	10
Emoticons	–	–	492	492
Totals	1,421	530	3,103	2,102

4 Identifying Author Profiles

The project of figuring out writer profiles includes figuring out a few factors of someone together with their age, sex, or a few behavioral developments primarily based totally at the evaluation of textual content samples. Author profiling may be used in lots of areas, for example, in forensic technology to attain an outline of a suspect with the aid of using studying messages published on social networks, and in enterprise to customize commercials that seem on social networks or despatched through email [19].

In latest years, special techniques had been proposed to deal with the project of figuring out writer profiles, maximum of which use automated getting to know techniques, records mining and herbal language processing. From a self-getting to know factor of view, the project of writer profile identity may be taken into consideration as a multi-magnificence and multi-label class hassle, in which every S_i detail of a hard and fast of textual content samples $S = S1, S2$. If a couple of tags are assigned ($l1, l2, ..., lk$), every of them representing an thing of the writer (gender, age, behavioral developments) and the cost assigned in every tag represents a class withinside the corresponding thing [14]. The hassle is translated into the development of an M classifier that assigns numerous labels to the unlabeled texts.

The automated getting to know technique is split into stages: education and trying out. In the education stage, a vectoral illustration of every of the instance texts of every class is received, that is, vi = {v1, v2, . . .} in which vi is the vectoral illustration of the instance textual content Si [20].

Then, a sorter is skilled to apply the vector illustration of the classified samples. The studies applies a vector-primarily based totally classifier and generates special class fashions for every thing of an writer's profile, i.e., a version to decide age and some other version to decide gender are learnt.

The traits used on this paper are primarily based totally on a vector illustration of phrase frequency the usage of the usual bag of phrases (BOW) version, which indicates to be powerful in obligations associated with writer characterization in preceding papers [9]. In this paper best the frequency of phrases that arise withinside the education textual content set is used to construct the version of illustration.

In the trying out or assessment phase, the vectoral illustration of the unlabeled texts is received the usage of the equal traits extracted withinside the education stage. Then, the classifier is used to assign values to the labels of every thing of the writer profile of every person of the take a look at suite.

In order to assess the usefulness of the dictionaries, the corpus designed for the project of writer profile identity is used [18]. The corpus consists of tweets in 4 special languages: English, Spanish, Italian and Dutch. Each language has a hard and fast of tagged tweets similar to the age and gender of the writer of that tweet. The values of the gender magnificence tags may be: male or female. The values of the age magnificence tags may be: 18–24, 25–34, 35–49, 50–xx.

In this sense, the experiments were carried out using the training corpus and a 10-layer cross validation was performed to evaluate the proposal.

Tables 2 and 3 present the accuracy obtained for the gender and age classes respectively, with and without corpus pre-processing. One can conclude that for each language, the best results were obtained when preprocessing is done using these dictionaries.

The pre-processing stage consists basically of identifying, within the corpus, the words found in the dictionaries and replacing them with their respective meanings. It is worth mentioning that this work does not carry out any process of disambiguation of the meaning of the words and therefore, only the first available meaning for each term is selected.

Table 2. Results obtained for gender classification

Language	SVM Liblinear	
	No pre-processing	With pre-processing
English	73.47	76.14
English	83.04	83.25

Table 3. Results obtained for the age classification

Language	SVM Liblinear	
	No pre-processing	With pre-processing
English	73.66	76.85
English	71.73	71.13

5 Conclusions and Future Research

The paper affords a social community lexicon containing dictionaries of slang words, abbreviations, contractions and emoticons famous on social networks. The aid includes dictionaries in English, Spanish, Dutch, and Italian. In addition, the records series approach is described, in addition to the listing of URLs used as reassets for the introduction of every dictionary, explaining the system of standardization of the dictionaries. The take a look at presents facts approximately the shape of the dictionaries and an outline in their length.

When the use of the dictionaries for pre-processing texts the researchers found out that there are a few phrases generally utilized in social networks that are not gift withinside the internet reassets, specifically for the English, Italian and Dutch languages. Therefore, destiny research will intend to amplify the slang phrase dictionaries with manually accumulated entries for every language, withinside the equal manner as changed into completed for the Spanish slang phrase dictionary.

References

1. Gelpi Texeira, R.: Política 2.0: las redes sociales (Facebook y Twitter) como instrumento de comunicación política. Estudio: caso Uruguay. Doctoral dissertation, Universidad Complutense de Madrid (2018)
2. Ponte, J.J.V.: La terminología de las redes sociales digitales: estudio morfológico-semántico y lexicográfico. Doctoral dissertation, Universidade da Coruña (2018)
3. Lundberg, J., Laitinen, M.: Twitter trolls: a linguistic profile of anti-democratic discourse. Lang. Sci. **79**, 101268 (2020)
4. González, F.: Big data, algoritmos y política: las ciencias sociales en la era de las redes digitales. Cinta de moebio **65**, 267–280 (2019)
5. Gómez-Hurtado, I., García Prieto, F.J., Delgado-García, M.: Uso de la red social Facebook como Herramienta de aprendizaje en estudiantes Universitarios: estudio integrado sobre Percepciones. Perspectiva Educacional **57**(1), 99–119 (2018)
6. Moreno Fernández, F., Moreno Sandoval, A.: Configuración lingüística de anglicismos procedentes de Twitter en el español estadounidense. Revista signos **51**(98), 382–409 (2018)
7. Roldan Robles, P.R.: Desarrollo de una arquitectura conceptual para el análisis de contenidos en redes sociales sobre el tema del aborto usando Python. Bachelor's thesis (2019)
8. Pila Pila, L.E.: Incidencia ortográfica que generan las redes sociales en los adolecentes. Bachelor's thesis, Universidad Técnica de Cotopaxi, Facultad de Ciencias Humanas Y Educación, Licenciatura en Comunicación Social, Latacunga (2017)

9. Kharlamov, A.A., Orekhov, A.V., Bodrunova, S.S., Lyudkevich, N.S.: Social network sentiment analysis and message clustering. In: El Yacoubi, S., Bagnoli, F., Pacini, G. (eds.) Internet Science. Lecture Notes in Computer Science, vol. 11938, pp. 18–31. Springer, Cham (2019). https://doi.org/10.1007/978-3-030-34770-3_2

10. Aljarah, I., et al.: Intelligent detection of hate speech in Arabic social network: a machine learning approach. J. Inf. Sci. 0165551520917651 (2020)

11. López-Monroy, A.P., González, F.A., Solorio, T.: Early author profiling on Twitter using profile features with multi-resolution. Expert Syst. Appl. **140**, 112909 (2020)

12. Hilte, L., Daelemans, W., Vandekerckhove, R.: Lexical patterns in adolescents' online writing: the impact of age, gender, and education. Written Commun. 0741088320-917921 (2020)

13. Bi, Q., et al.: Determining the topic evolution and sentiment polarity for albinism in a chinese online health community: machine learning and social network analysis. JMIR Med. Inf. **8**(5), e17813 (2020)

14. Bayrakdar, S., Yucedag, I., Simsek, M., Dogru, I.A.: Semantic analysis on social networks: a survey. Int. J. Commun. Syst. e4424 (2020)

15. Rosso, P., et al.: A survey on author profiling, deception, and irony detection for the arabic language. Lang. Linguis. Compass **12**(4), e12275 (2018)

16. Gómez-Adorno, H., Markov, I., Sidorov, G., Posadas-Durán, J.P., Arias, C.F.: Compilación de un lexicón de redes sociales para la identificación de perfiles de autor. Res. Comput. Sci. **115**, 19–27 (2016)

17. Viloria, A., et al.: Integration of data mining techniques to PostgreSQL database manager system. Proc. Comput. Sci. **155**, 575–580 (2019)

18. Hayon, S., et al.: Twitter mentions and academic citations in the urologic literature. Urology **123**, 28–33 (2019)

19. Viloria, A., Robayo, P.V.: Virtual network level of application composed IP networks connected with systems-(NETS Peer-to-Peer). Ind. J. Sci. Technol. **9**, 46 (2016)

20. Terán, L., Mancera, J.: Dynamic profiles using sentiment analysis and twitter data for voting advice applications. Govern. Inf. Q. **36**(3), 520–535 (2019)

Generalized Constraint Representation of Comparative Adjectives and Its Type-2 Fuzzy Modeling in PNL

Bushra Siddique[✉] and M. M. Sufyan Beg

Aligarh Muslim University, Aligarh, India
bushrasiddique006@gmail.com, mmsbeg@hotmail.com

Abstract. This paper deals with Zadeh's concept of Precisiated Natural Language (PNL) based upon the paradigm of Computational Theory of Perceptions (CTP). In order to employ PNL to handle imprecise information in the Natural Language (NL) propositions, the prerequisites are: to be able to convert the NL propositions in a form suitable for computations and to be able to model the same to carry out the computations. In this paper, we have dealt with these subjects particularly for the comparative form of the lexical category of adjectives. The objective of the paper is twofold: first is to propose a Generalized Constraint Representation (GCR) for the comparative adjectives in PNL, and the second is to outline the General Type-2 modeling of the same. In both the mentioned objectives, we have incorporated the effect of linguistic hedges as well. To signify our proposal and the correctness of the corresponding modeling, we have implemented the same for a set of adjectives and linguistic hedges and demonstrated it to an application scenario.

Keywords: Computing with words · CWW · Precisiated Natural Language · PNL · Generalized Constraint Representation · GCR · Comparative adjectives · Type-2 fuzzy sets

1 Introduction

A Natural Language (NL) is a system to describe perceptions. Thus, perception-based data constitute a large amount of information in NL propositions. While the traditional paradigms which treat numbers as objects of computation are not capable to deal with perception-based information, the paradigm of Computational Theory of Perceptions (CTP) proposed by Zadeh [14,15] offers this unique capability. In this paradigm, in contrast to numbers, the objects of computation are words/propositions of the NL. CTP thus offers to precisiate the NL statements in meaning and makes the contained information accessible to machines. This precisiation in meaning could be carried out for a subset of NL and is termed as the Precisiated Natural Language (PNL) [16].

To be able to treat NL propositions as objects of computation, one of the primary prerequisites is to convert the NL propositions into a suitable form.

© Springer Nature Singapore Pte Ltd. 2020
C. Badica et al. (Eds.): ICICCT 2020, CCIS 1170, pp. 269–283, 2020.
https://doi.org/10.1007/978-981-15-9671-1_24

In reference to PNL, this form is called the Generalized Constraint Representation (GCR). Furthermore, once the GCR corresponding to the NL propositions has been identified, what is needed is to model the fuzzy representations of the same (maybe understood as the perception-based words occurring in the GCR) to carry out the necessary computations. In this paper, we have addressed these subjects in the context of *comparative adjectives*. The objective of this paper is thus two-fold: first is to propose a Generalized Constraint Representation (GCR) for the comparative form of the lexical category of adjectives, and second is to present the General Type-2 modeling for the same. In both the mentioned objectives, we have incorporated the effect of linguistic hedges as well.

The work carried out is novel and significant in view of the following considerations:

- While GCR for lexical categories of adjectives and adverbs have been reported in the literature [11,12], the lexical category of comparative adjective has not yet been addressed. The proposed GCR thus offers to handle a simple NL proposition containing comparative adjectives and linguistic hedges (if present). Sample propositions are *John is taller than Sam, Monika is somewhat taller than Mary* etc.
- In view that Type-1 fuzzy representations for word modeling are rendered scientifically incorrect [7], we have outlined the General Type-2 [8,10] modeling for the comparative adjectives as well as its hedged form (i.e., adjectives preceded by a linguistic hedge). Particularly, we have used the Linear General Type-2 representation [2,3] of the linear adjectives, reported lately in the literature and identified to be the most appropriate over other representations to the best of our knowledge. The presented modeling, thus, offers to obtain the Type-2 representation of the comparative adjectives such as *taller, shorter*, as well as the hedged comparative adjectives such as such as *extremely taller, somewhat shorter* etc.

Table 1. Construction of comparative form of adjective from its absolute form

Absolute form	Comparative form	Sample pair
Most of one-syllable	Add -*er* at end (always)	*small-smaller*
Two syllables ending in -*y*	Add -*er* at end (asually)	*lucky-luckier*
Some of one syllable	Add -*er* at end	*clear-clearer*
Some of two syllables	Add *more* in front	*common-more common*
One syllable ending in -*ed*	Add *more* in front (always)	*pleased-more pleased*
Most of two syllables	Add *more* in front (always)	*careful-more careful*
Three or more syllables	Add *more* in front (always)	*magnificent-more magnificent*

While the proposed GCR and the corresponding modeling could be applied to solve complex CWW problems (which is not the objective of this paper), we have carried out the implementation and demonstrated a less comprehensive application scenario. The objective of the reported implementation is to justify the correctness of the proposed modeling. Particularly, given the perception-based information like *John is somewhat taller than Sam* (consisting of the comparative adjective taller and the linguistic hedge somewhat), the application scenario answers the following question: What is the truth value for Sam's height to be a if John's height is b (or vice versa, such that a and b can assume singleton as well ranged values)? Following, we outline the contributions of this paper:

- We have proposed the Generalized Constraint Representation (GCR) and the corresponding protoformal representation for the *comparative form* of the lexical category of adjectives.
- We have outlined the Type-2 fuzzy representation of the *comparative adjectives* using the Linear General Type-2 fuzzy representation of linear adjectives reported in the literature.
- We have incorporated the effect of linguistic hedges as well (which could additionally be present with the comparative adjectives) in the GCR proposal as well as in the modeling.
- To signify the GCR proposal and the correctness of the corresponding modeling, we have implemented the same and demonstrated its application to a less comprehensive scenario.

The paper is organized as follows. In Sect. 2, we briefly describe the comparative adjectives in the English language. In Sect. 3, we present the proposed Generalized Constraint Representation and the corresponding protoform for the comparative adjectives in PNL. In Sect. 4, we outline the Type-2 fuzzy modeling of the comparative adjectives. In Sect. 5, we study the effect of linguistic hedges on the comparative adjectives. In Sect. 6, we report the implementation of the proposal and the modeling to an application scenario. Finally, we conclude the paper.

2   Comparative Adjectives in English

In English grammar, an adjective is a lexical category of words that describes the attribute of a noun object. For example, in the sentence 'John is tall', the adjective *tall* describes the attribute *height* of the noun object John. The adjectives (particularly, gradable adjectives), termed to be in the absolute form, have comparative as well as superlative forms of which the former is the subject of this paper and is described next.

Comparative Adjectives: The comparative form of the adjective is used to compare the same attribute of two different noun objects [4]. It expresses a higher degree of the attribute denoted by the absolute form of the adjective [1]. The comparative adjectives can take either attributive or predicative positions in the sentence. The general form of predicative usage of the comparative adjective in a sentence is:

Noun 1 (subject) + verb + comparative adjective + than + noun 2 (object). For example, considering the comparative form of the adjective *tall* mentioned in the previous example, a sample sentence containing its comparative form could be 'John is taller than Sam', in which two noun objects *John* and *Sam* are compared based on the attribute *height* by the comparative adjective *taller*.

Depending upon the number of syllables (a unit of pronunciation constituting the word itself or a part of it having a vowel sound with/without surrounding consonants) in the given adjective, its comparative form could be constructed as outlined in the Table 1 (compiled using the contents in [4]) Moreover, there are some adjectives that have completely irregular comparative forms. For instance, the comparative form of the adjectives *good, little* and *far* are *better, less* and *farther* respectively.

3 Generalized Constraint Representation (GCR) of Comparative Adjectives in PNL

3.1 Overview of the Generalized Constraint Representation (GCR) in PNL

The GCR of an NL proposition conveys the information contained in it. This representation is formed by assuming that the given NL proposition is an answer to an implicit question. The GCR of a proposition extracts the implicit semantics in the form of three parameters: 1) the variable whose meaning is constrained, 2) the manner in which the variable is constrained and, 3) the constrained value. These three parameters are accordingly termed as the constrained variable, the modality of the constraint and the constraining relation represented by X, r and R respectively. The GCR of a given NL proposition p, $GCR(p)$ is represented as [16]:

$$X \; isr \; R \tag{1}$$

Considering Eq. 1, X and r may take different forms depending upon the nature of the information contained in the NL proposition. Some of the possible forms of X and r are listed in Fig. 1.

In line with the above discussion, consider, for instance, the proposition: *Monika is young.* Assuming the implicit question to be *What is the age of Monika?*, its GCR could be written as follows:

$$age \; (Monika) \; is \; young \tag{2}$$

In the just mentioned example, the constraining relation is a function of another variable, $f(X)$, the modality of the constraint is possibilistic and the constraining relation is the fuzzy set labeled 'young' depicting the possibility distribution of the age values.

Possible forms of:	
CONSTRAINING VARIABLE: 'X'	**MODALITY OF THE CONSTRAINT: 'r'**
• *An n-ary variable, $X = (X_1, ..., X_n)$* • *A conditional variable, $X|Y$* • *A structured variable, $A(B(X))$* • *A function of another variable, $f(X)$* ...	• *Possibilistic (r = blank)* • *Probabilistic (r = p)* • *Veristic (r = v)* • *Usuality (r = u)* • *Random set (r = rs)* • *Fuzzy graph (r =fg)* • *Bi-modal (r = bm)* • *Pawlak set (r = ps)* ...

Fig. 1. Possible forms of the constraining variable X and the modality of the constraint r in PNL

3.2 Proposed Generalized Constraint Representation (GCR) for Comparative Adjectives

Considering the nature of the comparative adjectives, the chosen form for the constraining variable is $f(X)$ (refer Fig. 1), such that X is a binary variable depicting the two noun objects that are compared and f is the characteristic feature of the noun described by the adjective. The proposed GCR for the comparative adjectives, thus, takes the following form (as in Eq. 3):

$$f(x_1, x_2) \ is \ R \tag{3}$$

In the above equation, the constraining relation R is a *binary fuzzy relation* depicting the comparative adjective of concern. We outline the detailed computation of the constraining relation R i.e. modeling of the comparative adjective, in the following section (Sect. 4). As an example, consider the proposition: *John is taller than Sam*. In line with Eq. 3, its GCR is represented as:

$$Height(John, Sam) \ is \ taller \tag{4}$$

Following Eq. 3, the corresponding protoform for the comparative adjective takes the following form:

$$A(B, C) \ is \ D \tag{5}$$

where A, B, C, and D are correspondingly the abstractions for the characteristic function described by the adjective, first noun object, second noun object and the comparative adjective respectively.

4 Modeling of the Comparative Adjectives

In this section, we discuss how the *binary fuzzy relation* corresponding to the comparative form of the adjective in the proposed GCR (refer Eq. 3) could be modeled given a fuzzy representation of the adjective itself. Limiting the scope to

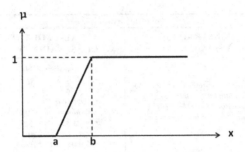

Fig. 2. Type-1 representation of the linear adjective *tall*

linear adjectives [6], we first present the modeling of the comparative form w.r.t. to a Type-1 fuzzy representation of the adjective (Sect. 4.1). However, in view that the Type-1 fuzzy modeling of words is rendered scientifically incorrect [7], we extend the basic idea of the Type-1 modeled comparative adjectives to outline its Type-2 modeling w.r.t. to a given Type-2 fuzzy representation of the adjective (Sect. 4.2). Particularly, we chose the Linear General Type-2 (LGT2) representation of the linear adjectives from the literature proposed by Bilgin et al. [2,3]. We have presented the discussion considering the linear adjective *tall* in the following subsections. However, it is to be noted that the formulation holds for any linear adjective, in general.

4.1 Type-1 Modeling of the Comparative Adjectives

Considering the realistic assumption that an individual is considered to be tall if he/she crosses a certain height value, let the Type-1 representation of the linear adjective *tall* to be a right shoulder membership function as given in the following equation (Eq. 6, and illustrated in Fig. 2):

$$\mu_{tall}(x) = \begin{cases} 0 & x < a \\ (x-a)/(b-a) & a \leq x \leq b \\ 1 & x > b \end{cases} \tag{6}$$

Let the range of the height be discretized into n points and matrix M having dimensions $n x n$ denote the binary fuzzy relation corresponding to the comparative adjective *taller*. The membership grades at each cell value (i, j) in this matrix depicts the degree to which the object having height i is taller that the object having height j. Thus, the membership grades of height value pair (i, j) in the binary fuzzy relation corresponding to the comparative adjective *taller* could be computed as follows (Eq. 7):

$$\mu_{taller}(x_i, x_j) = \begin{cases} 0 & if\ x_i \leq x_j \\ \mu_{tall}(x_i) - \mu_{tall}(x_j) & if\ x_i > x_j \end{cases} \tag{7}$$

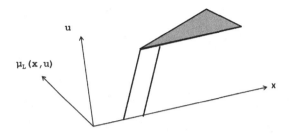

Fig. 3. 3-D view of the Linear General Type-2 representation of the linear adjective *tall*

4.2   Type-2 Modeling of Comparative Adjectives

We briefly describe the chosen Linear General Type-2 (LGT2) representation of the linear adjectives (Sect. 4.2) following which we outline the computation for the comparative form of the same (Sect. 4.2).

Linear General Type-2 (LGT2) Representation of Linear Adjectives. In view of the shortcomings of the Type-1 and the Interval Type-2 (IT2) [9] fuzzy representation to model the linear adjectives as highlighted in [6] and [5] respectively, authors [2,3] have proposed a Linear General Type-2 (LGT2) representation for the same, the 3D illustration of which is shown in Fig. 3. As shown, the secondary grades of LGT2 representation range in the interval [0, 1]. Thus, it offers to maintain the linear ordering of objects as required by the linear adjectives.

The front view and top view of the LGT2 representation is illustrated in Fig. 4a and 4b respectively. As shown, while the front view (Fig. 4a) of the LGT2 representation is similar to the Interval Type-2 representation, the point of difference is highlighted in the top view (Fig. 4b) which is a right edged right triangle in case of LGT2 in contrast to a horizontal line (at grade 1) in case of IT2 representation. Following, we outline the membership calculation of a singleton input x' in the LGT2 representation.

The singleton input x' in the LGT2 fuzzy representation of adjectives yields a vertical slice. The membership grade for a singleton input can be computed taking into account the support of the upper membership and lower membership functions. Based on this, the following conditions are distinguished:

- Condition 1) When $\bar{\mu}_{\tilde{L}}(x') = \underline{\mu}_{\tilde{L}}(x')$: In this case, the secondary grade is the length of the vertical line (as shown in Fig. 5a). Using the concept of similarity of triangles and accounting the fact that the secondary grades range from 0 to 1, the length of the vertical line depicting the secondary grade for x', could be calculated as follows (Eq. 8):

$$\mu_{\tilde{L}}(x', u) = \frac{x' - x_1}{x_2 - x_1} \tag{8}$$

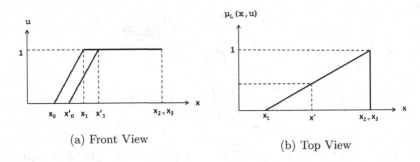

(a) Front View

(b) Top View

Fig. 4. Front and Top view of the Linear General Type-2 representation of the linear adjective *tall*

– Condition 2) When $\bar{\mu}_{\tilde{L}}(x') \neq \underline{\mu}_{\tilde{L}}(x')$: This further distinguishes two conditions as mentioned below:
  - Condition 2.1) $\bar{\mu}_{\tilde{L}}(x') < 1$: In this case, the vertical slice is in the shape of a triangle (as shown in Fig. 5b).
  - Condition 2.2) when $\bar{\mu}_{\tilde{L}}(x') = 1$: In this case, the vertical slice is in the shape of a trapezoid (as shown in Fig. 5c).

The secondary grade for the above conditions (Condition 2.1 and 2.2) can be calculated by computing the COG/centroid of the corresponding shape using the following equation (Eq. 9):

$$\mu_{\tilde{L}}(x', u) = f_{x'}^{cg}(\tilde{L}) = \frac{\sum_{k=1}^{M} u_k * \mu_{\tilde{L}}(x', u_k)}{\sum_{k=1}^{M} u_k} \tag{9}$$

where $u_k \in [\underline{\mu}_{\tilde{L}}(x'), \bar{\mu}_{\tilde{L}}(x')]$

Computations for Type-2 Modeling of Comparative Adjectives. The membership grade of a given input element x in a Type-1 fuzzy set F, $\mu_F(x)$ yields a crisp value, whereas its membership grade in a Type-2 fuzzy set $\tilde{F}$, $\mu_{\tilde{F}}(x)$ yields a Type-1 fuzzy set such that the elements and the membership values of this T1 set correspond to the primary membership grade and the secondary membership grade in $\tilde{F}$ respectively. In consideration of this, we extend the idea of forming the *binary fuzzy relation* corresponding to the comparative adjectives given the Type-1 representation of the linear adjective (as given in Eq. 7) to present the computation for the same given the Type-2 representation of the linear adjective.

Let $\widetilde{tall}$ denote the Linear General Type-2 representation of the linear adjective 'tall'. Now, the grade of membership of singleton input x in $\widetilde{tall}$ is a Type-1 fuzzy set A_x, such that its elements and the membership values correspond to the primary membership grade and the secondary membership grade in $\widetilde{tall}$ respectively. Let A_{x_i} and A_{x_j} be the Type-1 FS depicting the membership grade

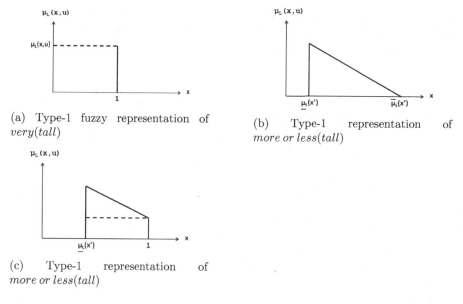

(a) Type-1 fuzzy representation of *very(tall)*

(b) Type-1 representation of *more or less(tall)*

(c) Type-1 representation of *more or less(tall)*

Fig. 5. Effect of concentrator and dilator on Type-1 fuzzy representation of linear adjective *tall*

in $\widetilde{tall}$ corresponding to heights x_i and x_j. Then, in line with Eq. 7, the membership grade of the height value pair (x_i, x_j) in the binary fuzzy relation matrix corresponding to the comparative form of $\widetilde{tall}$ is computed using the bounded difference of A_{x_i} and A_{x_j} as given in Eq. 10.

$$\mu_{\widetilde{taller}}(x_i, x_j) = A_{x_i} - A_{x_j} = min(0, \ \mu_{A_{x_i}}(x) - \mu_{A_{x_j}}(x)), \forall x \in X \quad (10)$$

where '−' denotes the bounded difference operation [17] on two fuzzy sets the computation for which is shown in Eq. 10.

5   Linguistic Hedges and Comparative Adjectives

In linguistics, hedges are put to use when the topic of utterance is to be specified more or less closely. Specifically, in English grammar, hedges are special kind of adverbs which modify the meaning of the adjective to which they are attached. For example, consider the sentence: *John is extremely taller than Sam*, in which the hedge *extremely* modifies the comparative adjective *taller* by intensifying its meaning.

As mentioned in the discussion of Sect. 3.2, the GCR for such NL propositions consisting of a comparative adjective preceded by a hedge takes the form as mentioned in Eq. 3 with the difference that the constraining relation now is the *modified* binary fuzzy relation due to the effect of the linguistic hedge on it. To highlight this difference, we write the GCR of the just mentioned sample NL proposition in the following form:

$$Height(John, Sam)\ is\ extremely.taller \tag{11}$$

Following we present a brief mathematical interpretation of linguistic hedges (Sect. 5.1). We have already presented the computation of the Type-1 and Type-2 binary fuzzy relation matrix corresponding to the comparative adjective in Sect. 4.1 and 4.2 respectively. In reference to the later representation, i.e. Type-2 representation of the comparative adjective, we outline the computations which govern the effect of the linguistic hedges on it (Sect. 5.2).

5.1   Mathematical Interpretation of Linguistic Hedges

In fuzzy logic, a hedge is interpreted as an operation on a fuzzy set such that it modifies its grade of membership resulting into another fuzzy set. The modification made on the operated fuzzy set depends upon the nature of the hedge, and accordingly, the hedges are of different types. We the following types of the linguistic hedges in this paper:

- Concentrators: "The result of applying a concentrator to a fuzzy set A is a fuzzy subset of A such that the reduction in the magnitude of the grade of membership of x in A is relatively smaller for those x which have a high grade of membership in A and relatively large for the x with low membership [13]".
- Dilators: The effect of dilation is opposite to that of concentration operation as mentioned above.

Let *con* and *dil* denote the concentrator and the dilator hedge respectively. Let F be the Type-1 fuzzy set on which the hedge (concentrator or dilator) is operated upon. This results in the modified fuzzy set represented as $con(F)$ or $dil(F)$, the membership grades for which are given respectively by the following equations (Eq. 12 and 13):

$$\mu_{con(F)}(x) = (\mu_F(x))^c \tag{12}$$

$$\mu_{dil(F)}(x) = (\mu_F(x))^d \tag{13}$$

where c and d assume values depending upon the strength of the corresponding concentrator and dilator respectively. From the literature, for example, the value of c for the concentrators 'very' and 'extremely' are found to be 2 and 3 respectively and, the value of d for the dilators 'more or less' and 'somewhat' are found to be $\frac{1}{2}$ and $\frac{1}{4}$ respectively.

Table 2. Results for comparative adjective *taller* and the effect of linguistic hedges on it

S.No. ↓	Value 1 x_i (in cm)	Value 2 x_j (in cm)	$\mu_{\tilde{F}=taller}(x_i, x_j)$ F	very.F	extremely.F	moreOrLess.F	somewhat.F
1.1	158	150	0.01577	0.00180	0.00021	0.04665	0.08023
1.2	200	180	0.42857	0.18367	0.07872	0.65465	0.80911
1.3	168	160	0.10335	0.01181	0.00135	0.30571	0.52579
1.4	200	165	0.20413	0.09502	0.04431	0.29941	0.36269
2.1	200	[180–200]	0.64286	0.45918	0.35423	0.79024	0.88565
2.2	[160–165]	155	0.01486	0.00106	0.00008	0.05561	0.10756
2.3	200	[160–165]	0.29266	0.14467	0.07199	0.41729	0.49858
2.4	[200–230]	165	0.29828	0.22285	0.17893	0.35732	0.39491
3.1	[200–230]	[180–200]	0.42857	0.18367	0.07872	0.65465	0.80911
3.2	[160–165]	[155–158]	0.04314	0.00389	0.00036	0.14502	0.26657
3.2	[180–200]	[160–165]	0.13141	0.05041	0.02247	0.24956	0.37107

Table 3. Results for comparative adjective *shorter* and the effect of linguistic hedges on it

S.No. ↓	Value 1 x_i (in cm)	Value 2 x_j (in cm)	$\mu_{\tilde{F}=shorter}(x_i, x_j)$ F	very.F	extremely.F	moreOrLess.F	somewhat.F
1.1	145	150	0.01335	0.00048	0.00002	0.07063	0.16247
1.2	135	140	0.03571	0.00128	0.00005	0.18898	0.43472
1.3	80	130	0.35714	0.12755	0.04555	0.59761	0.77306
1.4	100	145	0.20413	0.09502	0.04431	0.29941	0.36269
2.1	[80–100]	130	0.28571	0.08673	0.02770	0.53026	0.72672
2.2	[138–140]	145	0.01533	0.00066	0.00003	0.07465	0.16517
2.3	100	[135–140]	0.14633	0.03617	0.00900	0.29507	0.41926
2.4	[100–130]	135	0.05499	0.01197	0.00277	0.13348	0.22790
3.1	[80–100]	[100–130]	0.17857	0.03316	0.00638	0.42044	0.64758
3.2	[138–140]	[145–148]	0.01124	0.00055	0.00003	0.05093	0.10848
3.2	[80–100]	[135–140]	0.1777	0.05523	0.01785	0.32376	0.43869

5.2 Effect of Linguistic Hedges on Type-2 Representation of Comparative Adjectives

Let A be the Type-1 fuzzy set denoting the membership grade of the height value pair (x_i, x_j) in the Type-2 binary fuzzy relation matrix corresponding to the comparative adjective *taller*. Furthermore, let *con.taller* and *dil.taller* denote the modified binary fuzzy relation matrix due to the effect of concentrator *con* and dilator *dil* on the comparative adjective *taller*. Then, in line with Eqs. 13–14, the membership grade of the height value pair (x_i, x_j) in the modified binary fuzzy relation matrix *con.taller* and *dil.taller* is computed using following set of equations (Eqs. 14–17):

$$\mu_{con.taller}(x_i, x_j) = con(A) \tag{14}$$
$$= [\mu_A(u)]^c, \ \forall u \in domain(A) \tag{15}$$

$$\mu_{dil.taller}(x_i, x_j) = dil(A) \tag{16}$$
$$= [\mu_A(u)]^d, \ \forall u \in domain(A) \tag{17}$$

6   Implementation Results

Since the objective of this paper is not to solve a complex CWW problem, we have chosen a less comprehensive scenario to demonstrate the application of the proposal and the correctness of the corresponding modeling.

The considered application scenario is as follows: Assuming the attribute described by the comparative adjective (or its hedged form, if any linguistic hedge is present) is *att*, and the objects compared by it are X and Y, the considered application scenario aims to answer the questions such as follows:

– *What is the truth value for 'att' of X to be 'a' if 'att' of Y is given as 'b'?*
– *What is the truth value for 'att' of X and Y to be 'a' and 'b' respectively?*

In the implementation, we have considered singleton as well as ranged value for a and b.

Given simple NL propositions containing the comparative adjectives (and linguistic hedges, if present), we convert them into the proposed GCR using parsing techniques (we have used the Stanford parser and the relevant POS tag for identification of comparative adjectives). Following, we model the identified comparative adjective using the proposed general Type-2 modeling. In the implementation reported, we have performed the modeling of two comparative adjectives *taller* and *shorter* using the LGT2 representation of the corresponding linear adjective *tall* and *short*. The considered linguistic hedges are four, namely, *very*, *extremely*, *more or less* and *somewhat*, of which the former two are concentrators and the latter two are dilators. The specifications considered for the Upper Membership Function (UMF) and the Lower Membership Function (LMF) of the LGT2 representation of tall and short are as follows:

– UMF coordinates for *tall*: [140, 160, 230, 230]
– LMF coordinates for *tall*: [150, 170, 230, 230]
– UMF coordinates for *short*: [0, 0, 140, 160]
– LMF coordinates for *short*: [0, 0, 130, 150]

Results Discussion
The results obtained are reported in Table 2 and 3 for the comparative adjective *taller* and *shorter* respectively. The tables list three types of sample pairs:

1. Pairs indexed as 1.x correspond to both the input values as a singleton,
2. Pairs indexed as 2.x correspond to one input value as a singleton and the other as an interval (or vice versa),
3. Pairs indexed as 3.x correspond to both the input values as intervals.

We have chosen sample singleton values and intervals for each of the conditions highlighted in Sect. 4.2 in reference to the specifications of the LGT2 representation of the adjectives, as mentioned above. The intervals are treated as a pair of singleton values and the resulting grade is the mean of the obtained individual grades.

It is to be noted that some membership grades obtained in the result tables are too low to be meaningful, however, as mentioned, we have reported this implementation to verify the correctness of the outlined modeling. To support this claim, we highlight the following points in the interpretation of the obtained results:

1. Considering that the perception of the degree of tallness/shortness of an individual from another depends not only on the difference of height values but also on the range in which the individual heights are, we conclude that the modeling results are in agreement with human-based perceptions. For instance, consider the sample pairs 1.1 and 1.3 of Table 2. Although the height difference between both the input pairs is the same (equal to 8 cm), the corresponding membership grade obtained for both is different. In contrast, for sample pairs, 1.2 and 3.1 of Table 2, although the nature of input (one is singleton pair and the other is interval pair) as well as height difference for the values in pair is different, the membership grade obtained is same.
2. The degree of tallness/shortness for the taller/shorter individual is more if the difference between the height of the other individual that is being compared is more (and vice versa). This is in agreement in view of the sample pairs 2.1 and 3.1 of Table 3. For the height interval [80–100] cm, the degree of shortness for the interval [100–130] cm (which is closer, hence the difference is less) is less than that for 130 cm (which is farther, hence the difference is high).
3. The membership grade of any pair of height values in the comparative adjective is greater than its grade in the comparative adjective modified due to a concentrator. This is in agreement with the nature of the modification carried out by the concentrator operator. Similarly, for the dilator hedge, the membership grade of any pair in the comparative adjective is lesser than its grade in the comparative adjective modified due to a dilator. This is justified for all the sample observations in both the result tables.
4. The higher is the strength of the concentrator, the lower is the membership grade of an input pair in it. Similarly, the higher is the strength of the dilator, the greater is the membership grade of an input pair in it. This is in agreement with the nature of the effect of concentrators/dilators. The grades obtained for all the sample pairs in both the result tables are in conformance with this.

The discussion highlights four points. The former two are in reference to the comparative adjectives and the latter two are in reference to the linguistic hedges. In light of the above discussion, we conclude that the modeling presented for the comparative adjectives and the effect of linguistic hedges on it is in agreement with human reasoning as well as the mathematical interpretation.

7   Conclusion

In this paper, we have addressed the subject of comparative adjectives in PNL. We have proposed a Generalized Constraint Representation (GCR) and the corresponding General Type-2 modeling for the same. We have implemented the proposal and the modeling and applied it to a less comprehensive application scenario. Since perception-based inputs are more realistic, we aim to include the non-singleton inputs as well to enhance the considered application scenario. While the study conducted is complete in its respect, we highlight the following related works which could be carried out. First, to outline an automatic and more effective procedure for identifying GCRs in the simple as well as the complex NL propositions (using language models etc.) and second, to apply the proposal and the modeling to solve more complex CWW problem.

References

1. Aarts, B., Chalker, S., Edmund, W.: The Oxford Dictionary of English Grammar. Oxford University Press, Oxford (2014)
2. Bilgin, A., Hagras, H., Malibari, A., Alhaddad, M.J., Alghazzawi, D.: Towards a general type-2 fuzzy logic approach for computing with words using linear adjectives. In: 2012 IEEE International Conference on Fuzzy Systems, pp. 1–8. IEEE (2012)
3. Bilgin, A., Hagras, H., Malibari, A., Alhaddad, M.J., Alghazzawi, D.: Towards a linear general type-2 fuzzy logic based approach for computing with words. Soft. Comput. 17(12), 2203–2222 (2013). https://doi.org/10.1007/s00500-013-1046-2
4. Eastwood, J.: Oxford Guide to English Grammar. Oxford University Press, Oxford (1994)
5. Greenfield, S., John, R.I.: The uncertainty associated with a type-2 fuzzy set. In: Seising, R. (ed.) Views on Fuzzy Sets and Systems from Different Perspectives. STUDFUZZ, vol. 243, pp. 471–483. Springer, Heidelberg (2009). https://doi.org/10.1007/978-3-540-93802-6_23
6. Klein, E.: A semantics for positive and comparative adjectives. Linguist. Philos. 4(1), 1–45 (1980)
7. Mendel, J.M.: Fuzzy sets for words: a new beginning. In: The 12th IEEE International Conference on Fuzzy Systems, FUZZ 2003, vol. 1, pp. 37–42. IEEE (2003)
8. Mendel, J.M.: Type-2 fuzzy sets and systems: an overview. IEEE Comput. Intell. Mag. 2(1), 20–29 (2007)
9. Mendel, J.M.: Type-2 fuzzy sets as well as computing with words. IEEE Comput. Intell. Mag. 14(1), 82–95 (2019)
10. Mendel, J.M., John, R.B.: Type-2 fuzzy sets made simple. IEEE Trans. Fuzzy Syst. 10(2), 117–127 (2002)
11. Soto, A., Olivas, J.A., Prieto, M.E.: Using generalized constraints and protoforms to deal with adjectives. In: 2007 IEEE International Fuzzy Systems Conference, pp. 1–6. IEEE (2007)
12. Soto, A., Olivas, J.A., Prieto, M.E.: Using generalized constraints and protoforms to deal with adverbs. In: EUSFLAT Conference (2), pp. 119–126 (2007)
13. Zadeh, L.A.: A fuzzy-set-theoretic interpretation of linguistic hedges (1972)

14. Zadeh, L.A.: A new direction in AI: toward a computational theory of perceptions. AI Mag. **22**(1), 73–84 (2001)
15. Zadeh, L.A.: From computing with numbers to computing with words: from manipulation of measurements to manipulation of perceptions. In: MacCrimmon, M., Tillers, P. (eds.) The Dynamics of Judicial Proof. STUDFUZZ, vol. 94, pp. 81–117. Physica, Heidelberg (2002). https://doi.org/10.1007/978-3-7908-1792-8_5
16. Zadeh, L.A.: Precisiated natural language (PNL). AI Mag. **25**(3), 74–92 (2004)
17. Zadeh, L.A.: Calculus of fuzzy restrictions. In: Fuzzy Sets and Their Applications to Cognitive and Decision Processes, pp. 1–39. Elsevier (1975)

Homogeneous Pools to Heterogeneous Ensembles for Unsupervised Outlier Detection

Akanksha Mukhriya$^{(\boxtimes)}$ and Rajeev Kumar

School of Computer and Systems Sciences,
Jawaharlal Nehru University, New Delhi, India
akankshamukhriya@gmail.com

Abstract. A member selection method is presented here for ensembles of unsupervised outlier detection. The key challenge of ensemble construction in unsupervised scenario is the absence of labeled training set. Thus, an alleged outlier set needs to be formed first. Existing methods construct this set, called as target set, comprising all random detectors at input. Our argument is that such target formation may itself be erroneous as an outcome of such no filtered random results. Hence, complete reliance on it may mislead entire selection process. Herein, we propose an ensemble construction approach HEnS (Heterogeneous Ensemble Selector), which selects members from different sets of homogeneous detectors to build a heterogeneous one. Heterogeneity is ensured to induce diversity to form a good target outlier set, first, by considering those detectors at input which are characteristically distinct, and second, by selecting minimal subset of detectors of each type. Accuracy is maintained, first by pruning the relatively highly inaccurate detectors out of the process, and second, by forming a better target which includes only two extreme parameter instantiations from each type. This work primarily aims at building a heterogeneous ensemble which comprises of best or relatively better detectors from each of the homogeneous groups. Experimental results on benchmark datasets show notably improved prediction accuracy of ensembles constructed using proposed method, which in turn supports our claim of better target construction and enhanced diversity.

Keywords: Outlier detection · Outlier ensembles · Ensemble member selection

1 Introduction

Outlier detection is finding out abnormal data observations. Unmasking of outliers provides important insights about some unusual system activity, e.g. fraudulent transactions in a banking system. Since outliers are rare data patterns, their detection is highly challenging. Additionally, all outliers can be notably different to each other in characteristics, hence may not be discovered by any single detection method. Therefore, ensemble learning is being used in recent years for outlier detection [1–5].

The primary goal of ensemble learning is to get more robust results with the help of divergent and accurate members. Thus, an ensemble that comprises of randomly chosen members is not preferable, and hence, members are selected first based on some

© Springer Nature Singapore Pte Ltd. 2020
C. Badica et al. (Eds.): ICICCT 2020, CCIS 1170, pp. 284–295, 2020.
https://doi.org/10.1007/978-981-15-9671-1_25

criteria before combination. In context of outlier detection, member selection for ensembles is extremely difficult because of unsupervised nature of the problem. Due to the same reason of unavailability for samples with known class labels, member selection methods for classification ensembles are also not applicable here. A very few attempts have been made in recent past to build at least better than random ensembles for outlier detection [4–6].

Existing selection methods for outlier detection ensembles make their assessments based on a target set which is produced by some combination of all random input detectors. Even if a small proportion of input detectors are inaccurate, then also, not only union of top points [4], but average score [5] also gets affected heavily. Unquestionably, identifying inaccurate detectors at the input of a selector is as difficult as selecting accurate ones. However, by using existing measures, highly inaccurate detectors can be caught, if used with a bunch of distinct types, unless the underlying data is quite hard. Although, a set of detectors which are very dissimilar to each other in characteristics and formulations, may also result similarly at times, or for some data. Yet, there are higher chances of them resulting diversely e.g., LOF [7], ABOD [8], SOD [9], KDEOS [10] etc. detectors.

In this work, an attempt is made to fill these gaps by focusing on the above two aspects of a good selector. First, to block the highly inaccurate detectors at selector's input from further processing, to avoid the target being more erroneous. Second, to possibly try to maintain distinctiveness of results while target construction, in order to get the better oracle output for further selection assessments. Contributions of this work are summarized as follows.

- We propose an ensemble member selection method for unsupervised outlier detection: HEnS (Heterogeneous Ensemble Selector). It selects members belong to h distinct types of detection methods, from a homogeneous pool of size m for each type. It works in two phases, where each phase corresponds to the above two requirements.
- The first phase of pruning i.e. Selector 1 filters out relatively highly inaccurate detectors from further selection process, using global average.
- The second phase of Selector 2 corresponds to maintain required distinctiveness at the input by building a heterogeneous ensemble while selecting minimal detectors of each type. The double-fault measure [11] is also used for this purpose.
- Our approach overall aims to maintain a minimal but accurate homogeneous subsets of each type to avoid the accuracy target being biased and misleading.

2   Related Work

Building a good ensemble lies on two pillars, accuracy of its members and diversity between them. Since outlier detection is mostly unsupervised in practice, it is extremely difficult to assess accuracy of a detector in absence of class labels. Additionally, since outliers are very rare observations in data, this challenge gets intensified further. With the increasing attention to ensemble learning for outlier detection, only a handful of methods have been proposed by far for member selection. A brief discussion about those is given in this section, as follows.

Greedy Selection [4] is the very first method presented for selecting members of an outlier detection ensemble. As the name suggests, this method greedily selects detectors on the basis of their similarity to a calculated oracle set i.e. target. It is a union of top-k points resulted as outliers by all detectors at the input. Detector that results in maximum similarity to this target is included first in the ensemble. Similarity computation is done by Weighted Pearson Correlation (WPC) between the score list of a detector in question and the target set. After first selection, all remaining detectors are picked one by one in order of their dissimilarity to the currently selected ensemble at that point. If the detector in question improves current ensemble's correlation to the target upon inclusion, it gets selected, rejected otherwise. Since, the method works greedily, selection decision regarding a detector will not be revisited again. The primary issue with greedy selection is the central target set itself, as the union of all random input detectors is highly sensitive to those are inaccurate. As a result, entire selection process gets completely misleading in such cases.

Vertical Selection [5] is the next proposed method for member selection. Similar to greedy selection, this method's center is also a target set, which is the average score vector of all random inputs. Same as in case of greedy selection, detector which has maximum similarity to this target is selected first. Similarity computation is done by Weighted Pearson Correlation (WPC) here as well, but weights are the reciprocal of ranks as per average. It also works in a greedy fashion, but unlike the earlier method, here detectors are picked in the order of their similarity to the target. Hence, it is evident that vertical selection does only contributes to accuracy not diversity.

Horizontal Selection [5] is the next proposed method which is an element based approach. First, mixture modeling is used to label detectors' results as outlier or inliers, and then target set is computed by majority voting. It then uses order statistics to compute that, for a given outlier point, what is the probability that a given ordering of ranks across all input detectors is generated by a null model. Candidate detectors those do not result in sufficiently higher ranks for most of these alleged outliers, are discarded. This approach though contributes to accuracy better, but its diversity contribution is limited only to majority voting.

Boost-select [6] is the next and most recent selection method, which is inspired by the popular boosting algorithm for classification ensembles [12]. It is an unsupervised boosting procedure for outlier detection ensembles, where target is the set of top-k points according to average score of all input detectors. Similar to greedy selector, it also picks up detector which is most similar to target first. Further as well, detectors are considered one by one in the order of their dissimilarity to the partially selected ensemble. If it improves correlation of ensemble to the target, it gets selected.

The boosting procedure steps in when a selection happens. All the top-k points of a selected detector, if included in target, are assigned lesser weights for further similarity assessments by a drop rate of d. The idea behind is to consider detectors further-on on the basis of the yet uncovered points of the target. Target computation in this method empirically shows better contribution to accuracy, but still limited to the accuracy of all random input detectors. Diversity contribution is both in the order of assessments, and due to boosting as well.

Overall, greedy selection is only suitable, if there is some prior knowledge about the accuracy of input detectors, not otherwise. Vertical selection is since only accuracy focused, there are higher chances of getting similar results by the ensemble. This in turn may sometimes lose the purpose of using an ensemble. Same is the case with horizontal selection. Boost-select is basically a good balance between accuracy and diversity, only if most of the random input detectors are accurate.

Other than above, a few ensemble construction methods for outlier detection are based on subsampling of data e.g. variable subsampling [2], rotated bagging [2], variable rotated bagging [2], subsampling ensembles [13], smart sampling [14] etc. Additionally, there is a sequential ensemble learning method for unsupervised outlier detection, CARE [15], which generates feature-bagged outlier detectors as members and improves these iteratively. It works by removing outliers sequentially from the data to build a better data model, on which outlierness is assessed later.

3 Proposed Work

In this section, a member selection method is presented for unsupervised outlier detection ensembles. The key focus of our approach is to select good members from a set of homogeneous detectors to get a good heterogeneous ensemble. The more distinct types of errors will be resulted by selected members of an ensemble, the more will be the diversity, and the more will be the chances of better predictions by the combined ensemble. The workflow is given in pseudocode 1. Before proceeding to its description, a brief discussion is given here about double-fault diversity measure, which is used in this work.

The Double-Fault Measure: This measure is proposed by Giacinto and Roli [11] to select most diverse classifiers from a set of classifiers. It works by finding the pairwise diversity between classifiers based on a set of training samples. The idea behind is that chances of any two given classifiers of being similar are more if they are wrong together than if they are correct together. For a pair of two classifiers a and b, double fault equals to the proportion of training samples those are misclassified by both of them simultaneously. If 0 denotes incorrect classifications and 1 implies the correct one, then double fault value between classifiers a and b i.e. $DF_{a,b}$ can be calculated as:

$$DF_{a,b} = \frac{n_{a,b}(0,0)}{n_{a,b}(1,1) + n_{a,b}(0,1) + n_{a,b}(1,0) + n_{a,b}(0,0)} \tag{1}$$

where, $n_{a,b}(0,0)$ is the number of simultaneous misclassifications by a and b. The higher is the value of DF, the lesser is the diversity. To calculate diversity value of the complete ensemble, values are averaged over the pairwise diversity matrix.

Since, to use any of the classification principles in context of outlier detection, the biggest challenge is its unsupervised nature. Similar is the case with the above measure as in Eq. 1, where correctness or incorrectness is being assessed as per the training set, which is labeled. However, with the extremely limited ways suggested in recent years [4–6, 13–15], getting a moderately better or even slightly better results than a random guess is certainly a win-win case, particularly for detecting rare patterns from data.

Therefore, similar to [6], in this work we use top-k points by average score of a pruned subset of input detectors as the oracle or target set. The prediction accuracy (0/1) of an outlier detector a w.r.t. a point x from the target set can be calculated as:

$$D_a(x \in Target) = \begin{cases} 1 & if \ rank_a(x) \leq k(correct\,prediction) \\ 0 & otherwise \ (incorrect\,prediction) \end{cases} \qquad (2)$$

To calculate diversity of complete ensemble, similar to that in case of classification, first, proportion of simultaneous incorrect predictions over the target set is calculated, for all pairs of detectors. These proportions are then aggregated for each detector. For an ensemble of D detectors, the double fault vector i.e. DF vector in which each value corresponds to the DF value of a detector, can be calculated as:

$$DF(D, Target)_{[1*|D|]} = \forall_{a=1}^{|D|} \sum_{b=1 \neq a}^{|D|} \frac{n_{a,b}(0,0)}{|Target|} \qquad (3)$$

As discussed earlier that higher DF value indicates lower diversity, so rather than averaging all these DF values (Eq. 3) to get the ensemble diversity, their reciprocals are averaged. The reciprocal vector directly indicates diversity of corresponding detector. The ensemble diversity DV is calculated as:

$$DV(D, Target) = \sum_{j=1}^{|D|} \frac{1}{DF(D_j, Target)} \qquad (4)$$

DV value is used here to assess the dissimilarity between members of an ensemble in question, during the selection process. Moreover, the motivation behind the use of double-fault measure is to get more concrete view of element based dissimilarities between detectors.

Description of Method: The main work flow is given in pseudocode 1. Given an input set O of h heterogeneous types of outlier detectors, with each type set having m outlier score lists corresponding to its m parameter instantiations. These m parameter values are distant k values such that $k1 < k2 < ... < km$. The reason for choosing a number of parameter instantiations of a same method is to allow selectors to assess performance of a given detection method using a wide enough range of parameters.

Further, it has been observed experimentally that for a given dataset, usually detection performance of a method either gets improved or degrades with the increasing parameter value, up to a certain point. Since, this saturation point cannot be predicted easily when data labels are missing, we approach to at least avoid selection of the inaccurate instantiations for each of these h types using this wide range. Although, it may not be the case always due to the very challenging nature of outlier detection. Yet, most of the time, such range of parameters not only allow to avoid the worst ones, but also to pick up slightly better accurate instantiations.

Coming back to pseudocode 1, it is a two-phase process. The first phase is the Selector 1 (pseudocode 2), which is basically a pruning phase applied to all $h * m$ score lists.

Pseudocode 1: <u>H</u>eterogeneous <u>E</u>nsemble <u>S</u>elector (HEnS)

Input: $O_{[h*m]} :=$ h-sets of m-normalized score lists, corresponding to same method but different parameters k = $(k_1, k_2,..., k_m)$ such that $k_1 < k_2 < ... < k_m$, and $t_c :=$ correlation threshold

Output: E := selected Ensemble

1. E := $\emptyset$

2. A := Selector1(O, t_c)

3. E := Selector2(A, K)

4. **Return**(E)

Pseudocode 2: Selector1

Input: $O_{[h*m]} :=$ h-sets of m-normalized score lists, corresponding to same method but different parameters k = $(k_1, k_2,..., k_m)$, and $t_c :=$ correlation threshold

Output: P: h'-sets of normalized score lists P:= $\{P_1, P_2,..., P_{h'}\}$ where, each P_i = $\{P_{lb(i)}, P_{ub(i)}\} \forall_{i=1}^{h'}$

1. T_1 := average($O_1, O_2,..., O_h$)   /* average score vector of all candidates */

2. R := rank-list after sorting T_1 in descending order

3. **For each** of s outlier score-lists in O **do**

4.   **If** WPC(s, T_1) < t_c (threshold) **Then**   /* accuracy threshold for pruning */

5.   Remove s from O

6.   **End If**

7. **End For**

8. P = $\emptyset$

9. **For each** of h'-heterogeneous type set $q \in$ pruned set O **do**

10.   P = P ∪ score lists of both parameter extremes (q)

11. **End For**

12. **Return**(P)

This phase helps in filtering out any of the detectors those are highly inaccurate w.r. t. process. This is achieved by assessing their correlations to the global average score i.e. average score of all $h * m$ score lists. For this, weighted Pearson Correlation (WPC) is used, with the weights used in vertical selection [5]. If WPC of any detector is less than the correlation threshold, it is removed from the original set (line 3–7). This threshold t_c is to be set very low (0.2 in our experiments) to only let the highly inaccurate ones blocked, not the distinct ones. After pruning, for each of h type sets, score lists of the lowest and highest parameter values instantiations from the updated list-set will be passed to the next step (line 8–12). Hence, P is a set of h' sets of score-lists, corresponding to the two instantiation extremes of each.

Pseudocode 3: Selector2

Input: P: h'-sets of extreme instantiations for each heterogeneous types P := {P$_1$, P$_2$,...,
P$_{h'}$} where, P$_i$:= {P$_{lb(i)}$, P$_{ub(i)}$}, and K := number of top-outliers for target
Output: E$_1$:= selected ensemble
1. T$_2$:= average(P$_1$, P$_2$,..., P$_{h'}$)   /* average scores of extreme instantiations */
2. *Target* := top-K points by sorting T$_2$ in descending order
3. E$_1$:= ∅
4. **For each** set P$_i$ ∈ P
5.   L$_1$:= P - P$_{lb(i)}$ /*excluding lower end of instantiations for P$_i$ */
6.   L$_2$:= P - P$_{ub(i)}$ /*excluding upper end of instantiations for P$_i$ */
7.   DV$_1$:= DV(L$_1$, *Target*)   /* using equations 2-4 */
8.   DV$_2$:= DV(L$_2$, *Target*)
/* Selection step: the instantiation end whose removal results in lower ensemble diversity w.r.t. *Target*, gets selected */
9.   **If** (DV$_1$ < DV$_2$) **Then,**
10.   Add P$_{lb(i)}$ to E$_1$
11.   **Else** Add P$_{ub(i)}$ to E$_1$
12.   **End If**
13. **End For**
14. **Return**(E$_1$)

It is interesting to note here that from this step, only pruned instantiations of extreme parameter values will be passed further. The reason is, since the objective of this entire selection process is to get the better accurate parameter end for a given method, so considering all intermediate ones as well will not allow so by creating a bias of majority. Secondly, results of heterogeneous methods are combined in ensembles in a hope to get a more accurate prediction than the individuals by combining diverse errors. If more number of detectors from the same method are used for final selection decision, then their decision target will itself be biased towards those. As a result, the selections may suffer in diversity and in turn the purpose of ensemble as well.

Next, HEnS (pseudocode 1) calls the Selector 2 (pseudocode 3) with the set of h' parameter extremes having $2 * h'$ score lists in total. A new target is calculated for selection, which is average of all these $2 * h'$ score lists. From this average, top-K points are picked up as the new *Target* (lines 1–2). Next, from each of the h' sets, score lists corresponding to both parameter ends in P are removed one by one without replacement (lines 5 and 6). Such temporary removals are done to assess their impacts on overall ensemble diversity (Eqs. 2–4). The idea is to retain that parameter instantiation of each type h', whose removal degrades the ensemble diversity more (lines 9–12). E is the final selected ensemble, which includes exactly one detector of each of the h types from the initial set of candidate detectors, if these have passed the pruning of Selector 1.

Table 1. Summary of datasets

Dataset	# Instances	# Outliers	# Attributes	Outlier vs. Normal class
KDD Cup 1999	60839	246	79	U2R vs. Normal
ALOI	49534	1508	27	Outlier vs. Inlier images
ANN-thyroid	7200	534	21	Others vs. Normal
Satimage-2	5803	71	36	Class 2 vs. Others
Optical digits	5216	150	64	Class 0 vs. Others
Spambase	4601	1813	57	Spam vs. Non-spam emails

Note that, certainly this selection method does not ensure to pick up the most accurate instantiations for each of heterogeneous types. Yet, experiments show that even if more accurate parameter ends get selected for some types of detection methods, ensemble predictions get improved. One clear reasoning about this is the better estimation of final *Target*, due to first pruning and second, less bias and more diversity, resulted by several heterogeneous outlier detectors and very distant or extreme parameter values for a single type.

Novelty of this work can be summarized as the following key points. First, our method approaches to better target construction in the presence of random detectors at input. Pruning is initially used for this purpose, to exclude the highly inaccurate ones (relatively) from the selection process. Then, the final target is constructed by averaging scores of distant extremes of several heterogeneous detection methods. Hence, average of only a selective and lesser number of distinct and relatively diverse scores certainly leads to a better target, at least better than the target build from all random input detectors, as used in literature. The better is the target, the better will be the selected ensemble. Additionally, use of double-fault measure with top-k outliers by such enhanced target gives a better picture of element-based dissimilarity.

4   Experiments

In this section, the proposed member-selection method is evaluated on a set of benchmark datasets. The detection performance is compared with the state-of-art methods to highlight the effectiveness.

4.1   Description of Datasets and Ensembles

Experiments are conducted on six benchmark datasets from UCI machine learning repository[1]. Their summarized details are given in Table 1. The KDD Cup 1999 dataset consists of a set of network connections, where good connections are referred as normal and bad connections as intrusions. Here one of its variants are used as per Campos et al. [16], where 1-of-n encoding is used for categorical attributes and real-valued attributes are normalized. The Amsterdam Library of Object Images (ALOI) is a

---

[1] http://archive.ics.uci.edu/ml/datasets.html.

Table 2. Performance of member-selection methods (ROC AUC)

Dataset	Vertical selection [5]	Boost-select [6] (t = 5%, d = 25%)	All pruned extremes (O/P of Selector 1)	HEnS (Pseudocode 1)
KDD Cup 1999	0.9143	0.9341	0.9599	**0.9715**
ALOI	0.7502	0.7193	0.7381	**0.7636**
ANN-thyroid	0.6328	0.6046	0.6421	**0.6770**
Satimage-2	0.8846	0.9105	0.9129	**0.9304**
Optical digits	0.4992	0.5210	0.4972	**0.5371**
Spambase	0.5606	0.6188	0.6034	**0.6278**

collection of color images of small objects, used widely in literature. Here, its pre-processed variant with duplicates removed is used, as given in [16]. For ANN-thyroid dataset, the origin version as per UCI is used. The Satimage-2 dataset here is a pre-processed version of Statlog dataset from UCI, as used in [2]. The first 71 instances from class-2 are labeled as outliers, and rest as normal. Optical-digits dataset used here is also the same preprocessed version similar to [2]. A total of 150 outliers are instances those are down-sampled from class-0, and those belong to digits 1 to 9 are labeled as normal. For Spambase, the same variant as in UCI is used. Here, the spam emails are outliers and non-spam emails are inliers.

For ensemble of each dataset, three popular outlier detection methods are used as heterogeneous base detectors: Average k-NN, Local Outlier Factor (LOF), and Subspace Outlier Degree (SOD). For each of these three methods, eleven instantiations are used to create a pool of homogeneous detectors, where $k = 5, 10, 20, 30, 40, 50, 60, 70, 80, 90, 100$. The motive behind considering such large range of k for every single method is to allow the selector to pick an accurate instantiation for a given detection algorithm. ELKI framework[2] is used to evaluate LOF and SOD detectors.

For LOF, infinite scores are considered as outlying and thus we handle those by replacing with the maximum non-infinite score of the corresponding detector. For SOD detectors, the parameter value for shared nearest neighbor (snn) is same as that of k, and α is used as 0.8, as suggested in [9]. Overall, for each dataset, there is one ensemble with three heterogeneous detectors, each of which is a pool of eleven homogeneous ones i.e., detectors those belong to same method but varying parameters values.

4.2   Results

Detection performances of ensembles with members selected through different selectors are given in Table 2. It shows ROC AUC values of the selected ensembles. Effectiveness of proposed method is compared against two literature methods namely,

---

[2] https://elki-project.github.io/algorithms/.

vertical selection [5] and boost-select [6]. As discussed in [2, 3] that greedy selection [4] is highly sensitive to the presence of inaccurate detectors at the input and hence we have not included it for comparison. Since our selection approach is neither subsampling based nor subspace based, those approaches are also not included for comparison. In addition, ensemble performances of buildup from the extreme instantiations of all the three homogeneous pools, which is actually the outcome of Selector 1, are also given for comparison. Results in bold indicate the best preforming ensemble.

It can be clearly observed that for all datasets, the proposed method outperforms both vertical and boosting selectors. Performance improvements on KDD Cup, ANN-thyroid, and Satimage-2 datasets are highly significant. Evidently, by selecting good detectors (best or moderately accurate) from even some set of homogeneous pools results in better individual accuracy and better ensemble diversity and hence an enhanced ensemble.

Furthermore, with KDD Cup, ANN-thyroid and Satimage-2 datasets, ensemble of all extreme parameter detectors works notably better than vertical and boosting selectors. It simply signifies that the fewer is better from a single detection method, as target construction is less biased.

5   Conclusion

In this study, a heterogeneous outlier detection ensemble is constructed from a set of distinct types of homogeneous pools. For this purpose, a set of detectors with dissimilar formulations and characteristics are considered at input. For each type, a number of detectors with a wide range of varying parameter values are used. Such homogeneous pools are used to get a good detector of each type, at least better than random. Pruning is done first to prevent highly inaccurate detectors from any further consideration. From the pruned output set of detectors, only two instantiations are passed further for each type, those correspond to the two extreme parameter values.

Diversification is achieved as first, these two instantiations will themselves be resulting differently due to much distinct parameter values. Second, by not including more number of detectors of one type avoids unnecessary biasing of target set towards results of the same method (Selector 2). Also, it does not let hinder the good and distinct results of a good instantiation due to majority voting from similar results. The use of double-fault measure w.r.t final target of Selector 2 contributes to both, accuracy due to the use of better target, and to ensemble diversity by assessing element-based distinctiveness of detectors for points of this target. The positive contributions to accuracy and diversity are evident from experimental results, which conclude better ensemble constructions.

Acknowledgement. One of the author acknowledges Council of Scientific & Industrial Research (CSIR), India for fellowship assistance during the course of this work.

References

1. Zimek, A., Campello, R.J., Sander, J.: Ensembles for unsupervised outlier detection: challenges and research questions: position paper. ACM SIGKDD Explor. Newsl. **15**(1), 11–22 (2014)
2. Aggarwal, C.C., Sathe, S.: Theoretical foundations and algorithms for outlier ensembles. ACM SIGKDD Explor. Newsl. **17**(1), 24–47 (2015)
3. Mukhriya, A., Kumar, R.: Exploring ensembles for unsupervised outlier detection: an empirical analysis. In: Chakraverty, S., Goel, A., Misra, S. (eds.) Towards Extensible and Adaptable Methods in Computing, pp. 225–237. Springer, Singapore (2018). https://doi.org/10.1007/978-981-13-2348-5_17
4. Schubert, E., Wojdanowski, R., Zimek, A., Kriegel, H.: On evaluation of outlier rankings and outlier scores. In: Proceedings of the 12th SIAM International Conference on Data Mining, pp. 1047–1058 (2012)
5. Rayana, S., Akoglu, L.: Less is more: building selective anomaly ensembles with application to event detection in temporal graphs. In: Proceedings of the 15th SIAM International Conference on Data Mining, pp. 622–630 (2015)
6. Campos, G.O., Zimek, A., Meira, W.: An unsupervised boosting strategy for outlier detection ensembles. In: Phung, D., Tseng, V.S., Webb, G.I., Ho, B., Ganji, M., Rashidi, L. (eds.) PAKDD 2018. LNCS (LNAI), vol. 10937, pp. 564–576. Springer, Cham (2018). https://doi.org/10.1007/978-3-319-93034-3_45
7. Breunig, M.M., Kriegel, H.-P., Ng, R.T., Sander, J.: LOF: identifying density based local outliers. In: Proceedings of the 2000 ACM International Conference on Management of Data, pp. 93–104 (2000)
8. Kriegel, H.P., Schubert, M., Zimek, A.: Angle-based outlier detection in high-dimensional data. In: Proceedings of the 14th ACM SIGKDD International Conference on Knowledge Discovery and Data Mining, pp. 444–452 (2008)
9. Kriegel, H.-P., Kröger, P., Schubert, E., Zimek, A.: Outlier detection in axis-parallel subspaces of high dimensional data. In: Theeramunkong, T., Kijsirikul, B., Cercone, N., Ho, T.-B. (eds.) PAKDD 2009. LNCS (LNAI), vol. 5476, pp. 831–838. Springer, Heidelberg (2009). https://doi.org/10.1007/978-3-642-01307-2_86
10. Schubert, E., Zimek, A., Kriegel, H.P.: Generalized outlier detection with flexible kernel density estimates. In: Proceedings of the 2014 SIAM International Conference on Data Mining, pp. 542–550 (2014)
11. Giacinto, G., Roli, F.: Design of effective neural network ensembles for image classification purposes. Image Vis. Comput. **19**(9–10), 699–707 (2000)
12. Schapire, R.E., Freund, Y.: Boosting: Foundations and Algorithms. MIT Press, Cambridge (2012)
13. Zimek, A., Gaudet, M., Campello, R.J., Sander, J.: Subsampling for efficient and effective unsupervised outlier detection ensembles. In: Proceedings of the 19th ACM SIGKDD International Conference on Knowledge Discovery and Data Mining, pp. 428–436 (2013)
14. Salehi, M., Zhang, X., Bezdek, J.C., Leckie, C.: Smart sampling: a novel unsupervised boosting approach for outlier detection. In: Kang, B.H., Bai, Q. (eds.) AI 2016. LNCS (LNAI), vol. 9992, pp. 469–481. Springer, Cham (2016). https://doi.org/10.1007/978-3-319-50127-7_40

15. Rayana, S., Zhong, W., Akoglu, L.: Sequential ensemble learning for outlier detection: a bias-variance perspective. In: Proceedings of the 16th International Conference on Data Mining, pp. 1167–1172 (2016)

16. Campos, G.O., et al.: On the evaluation of unsupervised outlier detection: measures, datasets, and an empirical study. Data Min. Knowl. Disc. **30**(4), 891–927 (2016). https://doi.org/10.1007/s10618-015-0444-8

Author Index

Printed in the United States
By Bookmasters